The extreme right
in Western Europe

Manchester University Press

The extreme right in Western Europe

Success or failure?

Elisabeth Carter

Manchester University Press

Manchester and New York

distributed exclusively in the USA by Palgrave

The right of Elisabeth Carter to be identified as the author of this work has
been asserted by her in accordance with the Copyright, Designs and Patents
Act 1988.

Published by Manchester University Press
Oxford Road, Manchester M13 9NR, UK
and Room 400, 175 Fifth Avenue, New York, NY 10010, USA
www.manchesteruniversitypress.co.uk

Distributed exclusively in the USA by
Palgrave, 175 Fifth Avenue, New York NY 10010, USA

Distributed exclusively in Canada by
UBC Press, University of British Columbia, 2029 West Mall,
Vancouver, BC, Canada V6T 1Z2

British Library Cataloguing-in-Publication Data
A catalogue record for this book is available from the British Library

Library of Congress Cataloging-in-Publication Data
A catalog record for this book is available from the Library of Congress

ISBN 13: 978 0 7190 7049 5

First published in hardback 2005 by Manchester University Press

This paperback edition first published 2011

Printed by Lightning Source

Contents

List of tables and figures   *page* ix
Acknowledgements   xi
Abbreviations: right-wing extremist parties   xiii

1   The varying electoral fortunes of the West European parties of
    the extreme right   1
      Accounting for variation in the extreme right party vote   2
      Right-wing extremist parties in Western Europe since 1979   8
      Four explanations for the variation in the right-wing extremist
        party vote   10

2   Party ideology   13
      The concept of right-wing extremism   14
      Terminology   20
      The study of right-wing extremist party ideology: existing
        typologies and their limitations   24
      An alternative typology of right-wing extremist parties   28
        Importance attached to the issue of immigration   29
        Racist attitudes   35
        Attitudes towards democracy, parliamentarism and
          pluralism   41
      Five types of right-wing extremist party   50
      Right-wing extremist party ideology and electoral success   54
      Concluding remarks   60

3   Party organization and leadership   64
      The influence of party organization and party leadership   64
      Organization, leadership and factionalism: three types of
        right-wing extremist party   66
        Weakly organized, poorly led and divided parties   66
        Weakly organized, poorly led but united parties   77

Strongly organized, well-led but factionalized parties   80
Party organization, party leadership and the right-wing
    extremist party vote   91
Concluding remarks   98

4   Party competition   102
The concept of political space and the space of party
    competition   103
Mapping the political space and estimating party positions:
    five approaches   105
    Government expenditure flows   105
    Elite studies   106
    Voter attitudes   107
    Internal analysis of party election programmes   109
    Expert judgements   111
Data and methodology   112
Patterns of party competition: the mainstream right and the
    right-wing extremist party vote   114
Patterns of party competition: the extreme right and the
    right-wing extremist party vote   125
Patterns of party competition: the interaction of the
    mainstream right and the extreme right, and the right-wing
    extremist party vote   129
Patterns of party competition: convergence of the
    mainstream parties   136
Concluding remarks   141

5   The institutional environment   146
Electoral systems   147
    District magnitude and legal thresholds   148
    Electoral formulae   155
    The overall mechanical effect of electoral systems:
      measuring disproportionality   160
Other electoral laws   162
    Party/candidate access to the electoral process   163
    Access to the broadcast media   168
    Access to state subventions   176
    Ballot access, media access and state subvention rules:
      the overall impact of other electoral laws   192
Concluding remarks   195

6   Accounting for varying electoral fortunes   201
Explanations for the variation in the right-wing extremist
    party vote: the story so far   201

Explanations for the variation in the right-wing extremist party
        vote: putting the pieces together   205
    Concluding remarks   212

Appendix A: The ideological positions of West European political
        parties   216

Appendix B: The political space in the different countries of
        Western Europe   227

Appendix C: The disproportionality of elections, 1979–2003   233

Bibliography   236
Index   261

List of tables and figures

Tables

1.1 Electoral scores of the West European parties of the extreme
 right, 1979–2003 *page* 4
2.1 Importance attached to immigration in the ideologies of the
 different right-wing extremist parties of Western Europe 30
2.2 Racist attitudes of the different right-wing extremist parties of
 Western Europe 36
2.3 Attitudes of the different right-wing extremist parties of
 Western Europe towards democracy, parliamentarism and
 pluralism 42
2.4 Five types of right-wing extremist parties in Western Europe 50
2.5 Effect of ideology on the right-wing extremist party vote
 (OLS dummy regression) 58
2.6 Mean electoral scores of the different types of right-wing
 extremist parties in Western Europe, 1979–2003 59
3.1 Weakly organized, poorly led and divided right-wing
 extremist parties 67
3.2 Weakly organized, poorly led but united right-wing extremist
 parties 77
3.3 Strongly organized, well-led but factionalized right-wing
 extremist parties 80
3.4 Effects of organization, leadership and factionalism on the
 right-wing extremist party vote: one-way analysis of variance
 (ANOVA) 94
3.5 Effects of organization, leadership and factionalism on the
 right-wing extremist party vote: means test 95
3.6 Effects of organization and leadership on the right-wing
 extremist party vote (OLS dummy regression) 97
5.1 Dimensions of electoral systems in Western Europe,
 1979–2003 149

5.2   Electoral formulae and the mean right-wing extremist party
      vote, 1979–2003   159
5.3   Requirements for ballot access   164
5.4   Requirements for media access   170
5.5   Requirements for state subventions   178
5.6   Electoral laws and their impact on right-wing extremist
      parties, 1979–2003   192
6.1   Effects of party ideology, party organization and leadership,
      party competition and electoral institutions on the right-wing
      extremist party vote (OLS regression): Model 1   206
6.2   Effects of party ideology, party organization and leadership,
      party competition and electoral institutions on the right-wing
      extremist party vote (OLS regression): Model 2   208

Figures

2.1   Electoral success of the West European parties of the extreme
      right, 1979–2003: by ideological type   55
2.2   Extreme right party family   61
3.1   Electoral scores of the West European parties of the extreme
      right, 1979–2003: by type of party organization and
      leadership, and level of factionalism   92
4.1   Political space in France, 1982–2000   116
4.2   Political space in Denmark, 1982–2000   118
4.3   Political space in Austria, 1982–2000   120
4.4   Political space in Italy, 1982–2000   122
4.5   Political space in Norway, 1982–2000   122
4.6   Political space in Spain, 1982–2000   123
4.7   Political space in Switzerland, 1993–2000   127
4.8   Political space in Germany, 1982–2000   128
4.9   Ideological moderation and the right-wing extremist party
      vote   130
4.10 Ideological radicalization and the right-wing extremist party
      vote   131
4.11 Political space in Britain, 1982–2000   137
5.1   Electoral formula and mean votes for extreme right parties,
      1979–2003   157

Acknowledgements

Along the long road to completing this book I have received an immense amount of advice, help and support from a great number of people. First and foremost I am deeply indebted to David Farrell, who has provided me with extremely sound and dependable advice and guidance throughout this entire project. He has also exhibited unfailing patience and good humour, and he has never ceased to be encouraging. I could not have asked for more in a supervisor. I am also particularly grateful to Thomas Poguntke for all the help and support he has given me since he first set eyes on this project. He has been extremely generous in offering me advice whenever I have asked for it, and his judgement and suggestions have always been sound.

A number of other people at Keele, at Manchester and further afield have also helped me in various ways as I have been completing this project. At Keele I would like to thank Richard Luther and Robert Ladrech for their encouragement and their enthusiasm, and for giving me the opportunity to complete this book when I probably should have been doing other things. At Manchester I am grateful to Simon Bulmer, Geoffrey Roberts, Andrew Russell, Elisa Roller and Alan Trickett for helpful advice and suggestions. From elsewhere, I would like to thank Jocelyn Evans and Kai Arzheimer for their general help and very valuable feedback, and Roger Eatwell and Ingrid van Biezen for their useful comments.

I am also indebted to many people for much of the data on which this project is based. For patiently answering my questions about the intricacies of little-known electoral laws I would like to thank Luciano Bardi, Michael Brändle, Michael Bützer, Hans Hirter, Romain Lachat, Andreas Ladner, Paul Lucardie, Georg Lutz, José Magone, José Ramon Montero, Gerassimos Moschonas, Wolfgang C. Müller, Luis Ramiro, Pascal Sciarini and Lars Svåsand. For data and advice on the positioning of parties I would like to thank Michael Laver, Marcel Lubbers, Hanne Marthe Narud and Leonard Ray. Of course, any errors of fact and any misinterpretations are entirely my own responsibility.

I am also very grateful to the good people at Manchester University Press for their willingness to publish this book and for their professional approach to preparing the manuscript for publication. I also wish to thank Fiona Sewell for her care in copy-editing the manuscript.

In addition to all those people who have helped me directly with the researching and the writing this book, I would like to acknowledge the support of my friends who studied in the Department of Government at the University of Manchester at the same time as me. The whole process of completing this project would have been far more painful and difficult had it not been for their interest, encouragement and understanding. I am particularly thankful to Peter Stafford, Richard Whitaker, Adam McCarthy, Chris Agius, Paul Beeckmans, Sophia Price and Pat MacKenzie.

Finally, I would like to thank my family. Throughout this seemingly unending process they have shown enormous understanding and have been an unfailing source of encouragement, sound reason and emotional support. In recognition of all their help, I would like to dedicate this work to them.

Abbreviations: right-wing extremist parties

Party	Country	Full name	English translation
Agir	Wallonia	Agir	To Act
AN	Italy	Alleanza Nazionale	National Alliance
APS	Switzerland	Autopartei der Schweiz	Car Party of Switzerland
BNP	Britain	British National Party	
CD	Netherlands	Centrumdemocraten	Centre Democrats
CP	Netherlands	Centrumpartij	Centre Party
CP'86	Netherlands	Centrumpartij'86	Centre Party'86
DF	Denmark	Dansk Folkeparti	Danish People's Party
DNP	Sweden	Det Nya Partiet	The New Party
DVU	Germany	Deutsche Volksunion	German People's Union
EK	Greece	Ethniko Komma	National Party
EPEN	Greece	Ethniki Politiki Enosis	National Political Union
Falangistas	Spain	Falangistas	Phalanxes
FLP	Norway	Fedrelandspartiet	Fatherland Party
FN	France	Front National	National Front
FN(b)	Wallonia	Front National/Front voor die Natie	National Front
FNB	Wallonia	Front Nouveau de Belgique	New Belgian Front
FPÖ	Austria	Freiheitliche Partei Österreichs	Freedom Party of Austria
FPS	Switzerland	Freiheitspartei der Schweiz	Freedom Party of Switzerland
Frente Nacional	Spain	Frente Nacional	National Front
FRPd	Denmark	Fremskridtspartiet	Progress Party
FRPn	Norway	Fremskrittspartiet	Progress Party
Fuerza Nueva	Spain	Fuerza Nueva	New Force
KP	Greece	Komma Proodeftikon	Progress Party
LdT	Switzerland	Lega dei Ticinesi	Ticino League
LN	Italy	Lega Nord	Northern League
MNR	France	Mouvement National Républicain	National Republican Movement
Ms-Ft	Italy	Movimento Sociale–Fiamma Tricolore	Social Movement–Tricolour Flame
MSI	Italy	Movimento Sociale Italiano	Italian Social Movement
NA	Switzerland	Nationale Aktion für Volk und Heimat	National Action for People and Homeland
ND	Sweden	Ny Demokrati	New Democracy
NF	Britain	National Front	

Party	Country	Full name	English translation
NPD	Germany	Nationaldemokratische Partei Deutschlands	National Democratic Party of Germany
NVU	Netherlands	Nederlandse Volksunie	Dutch People's Union
PDC	Portugal	Partido da Democracia Cristã	Party of Christian Democracy
PFNb	Wallonia	Parti des Forces Nouvelles	Party of the New Forces
Republikaner	Germany	Die Republikaner	The Republicans
SD	Switzerland	Schweizer Demokraten	Swiss Democrats
SDk	Sweden	Sverigedemokraterna	Sweden Democrats
VB	Flanders	Vlaams Blok	Flemish Bloc

1

The varying electoral fortunes of the West European parties of the extreme right

Right-wing extremist parties have experienced a dramatic rise in electoral support in many West European democracies since the late 1970s. One of the most prominent such parties, the French Front National (FN), won nearly 10 percent of the vote in both the 1986 and 1988 national legislative contests, and in 1993 and 1997 its share of the ballots grew even further, first to 12.7 percent and then to 14.9 percent. Similarly, in Austria, the Freiheitliche Partei Österreichs (FPÖ) recorded close to 10 percent of the vote in 1986, and then saw its electoral score rise first to 16.6 percent in 1990, then to 22.5 percent in 1994, and then to a massive 26.9 percent in 1999. The Vlaams Blok (VB) has also performed well at the polls in this time period, recently securing over 16 percent of the vote in Flanders. In Scandinavia, the Fremskridtspartiet (FRPd) and the Fremskrittspartiet (FRPn) (Danish and Norwegian Progress Parties) have received over 10 percent of the vote on a number of occasions since the late 1970s, and the Dansk Folkeparti (DF) has also been successful at the polls since its foundation in 1995. Likewise, in Italy, the Alleanza Nazionale (AN) and the Lega Nord (LN) have both secured vote shares of over 10 percent in a number of elections since the early 1990s.

By the mid-1990s some of these parties had acquired sufficient electoral strength to become relevant players in the formation of governmental majorities. In Italy, the AN and the LN both entered office in 1994, as junior partners in Silvio Berlusconi's first government, and in 2001 they once again formed part of the governing coalition when the alliance with Forza Italia was renewed. In a move that sparked widespread international criticism, the Austrian FPÖ also assumed office when it entered into coalition with the Österreichische Volkspartei (ÖVP) in 1999. The party remained in government after the 2002 elections when the ÖVP–FPÖ coalition continued. In Norway and in Denmark, right-wing extremist parties similarly play a role in the formation of parliamentary majorities. Although they do not form part of the governing coalition, since the elections of 2001, both the Norwegian FPRn and the Danish DF have periodically lent their support to the minority bourgeois governments.

The considerable attention that these more successful right-wing extremist parties have received both in the media and in the academic literature has sometimes obscured the fact that parties of the extreme right have not been successful at the polls in all West European countries, however. Indeed, looking at Table 1.1, which documents the electoral scores of all the parties of the extreme right in Western Europe in the period since the late 1970s, it is clear that, alongside the successful parties mentioned above, there are a number of other parties that have experienced relative electoral failure. The German parties of the extreme right, for example, have remained electorally unsuccessful over this period. Even at their peak in 1990, the Republikaner only managed to secure 2.1 percent of the national vote. In the Netherlands, too, the extreme right has remained marginalized. The Centrumdemocraten (CD) polled only 2.5 percent of the vote at their height in 1994. In Greece, in Portugal and in Spain the parties of the extreme right have been similarly unsuccessful at the polls, while in Britain they have performed even more poorly. The National Front (NF) won a mere 0.7 percent of the vote in 1979 and has never managed to secure more than 0.1 percent of the vote since then, and the British National Party (BNP) has never recorded more than 0.2 percent of the national vote.

In addition to varying across countries, the electoral scores of individual parties of the extreme right have varied over time. It has been quite common for the same party to record low electoral scores in one election but to secure high electoral scores in another. For instance, as Table 1.1 illustrates, in 1983 the Austrian FPÖ polled only 5 percent of the vote. Yet in 1999 its vote soared to 26.9 percent. It then fell again in 2002, to 10.0 percent. Similarly, in Italy the Movimeto Sociale Italiano (MSI) recorded a mere 5.3 percent of the vote in 1979, but in 1996 (under the new guise of the AN) its vote stood at 15.7 percent. In the same way, in Norway, the FRPn polled only 3.7 percent of the vote in 1985, but secured 15.3 percent of the vote in 1997. In contrast, the Danish FRPd won 11.0 percent of the vote in 1979, but in 2001 its vote was only 0.6 percent.

Whereas the electoral breakthrough and the subsequent progress of the more successful parties of the extreme right have been extensively analysed in the existing academic literature, the issue of the variation in the electoral scores of the right-wing extremist parties across Western Europe has received only limited attention. In other words, while numerous studies exist that illustrate and help account for the rise of right-wing extremism, there are few analyses that seek to explain the reasons for the uneven electoral success of the West European parties of the extreme right.

Accounting for variation in the extreme right party vote

This book examines this question of the variation in the right-wing extremist party vote across Western Europe in a comprehensive and comparative manner. Drawing on the few existing studies that have already explored this issue, it investigates a broad set of political, supply-side reasons why the elect-oral scores of the West European parties of the extreme right have varied so considerably since the late 1970s. More specifically it explores whether the disparity in the electoral fortunes of the parties of the extreme right can be explained, to some extent, by the fact that the parties embrace different types of right-wing extremist ideology, and by the fact that they have different forms of party organization and leadership. It also investigates whether the varying vote scores of the parties of the extreme right can be accounted for, in part at least, by the different patterns of party competition at work in each of the party systems in which the right-wing extremist parties operate, and by the different institutional environments present in each of the countries in which the parties compete.

These are the factors that have tended to be overlooked in the wider litera-ture on right-wing extremism. Indeed, the majority of existing studies have focused on demand-side explanations for the rise of right-wing extremism, which concentrate on the socio-demographic characteristics and attitudes of right-wing extremist voters, and the effects that socio-economic change has had on this section of the electorate. Among these demand-side explanations, different studies have emphasized the rise of immigration, the growth of voter dissatisfaction with the established political parties and/or democratic system, the breakdown of social ties and the resultant feelings of insecurity and anomie, the calls for a return to more traditional and paternalistic modes of social organization, and the rise of social deprivation and exclusion.[1] Supply-side explanations for the growth of right-wing extremism, which focus on the supply of extreme right alternatives, and which examine the parties of the extreme right as strategic actors attempting to best respond their political and institutional environments, have, by contrast, received much less attention.[2]

The prevalence of demand-side explanations for the rise of right-wing extremism has also meant that while the social and economic reasons for the growth of this phenomenon have been well discussed and documented, the influence of political factors on the fortunes of the parties of the extreme right has attracted less coverage. Political explanations have remained rather under-researched, especially in the comparative perspective. Furthermore, there has been a tendency for these explanations to be characterized by assumption, rather than by fact and empirical analysis. It has often been claimed, for example, that right-wing extremism has been allowed to flour-ish in countries that employ proportional electoral systems (Hermens, 1941; Hain, 1986), and yet there is little empirical analysis that supports this assertion.

A further reason why this study focuses on political explanations for the uneven electoral success of the right-wing extremist parties is that while social and economic factors are important in explaining the rise of right-wing

Table 1.1   Electoral scores of the West European parties of the extreme right, 1979–2003 (%)

Party	Country	1979	1980	1981	1982	1983	1984	1985	1986	1987	1988
FPÖ	Austria	6.1				5.0			9.7		
VB	Belgium: Flanders[a]			1.6				2.0		2.7	
Agir	Belgium: Wallonia[a]			*				*		*	
FN(b)	Belgium: Wallonia[a]			*				0.1		0.3	
FNB	Belgium: Wallonia[a]			*				*		*	
PFNb	Belgium: Wallonia[a]			–				0.3		0.3	
BNP	Britain	*				0.0				0.0	
NF	Britain	0.7				0.1				0.0	
DF	Denmark	*		*			*			*	*
FRPd	Denmark	11.0		8.9			3.6			4.8	9.0
FN	France			0.2					9.8		9.8
MNR	France			*					*		*
DVU	Germany		–			–				0.6[b]	
NPD	Germany		0.2			0.2				0.6[b]	
Republikaner	Germany		*			–				–	
KP/EPEN/EK	Greece			1.7[c]				0.6[d]			
LN	Italy	*				*				0.5[g]	
Ms-Ft	Italy	*				*				*	
MSI/AN	Italy	5.3				6.8				5.9	
CD	Netherlands				*	*			0.1		
CP	Netherlands			0.1	0.8				0.4		
CP'86	Netherlands			*	*				*		
NVU	Netherlands			0.1	0.0				*		
FLP	Norway			*				*			
FRPn	Norway			4.5				3.7			
PDC	Portugal	1.1	0.4[h]				0.7	0.7		0.6	
Falangistas[i]	Spain	2.3[j]			0.0				0.2		
Fuerza Nueva/ Frente Nacional	Spain	2.3[j]			0.5				–		
DNP	Sweden	*				*		*			
ND	Sweden	*				*		*			
SDk	Sweden	*				*		*			
APS/FPS	Switzerland	*					*			2.6	
LdT	Switzerland	*					*			*	
NA/SD	Switzerland	1.3				2.9				3.0	

Notes: For full right-wing extremist party names, see Abbreviations (pp. xiii–xiv). *Party did not exist at this time. –Party did not contest election. [a]Flanders and Wallonia are treated as two separate political systems as Belgian political parties compete in only one of the two regions. The vote scores of the parties reflect their share of the vote in either Flanders and Brussels, or Wallonia and Brussels (see note 4). [b]From 1987 to 1990 the DVU and the NPD joined forces and contested elections under the banner DVU-Liste D. [c]KP. [d]EPEN. [e]Election of June 1989; party did not compete in election of November 1989. [f]EPEN and EK. [g]Lega Lombarda (Lombard League). The Lega Lombarda (led by Bossi) united with other regional leagues in 1991 to form the Lega Nord. [h]In alliance with the Independent Movement for National Reconstruction (Movimento Independente para a Reconstrução Nacional, MIRN). [i]The Falangistas (Phalanxes) include the Falange Española de las Juntas de Ofensiva Nacional-Sindicalista (the Spanish Phalanx of Committees for Nationalist Syndicalist Attack, FE de las JONS), the Falange Española (Unificación Falangista) (the Spanish

1989	1990	1991	1992	1993	1994	1995	1996	1997	1998	1999	2000	2001	2002	2003
	16.6				22.5	21.9				26.9			10.0	
		9.5				11.9				14.2				16.8
		0.4				0.8				*				*
		-2.4				6.9				3.4				5.3
		*				*				0.8				0.3
		0.1				*				*				*
			0.0					0.1				0.2		
			0.0					0.0				0.0		
	*				*				7.4			12.0		
	6.4				6.4				2.4			0.6		
			12.7					14.9					11.3	
				*				*					1.1	
	0.3[b]			–						1.2			–	
	0.3[b]				0.3					0.3			0.4	
		2.1			1.9					1.8			0.6	
0.3[de]	0.1[f]			0.1[f]			0.2[f]				–			
			8.7		8.4			10.1				3.9		
			*		*			0.9				0.4		
			5.4		13.5			15.7				12.0		
0.9					2.5				0.6				*	*
*					*				*				*	*
–					0.4				*				*	*
*					*				*				*	*
*				0.5				0.2				0.1		
13.0				6.3				15.3				14.6		
		*				*				*			*	
0.2				0.0			0.1				0.1			
–				–			*				*			
*		*			*				0.5				*	
*		6.7			1.2				0.2				0.0	
*		0.1			0.2				0.4				1.4	
		5.1					4.0			0.9				0.2
		1.9					1.8			0.9				0.4
		3.3					3.1			1.8				1.0

Phalanx (Phalangeal Unification, FE(UF)), the Falange Asturiana (Asturian Phalanx, FA), the Falange Española de las Juntas de Ofensiva Nacional-Sindicalista – Auténtica (the Authentic Spanish Phalanx of Committees for Nationalist Syndicalist Attack, FE de las JONS (a)), the Falange Española Independiente (the Independent Spanish Phalanx, FEI), the Falange Española Auténtica (the Authentic Spanish Phalanx, FEA), the Falange Española de las Juntas de Ofensiva Nacional-Sindicalista – sector Diego Marquez (the Spanish Phalanx of Committees for Nationalist Syndicalist Attack – sector Diego Marquez, FE de las JONS sector DM) and La Falange (the Phalanx, FE). All these groups have extremely similar ideologies and contest elections together. Collectively they are known as the Falangistas (see Casals, 2001). [i]Fuerza Nueva and the Falangistas formed a coalition under the banner of the Unión Nacional (National Union)

Source: Mackie and Rose (1991, 1997); Cheles et al., (1995); Betz and Immerfall (1998); Hainsworth (2000a); Elections around the World; Parties and Elections in Europe.

extremism as a general phenomenon, and are also crucial in accounting for individual voting decisions, they help little in understanding why some parties of the extreme right have fared better at the ballot box than others. At the aggregate level at least, little difference exists in the socio-economic make-up of the countries under investigation, and so there is little reason to expect aggregate levels of social and value change to differ significantly across these countries. It is therefore unlikely that the pronounced variation in the right-wing extremist parties' electoral fortunes will be explained satisfactorily by different levels of social and value change.

By focusing squarely on the political explanations for the disparity in the electoral fortunes of the parties of the extreme right, this study does not examine the influence of culture or history on the right-wing extremist party vote. Though clearly of importance in an overall account of the variation in the electoral scores of the parties of the extreme right, cultural and histor--ical explanations are notoriously difficult to operationalize and test, especially in a comparative perspective. Even at the level of a single-country case study there is little agreement over the factors that should be included in such explanations.

Four sets of political, supply-side explanations for the disparity in the electoral fortunes of the West European parties of the extreme right are put forward, examined and tested in the course of this book. In the first instance it investigates the ideologies of the different right-wing extremist parties, since, regardless of the nature of the institutional and political environments in which the parties find themselves, the electoral fortunes of the parties of the extreme right may depend, to a certain extent, on the nature of the message and policies that they put forward. Rather than there being a uniform right-wing extremist ideology, the ideas and policies of the different parties vary quite considerably, with some of these being more popular with electorates than others. Consequently, it is quite possible that the variation in the electoral success of the parties of the extreme right across Western Europe may be partly explained by the presence of different ideologies, with the more successful right-wing extremist parties embracing one type of ideology and the less successful ones adopting another.

The electoral fortunes of the parties of the extreme right are also likely to be affected by the parties' internal organization and leadership, and by the consequences of these internal dynamics. In fact, a general consensus in the literature on right-wing extremist parties suggests that 'one of the most important determinants of success is party organization' (Betz, 1998a: 9). More specifically, right-wing extremist parties with strong, charismatic leaders, centralized organizational structures and efficient mechanisms for enforcing party discipline are likely to perform better at the polls than parties with weaker and uncharismatic leaderships, less centralized internal structures and lower levels of party discipline. The former parties are expected to exhibit greater internal cohesion, and thus greater levels of programmatic and electoral coherence. In turn, these attributes are expected to enhance the parties' credibility and result in higher levels of electoral success.

In addition to being influenced by party-centric factors, the electoral fortunes of the parties of the extreme right are likely to be affected by party system factors. In particular, they are expected to be influenced by the patterns of party competition in the party system. On the one hand, the dynamics of party competition on the right side of the political spectrum are likely to be important in explaining the variation in the right-wing extremist party vote. The ideological proximity of the parties of the mainstream right (the extreme right parties' nearest competitors) determines how much political space is available to the parties of the extreme right, and this space may well be related to how successful the extreme right parties are at the polls. Furthermore, the electoral fortunes of the right-wing extremist parties may also depend on the positions that these parties choose to adopt for themselves within the political space available to them. On the other hand, the patterns of party competition at the centre of the political spectrum are also likely to influence how well the parties of the extreme right perform at the polls. In other words, the degree of ideological convergence between the mainstream right and the mainstream left may well affect the right-wing extremist party vote.

As well as being influenced by the dynamics of the party system in which they compete, right-wing extremist parties are also conditioned to a greater or lesser extent by the 'rules of the game' of the political system in which they operate. More specifically, the right-wing extremist party vote is likely to be influenced by the proportionality of the electoral systems in operation in the countries in which they compete, and by the broader electoral laws governing how parties and candidates may gain access to the ballot, to the broadcast media and to state subventions.

By considering this broad range of factors the book presents a comprehensive examination of the political, supply-side factors that may influence the electoral scores of the parties of the extreme right across Western Europe. This contrasts with the analyses carried out in the existing studies that have examined the issue of variation in the right-wing extremist party vote at the macro (rather than the voter) level. While between them these analyses have identified and tested many of the factors that help explain the uneven electoral fortunes of the parties of the extreme right, individually the existing studies have chosen to concentrate on sub-sets of explanations and have thus focused on only some of the possible reasons why the parties of the extreme right across Western Europe have recorded such divergent electoral results. For example, Jackman and Volpert's analysis (1996) examines the influence of the political and economic environment on the right-wing extremist party vote, but does not investigate the effects that party-centric factors such as ideology and organization have on the electoral fortunes of the parties of the extreme right. By contrast, the studies by Ignazi (1992, 1997a), Betz (1993b,

1994) and Mudde (2000) concentrate on party ideology, and the study by Taggart (1995) examines party ideology and party organization, but they do not consider how party system factors and electoral institutions affect the right-wing extremist party vote.

Even the more comprehensive of the existing studies do not consider all the supply-side factors that may affect the right-wing extremist party vote. Golder (2003a, 2003b) investigates the influence of electoral systems, and the effect of the level of unemployment and immigration on the electoral scores of the parties of the extreme right, for example, but does not examine the influence of party system factors. Similarly, Kitschelt (1995) suggests that party ideology and party organization are important factors in explaining the variation in the right-wing extremist party vote, and also points to the impact of party system factors as well as to the influence of individual-level variables such as voters' social characteristics and attitudes, but he does not consider the effects of electoral institutions. Likewise, Lubbers *et al.* (2002) consider a whole host of variables (including individual-level ones) that may affect the vote scores of the parties of the extreme right, but do not take into account the impact of party ideology or the influence of electoral institutions on the right-wing extremist party vote.

In addition to offering a comprehensive coverage of the political, supply-side factors that may help explain the uneven electoral success of the parties of the extreme right, this analysis builds on the existing studies by offering substance for the different explanations for the variation in the right-wing extremist party vote. With the exception of the work by Kitschelt, all the existing studies mentioned above are journal articles, which test the various hypotheses by way of integrated statistical models. They therefore contain limited information on the individual right-wing extremist parties and provide no detailed coverage of the national contexts in which these parties compete. This analysis, by contrast, is able to examine the different factors that affect the right-wing extremist party vote in significant detail, and to investigate the individual parties and their national contexts in considerable depth.

Right-wing extremist parties in Western Europe since 1979

All right-wing extremist parties that have contested elections at the national level are included in this study, regardless of their size.[3] The analysis examines 40 right-wing extremist parties across 14 countries (see Table 1.1). This considerably exceeds the number of parties and countries examined in some of the existing studies, and means that the conclusions reached throughout this analysis provide a sound base for generalization.

As a result of the inclusive approach adopted in this book, a number of parties that have been omitted from some other studies of the extreme right are examined here. The Italian LN, for example, is included in this study even though it has sometimes been considered 'on the border of the extreme right family' (Ignazi, 2003: 61). Similarly, the Italian AN is examined here although it is excluded from the study by Lubbers and his colleagues, and has been described as being 'on the fringe of the contemporary extreme right, on the threshold of its exit' (Ignazi, 2003: 52). By contrast, neither the Finnish Suomen Maaseudun Puolue (SMP), which went on to became the Perussuomalaiset (PS) in 1995, nor the Dutch Lijst Pim Fortuyn (LPF), nor the Swiss Schweizerische Volkspartei/Union Démocratique du Centre (SVP/UDC) is included in the analysis, even though these parties have sometimes been portrayed (especially in the media) as being of the extreme right. There is a consensus in the academic literature that although the Finnish party 'followed a somewhat populist and xenophobic line [it] cannot be associated with right-wing extremism' (Ignazi, 2003: 160). Instead, 'it emerged as another type of party, which basically represented a traditional populist protest against modernization' (Andersen and Bjørklund, 2000: 193–4). As for the LPF, Dutch observers have been keen to stress that even though this party has 'mobilized electoral support by making the mix of immigration and crime [its] core campaign issue', it is misleading to consider it part of the extreme right (Van der Brug, 2003: 89–90). Similarly, while the Swiss SVP/UDC has 'recently cultivated xenophobic mobilisation [and has] co-opted the immigration/ asylum issue', scholars argue that it 'would be inaccurate and simplistic' to equate it with other extreme right parties in Western Europe (Husbands, 2000: 508–15). Despite its populist character, it remains part of the mainstream (Husbands, 2000).

Of all the countries in Western Europe, only Finland, Iceland and Ireland do not feature in this analysis. This is because they do not have a right-wing extremist political party that has contested national elections (in fact no extreme right parties exist at all in Iceland and Ireland, and in Finland the tiny Isänmaallinen Kansallis-Liitto [IKL] has not participated in any national parliamentary elections). The other 14 West European countries are included in the study, with Belgium treated as two separate political systems on the grounds that Flanders and Wallonia have two separate party systems.[4]

The time period under investigation in this analysis is 1979–2003, representing what von Beyme (1988) has termed the 'third wave' of right-wing extremism, a phase distinct from the neo-fascism of the post-war years and from the social deprivation of the 1950s, 1960s and early 1970s. The analysis begins in 1979 because general elections were held in that year in many of the countries under investigation, including Austria, Britain, Denmark, Italy, Portugal, Spain and Switzerland.

By covering such a uniquely long period of time, stretching from the late 1970s up to the present, the analysis provides a comprehensive and solid basis from which to draw generalizable conclusions. In addition to testing the different explanations for the variation in the extreme right party vote over a longer period of time than has been the case in the majority of existing studies, the book is also able to update the existing works, many of which focus only on the early years of the so-called 'third wave' of extreme right party activity. It takes account of the more recent developments in the extreme right which the existing studies do not cover, including the emergence of the Danish DF and the transformation of the Italian MSI into the AN in 1995, the split of the French FN in 1998–99, and the disappearance of the Dutch extreme right in 2002.

The book explains the variation in the electoral fortunes of the right-wing extremist parties in national legislative elections (to the lower house of parliament). These elections provide the best basis from which to compare the levels of success of the right-wing extremist parties across the countries under observation. Other types of elections – such as presidential elections – do not occur in all of the countries under investigation. Therefore, although they are undoubtedly of importance to the parties of the extreme right, the vote shares obtained by the parties in other types of election are less suitable for comparison.

In terms of its methodology, this analysis adopts a thematic-comparative framework rather than the traditional case study approach that has tended to characterize studies of the extreme right. Each chapter examines a different set of political explanations for the variation in the right-wing extremist party vote across Western Europe. The precise methodology adopted for each set of explanations is discussed in detail in each of the chapters.

Four explanations for the variation in the right-wing extremist party vote

The investigation into the variation of the right-wing extremist party vote across Western Europe begins with an examination of right-wing extremist party ideology. After a discussion of the concept of right-wing extremism and of the terminology used to describe the various parties, Chapter 2 considers the existing studies that have sought to illustrate the diversity that exists among the West European parties of the extreme right (Stöss, 1988; Ignazi, 1992; Husbands, 1992a; Betz, 1993b; Taggart, 1995; Kitschelt, 1995). On the basis that these suffer from a number of limitations, the chapter then develops an alternative typology of right-wing extremist parties, which takes account of the full diversity that exists among the parties of the extreme right and which investigates the link between the parties' ideology and their electoral success. From this typology, it becomes possible to ascertain whether right-wing extremist party success is linked to a specific type of ideology, or whether, conversely, the nature of a party's ideology matters little to its electoral success.

Chapter 3 turns to discussing the impact of the parties' organizational structures and leaderships on their electoral performance. It explains the ways in which organization and leadership may influence the success of parties at the polls and puts forward a number of hypotheses as to the

expected effect of party organization on the electoral fortunes of the different right-wing extremist parties. Drawing on the literature on right-wing
extremism, the chapter examines the parties' internal dynamics in detail and
identifies different groups of parties according to how well they are organized, how well they are led, and how disciplined and united they are. Having
categorized the parties in such a way, the chapter investigates the link
between party organization, leadership and cohesion on the one hand, and
electoral success on the other, and draws conclusions about the extent to
which these factors may help explain the uneven electoral success of the
parties of the extreme right across Western Europe.

Having explored the extent to which party-centric factors may help explain
the variation in the right-wing extremist party vote across Western Europe, the
analysis then turns its attention to contextual factors. In Chapter 4, it moves
to consider the influence of different patterns of party competition on the
right-wing extremist party vote. The chapter first investigates the ideological
proximity of the parties of the mainstream right so as to establish how much
political space is available to the right-wing extremist parties, and explores
whether this political space is in any way related to how well these parties
perform at the polls. Since the electoral fortunes of the right-wing extremist
parties are also likely to depend on the positions that these parties choose to
adopt for themselves, the chapter examines the location of the right-wing
extremist parties within the political space, and investigates whether their
electoral scores are in any way affected by their own ideological positions. It
also considers the ways in which the parties of the mainstream right and the
parties of the extreme right interact, and explores how these interactions affect
the extreme right party vote. Lastly, Chapter 4 examines the influence of party
competition at the centre of the political spectrum, and investigates whether
ideological convergence between the mainstream right and the mainstream left
impacts on the right-wing extremist party vote in any way.

Chapter 5 continues the investigation into the effects of contextual factors
and explores the influence of electoral institutions on the right-wing extremist party vote. It assesses the impact of different electoral systems, including
the effects of district magnitudes, legal thresholds and electoral formulae as
well as the influence of the overall proportionality profile of the electoral
system. It also examines the impact of other electoral laws, namely ballot
access requirements, media access requirements and the laws regulating
access to state subventions.

The final chapter of the book – Chapter 6 – synthesizes the four sets of
explanations examined throughout the previous chapters. It investigates the relative weight of each of the different explanations, and discusses which factors
are most powerful in accounting for the variation in the right-wing extremist
party vote. It also explores the extent to which all four sets of explanations
may, together, account for why right-wing extremist parties in Western Europe
have experienced such varying levels of electoral success since the late 1970s.

Given that so many right-wing extremist parties are examined in the course of this study, for ease of reference, a list of commonly used abbreviations appears at the beginning of the book. In addition, the data used in Chapter 4 to locate the parties in their respective party systems and the data pertaining to the disproportionality of electoral systems employed in Chapter 5 are reported in full in the appendices.

As will become clear in the analysis that follows, the factors examined throughout this book together account for a significant amount of the variation in the extreme right party vote across Western Europe in the period under investigation. However, only three of the four sets of factors emerge as being important in an overall explanation of the uneven electoral fortunes of these parties. Differences in the type of ideology that the right-wing extremist parties embrace, differences in their organization and leadership, and differences in the patterns of party competition in the party systems in which they compete all help account for the variation in the right-wing extremist party vote. By contrast, differences in the institutional environments in which the parties find themselves add little to an overall explanation for the uneven electoral success of the parties of the extreme right across Western Europe.

Notes

1 See for example the studies by Ignazi, 1992, 1997a, 2003; Betz, 1993a, 1994, 1998a; Perrineau, 1997; Knigge, 1998; Mayer, 1999; for studies that examine the attitudes and policy preferences of extreme right voters see Falter and Schumann, 1988; Mayer and Perrineau, 1992; Westle and Niedermayer, 1992; Billiet and De Witte, 1995; Van der Brug et al., 2000; Van der Brug and Fennema, 2003.

2 For a useful review of the different demand- and supply-side approaches to explaining right-wing extremism see Eatwell, 2003.

3 As Table 1.1 illustrates, this includes even parties that have recorded negligible electoral scores. Ephemeral groupuscules that have been able to partake in the odd electoral contest due mainly to very low entry requirements are excluded from the analysis, however. Such groups have very little visibility. Furthermore, they have no nationwide base and no discernible ideology or identifiable party organization. This makes them unsuitable for this type of analysis.

4 Even in national legislative elections, political parties in Belgium contest seats in either Flanders and Brussels, or Wallonia and Brussels. Therefore, as Swyngedouw observes, it makes little sense to express the electoral strength of Belgian parties as a percentage of the national vote. It is preferable to calculate their strength on the basis of their vote in Flanders and Brussels (in the case of Flemish parties) or Wallonia and Brussels (in the case of Wallonian parties) (Swyngedouw, 1998: 68–9), even though this does mean that the Brussels electorate is included in the calculations of the scores for both the Flemish and Wallonian parties. In this analysis Flanders and Wallonia are thus treated as two separate political systems and the vote scores of the Flemish VB and the Wallonian right-wing extremist parties reflect the parties' strength in each separate part of the country.

2

Party ideology

Parties of the extreme right are to some extent 'masters of their own success'. That is, regardless of the political environment in which they operate and regardless of the institutional contexts within which they find themselves, their electoral success will depend, in part, on the ideology they espouse and the policies they put forward, and on the way in which they are organized and led. This chapter focuses on the first of these party-centric factors, and examines the extent to which the ideologies of the extreme right parties influence their fortunes at the polls. Rather than there being a uniform right-wing extremist ideology, the ideas and policies of the different parties vary quite considerably, with some of these being more popular with the electorate than others. Consequently, it is quite possible that the variation in the electoral success of the parties of the extreme right across Western Europe may be partly explained by the presence of different ideologies, with the more successful right-wing extremist parties embracing one type of ideology and the less successful ones adopting another.

The chapter begins by discussing the much-debated concept of right-wing extremism and by examining the different terminology used to describe the parties. Then it considers the existing studies of right-wing extremist party ideology, and investigates the ways in which these works have sought to illustrate the diversity that exists among the West European parties of the extreme right. As will become clear from this discussion, these existing studies suffer from a number of limitations and, in the light of this, the chapter puts forward an alternative typology of right-wing extremist parties. Five different types of right-wing extremist party are identified. On the one hand, this typology allows for the full diversity that exists within the right-wing extremist party family to be illustrated. On the other, it means that the link between the parties' ideology and their electoral scores can be investigated. In this way it becomes possible to ascertain whether right-wing extremist party success is linked to a specific type of ideology, or whether, conversely, the nature of a party's ideology matters little to its electoral success. The chapter concludes with some thoughts on the importance of party ideology in an overall explanation of the disparity in the electoral fortunes of the West European parties of the extreme right.

The concept of right-wing extremism

he fact that right-wing extremism has been extensively analyzed by academics, journalists and other observers alike, it remains the case that an unequivocal definition of this concept is still lacking. Indeed, almost every scholar of right-wing extremism has pointed to the difficulties associated with defining the concept: Billig refers to the term 'extreme right' as 'a particularly troubling one' (1989: 146); Roberts speaks of the lack of 'satisfactory operational indicators of extremism' (1994: 466); and von Beyme argues that 'formal definitions or derivations based on the history of ideas [have] largely failed to provide a convincing concept for "right-wing extremism"', while other frequently used criteria for labelling these parties have also been problematic (1988: 1–3).

The absence of an agreed-upon definition of right-wing extremism means that scholars continue to disagree over which attributes a party should possess if it is to be considered as being of the extreme right. As Hainsworth argues, 'essentialist categorizations of the extreme right [are] fraught with problems' and it is thus 'not easy to provide neat, self-contained and irrefutable models of extreme rightism which might successfully accommodate or disqualify each concrete example or candidate deemed to belong to this party family' (2000a: 4).

Surveying the different definitions of right-wing extremism that can be found in the academic literature, a consensus does nonetheless emerge that right-wing extremism refers to a particular form of *ideology* (Mudde, 1995a: 203–5). A few scholars have also pointed to a certain type of political style, behaviour, strategy or organization, or a certain electoral base as constituting facets of right-wing extremism (e.g. Herz, 1975: 30–1; Betz, 1994, 1998a; Taggart, 1995). These must be considered additional or secondary dimensions of the concept rather than defining features, however, since they are all informed first and foremost by the parties' ideology. As Backes notes,

> there are no organizational or strategic traits that would take into account the multiplicity of the phenomena that we generally call 'right-wing extremism', and that would act as a common denominator . . . The organizational structures of the parties of the extreme right are important for an exact description of this phenomenon, but they are totally inappropriate in reaching a definition of this concept. (2001: 24, 29, this author's translation)

A few authors have argued that right-wing extremism may be defined by reference to one single ideological feature. Husbands (1981), for example, points to 'racial exclusionism' as constituting the common ideological core of the West European extreme right, while more recently, Eatwell cites nationalism (in various forms) as being *the* defining feature of the parties of the extreme right in Western Europe (2000a: 412). The majority of scholars define right-wing extremism with reference to more than one ideological feature, however, although they fail to agree on which features these are.

Indeed, following an extensive review of the literature, Mudde found no fewer than 58 different features were mentioned in the existing definitions of right-wing extremism. That said, he also found that certain features appeared more frequently than others in the existing definitions, and that five features were cited in over half the definitions. These are nationalism, xenophobia, racism, anti-democratic sentiment and a call for a strong state (1995a: 206–7).

Just because these five features appear more frequently than others in the existing definitions of the concept of right-wing extremism does not mean that they can be considered as constituting the foundations of a generally accepted definition, however. It would, in fact, be misleading to consider them as such, because these five features do not all occupy the same place on the conceptual ladder of abstraction. More specifically, four of the five features – nationalism, xenophobia, racism and a call for a strong state – are all further down the ladder of abstraction than the fifth concept – anti-democratic sentiment. Put differently, nationalism, xenophobia, racism and a call for a strong state are all manifestations of the higher concept of anti-democratic sentiment.

The disparity in the level of abstraction of these five features is problematic because it means that possible (or even sufficient) features of right-wing extremism are mixed with its necessary features. Nationalism, xenophobia, racism and a call for a strong state are all possible (and sometimes even sufficient) features of right-wing extremism, but they are not necessary ones. Anti-democratic sentiment, by contrast, is a necessary (though not a sufficient) feature of right-wing extremism. Cumbersome though it may be, this distinction between necessary and possible features of right-wing extremism is important because it underlines the fact that while a racist party, for example, is indeed a right-wing extremist party, not all right-wing extremist parties are racist. Thus, to argue that nationalism, xenophobia, racism or a call for a strong state are defining features of right-wing extremism is misleading. To maintain that anti-democratic sentiment is a defining feature of right-wing extremism is not problematic, however, because all right-wing extremist parties do indeed embrace anti-democratic sentiment, though it is important to note that not all parties that embrace anti-democratic sentiment are right-wing extremist.

To get closer to identifying the defining features of right-wing extremism – that is, features that are common to *all* right-wing extremist parties – and to make out which parties belong to an extreme right party family, it is therefore important to focus on necessary features of right-wing extremism rather than on possible ones. Possible features only become important later on, when the extreme right party family is subdivided in some way or another. To begin identifying the necessary features of right-wing extremism it is useful to go back to the concept of extremism, *tout court*, and for the most part, it is scholars from (or linked with) the German tradition who have engaged in such a task, not least because of the consequences a German party must face if it is deemed to be extremist (see below).

As Backes explains, the concept of extremism originates from an Aristotelian tradition, in which the just moral and politico-institutional sphere is set against the excessive exercise of power (2001: 21). It is thus concerned with negative constitutional notions and with the domination of one group over another, and hence involves both anti-constitutional and anti-democratic elements. In the more modern era, and since the advent of the totalitarian regimes of the twentieth century in particular, extremism is most often conceptualized as the antithesis of liberal democracy. This means that on the one hand, it is characterized by its rejection of the 'fundamental values (human rights), procedures and institutions (free, equal, direct and secret elections; party competition; pluralism; parliamentarism; a state based on the rule of law; separation of powers) of the democratic constitutional state' (Backes and Moreau, cited in Roberts, 1994: 463), while on the other, it is distinguishable by what it embraces: absolutism and dogmatism (Backes, 2001: 22).

A definition of extremism as an ideology that incorporates anti-constitutional and anti-democratic features has also been adopted by the German Federal Constitutional Court in its interpretation of the Basic Law. As Saalfeld observes,

> in addition to the principles of political pluralism, the Court has emphasised the rule of law, respect for human rights and civil liberties, free and universal democratic elections, a limitation of government powers through a system of checks and balances, the accountability of government, and independence of the judiciary as fundamental elements of liberal democracy. Furthermore, it has pointed out that liberal democracy is incompatible with the violent or arbitrary exercise of power. Parties whose principles violate one or more of these fundamental characteristics are considered extremist and can be banned by the Federal Constitutional Court. (1993: 180–1)

Since anti-constitutional and anti-democratic elements can be part of a left-wing ideology just as they can be part of a right-wing ideology, political extremism can be of the left or of the right. Right-wing extremism is therefore a particular type of political extremism, and is distinguishable from left-wing extremism. The distinction between the two types of extremism can be made by reference to attitudes towards the principle of fundamental human equality, a principle that lies at the very core of liberal democracy. Whereas left-wing extremism accepts and supports this principle even though it interprets it 'with consequences that mean the principle of total equality destroys the freedoms guaranteed by the rules and institutions of the state of law' (Backes, 2001: 24, this author's translation), right-wing extremism strongly rejects it. Instead, right-wing extremism emphasizes the notion of inequality of individuals, and 'extreme right-wing models of political and social order are rooted in a belief in the necessity of *institutionalised* social *and* political inequality' (Saalfeld, 1993: 181 italics in original).

Such institutionalized social and political inequality may be based on a number of different criteria, but those overwhelmingly favoured by parties and movements of the extreme right have been nationality, race, ethnic group and/or religious denomination. This, to a great extent, helps explain why nationalism, xenophobia, racism and ethnocentrism appear in so many of the existing definitions of right-wing extremism. It remains the case, however, that although these features may help characterize and describe the extreme right, they do not help define it. They are mere manifestations of the principle of fundamental human inequality, which lies at the heart of right-wing extremism.

In the same way as it is misleading to consider nationalism, xenophobia, racism and a call for the strong state as defining features of right-wing extremism, so too is it inaccurate to view an adherence to the legacy of fascism as a defining feature of right-wing extremism. This is because the characteristics of fascism or neo-fascism (to use a term frequently assigned to the post-war extreme right, which drew on the legacy of historical fascism) are also merely manifestations of the higher concept of right-wing extremism.[1] These characteristics (over which there is significant debate but which include extreme nationalism, anti-parliamentarism, anti-pluralism, and the subordination of the individual to the will of the nation or state, to name but a few) are thus only possible features of right-wing extremism rather than necessary ones. While fascist or neo-fascist movements or parties should indeed be considered right-wing extremist, not all right-wing extremist movements or parties may be considered fascist or neo-fascist.

This point is accepted by the vast majority of scholars studying the contemporary extreme right. Billig is explicit on this matter, and argues that 'fascist regimes can be seen as the paradigmatic instances of extreme right-wing politics, but this should not be taken as implying that all extreme right-wing movements are necessarily fascist' (1989: 146). Similarly, Hainsworth maintains that although 'the label "neo-fascism" may be appropriate in some extreme right cases . . . it would be erroneous and reductionist to stereotype the post-war extreme right as parodies of earlier fascist movements' (1992a: 5). Thus, just as racist parties should be seen as a particular type of right-wing extremist party, as was argued above, so too should fascist or neo-fascist parties.

To be absolutely clear, therefore, right-wing extremism is defined by two anti-constitutional and anti-democratic elements:

1 a rejection of the fundamental values, procedures and institutions of the democratic constitutional state (a feature that makes right-wing extremism extremist);
2 a rejection of the principle of fundamental human equality (a feature that makes right-wing extremism right wing).

Of the numerous features that appear in the existing definitions of right-wing extremism, most are mere manifestations of one or other of these two elements. Anti-partyism, anti-pluralism, anti-parliamentarism, a call for a strong state, a demand for a strong leader, an emphasis on law and order, and a call for militarism are all manifestations of the rejection of the fundamental values, procedures and institutions of the democratic constitutional state (i.e. they are all manifestations of extremism), while nationalism, xenophobia, racism, ethnocentrism and exclusionism are all manifestations of the principle of fundamental human inequality (i.e. they are all manifestations of right-wing extremism). These elements are possible features of right-wing extremism rather than necessary ones, and while they help describe and sub-categorize the extreme right, they do not define it.

The assertion that right-wing extremism may be defined by (1) a rejection of the fundamental values, procedures and institutions of the democratic constitutional state and (2) a rejection of the principle of fundamental human equality does not mean that the concept is free from definitional problems, however. On the contrary, the concept remains a difficult one because, as Roberts explains, 'satisfactory operational indicators of extremism are [still] lacking' (1994: 466). The reason for this is that the concept of extremism refers, in the first instance, to what Roberts calls 'structural elements', rather than to the programme or policies of movements or parties. Indeed, he observes that 'the stipulative definition of "extremism" applying to groups opposed to the values, procedures, and institutions of the democratic constitutional state says nothing, in itself, about the programme and policies of organisations or movements that qualify as "extremist"' (1994: 465).

Yet, to operationalize the concept of extremism, scholars have turned to the policies and programmes of the movements and parties, and have made the assumption that 'the content of policy statements of such extremist groups *in themselves* necessitate breaches of the democratic constitutional order' (Roberts, 1994: 465, italics in original). This assumption is, in some instances, not overly problematic. Policy statements that call for the expulsion of all non-whites, such as those put forward by the British NF in the early 1980s, for example, clearly result in a violation of the democratic constitutional order because they give rise to the breaching of the fundamental values of that order, including the principle of fundamental human equality. However, the presumption is more difficult with regard to many other policy statements, as it is less evident whether a violation of the democratic constitutional order will inevitably occur.

This is particularly the case in the contemporary period as most movements and parties described as extremist by academics and other observers regularly underline their commitment to the existing democratic constitutional order and to its values. As Betz notes, 'if not out of conviction then out of expediency, they have tended to abandon much ideological baggage that might sound too extremist [as] parties that have transgressed the boundaries of the permissible and acceptable political discourse soon found themselves penalized in public opinion, at the polls, or in parliament' (1998a: 3).

Though well aware of the problem this presents to the operationalization of right-wing extremism, many scholars argue that the parties' expressions of commitment to the democratic constitutional order should not be taken at face value, however. As Hainsworth puts it, 'nominal commitment to democracy and constitutionalism should not simply be taken as evidence of its actual realization' (2000a: 8). Instead, scholars believe that beneath the homage to the rules of the game lie a discourse and a political culture that clearly undermine the legitimacy of the democratic system. In other words, scholars consider these parties examples of what Sartori (1976) terms 'anti-system' parties or what Kirchheimer refers to as parties that display an 'opposition of principle' (1966: 237).

Gardberg sums up the political culture of the extreme right as one that can be interpreted as a 'subversive stream that is anti-egalitarian and anti-pluralist and that opposes the principle of democratic constitutional states' (1993: 32). Similarly, Voerman and Lucardie argue that 'even if extremists accept the formal constitution, they reject the dominant political culture and party system'. These authors go on to say that, in the case of many modern right-wing extremist parties, they 'seem to accept parliamentary democracy, but reject the prevailing "cosmopolitan" and liberal political culture' (1992: 35–6).

The lack of operational indicators of extremism means that it is very difficult to establish a dividing line between the extreme right and the mainstream right. In fact, Roberts argues that since 'there is an analytic continuity linking democratic parties and organisations to those classified as extremist . . . it is impossible to draw a firm boundary line and say that on one side of the line everything is democratic, on the other everything is "extreme"' (1994: 480). Von Beyme is not quite so categorical but nonetheless maintains that, as right-wing extremist parties have evolved and as more and more parties reject any adherence to the legacy of fascism, 'the dividing line between conservatives and right-wing extremists has become even more blurred' (1988: 2).

Two points can nevertheless be made about this dividing line. First, as the above discussion has shown, the dividing line should be conceived in terms of a party's acceptance or rejection of the fundamental values, procedures and institutions of the democratic order rather than in terms of its spatial location. In other words, a party does not qualify as being of the extreme right just because it is the party furthest to the right in its party system. Instead, it qualifies as being of the extreme right because it rejects or undermines the democratic constitutional order in which it operates. The examples of Iceland or Ireland illustrate this point: although one party in each party system is further to the right than all others, no party in either party system may be considered right-wing extremist because no right-wing party in either party system undermines or rejects the respective democratic constitutional order.

The second point to make about this dividing line is that it is country specific, since the values, procedures and institutions that make-up the democratic constitutional order of each country are specific to that country. Indeed, Roberts questions the universal validity of the concept of right-wing extremism and suggests instead that the concept has a '"relative" quality'. He argues that

> since the basic rights and pattern of democratic institutions and procedures vary not insignificantly from democratic constitution to democratic constitution . . . surely a group which might be extremist in one country might not be so described in another. [Thus] for all the claims to be dealing with a concept of universal validity, 'extremism' is primarily a concept defined in relation to the particular version of the democratic constitutional order. (1994: 467)

The relative nature of the concept is well illustrated if the Scandinavian parties of the extreme right – the Danish FRPd, Norwegian FRPn and Danish DF – are compared to their counterparts elsewhere in Western Europe. The ideology of these parties is somewhat less extreme than that of other right-wing extremist parties. As Ignazi observes, they have 'never made a frontal attack on democracy involving authoritarian solutions' in the way that other extreme right parties have (2003: 148). However, this does not mean that they are not extreme within their own party systems and political culture. Rather, as Ignazi goes on to argue, 'they certainly undermined the system's legitimacy, not just by displaying contempt towards the parties and the politicians, but also by considering the parties as useless, backward, and even harmful' (2003: 148). Thus, 'although their anti-system profile is quite limited compared to that of their other European counterparts', they nonetheless 'qualify for inclusion in [the extreme right] political family' (Ignazi, 2003: 140).

The difficulty – if not impossibility – in establishing where the dividing line between the extreme right and the moderate right lies does not mean that parties of the extreme right cannot be identified and analysed. To be sure, borderline cases exist and scholars continue to disagree over whether these should be considered part of the extreme right party family or not. Yet 'there is a large number of political parties whose extreme right status is not debated' (Mudde, 2000: 16), and an extreme right party family, distinct from the mainstream right, is indeed discernible (Hainsworth, 2000a: 6; Mudde, 2000: 16–17).

Terminology

Before embarking on a detailed examination of the different ideologies of the parties of the extreme right, a few words must be said about terminology.

As the above discussion has shown, the term 'extreme right' is clearly favoured in this book, but a number of other authors have preferred to assign other terminological labels to the parties in question. Indeed, a plethora of terms has been used in conjunction with these parties. As well as being termed extreme right, these parties have been labelled fascist, neo-fascist, Nazi, neo-Nazi, totalitarian, fundamentalist, radical right, new radical right, populist right, neo-populist right, new populist, far right and even simply rightist. And long though it is, this list is probably not exhaustive.

There is a growing consensus in the more recent literature that a number of these terms can be misleading and unhelpful. Perhaps the most unhelpful are 'totalitarian' and 'fundamentalist'. Von Beyme notes the unsuitability of applying the first to the modern parties of the extreme right when he observes 'it is difficult to argue that totalitarianism is possible without the access to power in a given society' (1988: 2). As for the term 'fundamentalist', it has been linked above all to religious movements, and has the unity of the state and the religious order as a central element. Therefore, as Backes explains, it is inappropriate to apply this term to non-religious movements such as the contemporary parties of the extreme right. The term is further unsuitable because it does not denote movements or parties that are specifically of the right (Backes, 2001: 18).

The terms 'fascist', 'neo-fascist', 'Nazi' and 'neo-Nazi' are not without their problems either. To return to a point made earlier, many authors agree that 'fascist' or 'neo-fascist' are no longer accurate labels for the contemporary parties of the extreme right, since many of these have abandoned all references to the legacy of fascism. Most authors instead argue that fascism or neo-fascism is a sub-phenomenon of the extreme right and that fascist or neo-fascist parties are therefore only a particular type of extreme right party (see Billig, 1989; Hainsworth, 1992a; Fennema, 1997; and Backes, 2001, among others). The same is even more true for Nazi or neo-Nazi parties: not only can these parties be considered a sub-type of the extreme right, but they have also been judged to be a sub-type of fascist parties (Billig, 1989).

More common in the recent literature is the use of the terms 'radical right' or 'new radical right'. Indeed, Herbert Kitschelt's influential analysis (1995) is entitled *The Radical Right in Western Europe*, while Hans-Georg Betz famously coined the term 'radical right-wing populist parties', though in more recent work he appears to have dropped the label 'populist' and refers to the parties simply as 'radical right-wing' (e.g. Betz, 2003). Peter Merkl (1997, 2003) has also used the term 'radical right', though he does seem to use it interchangeably with the term 'extreme right'.

A number of other authors take issue with the term 'radical' being used to refer to the contemporary parties of the extreme right, however. The main objection they have is that the term has been used to refer to a wide variety of movements, most of which have been quite distinct from the modern parties of the extreme right. As Backes explains, the term originated in eighteenth-century England but was soon used on the other side of the Atlantic to refer to advocates of Utilitarianism. It was then swiftly adopted by left-liberal and republican parties in France and Italy (2001: 17). In the twentieth century, however, the term was applied to rather different movements. In the United States it was used in the immediate post-World War II period to refer to extreme conservative movements that were 'characterized by strict moral traditionalism and an obsessive anticommunism' (Ignazi, 2003: 28). As Ignazi notes, therefore, its varied usage means that the term 'radical' has taken on 'ambiguous connotations'. Furthermore, the fact that it has been applied to movements that did not display anti-system tendencies means that it is 'too loose [to] be fruitfully applied to the analysis of extreme right parties' (2003: 28).

This last point finds resonance in the German usage of the term. Since 1974, the Federal Office for the Protection of the Constitution has labelled 'radical' those groups or parties that display a critique of the constitutional order without any anti-democratic behaviour or intention. By contrast, those that exhibit anti-democratic, anti-constitutional or anti-liberal values or intent are labelled 'extremist' and, as was noted above, such parties can be banned by the Federal Constitutional Court. As Roberts (1994) has argued, and as was discussed above, the lack of satisfactory operational indicators of extremism means that, in practice, making the distinction between radicalism and extremism is very difficult, and it remains the case that the contemporary German parties of the extreme right have not (yet) been officially defined as extremist, and have thus not (yet) been banned. However, if 'anti-system' is taken to mean behaviour or values that undermine the legitimacy of the democratic system, the parties in question are clearly parties that display anti-system tendencies, and as such they should not be labelled 'radical', as this term does not capture their anti-systemness. As Westle and Niedermayer note, this explains why, despite the fact that these parties have not been officially defined as extremist by the Federal Office for the Protection of the Constitution, 'in the scientific literature [they] are predominantly judged as being clearly on the extreme right' (1992: 87).

The preference for the term 'extreme right' over 'radical right' that is apparent in the German or German-based literature has been mirrored elsewhere. As a result of the different connotations of the term 'radical' and the fact that it does not denote movements or parties that display an anti-systemness, it has been increasingly replaced in the literature by the term 'extreme right'.

Another term increasingly used in recent years to refer to the contemporary parties of the extreme right is 'populist', or its derivative 'neo-populist'. As was just observed, Hans-Georg Betz (1993a, 1993b, 1994) has shown a preference for this term over the label 'extreme right' and has referred to the modern parties as radical right-wing populist parties. French authors have also favoured this term, and have tended to refer to the contemporary parties as national-populist parties (see Taguieff, 1984, 1986, 1995; Winock, 1993;

Perrineau, 1997, among others). Other authors have used the term 'populist' to refer to a specific type of right-wing extremist party. Taggart, for example, identifies as 'New Populist' those extreme right parties that fuse 'the anti-politics stance of the New Politics with the broad-based protest of the populist right' (1995: 35). Similarly, Kitschelt (1995) uses the term 'populist' to describe certain parties of the extreme right, notably the Austrian FPÖ and the Italian LN.

The term 'populism' is not unproblematic, however, especially when it is applied to the contemporary parties of the extreme right. While the term may be used meaningfully to describe or characterize certain parties of the extreme right, it is of little use to denote or identify a separate party family. This is because populism refers to a particular political style or form rather than to a specific political ideology (Taguieff, 1995; Mudde, 1996a: 231; Backes, 2001: 20). It therefore brings together parties that are ideologically quite distinct from each other, and within the populist group many parties that are not of the extreme right (and that do not espouse anti-democratic sentiments) sit alongside ones that are. The usefulness of the term is further limited when it is applied to the parties of the extreme right because, just as not all populist parties are of the extreme right (or even of the right), not all parties of the extreme right have adopted a political style that may be described as populist.

The term 'far right' is also problematic, even though it is used quite widely in both the academic literature and the media. Its limitation lies in the fact that it suggests that cases are selected according to their relative spatial location. However, as was discussed above, a party should be considered for inclusion in the extreme right party family according to its acceptance or rejection of the fundamental values, procedures and institutions of the democratic constitutional order, and according to its acceptance or rejection of the principle of fundamental human equality, rather than in terms of its spatial location. A party does not qualify as being of the extreme right just because it is the party furthest to the right in its party system. As for the term 'rightist', which is used frequently in the study by Kitschelt, for example, it is simply too imprecise to be used to describe the parties of the extreme right, as it fails to distinguish them from their mainstream counterparts.

In the light of these discussions, the term 'extreme right' is clearly favoured in this book. Not only does it overcome the problems associated with the alternative terms, but it also has the advantage of being squarely concerned with party ideology and of evoking notions of anti-democracy and anti-systemness, which lie at the very heart of the concept of right-wing extremism. Some of the other terms discussed above are used within the book, but they are not employed interchangeably with the term 'extreme right' as they have been in some of the other studies of right-wing extremism. Instead, they are used, where appropriate, to describe sub-groups of the wider extreme right party family only.

The study of right-wing extremist party ideology:
existing typologies and their limitations

In view of the continuing debates over what constitutes right-wing extremism and over what terminology should be used to describe the parties, more and more studies have sought to turn attention away from conceptual definitions and instead have endeavoured to examine the actual object in question – that is, they have focused on the nature of the right-wing extremist parties themselves. The single-party case study is the most common approach to this kind of research, but in addition to such works, a handful of comparative analyses of the ideologies of the parties of the extreme right exists.

The main impetus behind most of these comparative studies of right-wing extremist ideology is the desire to illustrate the diversity that exists among these parties. In particular, the parties that have emerged and prospered during the 'third wave' of post-war right-wing extremist activity are, for the most part, distinct from those older parties that embrace some form of historical legacy, be it of a fascist or some other kind. The French FN and the Austrian FPÖ, for instance, are markedly different in nature from the British NF or the Italian MSI. Therefore, through their examination of the ideology of the parties, the existing comparative studies have shown that the combination of the rise of newer parties and the continued survival of older parties has rendered the extreme right party family increasingly diverse in composition.

In addition to illustrating the variety that exists within the extreme right party family – something that is clearly of interest and importance in itself – these comparative studies also shed some light on which type or types of right-wing extremist ideology are most commonly associated with electoral success. Whereas the connection between ideology and electoral success is only implicit in some of these studies, in others it is wholly explicit. For example, Richard Stöss's analysis of West German right-wing extremism (1988), Christopher Husbands's overview of the extreme right in Western Europe at the beginning of the 1990s (1992a), and Hans-Georg Betz's broader study of West European radical right-wing populism (1993b, 1994) all stop short of offering a discussion of which type of party is the most successful in electoral terms. In contrast, in his influential article on the emergence of right-wing extremist parties, Piero Ignazi (1992) discusses which of his two types of party ('old' and 'new') is electorally most successful. In a similar fashion, Paul Taggart (1995) observes that the right-wing extremist parties that he terms 'New Populist' are those that have experienced the greatest success at the polls. The link between ideology and electoral success is even more explicit in Herbert Kitschelt's analysis (1995), as a core objective of this study is precisely to explain why right-wing extremist parties have performed well at the polls in some countries but not in others. Ideology is therefore examined as one of the factors that might account for the uneven electoral success of these parties.

Although these existing comparative studies provide valuable insights into the diversity that exists within the extreme right party family, and although some of these works also point to which types of right-wing extremist parties are more successful at the polls, these existing typologies nonetheless suffer from a number of shortcomings, which limit the extent to which they can be used as a basis from which to examine the link between the parties' ideology and their electoral success in close detail. In the light of this, a new, alternative typology of right-wing extremist parties will be constructed in this chapter, with which it will be possible to investigate fully the influence of ideology on the parties' electoral success. In the first instance, however, it is useful to examine the limitations of the existing typologies in some depth and to draw lessons from these so that the typology put forward later in the chapter may avoid some of the pitfalls most commonly associated with this type of study.

A first limitation of the existing typologies is that the majority of them do not examine all of the parties of the extreme right that are of concern to this book. With the notable exceptions of Ignazi's and Taggart's studies, the existing analyses include only certain members of the extreme right party family. Stöss's categorization remains limited to the West German extreme right; the study by Betz fails to include older parties such as the Italian MSI, the German Nationaldemokratische Partei Deutschlands (NPD) and the British NF; and the works by Husbands and Kitschelt omit some of the smaller and less successful West European right-wing extremist parties such as the Belgian Front National/Front voor die Natie (FN(b)) or the Spanish Falangistas.

A second reason for not wishing to use the existing categorizations as a basis from which to examine the influence of ideology on the electoral scores of the parties of the extreme right is that they are now all to varying degrees out of date. With the exception of Stöss's study, which has a historical focus and concentrates on the West German extreme right of the 1950s and 1960s, all of the typologies referred to above examine the extreme right in Western Europe in the 1980s and in the first few years of the 1990s. Therefore, because they were compiled when they were, they do not take into account more recent developments in the West European extreme right, such as the split in the Danish FRPd in 1995 and the establishment of the rival DF, the transformation of the Italian MSI into the AN in the same year and the subsequent breakaway of Pino Rauti's Movimento Sociale-Fiamma Tricolore (Ms-Ft), or the formation of the Front Nouveau de Belgique (FNB) as a result of Marguerite Bastien's defection from the Belgian FN(b) in 1997. Making use of these studies to examine the link between ideology and extreme right-wing party success would therefore result in the investigation being out of date.

A further, more fundamental reason for deciding not to use the studies mentioned above to examine the influence of ideology on the parties' electoral success is that some of these analyses display methodological and theoretical shortcomings. More specifically, a number of the existing typologies fail to satisfy the conditions of exhaustiveness and mutual exclusiveness around which typologies should be built (Sartori, 1984; Marradi, 1990). In Betz's study, for example, the fact that two parties are not assigned to either of the two types suggests that a third type of party is possible, and that the typology is therefore not exhaustive in nature. As the typology stands, the Austrian FPÖ and the Swiss Autopartei der Schweiz (APS) are not included in either the 'neo-liberal populist' or the 'national populist' type because they 'place equal emphasis on both a neo-liberal and an anti-immigrant program' (1993b: 684). While this may indeed be the case, in order for the typology to be exhaustive, a third category would have to be created to accommodate such parties. The inclusion of this third category would mean that every possible state of the property that is being used as a basis of division (in this case the emphasis placed on the neo-liberal elements of the programme as compared to that placed on the anti-immigration elements) is allocated to one of the typology's categories.

In some of the other studies, the condition of mutual exclusiveness is not met. In Taggart's categorization, for instance, the German Republikaner, the French FN and the Flemish VB may, arguably, be accommodated in either one of the two categories of parties. Indeed, Taggart himself argues that these three competitors are 'examples of parties that blur the distinction' between 'neo-fascist' and 'New Populist' parties (1995: 40). In contrast to Betz's analysis, this problem with Taggart's study would not be solved even if a third category were constructed. Instead, the difficulty lies with the basis of division used. The features Taggart highlights as important in distinguishing between 'neo-fascist' and 'New Populist' parties do not reflect a particular property of the parties that may be categorized into all its various states. As such, these features are not sufficiently stringent to allocate parties to one type and one type only and, as a result, the two categories in the typology are not mutually exclusive. Taggart is clearly aware of this since he argues that 'New Populism and neo-fascism are not *necessarily* contradictory' (1995: 40, italics in original). This does not stop the principle of mutual exclusiveness from being violated, however.

The distinction between the categories in Kitschelt's typology is also somewhat unclear. The Italian MSI and the German NPD are described as 'likely to express shades of fascist thinking that range from a workerist (and now welfare chauvinist) "social fascism" . . . to a "corporatist capitalism"' (1995: 64). The apparent uncertainty over whether to locate these two parties in the 'welfare chauvinist' or in the 'fascist' category of parties suggests that, here too, the bases of division used to subdivide the extreme right party family are not stringent enough to ensure that all of the categories in this study are mutually exclusive.

Of all the existing typologies, Ignazi's arguably displays the most theoretical and methodological rigour. The bases of division that are used are such that the different categories are mutually exclusive and the typology is also exhaustive in nature. In addition, it is one of the most comprehensive of the existing comparative studies, since it includes the great majority of West European right-wing extremist parties. In spite of these attributes, however, in terms of providing a base from which this chapter may investigate the link between the parties' ideology and their electoral success, Ignazi's typology remains far from ideal.

The main reason for this is that Ignazi is primarily interested in examining the different parties of the extreme right from a democracy/anti-democracy perspective. In other words, he is concerned above all with whether the parties accept or reject the existing democratic consensus, something that leads him to consider both the parties' ideological legacy and their attitudes towards the system. This is in no way a criticism of the typology – on the contrary, as has been observed already, the study is extremely sound and, for that reason, has become very influential – but it does mean that the different parties within each of Ignazi's two groups ('old' and 'new') continue to exhibit significant variation when features other than their attitudes towards democracy are taken into account. For instance, even though their views on democracy are relatively similar, the British NF and the Spanish Frente Nacional, two of the parties located within Ignazi's 'old' extreme right category, differ markedly in their attitude towards foreigners and people of other ethnicities. Whereas racism and xenophobia lie at the heart of the NF's ideology, these features do not play a part in the belief structure of the Frente Nacional.

The fact that significant differences continue to exist between parties of the same group implies that, in Ignazi's typology, the diversity present within the extreme right party family is not illustrated as fully as it could have been had more bases of division been employed. This, in turn, suggests that, if such a model were to be used to examine the link between the parties' ideology and their electoral success, the extent to which ideology might be able to explain the disparity in the electoral fortunes of the parties would possibly be limited. In other words, with a model such as this, the explanatory power of ideology in an overall account of the disparity in the electoral fortunes of the parties of the extreme right could potentially be curtailed. This is because it may well be the case that some parties have been more electorally successful than others due to characteristics not mentioned in Ignazi's typology. For example, it is quite possible that the most successful right-wing extremist parties are those that have an ideology in which xenophobia (a feature not included in Ignazi's typology) is central. Therefore, in spite of its strengths, Ignazi's typology will not be used as a model on which to base an examination of the link between the ideology of the parties of the extreme right and their electoral success. In addition to his model being rather dated by now, it does not contain sufficient bases of division with which to fully illustrate the diversity that exists within the right-wing extremist party family.

From this examination of the limitations of the existing typologies, it has become clear that if the relationship between the ideology of the parties of the extreme right and their levels of electoral success is to be properly investigated a new typology is necessary. This typology, however, must be sure to draw on the lessons learned from the existing studies. Namely, it must:

- include all right-wing extremist parties in Western Europe;
- be as up to date as possible;
- be constructed so that its types are jointly exhaustive;
- be constructed so that its types are mutually exclusive;
- attempt to reflect the full diversity of the extreme right party family.

In addition, and in contrast to some of the existing studies, the logic behind the construction of the typology will be fully explained. It will be apparent what bases of division are being employed, and why. It should therefore also be clear why certain parties are grouped together, while others are not.

An alternative typology of right-wing extremist parties

To fully illustrate the diversity present within the right-wing extremist party family, three bases of division have been chosen with which to construct this typology. These are:

1 the importance attached by the parties to the issue of immigration;
2 the nature of the parties' racist attitudes;
3 the parties' attitudes towards democracy, parliamentarism and pluralism.

These criteria have been selected because they relate to elements of right-wing extremist ideology most frequently mentioned in the existing literature. Indeed, in his review of the existing definitions of right-wing extremism, which was referred to above, Mudde found that at least half the studies he examined pointed to xenophobia, racism, anti-democracy and the strong state (1995a: 206) as being key features of right-wing extremism.[2] While the above discussion of the concept of right-wing extremism argued that these elements are only possible features rather than necessary ones, and emphasized that they are therefore not appropriate for defining right-wing extremism, it nonetheless suggested that these features are useful for describing and sub-categorizing the extreme right party family.

Clearly, the first basis of division proposed for this typology relates to xenophobia, and the second to racism. The third encompasses both the parties' attitudes towards democracy and their views on the state. These two final features are merged into one basis of division because the views right-wing extremist parties have on democracy and on how society should be organized are closely related to their position on the role of the state.

These three bases of division also allow the typology to distance itself from examining the impact that the legacy of fascism (or any other historical ideology) has had on the different parties of the extreme right. This is an advantage because evaluating the importance of fascism in the ideologies of right-wing extremist parties is fraught with difficulties. In some instances, parties have referred to past legacies even though these have not formed a central part of their ideologies. This was the case, for example, when Jörg Haider, the leader of the Austrian FPÖ, commented on the Third Reich's 'competent employment policies' (Knight, 1992: 285). In contrast, parties that do draw on such historical traditions in their ideologies have, as Ignazi observes, frequently toned down symbolic references to fascism so as to avoid stigmatization (1992: 10). Given this behaviour, it is extremely difficult to assess the extent to which the ideologies of the parties are actually informed by such legacies.

Each basis of division will now be considered in turn. The ideologies of the right-wing extremist parties will be explored in detail and, in the first instance, the parties will be categorized along each basis of division separately. Then the three bases of division will be combined to produce the final typology. Once the separate types of right-wing extremist party are identified, the electoral success of the parties of each type will be examined so that it will become possible to ascertain whether the electoral performance of the different parties is in any way linked to their ideology.

Importance attached to the issue of immigration

Attitudes towards the issue of immigration reflect the importance of xenophobia in the ideologies of the different right-wing extremist parties. Moreover, a party's xenophobia – its fear, hatred of and hostility towards foreigners – reveals its concern for 'internal homogenization', which Koch (1991) argues is one of the two forms of the nationalist political programme.[3] As Table 2.1 illustrates, right-wing extremist parties can be divided into two groups according to the importance they attach to the issue of immigration. For some parties this issue is a priority, and they can thus be described as radically xenophobic. In contrast, xenophobia does not feature in the ideology of other right-wing extremist parties.

Parties of the first group view combating immigration as their overriding concern. The French FN, for example, has demanded the immediate expulsion of all illegal immigrants and the strict control of political refugees ever since the late 1970s when Jean-Pierre Stirbois (who later became the FN's secretary general) famously called on immigrants from beyond the Mediterranean to 'go back to your huts' (Hainsworth, 2000b: 24). The issue has remained central

Table 2.1   Importance attached to immigration in the ideologies of the different
right-wing extremist parties of Western Europe

Central to party's ideology	Not central to party's ideology
Freiheitliche Partei Österreichs (FPÖ) Austria	Fremskridtspartiet (FRPd) before
Vlaams Blok (VB) Belgium (Flanders)	mid-1980s, Denmark
Front National (FN(b)) Belgium (Wallonia)	Ethniko Komma (EK) Greece
Front Nouveau de Belgique (FNB) Belgium	Alleanza Nazionale (AN) Italy
(Wallonia)	Lega Nord (LN) before mid-1990s,
British National Party (BNP) Britain	Italy
National Front (NF) Britain	Movimento Sociale–Fiamma Tricolore
Dansk Folkeparti (DF) Denmark	(Ms-Ft) Italy
Fremskridtspartiet (FRPd) since mid-1980s,	Fremskrittspartiet (FRPn) before
Denmark	mid-1980s, Norway
Front National (FN) France	Falange Española Auténtica (FEA)
Mouvement National Républicain (MNR)	Spain
France	Falange Española de las Juntas de
Deutsche Volksunion (DVU) Germany	Ofensiva Nacional-Sindicalista
Nationaldemokratische Partei Deutschlands	(FE de las JONS) Spain
(NPD) Germany	Falange Española de las Juntas de
Republikaner Germany	Ofensiva Nacional-Sindicalista –
Lega Nord (LN) since mid-1990s, Italy	sector Diego Marquez (FE de las
Fedrelandspartiet (FLP) Norway	JONS sector DM) Spain
Fremskrittspartiet (FRPn) since mid-1980s,	Falange Española Independiente (FEI)
Norway	Spain
Ny Demokrati (ND) Sweden	Lega dei Ticinesi (LdT) Switzerland
Sverigedemokraterna (SDk) Sweden	
Freiheitspartei der Schweiz (FPS) Switzerland	[Ethniki Politiki Enosis (EPEN)
Schweizer Demokraten (SD) Switzerland	Greece]
	[Komma Proodeftikon (KP) Greece]
[Agir Belgium (Wallonia)]	[Movimento Sociale Italiano (MSI)
[Parti des Forces Nouvelles (PFNb) Belgium	Italy]
(Wallonia)]	[Partido da Democracia Cristã (PDC)
[Centrumdemocraten (CD) Netherlands]	Portugal]
[Centrumpartij (CP) Netherlands]	[Frente Nacional Spain]
[Centrumpartij'86 (CP'86) Netherlands]	[Fuerza Nueva Spain]
[Nederlandse Volksunie (NVU) Netherlands]	
[Det Nya Partiet (DNP) Sweden]	

Note: Parties in square brackets no longer exist.

in more recent years too. In both the 1993 and 1997 party programmes, immigration was addressed in the very first chapter (Marcus, 1995: 100; Front
National, 1997a). The FN seeks to reduce the length of employment contracts
for non-Europeans, rejects the automatic acquisition of French citizenship by
children born in France to foreign parents, and calls for an end to dual citizenship (Marcus, 1995: 107). Furthermore, the majority of the FN's other
policies – be they on the family, health, housing or law and order – all revolve
around this political issue, with the notion of national and European preference lying at the heart of the party's programme (Hainsworth, 1992b: 49;

Mayer, 1998: 16). As Marcus argues, immigration has thus become the FN's 'ideological aspic' (1995: 101).

The French Mouvement National Républicain (MNR), which split from the FN in 1998–99, has an attitude towards immigration that is very similar to that of the FN. In fact, the entire political programme of the MNR closely mirrors that of the pre-split FN, since Mégret, who now heads the MNR, drafted the majority of FN manifestos (Bastow, 2000).

With the election of Franz Schönhuber to the position of party chairman in 1985, and with the fall of the Berlin Wall, immigration also became the overriding concern for the German Republikaner. In its 1990 programme, the party called for the repatriation of the 4.5 million immigrants living in Germany and, like its French counterparts, it recommended that employment contracts for foreigners should not be granted indefinitely (Childs, 1995: 300). In addition, the party opposes the right of immigrants to permanent residence in Germany and objects to foreigners bringing their dependent families into the country (Backes, 1990: 10). It also recommends that the naturalization laws should be tightened and that dual nationality should be banned (Saalfeld, 1993: 191; Veen *et al.*, 1993: 16). Thus the issue of immigration informs the majority of the Republikaner's other policies, very much as it does the FN's (Backer, 2000: 100).

Immigration also occupies a central place in the ideologies of the German Deutsche Volksunion (DVU) and NPD (Mudde, 1995a: 213). Both parties demand a significant reduction in the number of immigrants and asylum-seekers, and favour measures such as repatriation schemes in order to 'solve' the immigration problem (Saalfeld, 1993: 183).

The attitude of the Austrian FPÖ towards immigration is similar to that of both the French and the German right-wing extremist parties. Jörg Haider and his party did not hesitate to exploit the sentiments of anxiety felt within Austria after the arrival of many foreigners from the former Communist countries of Eastern Europe in 1989 and 1990 (Morrow, 2000: 51). The FPÖ argued that this surge in immigration was leading to higher levels of unemployment, and demanded an immediate stop to foreigners entering the country. In addition, the party called for the repatriation of all foreigners already in residence in Austria. Although the tightening of immigration and asylum legislation by the socialist interior minister in the early 1990s deprived the FPÖ of some of its ammunition (Knight, 1992: 296–7), the party continues to place the issue of immigration very high on its agenda. This was evident in the 1997 party programme, which 'clearly stated the central role of national identity and the necessity to defend it from foreign invasion' (Ignazi, 2003: 119).

Immigration has also become the most important policy area for the Danish and Norwegian right-wing extremist parties in more recent years. The issue was of little concern until the mid-1980s, but following an increase in the number of foreigners entering both countries, the two Progress Parties (the FRPd and the FRPn) began to address the question of immigration more and more (Andersen and Bjørklund, 2000: 205). They began to demand that the number of immigrants should be sharply reduced, that integration into society should be strongly encouraged, and that immigrants should be sent home if they committed serious crimes or if conditions in their home countries improved sufficiently (Svåsand, 1998: 84). The parties' continued emphasis on these policies has been such that today xenophobia and immigration are key elements for both Progress Parties (Widfeldt, 2000: 491). The issue is also central to the ideology of the Danish DF, which was formed in 1995 when the FRPd split. It is key in the ideology of the Norwegian Fedrelandspartiet (FLP) too.

Like its Danish and Norwegian counterparts, the Swedish Ny Demokrati (ND) has been greatly concerned with the issue of immigration. During the 1991 election campaign, the party stood on a platform that included measures to repatriate immigrants (Arter, 1992: 357). It was also very critical of the government's policies towards immigration and asylum-seekers, linking immigration to crime, and describing refugees as welfare scroungers (Widfeldt, 2000: 496). Sweden's Sverigedemokraterna (SDk) and Ian Wachtmeister's Det Nya Partiet (DNP), which he formed in 1998 after he left Ny Demokrati but which has since been dissolved, are two other parties with views on the issue of non-European immigration that are similar to those of the ND (AXT, 2001: 8–10; Widfeldt, 2000: 496).

As the Scandinavian Progress Parties began to concern themselves more and more with the issue of immigration from the mid-1980s onwards, so likewise immigration has become central in the ideology of the Italian LN since the mid-1990s. Ignazi argues that by 1996 the LN had become the 'only Italian party openly to address a xenophobic discourse' and that 'the opposition to multiculturalism and the practice of making foreigners the scapegoats are constant themes of party propaganda' (2003: 59).

The issue of immigration also features centrally in the ideology of the Belgian right-wing extremist parties. The VB perceives the 'massive' presence of foreigners as 'the most important cause of moral decay' and claims that immigration is 'destroying Flemish culture' (Swyngedouw, 1998: 65–6). Accordingly, since the mid-1980s, the anti-immigrant issue has become the central plank of the party's electoral platform, overshadowing even the nationalist issue (Swyngedouw, 1998: 67; Mudde, 1995b: 11). The party calls for a 'watertight' end to immigration and demands the immediate expulsion of all immigrants who are found to have no papers, who have committed criminal offences, or who have been unemployed for more than three months (Hossay, 1996: 343). Although their ideologies are significantly less well-developed than that of the VB, the Belgian FN(b) and its offshoot, the FNB, have similarly virulent views on migrants and subscribe to many of the same policies as the VB, including the repatriation of immigrants (Fitzmaurice, 1992: 307; Swyngedouw, 1998: 59). The same is also true of the Parti des Forces Nouvelles (PFNb), and of Agir, two very small Wallonian parties that had ceased to contest elections by the 1990s.

Immigration was also a key element in the ideologies of the now defunct Dutch Nederlandse Volksunie (NVU), Centrumpartij (CP), Centrumpartij'86 (CP'86) and CD. The CP saw immigration from countries with a non-European culture as the root of a whole host of social problems, from environmental concerns to unemployment. In response, the party called for the immediate cessation of immigration, and for the expulsion of illegal immigrants (Voerman and Lucardie, 1992: 40). The CP'86 also demanded the repatriation of all foreigners, starting with those not legally entitled to be in the Netherlands and those with criminal records (Mudde, 2000: 151). As for the CD, its obsession with the dangers of multiculturalism was such that, as Mudde and Van Holsteyn argue, 'the ideology of the CD is almost exclusively focused on the immigration issue' (2000: 150). Like those of the French FN and the German Republikaner, all the CD's other policies were informed by the party's attitude towards immigration (Lucardie, 1998: 118).

The Swiss Schweizer Demokraten (SD) are also preoccupied by the immigration issue. As Gentile and Kriesi observe, even though the party has changed its name twice since it was first founded,[4] its programme has remained fundamentally the same and continues to emphasize anti-immigrant concerns (1998: 126). More specifically, 'since the early 1970s, the Swiss Democrats have sought to reduce or at least restrict the number of foreign residents in Switzerland [and] have also been involved in the movement to limit the right of foreigners to be recognized as refugees, especially for non-European nationals' (1998: 131). Anti-foreigner sentiment is similarly central in the ideology of the Swiss Freiheitspartei der Schweiz (FPS) (Husbands, 1992a: 281).

The British right-wing extremist parties are one last set of parties for which the fight against immigration is a priority. The NF's vehement xenophobia and anti-immigrant sentiment were illustrated in the party's most notorious policy – the compulsory repatriation of New Commonwealth immigrants (Thurlow, 1998: 262–3). The BNP's policies are similar, even though Nick Griffin, who assumed the party leadership in 1999, seems more guarded about the issue of forced repatriation (Eatwell, 2000b: 189).

All the parties just discussed are grouped together in Table 2.1. Since immigration is central to the ideologies of all these parties, and since they all perceive the fight against immigration to be a priority, all can be considered radically xenophobic.

In contrast to parties of the first group, the fight against immigration does not preoccupy the Italian MSI/AN and Movimento Sociale–Fiamma Tricolore (Ms-Ft), the Spanish Falangistas[5] and Fuerza Nueva/Frente Nacional, or the Portuguese Partido da Democracia Cristã (PDC). These parties therefore form part of a separate, second group. Commenting on the ideology of the Italian MSI, Griffin observes that 'in marked contrast to [the British NF and the German Republikaner] and to . . . Le Pen's Front

National, the MSI had in the late 1980s deliberately veered away from an overtly racist "anti-immigration" platform' (1996: 132). Furthermore, xenophobia remains insignificant in the ideology of the AN, the successor party to the MSI. As Ignazi notes, at the Fiuggi party congress of 1995, Fini, the party leader, 'clearly abandoned any tough standing regarding immigration' (1996a: 707).[6]

The lack of emphasis placed on the issue of immigration by the Spanish Falangistas and Fuerza Nueva/Frente Nacional can be explained, in part, by the fact that there was an absence of anti-immigrant rhetoric in the Franco era.[7] Furthermore, 'the anti-Muslim sentiment that pervades the European neo-populist movement may be difficult to mobilize in a country that was once part of the Islamic empire' (Davis, 1998: 161). With non-nationals accounting for less than 2 percent of the Spanish population, it is also very difficult for the parties to blame these individuals for the high level of unemployment (Ellwood, 1995: 103; Casals, 2001: 330). As for Portugal, even though there are significantly more black or mixed-race people here than in Spain, 'the anti-immigrant hysteria which has revived the far Right in France, Austria and elsewhere, has passed Portugal by' (Gallagher, 1992: 244).

The fight against immigration is also not central in the ideology of the Swiss Lega dei Ticinesi (LdT), nor was it in that of the Italian LN until the mid-1990s. Although the LdT has campaigned for the defence of the cultural autonomy of the Ticino region and has criticized other cultures in the process, and although its attitude towards refugees is not very favourable (Mazzoleni, 1999: 80–1), the party has never developed an ideology in which the fight against immigration is central and in which all other themes revolve around this issue. Similarly, until the mid-1990s the LN used the issue of immigration in order to attract votes. However, Bossi's xenophobic slurs in this period must be viewed as provocative arguments only, designed to shock and earn him public attention, rather than as expressions of the party's true beliefs (Kitschelt, 1995: 162, 175; Gallagher, 1993: 620).

The ideology of the Greek parties of the extreme right is not centred on the issue of immigration either. The Ethniko Komma (EK), like its predecessors the Ethniki Politiki Enosis (EPEN) and the Komma Proodeftikon (KP), is concerned above all with 'restoring Greece's national strength' and promoting a return to 'Hellenization' in public life rather than fighting immigration (Dimitras, 1992: 265). As in Spain, the lack of emphasis on the issue of immigration by the Greek parties of the extreme right may, in part, be explained by the high ethnic homogeneity of the Greek population.

As was mentioned earlier, the issue of immigration hardly featured in the ideologies of the Scandinavian Progress Parties until the mid-1980s. Indeed, in the 1973 FRPn and FRPd pamphlets the issue was not even referred to (Andersen and Bjørklund, 2000: 204). Therefore the Progress Parties of the 1970s and early 1980s are categorized in the second group of parties in Table 2.1 rather than the first.

Racist attitudes

Racism, which may be defined as the belief that natural and hereditary differences exist between groups of people, is another frequently mentioned characteristic of right-wing extremism (Miles and Phizacklea, 1979). That said, it is not a defining element of right-wing extremism, and the contemporary parties of the extreme right exhibit different types of racist attitudes. The views of the parties on race can therefore be used as a second basis of division in the present typology. More specifically, right-wing extremist parties can be divided into three categories according to their attitudes on race. Parties of a first group embrace classical racism; those of a second group espouse new racism or culturism; and parties of a third group adhere to ideologies in which racism plays no part. These three categories are illustrated in Table 2.2.

The first group consists of parties that distinguish groups solely on the grounds of race (rather than culture) and that embrace overtly anti-Semitic beliefs. These parties, which stress the inequalities of races, can be described as adhering to classical racism (Barker, 1981). The British NF and BNP espouse classically racist beliefs. John Tyndall and Martin Webster, who assumed control of the NF in its heyday in the 1970s, both had their roots in the tradition of British neo-Nazism that originated in the pre-war Imperial Fascist League. They were concerned above all with the racial purity of Britain and warned against the degeneration of the British race brought about by ethnic cross-breeding (Thurlow, 1998: 265–6). They were also distinctively anti-Semitic. Despite some change in direction when Nick Griffin and Joe Pierce took control of the NF in 1983, this type of racism still characterizes the party's inner core, although publicly the repatriation of blacks on the grounds of non-assimilation is emphasized (Husbands, 1988a: 71–2). The BNP also adheres to classical racism. This similarity is partly explained by the fact that it was Tyndall who set up the BNP, two years after he resigned from the NF in 1980 (Eatwell, 1992: 178).

The German NPD has also traditionally adhered to notions of classical racism. Admittedly, the importance the party attaches to the white race has been toned down in recent years, with echoes of biological racism being eliminated from its public programme in favour of greater emphasis on the importance of the German *Volk* (Backes, 1990: 15). This moderation stems mainly from the party's fears of being outlawed by the Federal Constitutional Court for exhibiting anti-democratic behaviour. An examination of the NPD's internal literature shows clear continuities with the prewar German extreme right tradition that fed into National Socialism, and that undeniably included vehement white supremacism and aggressive anti-Semitism. The racist sentiments of the DVU are similar to, if not more extreme than, those of the NPD. The DVU also embraces strong nationalism and patriotism. In addition, it overtly glorifies the National Socialist past and challenges the responsibility of the Nazis as regards the Holocaust. Its

Table 2.2 Racist attitudes of the different right-wing extremist parties of Western Europe

Adhere to classical racism	Adhere to culturism	Not racist
British National Party (BNP) Britain National Front (NF) Britain Deutsche Volksunion (DVU) Germany Nationaldemokratische Partei Deutschlands (NPD) Germany [Parti des Forces Nouvelles (PFNb) Belgium (Wallonia)] [Centrumpartij'86 (CP'86) Netherlands] [Nederlandse Volksunie (NVU) Netherlands]	Freiheitliche Partei Österreichs (FPÖ) Austria Vlaams Blok (VB) Belgium (Flanders) Front National (FN(b)) Belgium (Wallonia) Front Nouveau de Belgique (FNB) Belgium (Wallonia) Dansk Folkeparti (DF) Denmark Fremskridtspartiet (FRPd) since mid-1980s, Denmark Front National (FN) France Mouvement National Républicain (MNR) France Republikaner Germany Lega Nord (LN) since mid-1990s, Italy Fedrelandspartiet (FLP) Norway Fremskrittspartiet (FRPn) since mid-1980s, Norway Ny Demokrati (ND) Sweden Sverigedemokraterna (SDk) Sweden Freiheitspartei der Schweiz (FPS) Switzerland Schweizer Demokraten (SD) Switzerland [Agir Belgium (Wallonia)] [Centrumdemocraten (CD) Netherlands] [Centrumpartij (CP) Netherlands] [Det Nya Partiet (DNP) Sweden]	Fremskridtspartiet (FRPd) before mid-1980s, Denmark Ethniko Komma (EK) Greece Alleanza Nazionale (AN) Italy Lega Nord (LN) before mid-1990s, Italy Movimento Sociale-Fiamma Tricolore (Ms-Ft) Italy Fremskrittspartiet (FRPn) before mid-1980s, Norway Falange Española Auténtica (FEA) Spain Falange Española de las Juntas de Ofensiva Nacional-Sindicalista (FE de las JONS) Spain Falange Española de las Juntas de Ofensiva Nacional-Sindicalista – sector Diego Marquez (FE de las JONS sector DM) Spain Falange Española Independiente (FEI) Spain Lega dei Ticinesi (LdT) Switzerland [Ethniki Politiki Enosis (EPEN) Greece] [Komma Proodeftikon (KP) Greece] [Movimento Sociale Italiano (MSI) Italy] [Partido da Democracia Cristã (PDC) Portugal] [Frente Nacional Spain] [Fuerza Nueva Spain]

Note: Parties in square brackets no longer exist.

anti-Semitism is particularly fervent (Roberts, 1994: 335; Backes and Mudde, 2000: 462).

The former Dutch NVU was another right-wing extremist party that embraced classical racism. As Voerman and Lucardie observe, 'Glimmerveen [the party leader] and his comrades could be considered racists in the narrow, classical sense. They believed in the superiority of the white race in general and the Germanic and Northwest European race in particular' (1992: 38–9).

The Dutch CP'86, which was outlawed in 1998, also adhered to classical racism. Although the party's manifestos and programmes contained few references to the superiority of the white race, as Mudde notes, 'closer reading shows that one race is "more equal" than others. The superiority of the white race is implicated in [a number of party] slogans' and the inferiority of other races was implicitly referred to in the party paper, which spoke of '"jungle-people, "non-European underdeveloped nations" and [talked of] "degeneration" as a result of the mixing of races' (1995a: 211–12). In addition, the CP'86 displayed anti-Semitic tendencies (Voerman and Lucardie, 1992: 43).

The Belgian PFNb, which was dissolved in 1991, also embraced classical racism. In particular, the party engaged in fervent anti-Semitism and developed a revisionist ideology, the central tenet of which was the denial of the Holocaust (Husbands, 1992b: 133; Deslore, 1995: 253).

The parties that adhere to classical racism are grouped together in Table 2.2. As the table illustrates, however, contemporary right-wing extremist parties that embrace such attitudes are in the minority. Much more common are parties that may be termed culturist, or which espouse a 'new' racism. These parties believe that differences exist between groups of people but, in contrast to their counterparts who advocate classical racism, they argue that it is culture rather than race that marks these differences. Thus, they maintain that the indigenous people and the Western civilization are superior because of their culture rather than because they are part of the white race. They also stress that certain groups are incompatible because of differences in their culture rather than differences in race. Hence, culturist or new racist parties reject multiculturalism on the grounds that the mixing of cultures endangers the separate identity of each of the different groups (Barker, 1981: 23; Mudde, 1995a: 211). This contrasts with parties that adhere to classical racism, which view multiculturalism as leading to the 'degeneration' or 'pollution' of the white race.

The French FN is located within this second category of parties. Its leader, Jean-Marie Le Pen, is obsessed with the French nation's survival and with its identity, which, he argues, is threatened by increasing cosmopolitanism. He 'insists that a plurality of cultures and peoples must be preserved, but clearly not in France [and] he rejects the "Anglo-Saxon" and American models of integration – "multiculturalism" and the politics of the "melting-pot" – . . . as unrealistic and dangerous options' (Marcus, 1995: 106). These attitudes are reflected in the policies of the party. As Swyngedouw and Ivaldi contend, 'the key argument of the FN is that the culture and religion of the immigrants coming from North Africa or black African countries is irreconcilable with the European culture of which the French nation is part. There can only be adversarial coexistence between the two' (2001: 14). The party thus avoids 'blatantly racist formulations, stressing cultural differences between groups instead of their supposed inferiority' (Mayer, 1998: 17).

The MNR is similarly preoccupied with the preservation of France's identity, which it considers particularly threatened by Islam (Bastow, 2000: 7–9). The parallels with the FN's beliefs on multiculturalism and globalization are unsurprising, given that Mégret, the MNR's leader, was responsible for drafting many of the FN's policies before he left the FN to form the MNR. Indeed, he declared that the MNR had not abandoned 'one iota of the programme of the Front national' (Bastow, 2000: 7).

The German Republikaner display similar beliefs. As Backes makes clear, the party distances itself from the tradition of National Socialism and 'does not shroud its xenophobia in a biologically-based theory of race' (1990: 14). Instead, it rejects multiculturalism and argues that cultural diversity poses a threat to the national identity. Saalfeld explains that, for the Republikaner, 'foreigners and non-Germans are not officially classified as inferior, [but] they are seen as a threat to the cultural and ethnic identity of Germany' (1993: 191). Thus, like the FN, the Republikaner can be categorized as being culturist, rather than adhering to the tradition of classical racism.

The racism of the Belgian VB is also of the culturist variety. Although the party 'essentially maintains that peoples are not the same or equal . . ., the VB rarely allows itself to support a distinction on a purely biological (racial) basis' (Swyngedouw, 2000: 136). The party 'insists that it never speaks in terms of races and that, in its opinion, the Flemings are no better than other people' (Mudde, 1995b: 19). However, it does emphasize that different cultures are incompatible, and talks of non-Europeans as being 'incapable of assimilating into the Flemish community' (Mudde, 2000: 99). Furthermore, the party's paper 'is not completely free from claiming the inferiority of other cultures' (Mudde, 2000: 100).

The racism of the now-defunct Wallonian party Agir, which was formed in 1989 after a split in the PFNb, was similar. The founders of the party (Freson, Steuckers and Destordeur) made a point of distancing themselves from other extreme right groups by emphasizing a culurist belief structure rather than one based on biological racism (Ignazi, 2003: 128). In the same vein, the Wallonian FN(b) and FNB (the latter created after a split in the FN(b) in 1995) avoid any reference to biological racism, and instead emphasize their concern with the preservation of the nation's identity, which they believe is being particularly undermined by the presence of foreigners.

The Austrian FPÖ may also be regarded as culturist. Morrow notes that the party makes 'no explicit mention of traditional phrases such as *Volksgemeinschaft* ("the community of the *volk*", a core component of Nazi racial ideology). Instead, [it] substituted a determination to protect more pastoral and domestic notions like *Heimat* (hearth and home)' (2000: 54). The current party programme continues to reflect this preoccupation with *Heimat*, and as well as emphasizing Austria's right to a cultural identity, the programme also rejects 'multi-cultural experiments that bear social conflicts with them' (FPÖ, 2002a).

The racism of the contemporary Scandinavian right-wing extremist parties is also of the culturist kind. Writing about the Danish DF and the Norwegian FRPn, Widfeldt explains that both parties may be classified as new racist because of their clear opposition to multiculturalism. The Danish party 'objects to Denmark developing into a multi-ethnic society', while its Norwegian counterpart argues that the 'continued immigration of asylum-seekers . . . will lead to serious conflicts between ethnic groups in Norway' (2000: 491). The same is true of the other, smaller Scandinavian right-wing extremist parties – the present-day Danish FRPd, the Swedish ND, DNP and SDk, and the Norwegian FLP. This latter party, for example, calls for an end to multiculturalism on the grounds that the mixing of peoples of different cultures leads to murder, rape and the establishment of gangs (AXT, 2000: 8).

In the same way the Swiss FPS and SD distance themselves from any reference to biological racism but do, however, embrace a culturism which is underpinned by an aversion to multiculturalism. The two parties' involvement in initiatives against the antiracist law (which was finally passed in 1994) and in other similar public actions reflect their beliefs that the mixing of different cultures can only be detrimental to the preservation of the Swiss identity and culture.

The Dutch CP and CD – now both defunct – were similarly preoccupied with the threat posed by multiculturalism. In its internal papers the CD argued that 'the inclusion of people of a different culture . . . causes substantial problems, for both the Dutch culture and the people from the other cultures' (*CD-Actueel*, March 1990, quoted in Mudde, 2000: 134). One way in which the CD proposed to help 'combat' multiculturalism was by discouraging mixed marriages, and by making it easier for Dutch people married to foreigners to file for divorce (Mudde, 2000: 133).

The parties just discussed are grouped together in Table 2.2. All of these right-wing extremist parties can be described as culturist or new racist, as they all emphasize cultural rather than racial differences between groups. They also point to the incompatibility of these groups and, if they stress the superiority of one group over another, this is done on the grounds of culture rather than race.

As was the case with their attitude towards the issue of immigration, the Spanish, the Portuguese and the Greek right-wing extremist parties differ from their north European counterparts in that they do not adhere to any form of racist beliefs. They espouse neither racial supremacism nor any form of culturism. As Ellwood explains, there is no tradition of racism on the extreme right in Spain and none of the parties are white supremacist (1995: 103).[8] Racism has never been a feature of the Portuguese extreme right either (Davis, 1998: 161).

Racism is also absent from the ideology of the Italian AN, just as it was from that of its predecessor, the MSI. At the 1995 party congress, the party leader, Gianfranco Fini, unequivocally condemned any form of racism and anti-Semitism (Ignazi, 1996a: 707). This stance was reflected in the 'Fiuggi Theses', which were published shortly after the conference and in which the party declared its 'explicit, definitive and absolute condemnation of any form of anti-Semitism and anti-Hebrewism' (Griffin, 1996: 140).

Similarly, racism is absent from the ideology of the Ms-Ft, a party created in 1995 as a result of a split in the AN. Indeed, Pino Rauti, the leader of the Ms-Ft, was known for having emphasized a rejection of all forms of xenophobic and racist attitudes in his days as secretary of the MSI in the early 1990s, and had led a faction within the MSI that distanced itself from any type of racial discrimination (Ignazi, 2003: 42). When he left the AN and set up the Ms-Ft, Rauti's views on race remained fundamentally unchanged.

The Swiss LdT does not espouse racist views either. While it is intent on defending the regional interests of the Ticino region, and on safeguarding its cultural identity and autonomy, it does not do this by arguing that other cultures are inferior or that the mixing to different cultures is a threat to the region. Instead, the LdT believes that the interests of the Ticino region are being undermined by the federal political establishment, which pursues economic policies that discriminate against Ticino in favour of the richer Swiss-German regions (Mazzoleni, 1999: 80).

Given the absence of racism in their ideologies, the Spanish Falangistas, Fuerza Nueva and Frente Nacional, the Portuguese PDC, the Greek KP, EPEN and EK, the Italian AN (and its predecessor the MSI) and Ms-Ft, and the Swiss LdT are therefore all grouped together into a third category in Table 2.2, distinct from the previous two.

Until the mid-1990s the Italian LN did not hold racist beliefs either. Talking about the party in the early 1990s Kitschelt observed, 'Bossi's ethnoregional and xenophobic anti-immigration slurs . . . are not expressions of a biological or cultural racism as much as new efforts to attack the establishment' (1995: 175). More recently, however, opposition to multiculturalism has become a constant theme in the party's programmes and statements (Ignazi, 2003: 59). The LN is thus categorized in Table 2.2 as not racist in the period until the mid-1990s, and as culturist after that date.

Similarly, although the Scandinavian Progress Parties (FRPn and FRPd) of the contemporary period display a culturist form of racism as was just discussed, in the period up until the mid-1980s these parties did not hold any form of racist beliefs. They are therefore categorized as not racist in the period until the mid-1980s, but are placed in the culturist category of Table 2.2 thereafter.

Attitudes towards democracy, parliamentarism and pluralism

The contemporary right-wing extremist parties of Western Europe can also be categorized into three groups according to the kind of attitudes they have towards democracy, parliamentarism and pluralism. One group is made up of parties that reject outright the fundamental values, procedures and institutions of the democratic constitutional state and wish to see the existing democratic order replaced altogether. A second group comprises parties that also display an anti-systemness but that, rather than calling for a wholesale replacement of the existing democratic constitutional state and its values, procedures and institutions, demand significant reform that would strengthen the executive and would curtail the rights and freedoms of organized interests and of individuals. In other words, parties of this second group undermine the legitimacy of the existing constitutional state by calling for less democracy, weaker powers for parliament and less pluralism. Finally, a third group of parties also favour a reform of the existing democratic institutions and procedures but, unlike the parties of the second group, demand less state intervention rather than more, and call for more to be done to promote and safeguard the rights and freedoms of individuals. As will be discussed, the attitudes of these parties as regards democracy, parliamentarism and pluralism call into question their inclusion in the wider extreme right party family. Table 2.3 illustrates which right-wing extremist parties belong to which of the three groups.

The Italian MSI is part of the first group of parties. In the early 1980s it proposed the adoption of an entirely new constitution, which would establish a 'corporativist political system, based on compulsory trade unions, with a strong centralised state. [The party] also proposed the direct election of the head of state, with a seven-year term and strong executive powers, and a limited role for political parties' (Furlong, 1992: 349).

The MSI's successor party, the AN, is arguably still deeply embedded in the fascist tradition. Despite some modernization, it espouses deep-seated anti-democratic sentiments (Ignazi, 1996a: 706). Although the AN publicly maintains that it is the partocracy that it is against, rather than the democratic system itself, as Griffin observes, 'at a subtextual level self-evident to any fascist, the party-ocracy was a code-name for liberal democracy *per se*' (1996: 134). Similarly, even though the AN's 1995 programme talks of moves towards direct democracy and of 'new forms of participation through organisms linking to civil society and institutions', Griffin argues that '[h]istorically speaking, this scheme is nothing less than a "modernized" and muted form of the Fascist regime's leftist corporativism' (1996: 135). Such a system would leave little or no room for autonomous political parties and

Table 2.3   Attitudes of the different right-wing extremist parties of Western Europe
             towards democracy, parliamentarism and pluralism

Outright rejection of existing system	Reform of existing system: less democracy, more state	Reform of existing system: more democracy, less state
British National Party (BNP) Britain	Freiheitliche Partei Österreichs (FPÖ) Austria	Dansk Folkeparti (DF) Denmark
National Front (NF) Britain	Vlaams Blok (VB) Belgium (Flanders)	Fremskridtspartiet (FRPd) Denmark
Deutsche Volksunion (DVU) Germany	Front National (FN(b)) Belgium (Wallonia)	Ethniko Komma (EK) Greece
Nationaldemokratische Partei Deutschlands (NPD) Germany	Front Nouveau de Belgique (FNB) Belgium (Wallonia)	Lega Nord (LN) Italy
Alleanza Nazionale (AN) Italy	Front National (FN) France	Fedrelandspartiet (FLP) Norway
Movimento Sociale-Fiamma Tricolore (Ms-Ft) Italy	Mouvement National Républicain (MNR) France	Fremskrittspartiet (FRPn) Norway
Falange Española Auténtica (FEA) Spain	Republikaner Germany	Ny Demokrati (ND) Sweden
Falange Española de las Juntas de Ofensiva Nacional-Sindicalista (FE de las JONS) Spain	Schweizer Demokraten (SD) Switzerland	Sverigedemokraterna (SDk) Sweden
Falange Española de las Juntas de Ofensiva Nacional-Sindicalista – sector Diego Marquez (FE de las JONS sector DM) Spain	[Agir Belgium (Wallonia)]	Freiheitspartei der Schweiz (FPS) Switzerland
Falange Española Independiente (FEI) Spain	[Centrumdemocraten (CD) Netherlands]	Lega dei Ticinesi (LdT) Switzerland
	[Centrumpartij (CP) Netherlands]	
[Parti des Forces Nouvelles (PFNb) Belgium (Wallonia)]		[Ethniki Politiki Enosis (EPEN) Greece]
[Movimento Sociale Italiano (MSI) Italy]		[Komma Proodeftikon (KP) Greece]
[Centrumpartij'86 (CP'86) Netherlands]		[Det Nya Partiet (DNP) Sweden]
[Nederlandse Volksunie (NVU) Netherlands]		
[Partido da Democracia Cristã (PDC) Portugal]		
[Frente Nacional Spain]		
[Fuerza Nueva Spain]		

Note: Parties in square brackets no longer exist.

interest groups or even for parliament, which Fini would like to see 'demoted in importance' (Gallagher, 2000: 79). The Ms-Ft is even more hard-line, and even more loyal to the fascist legacy than the AN (Gallagher, 2000: 78). It strongly rejects the existing democratic order and expresses contempt for pluralism. It can therefore also be considered as belonging to this first group of parties.

The Spanish Falangistas have also shown themselves unwilling to support the principles of parliamentary democracy. Similarly, Piñar's Fuerza Nueva opposed democratic reform, and 'overtly manifested its affective, ideological, and political ties with Franco's regime' (Ignazi, 2003: 188). It also disapproved of 'most social liberalization laws including those dealing with abortion, divorce, and the freedom of religion and press' (Davis, 1998: 159). As Ellwood explains, the Spanish right-wing extremist parties 'drew their inspiration from the past and, as in the past, considered anathema precisely those things on which post-Francoist Spaniards pinned their hopes, such as the devolution of power to regional governments, class-based trades unions, a market-based economy, integration into the EC, and, above all, freedom of choice and expression in every sphere of life' (1992: 381). Even the more modern Frente Nacional 'lapsed back into its obsession with "Spain's problems", identifying these as disorder and lack of effective government; . . . liberalism; political parties, elections and democracy in general' (Ellwood, 1992: 383–4). A similar attitude towards democracy and parliamentarism, and a similar nostalgia for the past, characterized the now-defunct Portuguese PDC.

The British right-wing extremist parties also belong to this first group as they too reject the existing democratic institutions, procedures and values. Although the NF maintained that it never totally rejected democracy, as Eatwell explains, the party's democratic credentials were hardly sound, as 'most of its leaders felt that "democracy" was perfectly consistent with a one-party state that would reforge the holistic nation and overcome the threat from international capital' (i.e. Jewish interests) (1998a: 146–7). The legacy of Strasserism, which drew on the ideas and beliefs of the German inter-war fascists Otto and Gregor Strasser, and which advocated the replacement of parliamentary democracy by a corporate system and the rejection of capitalism, was still strong within the NF for much of the 1980s and early 1990s (Thurlow, 1998: 267).

As with other areas of policy, the BNP's views on democracy have been very similar to those of the NF, particularly in the 1980s and early 1990s. Tyndall, who led the party until 1999, was 'suspicious of the masses, seeing them as putty to be manipulated by the strong leader – whose task it is to set out a grand vision' (Eatwell, 1998a: 147).

Three other parties that rejected the established democratic order and that were suspicious of pluralism were the Dutch NVU and CP'86, and the Wallonian PFNb. The NVU favoured reinforcing the executive and weakening the legislature. It proposed that the prime minister should be appointed by the queen and should be able to veto any legislation passed by a parliament that would be partly elected and partly appointed. The party also suggested the creation of a corporatist socio-economic council (which would serve as a senate) and envisaged the end of all class conflict as a result of cooperation between workers and employers (Voerman and Lucardie, 1992: 38). All these proposals were very much in line with traditional fascist thought.

For its part, the CP'86 also viewed pluralism and individual rights with suspicion, maintaining that 'there will be no place for the "personal and group egoism [that] have led to an excessive deterioration of responsible thinking and acting"' (1989 party programme, *Nationaaldemocratische gedachten voor een menswaardige toekomst*, quoted in Mudde, 2000: 163). The Wallonian PFNb embraced similar views, expressing contempt for parliamentary parties and favouring the introduction of a new corporatist order (Ignazi, 2003: 128).

Assessing the German right-wing extremist parties' true beliefs about democracy is a somewhat difficult task, since, as Winkler and Schumann explain, a 'party's goals cannot necessarily be deduced from its official platform [because] for strategic reasons [parties] do not openly proclaim their ideas, in order to avoid being considered hostile to the constitution' (1998: 102). That said, it is quite evident from internal documents and from the party press that the NPD opposes the contemporary democratic system, its institutions and its values, even though the party often attempts to guard its true attitudes. Indeed, the very fact that it is currently under observation by the Office for the Protection of the Constitution bears witness to its anti-democratic character (Bundesamt für Verfassungsschutz, 1999). In its 1987 and 1992 manifestos, the NPD displayed 'a tight monistic vision of the state, in which there [was] neither place for "group-egoism" nor for the "*Volk*-hostile class-struggle"'. The party also argued that in order 'to uphold true democratic principles, individual and sectional interests should always be appointed and subordinated to the whole' (Mudde, 1995a: 215). In its 1987 programme, the NPD committed 'itself to the establishment of an ethnically defined "national community" based on corporatism and directed by a strong and non-partisan executive' (Saalfeld, 1993: 183). As far as the institutions of democracy are concerned, 'the line taken by the NPD party press is that the party still serves a public fundamentally opposed to the parliamentary system which it often subjects to vicious attacks' (Backes, 1990: 15).

The DVU's attitudes towards the democratic system and towards individual rights and freedoms are similar to those of the NPD, although the DVU's party programmes tend to be much less detailed than those of the NPD (Mudde, 2000: 78). Like the NPD, the DVU calls for a strong, authoritarian state, whose interests should come first, before those of the individual citizen (Winkler and Schumann, 1998: 102). Given their attitudes on democracy, parliamentarism and pluralism, it is appropriate to locate the NPD and the DVU in the first group of parties (see Table 2.3), even though they may at times temper their anti-democratic remarks so as to avoid prosecution by the Office for the Protection of the Constitution.

Not all contemporary right-wing extremist parties reject outright the existing democratic order, its values, procedures and institutions, however. In contrast to the parties just discussed, some parties of the extreme right tolerate the established liberal democratic system, but at the same time they call for significant reform that would strengthen the executive, weaken the power of parliament and organized interests, and curtail the rights and freedoms of individuals. These parties can be grouped together in a second category.

One such party is the French FN. Jean-Marie Le Pen and the FN have not only accepted the electoral path to power, but also claim to have consented to the parliamentary method of achieving this. Nevertheless, while the party takes care not to question the legitimacy of the constitution and the established institutions, it is far from enamoured of the current state of French democracy (Marcus, 1995: 114; Swyngedouw and Ivaldi, 2001: 12–13). Indeed, Le Pen 'describes himself as a Churchillian democrat, i.e. not a great supporter of democracy, although knowing no better system' (Hainsworth, 1992b: 48). The FN's main argument is that the political system is in need of comprehensive reform. In particular, the party calls for the introduction of proportional representation for all legislative elections as a priority. In addition, it favours a significant extension of the use of direct democracy, including the increased use of referendums and the introduction of a system of popular initiatives through which a sufficient number of signatures could force a referendum. The party's programme suggests that immigration is an appropriate theme for the extension of referendums and insists that the introduction of popular initiatives would enable French people to voice their opinions openly on this subject (Hainsworth, 1992b: 49; Front National, 1997a; Mayer, 1998: 16).

While such recommendations may give the impression that the FN is above all concerned with individual rights and liberties, the party's attitude towards interest group activity suggests otherwise. In its programme, the FN condemns the strength of political lobbies and unions and accuses them of entering into a cosy relationship with the mainstream political parties for their mutual benefit (Front National, 1997a). Le Pen maintains that the rights of the individual should be subordinated to the 'sacred rights of the collective', which, in his worldview, refers to nothing less than the nation of France as a whole (Marcus, 1995: 103–4; Swyngedouw and Ivaldi, 2001: 16–18). Bearing these attitudes in mind, the FN's call for the extension of direct democracy therefore becomes more a vehicle for suppressing the organization of interests than a means of promoting a more participatory political system. Furthermore, far from giving power back to the people, the FN favours a strengthening of the presidency (Hainsworth, 1992b: 50).

Despite its criticisms of the established system, the FN does not aspire to change the political regime altogether (Minkenberg, 1997: 77). Instead, it presents proposals for reform that would strengthen the executive and weaken organized interests and that would curtail individual rights and freedoms. It therefore differs significantly from the parties of the first group that advocate a complete replacement of parliamentary democracy.

As is the case in all policy areas, the MNR's views on democracy, parliamentarism and pluralism are extremely similar to those of the FN. While the MNR supports the 'institutional principles of the Republic', it nonetheless calls for some significant reform of the system (Bastow, 2000: 11). The party also emphasizes 'the general interest over that of the particular' (Bastow, 2000: 14).

As has been the case in other areas of policy, the Republikaner's attitudes towards the existing democratic order are very similar to those of the FN. Like the FN, the Republikaner demand that referendums be used widely, especially in situations where there are proposed amendments to the German Basic Law. This request is particularly significant in view of the fact that plebiscitary forms of decision-making and referendums are outlawed under the Basic Law. Furthermore, the party recommends that the present system should be altered so that the presidency gains full political powers, and it suggests that the incumbent should be elected directly by the people (Minkenberg, 1997: 82; Die Republikaner, 1998).

The Republikaner, just like the FN, also call for a stronger state, the restriction of the power of trade unions and other interest groups, and the subordination of individual and group interests to the common, national interest. In addition, the party demands that the mass media be subject to greater control (Westle and Niedermayer, 1992: 90–1; Saalfeld, 1993: 185). In short, therefore, the Republikaner do not wholeheartedly accept the existing political system, and, like their French counterpart, they demand considerable reform in many areas. However, unlike parties of the first group discussed earlier, the Republikaner do not reject democracy outright. On the contrary, the party makes sure it continually emphasizes its loyalty to the constitution and its commitment to the existing democratic arrangements.

The Belgian VB has similar views on democracy and on individual rights. The party does 'not outwardly reject the multi-party system, free expression, or parliamentary democracy' (Swyngedouw, 1998: 65), but at the same time, it calls for 'effective measures which bring about an upgrading of political life and parliamentary activities, [and argues that] politics must be withdrawn from the atmosphere of small-mindedness, cliques, and calculation in which it has currently been marooned by democracy and the malady of parliamentarism' (*Principles of the VB*, quoted in Swyngedouw, 1998: 65). As for the rights of individuals, the VB maintains that 'the ethnic community takes absolute precedence over the individual [and that] individuals have no separate existence from which they could draw universal rights' (Swyngedouw and Ivaldi, 2001: 16).

The Belgian FN(b) and FNB embrace similar beliefs to those of the parties just discussed. This likeness is unsurprising in view of the fact that the FN(b) has tried to model itself on the French FN (Deslore, 1995: 253). It too calls for a stronger state and a stricter policy on law and order, and it also criticizes the immobilism of the traditional democratic parties and emphasizes the need for stronger leadership. Agir, which merged with the FN(b) in 1997, held similar attitudes too. It distanced itself from elements that called for a wholesale replacement of the existing democratic system, such as those inside the PFNb (Ignazi, 2003: 128), yet was critical of the established parties and favoured significant institutional reform.

The Dutch CD and CP also advocated democracy, yet they criticized the existing system and argued that it was in need of reform. As Voerman and Lucardie explain, the leaders of the CP and the CD seemed 'to accept the institutions of liberal democracy but [rejected] the dominant liberal values with respect to ethnic minorities and cultural pluralism' (1992: 52). The CD called for a stronger state, more police and stricter sentencing (Voerman and Lucardie, 1992: 45). At the same time, however, just like the French FN and the German Republikaner, the party maintained that it wanted to give more power to the people by introducing referendums (Lucardie, 1998: 117–18).

The Austrian FPÖ is another party that belongs to this second group, as its attitudes towards democracy and the existing institutions and norms are similar to those of the French FN, the German Republikaner, the Belgian VB and the Dutch CD and CP. More specifically, the FPÖ has called for a stronger executive, suggesting that the position of chancellor should be abolished and that, in its place, a powerful presidency should be created. The party has also proposed that the cabinet should be reduced in size (Morrow, 2000: 54). In addition, the FPÖ has shown itself in favour of an increased use of plebiscites, and has voiced its objection to the power that political parties have in the Austrian system (FPÖ, 2002b).

The Swiss SD is one final party that belongs to this second group. It too calls for a strong state, whose role is perceived as guaranteeing 'the well-being of the Swiss collectivity and not of the business community'. The party maintains that to do this 'the state has to be strong and ready to intervene in the social and economic spheres' (Gentile and Kriesi, 1998: 131). The party also demands that the Swiss system of direct democracy be protected, and in line with this it opposes Swiss membership of the EU, UN and IMF (Gentile and Kriesi, 1998: 131).

All the parties just discussed are grouped together in Table 2.3. All tolerate the established democratic order, but they nonetheless recommend significant levels of reform that would strengthen the executive and weaken the rights and freedoms of organized interests and individuals. They thus call for less democracy, less pluralism and a stronger state, and in doing so, they undermine the legitimacy of the procedures, institutions and values upon which the existing constitutional state is built.

A third group of contemporary West European right-wing extremist parties also calls for significant reform of the existing democratic order, but unlike the second group of parties just discussed, parties in this third group believe that existing democratic institutions and procedures make for too little democracy rather than too much. In particular, parties of this third group are critical of the established parliamentary system and of the existing parties for not representing citizens adequately, and they call for substantial reforms to address these issues. Parties in this third group also favour a reduction (rather than a strengthening) of the role and reach of the state. They also differ from the first two groups of parties in that they do not maintain that individual rights and freedoms should be subordinated to the greater national interest.

The Danish and Norwegian Progress Parties (FRPd and FRPn) and the Danish DF emphasize their commitment to safeguarding the personal freedom of the indigenous population, which they believe is currently undermined by the size and reach of the state apparatus (Fremskridtspartiet, 1998). Both Progress Parties call for a reduction in the size of the public sector and argue that 'politically, the state or other public authorities should have less opportunity to regulate the activities of citizens, and economically, the public sector should be scaled down [and] should retreat from many of its regulating activities' (Svåsand, 1998: 83). According to both Progress Parties, such measures will 'increase the freedom of the individual in society' (Svåsand, 1998: 83).

The Danish and Norwegian right-wing extremist parties also have a preference for more direct democracy, including increasing the use of referendums (Andersen and Bjørklund, 2000: 202). The FRPd also favours a reduction in the size of the Danish parliament (Svåsand, 1998: 83). In contrast to the parties of the second group, the demands of the Danish and Norwegian parties for more direct democracy and for reform of the parliamentary system must be viewed as efforts to increase the freedom of the individual rather than as methods by which to subordinate the rights of the individual in the greater interests of the collective.

The Swedish right-wing extremist party ND shares many of the views of the Progress Parties and of the Danish DF as regards democracy, parliamentarism and pluralism. It too calls for more referendums and fewer parliamentarians and it also favours the direct election of the prime minister (Svåsand, 1998: 84). It also demands a reduction in the size of the public sector and less state intervention (Svåsand, 1998: 84; Widfeldt, 2000: 495). The DNP, a short-lived party created as a result of a split in the ND in 1994 and led by a Ian Wachtmeister, one of the founders of the ND, embraced similar policies (Widfeldt, 2000: 496).

The Swedish SDk and the Norwegian FLP have little to say on the subject of democracy and pluralism, as their respective programmes are concerned, above all, with immigration and multiculturalism. That said, when they do touch upon issues that relate to the existing democratic system, the established parties or the rights of individuals, by and large these two parties seem to share the outlook of the other Scandinavian parties of the extreme right. The SDk, for example, has been keen to portray itself as a 'leftist' or 'progressive' party rather than a 'nationalist' one (Anti-Semitism Worldwide, 2000/1), thereby suggesting that it attaches some importance to the safeguarding of individual rights and freedoms.

The Swiss FPS (known as the APS until the party changed its name in 1992) has views on democracy that are similar to those of the Scandinavian right-wing extremist parties. The party fights all intervention by the state that restricts personal freedoms and that impinges on the workings of the free market. It argues that the state should exert no control over society and that, instead, the state's role should be kept to guaranteeing internal and external security and public order only (Gentile and Kriesi, 1998: 131–2).

The LdT is similarly critical of the existing democratic system. Although it sees some role for the state in the economy (in particular in providing social benefits such as pensions), it favours the reduction of taxes and administrative red tape so as to attract more businesses to the Ticino region. More importantly, however, it is extremely critical of the Swiss party system and of the established parties. It regards the party system as a 'power bloc' working against the interests of the people, and sees the mainstream parties as agents of clientalism (Mazzoleni, 1999: 80–6).

In its quest for a complete reorganization of the Italian political and economic system, the LN likewise calls for less state intervention. The party proposes the creation of a federal republic, a development that would entail radical devolution of power away from Rome (Betz, 1998b: 48).

Similarly, the Greek parties of the extreme right have called for less state intervention in people's daily lives. While the KP was particularly vocal about what it saw as excessive intervention by the state in economic affairs, its successor, EPEN, demanded, among other things, the 'restoration and cleansing of parliamentarism' as well as a return to the 'liberalized economy' (Dimitras, 1992: 265). Similarly, the EK, founded in 1989 after EPEN was disbanded, called 'for the abolishment of income taxes, a significant scaling back of the state's role in economic affairs, and the adoption of a simple system of proportional representation benefiting smaller parties' (Davis, 1998: 167).

The parties that belong to this third group are listed in Table 2.3. They differ from the two other groups of right-wing extremist parties discussed above in that they believe the existing democratic order does too little rather than too much to promote and safeguard the rights and freedoms of individuals. To address these issues they call for less state intervention and a reform of the parliamentary system and of the established parties.

As was mentioned above, the attitudes of the parties in this third group towards democracy and towards the rights and freedoms of individual citizens raise doubts over their inclusion in the wider right-wing extremist party family. Indeed, it is debatable whether the reforms that these parties call for undermine the legitimacy of the democratic constitutional state and the fundamental values, procedures and institutions on which it is built. After all, these parties are asking for more democracy rather than less. That said, before any judgements are made on whether these parties do or do not belong to the right-wing extremist party family, it should be remembered that, as the earlier discussion of the concept of right-wing extremism made clear, a party's attitude towards the principle of fundamental human equality is also crucial in determining whether it should be considered right-wing extremist. Thus, if the parties in this third group embrace xenophobic and/or racist attitudes, and thereby display a rejection of the principle of fundamental human rights, they qualify for inclusion in the extreme right party family regardless of their rather liberal views on democracy and on the rights and freedoms of individuals. This point will be returned to below.

Having discussed the attitudes of the different West European right-wing extremist parties towards immigration, towards race, and towards democracy, parliamentarism and pluralism, it is now possible to consider these three bases of division simultaneously rather than one by one. In other words, the alternative typology can now be constructed.

Five types of right-wing extremist party

The three bases of division examined above are sufficiently stringent to allow for the types in this new, alternative typology to be jointly exhaustive and mutually exclusive. In addition to satisfying these key theoretical and methodological conditions, the present typology also has the advantages of including all West European parties of the extreme right and of being as up-to-date as possible. In this way it reflects the full diversity of the extreme right party family in Western Europe.

Given the three bases of division just examined and given the number of classes within each of these (2, 3 and 3 respectively), 18 different types of right-wing extremist parties are theoretically possible (2 × 3 × 3). In practice, however, far fewer types exist. In fact, as Table 2.4 illustrates, only five types of right-wing extremist party are found in Western Europe in the contemporary period.

A first type of party is characterized by radically xenophobic attitudes, classical racism, and an outright rejection of democracy, parliamentarism

Table 2.4 Five types of right-wing extremist parties in Western Europe

---

1 Neo-Nazi parties *(radically xenophobic; adhere to classical racism; reject outright existing democratic system)*
  British National Party (BNP) Britain
  National Front (NF) Britain
  Deutsche Volksunion (DVU) Germany
  Nationaldemokratische Partei Deutschlands (NPD) Germany
  [Parti des Forces Nouvelles (PFNb) Belgium (Wallonia)]
  [Centrumpartij'86 (CP'86) Netherlands]
  [Nederlandse Volksunie (NVU) Netherlands]

Table 2.4 (continued)

2 **Neo-fascist parties** *(not xenophobic; not racist; reject outright existing democratic system)*
   Alleanza Nazionale (AN) Italy
   Movimento Sociale–Fiamma Tricolore (Ms-Ft) Italy
   Falange Española Auténtica (FEA) Spain
   Falange Española de las Juntas de Ofensiva Nacional-Sindicalista (FE de las JONS)
      Spain
   Falange Española de las Juntas de Ofensiva Nacional-Sindicalista – sector Diego
      Marquez (FE de las JONS sector DM) Spain
   Falange Española Independiente (FEI) Spain
   [Movimento Sociale Italiano (MSI) Italy]
   [Partido da Democracia Cristã (PDC) Portugal]
   [Frente Nacional Spain]
   [Fuerza Nueva Spain]

3 **Authoritarian xenophobic parties** *(radically xenophobic; culturist; demand reform of exisiting system: less democracy, less pluralism, more state)*
   Freiheitliche Partei Österreichs (FPÖ) Austria
   Vlaams Blok (VB) Belgium (Flanders)
   Front National (FN(b)) Belgium (Wallonia)
   Front Nouveau de Belgique (FNB) Belgium (Wallonia)
   Front National (FN) France
   Mouvement National Républicain (MNR) France
   Republikaner Germany
   Schweizer Demokraten (SD) Switzerland
   [Agir Belgium (Wallonia)]
   [Centrumdemocraten (CD) Netherlands]
   [Centrumpartij (CP) Netherlands]

4 **Neo-liberal xenophobic parties** *(radically xenophobic; culturist; demand reform of existing system: more democracy, less state)*
   Dansk Folkeparti (DF) Denmark
   Fremskridtspartiet (FRPd) since mid-1980s, Denmark
   Lega Nord (LN) since mid-1990s, Italy
   Fedrelandspartiet (FLP) Norway
   Fremskrittspartiet (FRPn) since mid-1980s, Norway
   Ny Demokrati (ND) Sweden
   Sverigedemokraterna (SDk) Sweden
   Freiheitspartei der Schweiz (FPS) Switzerland
   [Det Nya Partiet (DNP) Sweden]

5 **Neo-liberal populist parties** *(not xenophobic; not racist; demand reform of existing system: more democracy, less state)*
   Fremskridtspartiet (FRPd) before mid-1980s, Denmark
   Ethniko Komma (EK) Greece
   Lega Nord (LN) before mid-1990s, Italy
   Fremskrittspartiet (FRPn) before mid-1980s, Norway
   Lega dei Ticinesi (LdT) Switzerland
   [Ethniki Politiki Enosis (EPEN) Greece]
   [Komma Proodeftikon (KP) Greece]

Note: Parties in square brackets no longer exist.

and pluralism. The one feature that sets parties of this type apart from other right-wing extremist competitors is the nature of their racist attitudes: they adhere to classical racism. Since their racist attitudes are reminiscent of and highly influenced by that of the National Socialist German Workers' Party (Nazi Party), and because they renounce the established political and economic order, these parties can be referred to as 'neo-Nazi' parties.

A second type of right-wing extremist party also rejects democracy, parliamentarism and pluralism outright but, unlike the first type, this type of party is neither concerned with immigration nor racist. The parties of this type have tended to remain faithful to many of the legacies of Mussolini's Italy and Franco's Spain. Accordingly, they are labelled 'neo-fascist' parties.

Parties of a third type differ from the previous two in their attitudes towards democracy, parliamentarism and pluralism. Unlike the neo-Nazi and neo-fascist parties, parties of this third type do not reject the existing democratic order completely. Yet neither do they accept it. Instead, they are critical of many of the existing institutions and are also suspicious of interest group activity and of the promotion of individual rights and freedoms. These parties call for significant reforms that would strengthen the executive and would weaken the rights and freedoms of organized interests and individuals, and which, together, can be seen to undermine the legitimacy of the existing democratic order. Like members of the first group, parties of this third group are radically xenophobic, as the fight against immigration is central to their ideology. However, they do not embrace classical racism. Their racism is of a culturist kind. In the light of the emphasis these parties place on the issue of immigration, and in view of their attitudes towards democracy, pluralism and individual rights, these parties are termed 'authoritarian xenophobic' parties.

Parties of the fourth type share some of the characteristics of the authoritarian xenophobic parties: they are radically xenophobic and their racism is of a culturist variety. However, in contrast to authoritarian xenophobic parties, parties of this fourth type favour a reform of the existing democratic order that would make for more democracy rather than less. These parties call for less state intervention, for the reform of the existing parliamentary and party system to represent citizens better, and for a promotion of the rights and freedoms of individuals. Given these somewhat liberal attitudes towards democracy, parliamentarism and pluralism, and yet taking into account their strong emphasis on the fight against immigration, parties in this fourth group are referred to as 'neo-liberal xenophobic' parties.

A final type of right-wing extremist party is characterized by the absence of xenophobic and racist attitudes, and by the same liberal attitudes towards democracy and individual rights that the neo-liberal xenophobic parties embrace. Like the neo-liberal xenophobic parties, parties of this fifth group call for a reform of the parliamentary and party system and favour a substantial reduction in the size and reach of the state, all in the name of promoting individual rights and freedoms. In the light of their views on democracy and individual rights, but given that these parties have drawn on a whole range of issues for electoral profit – including immigration, even though xenophobia is not central to their ideology – parties in this fifth group are labelled 'neo-liberal populist' parties. The five types of parties and their constituent members are illustrated in Table 2.4.

The fact that neo-liberal populist parties embrace neither xenophobic nor racist attitudes, and the fact that they have rather liberal views on democracy and individual rights, clearly raise questions over whether these parties should be considered part of the wider extreme right party family. The absence of xenophobia or racism in their ideologies implies that these parties do not reject the principle of fundamental human equality, which, as the earlier discussion of the concept of right-wing extremism suggested, is one of the two anti-constitutional and anti-democratic elements of right-wing extremism. These parties' inclusion in the right-wing extremist party family therefore rests on the second element of right-wing extremism, namely the rejection or the undermining of the fundamental values, procedures and institutions of the democratic constitutional state.

At first sight, it appears somewhat debatable that the neo-liberal populist parties' calls for the extension of participatory democracy, and for the promotion of the rights and freedoms of the individual, can be seen as undermining the legitimacy of the democratic constitutional state and the fundamental values, procedures and institutions upon which it is built. After all, these demands suggest that these parties favour more democracy, rather than less, and more democracy can hardly be perceived as threatening the legitimacy of the existing democratic order.

On closer inspection, however, the ways in which the neo-liberal populist parties propose to carry out these reforms, and the attitudes these parties have towards the existing parliamentary and party system, indicate that, behind the calls for greater democracy and participation, lie a discourse and a political culture that do indeed undermine the legitimacy of the democratic system, and the legitimacy of its institutions and procedures in particular. The calls of the Scandinavian and the Greek right-wing extremist parties for the substantial reform of the existing parliamentary system (including a significant reduction in the size of parliament) demonstrate an opposition to the existing democratic institutions and the procedures by which citizens are represented, and the strong anti-partyism that all these parties exhibit points to a further rejection of the procedures and institutions of the existing constitutional democratic state (Gentile and Kriesi, 1998: 126; Ignazi, 2003: 55, 60–1).

Thus, although their anti-systemness is less strong than that of some of the other right-wing extremist parties, neo-liberal populist parties nonetheless display contempt for the institutions and procedures of the existing democratic system that results in it being undermined. Ignazi sums this up well when, speaking about the Danish FRPd, he argues:

> While Glistrup and the more moderate leadership never made a frontal attack on democracy by invoking authoritarian solutions, they certainly undermined the system's legitimacy, not just by displaying contempt towards the parties and the politicians, but also by considering the parties as useless, backward and even harmful. There is a substantial anti-partism [sic] circulating in the veins of the FRPd, clearly indicated by its irritation with parliamentary procedures. (2003: 148)

The fact that the neo-liberal populist parties exhibit a weaker anti-systemness than some of the other West European right-wing extremist parties is reflected in the debates in the literature. Indeed, a number of existing studies do not consider some of the neo-liberal populist parties to belong to the wider extreme right party family, precisely because they do not deem the anti-systemness of these parties to be sufficient to warrant their inclusion in this party family. Andersen and Bjørklund (2000), for example, have reservations over whether the Scandinavian parties (especially in their early years) should be considered full members of the extreme right party family. Other scholars, by contrast, believe that the anti-systemness of the neo-liberal populist parties is pronounced enough to justify their inclusion in the wider extreme right party family (e.g. Mazzoleni, 1999; Golder, 2003a; Ignazi, 2003). This present study concurs with this latter view, and believes that the contempt that the neo-liberal parties display towards the existing institutions and procedures of the democratic constitutional state constitutes an anti-systemness that is sufficient to undermine the legitimacy of that state. Thus, although they may be perceived as being on its fringes, the neo-liberal populist parties should nonetheless be considered as belonging to the wider extreme right party family.

Right-wing extremist party ideology and electoral success

Having identified the different types of right-wing extremist parties present in Western Europe, it is now possible to investigate whether electoral success is linked to a particular type of extreme right ideology, or whether, conversely, the type of ideology a party embraces is unrelated to its success at the polls.

Figure 2.1 illustrates the average electoral scores of the different right-wing extremist parties under observation, with the parties arranged according to their type of ideology. A number of patterns are immediately discernible from the bar chart. Particularly striking is the lack of success of the neo-Nazi parties. While parties of the other four types have experienced electoral success, none of the neo-Nazi ones has. In fact, they have all been extremely unsuccessful at the polls, never securing more than an average of 0.6 percent of the vote – this being the average score of the German DVU.

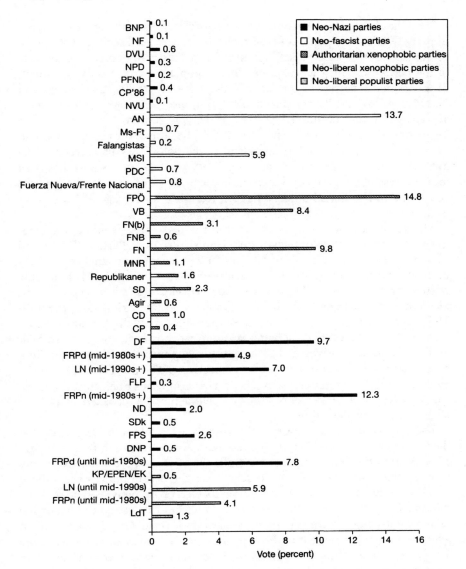

Figure 2.1 Electoral success of the West European parties of the extreme right, 1979–2003: by ideological type

Notes: For full right-wing extremist party names, see Abbreviations (pp. xiii–xiv). The figure illustrates the mean electoral scores of each party in the period 1979–2003. The mean score is calculated by summing the electoral scores of each party at all elections in which it competed and then dividing this total by the number of elections the party contested.

Sources: Mackie and Rose (1991, 1997); Cheles *et al.* (1995); Betz and Immerfall (1998); Hainsworth (2000a); Elections around the World; Parties and Elections in Europe.

There has been more variation in the electoral success of the other four types of party. While some parties of each type have experienced success at the polls, others have not. For example, the Italian LN averaged 5.9 percent of the vote in the period in which it was a neo-liberal populist party. Similarly, as neo-liberal populist parties in the late 1970s and early 1980s, the Danish and Norwegian Progress Parties (FRPd and FRPn) also performed relatively well, averaging 7.8 percent and 4.1 percent of the vote respectively. However, the Greek right-wing extremist parties (KP/EPEN/EK), also of the neo-liberal populist type, have been much less successful at the polls. They have recorded an average of only 0.5 percent of the vote. The Swiss LdT, for its part, has been more successful than the Greek parties, but less successful than the LN and the Scandinavian neo-liberal populist parties, recording an average of 1.3 percent of the vote.

The same variation is apparent within the neo-liberal xenophobic category of parties. The Norwegian and Danish Progress Parties (FRPn and FRPd) have secured averages of 12.3 and 4.9 percent of the vote respectively in the period since the mid-1980s when they became neo-liberal xenophobic parties, and the Danish DF has also enjoyed electoral success, polling an average of 9.7 percent of the ballots. Similarly, in the period since the mid-1990s when it became a neo-liberal xenophobic party, the LN has won an average of 7.0 percent of the vote. By contrast, however, the Swedish SDk and DNP and the Norwegian FLP have recorded low electoral scores, polling averages of 0.5, 0.5 and 0.3 percent respectively. The Swedish ND and the Swiss FPS fall between these two sets of parties in terms of electoral success. The ND averaged 2.0 percent of the vote, while the FPS recorded an average of 2.6 percent of the ballots.

The other two types of party – the authoritarian xenophobic parties and the neo-fascist parties – have also experienced both success and failure in elections. Within the first group, for example, the FPÖ has performed extremely well, polling an average of 14.8 percent over the period under observation. The French FN and the Belgium VB have also recorded high average scores – 9.8 and 8.4 percent respectively. However, within this group of parties the Dutch right-wing extremist parties have not performed well. The CP won an average of only 0.4 percent of the vote, and the CD polled an average of only 1.0 percent. The Wallonian parties of the extreme right have not been successful either. While the Belgian FN(b) recorded an average of 3.1 percent, the FNB and Agir secured averages of only 0.6 percent of the ballots. The German Republikaner and the Swiss SD fared poorly too. The two parties secured 1.6 and 2.3 percent of the vote respectively.

Of the neo-fascist parties, the Italian MSI/AN has enjoyed electoral success, polling an average of 5.9 percent of the vote as the MSI, and recording 13.7 percent as the AN. No other parties of this type have experienced such success. The Ms-Ft secured an average of only 0.7 percent of the vote; the Spanish Fuerza Nueva and Frente Nacional won an average of 0.8 percent of the vote; the Falangistas recorded an average of only 0.2 percent of the ballots; and the Portuguese PDC averaged a mere 0.7 percent.

The electoral success of the neo-fascist group of parties must be viewed with caution, however, as there is significant debate in the literature on right-wing extremism about the nature of the AN's ideology. Indeed, Newell talks of the AN 'standing at the crossroads', having not completely rejected its founding ideology but yet no longer talking of 'alternatives to the system' (2000: 483–4). Similarly, Griffin sees the AN as posing a 'taxonomic dilemma' to those who wish to compare it to other right-wing extremist parties. He too maintains that the AN falls between two distinguishable categories, and that it is 'a genuine hybrid' that embraces 'a reformist or democratic fascism' (1996: 142). Ignazi also describes the AN as moving away from neo-fascism, though at the same time he argues that the 'AN's governing and appeasing role still clashes with the lack of profound internal revision which leaves space for nostalgia. While the national leadership (with few exceptions) rapidly pursues the path away from neo-fascism, the middle-level elite and local militants remain imbued of [sic] the traditional MSI political culture' (2003: 223).

Within this present typology the AN has been included in the neo-fascist category of parties on the basis of its past behaviour and ideology rather than on forecasts of its future direction. However, if the party were to embrace the democratic system fully, and to disassociate itself finally from its original ideology, its inclusion in the neo-fascist category would clearly no longer be accurate. Following such a move, the party would need to be accommodated in a sixth category, the characteristics of which would be a rejection of xenophobia and racism and a full acceptance of the existing political and economic system. This move would further throw into question the inclusion of this party in the right-wing extremist party family and would suggest that it might instead have become a constituent of the mainstream right – a transition that Fini himself announced as having begun at the Verona party conference in March 1998 (Gallagher, 2000: 82–3).

The transformation of the AN into a conservative party would also mean that the neo-fascist category of parties would become markedly less successful. The MSI, which averaged 5.9 percent of the vote over the period under observation, would become the category's most successful party if the AN were no longer included, and the neo-fascist category of parties would be second only to the neo-Nazi parties in terms of its lack of success.

Overall, the patterns illustrated by Figure 2.1 suggest that successful right-wing extremist parties have tended to embrace an authoritarian xenophobic, a neo-liberal xenophobic or a neo-liberal populist ideology rather than a neo-Nazi or a neo-fascist one. These trends are further confirmed by a regression analysis. Taking the neo-Nazi parties as a reference group, the OLS (ordinary least squares) regression model reported in Table 2.5 estimates the right-wing extremist party vote as a function of ideology, represented by the

Table 2.5   Effect of ideology on the right-wing extremist party vote (OLS dummy
regression)

Type of party	Unstandardized coefficients	
	B	Std error
Constant	0.233	1.005
Neo-fascist parties	3.075**	1.469
Authoritarian xenophobic parties	5.489***	1.231
Neo-liberal xenophobic parties	4.172***	1.351
Neo-liberal populist parties	2.953*	1.554
Adjusted R^2	0.104	
n = 146		

Notes: Dependent variable: right-wing extremist party vote (in percent). Reference
group: neo-Nazi parties. *** coefficient significant at 0.01 level. ** coefficient
significant at 0.05 level. * coefficient significant at 0.1 level.

five types of ideology described above.[9] The value of the constant in this
regression, .233, reports the expected vote share for neo-Nazi parties (the
reference group). The other regression coefficients estimate the effect of
being in a particular category of ideology as compared with the reference
group. On average, therefore, neo-fascist parties are expected to win 3.075
percent more of the vote than neo-Nazi parties; authoritarian xenophobic
parties are expected to record 5.489 percent more of the vote than neo-Nazi
parties; neo-liberal xenophobic parties are expected to secure 4.172 percent
more of the vote than neo-Nazi parties; and neo-liberal populist parties are
expected to poll 2.953 percent more of the vote than neo-Nazi parties. All
these coefficients are statistically significant at the 0.1 level or better.

These broad patterns are further confirmed in Table 2.6, which displays
the mean electoral scores for each type of right-wing extremist party. The
table shows that when each party at each election is taken as the unit of analysis, the mean electoral score of the neo-Nazi parties is a mere 0.23 percent of
the vote (i.e. the constant in Table 2.5). The neo-fascist parties average a score
of 3.31 percent if the AN is included, but record a mean of only 1.66 percent
if this party is excluded. The authoritarian xenophobic parties poll an average
of 5.72 percent of the vote; the neo-liberal xenophobic parties register a
mean of 4.40 percent of the vote; and the neo-liberal populist parties average
3.19 percent of the ballots.[10]

In addition to reporting the mean electoral scores of the different types of
parties, Table 2.6 also illustrates how often the different types of parties have
competed in elections. The neo-liberal populist parties (of which there are 7)
have competed in the fewest elections – 18. By contrast, the 11 authoritarian xenophobic parties have contested 50 elections. The 7 neo-Nazi parties
have taken part in 25 electoral contests, the 6 neo-fascist parties (taking the
Falangistas as one single party) have competed in 22, and the 9 neo-liberal

Table 2.6   Mean electoral scores of the different types of right-wing extremist parties
in Western Europe, 1979–2003

Type of party	Number of cases (number of times parties of this type have competed in elections)	Mean electoral score (percent)
Neo-Nazi (7)	25	0.23
Neo-fascist (6)	22	3.31
[Neo-fascist excluding AN] (5)	19	1.66
Authoritarian xenophobic (11)	50	5.72
Neo-liberal xenophobic (9)	31	4.40
Neo-liberal populist (7)	18	3.19

Notes: Numbers in parentheses refer to the number of individual parties of each type.
(The Italian Movimento Sociale and Alleanza Nazionale are counted as one party
within the neo-fascist group; the Spanish Falangistas are counted as one party.)

xenophobic parties have contested 31 elections. The authoritarian xeno-phobic parties are therefore not only the most successful type of party in terms of their mean electoral score, but also the most common type of party and the most active type of party, as they have competed in the most elections.

As well as examining the mean electoral scores of the different types of right-wing extremist parties and the frequency with which they have contested elections, it is also useful to consider which parties have ceased to exist. A glance back at Table 2.4 shows that it is the neo-Nazi and the neo-fascist types of party that have seen the most casualties. Of the seven neo-Nazi parties featured in this study, three no longer exist – the CP'86, the NVU and the PFNb. Moreover, of those that continue to exist the NF currently faces disintegration (see Chapter 3). As for the neo-fascist parties, four of the six (counting the Falangistas as one party) no longer exist. The Spanish Fuerza Nueva and Frente Nacional, the Portuguese PDC and the Italian MSI have all been dissolved – although this last party was superseded by the AN, so did not disappear in quite the same way as the other parties. In the authoritarian xenophobic group, three of the eleven parties – the Dutch CP and CD and the Wallonian party Agir – no longer exist, while in the neo-liberal populist group of parties, two parties – the Greek KP and EPEN – have been dissolved. Only one of the neo-liberal xenophobic parties – the Swedish DNP – has ceased to exist.

These patterns are not surprising – they simply confirm that persistent electoral failure has led to a number of neo-Nazi and neo-fascist parties decid-ing (or being forced) to cease contesting elections. In many cases these parties have chosen to disband altogether. In contrast, the authoritarian xenophobic, the neo-liberal xenophobic and the neo-liberal populist parties have not fallen victim to such pressures to the same extent. They have seen fewer casualties: with the exception of three authoritarian xenophobic parties (the Dutch

CP and CD and the Wallonian party Agir), two neo-liberal populist parties (the Greek KP and EPEN) and one neo-liberal xenophobic party (the Swedish DNP), they all continue to compete in the electoral arena.

Concluding remarks

At the outset, this chapter suggested that ideology might potentially be important in helping to explain why some right-wing extremist parties in Western Europe have performed better in elections than others. To test this proposition a new typology of right-wing extremist parties was constructed, as it was argued that the existing studies were not adequate for the task at hand. More specifically, an overview of the existing typologies showed that these were out of date, were not comprehensive, and suffered from important methodological and theoretical limitations. The new typology, constructed using three bases of division, has identified five different types of right-wing extremist parties: (1) neo-Nazi parties, (2) neo-fascist parties, (3) authoritarian xenophobic parties, (4) neo-liberal xenophobic parties, and (5) neo-liberal populist parties.

In the first instance, by its in-depth examination of the ideologies of the different parties, the typology has illustrated the full diversity that exists within the West European extreme right party family. As well as highlighting this diversity, the typology also allows for some observations to be made as to the composition of this party family. It has demonstrated that the various types of right-wing extremist parties are related to each other in different ways. While some types of party are directly related to each other, others are not. For example, the neo-Nazi parties, the authoritarian xenophobic parties and the neo-liberal xenophobic parties all resemble each other in that they are all radically xenophobic. Similarly, the neo-Nazi parties and the neo-fascist parties share a number of characteristics as both types of party reject democracy, parliamentarism and pluralism outright. However, in contrast, neo-Nazi parties share no features with neo-populist parties. Likewise, neo-fascist parties share no characteristics with authoritarian xenophobic parties. Therefore, to pursue the analogy of the party family, the conclusion can be reached that while some right-wing extremist parties are directly related to each other rather like brothers and sisters, others are only cousins (see Figure 2.2, which illustrates the ways in which the different types of parties are related to each other). All these parties nonetheless belong to the same, wider party family.

In addition to shedding light on the composition of the extreme right party family, the typology has allowed for the link between right-wing extremist ideology and electoral success to be examined. The analysis undertaken in this chapter has shown that certain types of ideology are indeed linked with greater electoral success than other types of ideology. Specifically, the neo-Nazi and the neo-fascist type of right-wing extremist parties have tended to

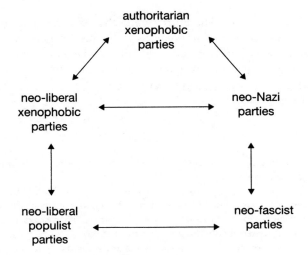

Figure 2.2 Extreme right party family

record low electoral scores, whereas the authoritarian xenophobic, the neo-liberal xenophobic and the neo-liberal populist types of parties have tended to experience greater levels of electoral success.

This said, having an authoritarian xenophobic, a neo-liberal xenophobic or a neo-liberal populist type of ideology is in no way a guarantee of electoral success. As well as performing well at the polls, these three types of parties have, on occasions, also recorded low electoral scores. By contrast, however, neo-Nazi and neo-fascist parties (with the notable exception of the MSI/AN) have nearly always experienced failure at the polls. In fact, all the neo-Nazi parties in the countries under observation in this study have experienced electoral failure. Neo-Nazi and neo-fascist parties have also had a tendency to disband – precisely because of their lack of electoral success.

Overall, therefore, this chapter has suggested that the type of ideology to which the different parties of the extreme right adhere is quite likely to help account for their levels of electoral success. The disparity in the electoral fortunes of the parties of the extreme right across Western Europe may thus be explained, at least in part, by the fact that the parties embrace different types of ideologies, some of which are more successful than others. More specifically, Table 2.5 suggested that, when no other factors are taken into consideration, approximately 10 percent of the variance in the right-wing extremist party vote could be explained by the presence of different types of right-wing extremist party ideology ($R^2 = .104$).

This said, however, ideology is clearly only one factor of many that may help explain why the parties of the extreme right have experienced uneven success at the polls. When other factors are taken into consideration, the influence of ideology on the electoral scores of the right-wing extremist parties may well change. Therefore, while the conclusions reached in this chapter are important in and of themselves, the precise influence of ideology on the right-wing extremist party vote will only be ascertained when other explanatory factors are also taken into consideration. One such set of factors refers to the parties' organization and leadership, and it is to these that the book now turns.

Notes

1 It is worth noting that Eatwell (1995) identifies a left-wing type of fascism as well as a right-wing type.

2 In addition, over half the authors mentioned nationalism. However, in this present typology nationalism has not been chosen as a basis of division because, since the great majority of right-wing extremist parties display this characteristic, it does not assist in sub-categorizing the extreme right party family.

3 Internal homogenization is achieved when only people belonging to a certain nation live within the borders of that state. For this to occur, all foreigners must leave that state. This helps ensure that the congruence of the nation and the state is attained – the traditional definition of the nationalist political doctrine (Gellner, 1983; Hobsbawm, 1990). Although this form of nationalism entails xenophobia, xenophobia and nationalism remain different concepts. This is because, in addition to internal homogenization, the congruence of the nation and the state may be reached through external exclusiveness, that is, the need to have all people belonging to a nation living within the borders of that state. Therefore, a political party can adhere to a nationalist ideology without necessarily espousing a xenophobic attitude if it pursues external exclusiveness only and remains unconcerned with internal homogenization.

4 The party (founded in 1961) was first called Nationale Aktion gegen die Überfremdung von Volk und Heimat (National Action against Excessive Foreign Influence on People and Homeland). Then in 1977 it changed its name to Nationale Aktion für Volk and Heimat (National Action for People and Homeland). It then changed its name again in the summer of 1990 to Schweizer Demokraten.

5 See below and note 7.

6 However, the ideology of the MSI and the AN clashes somewhat with the attitudes of a significant number of middle-level elites. On the basis of the results of a survey he carried out himself, Ignazi argues that many party cadres express concerns over the loss of national identity brought about by the presence of immigrants and favour the expulsion of illegal immigrants (Ignazi, 1996a: 707). Nonetheless, the party leadership continues to condemn such sentiments and insists that xenophobia has no place within the party's ideology.

7 After Franco's death a number of different groups all laid claim to the original title of the dictator's movement, Falange Española de las Juntas de Ofensiva Nacional-Sindicalista (FE de las JONS). These were the Frente Nacional Español, the Falange Española Auténtica, the Junta Coordinadora Nacional Sindicalista (which was made up of two groups: the Falange Española Independiente and the Círculos Doctrinales José Antonio), and a group without a name. The matter was

resolved in October 1976 when the title of FE de las JONS was assigned to the Frente Nacional Español (Ellwood, 1995: 92–3). Today, the parties with any visibility are the FE de las JONS, the Falange Española Independiente (FEI), the Falange Española Auténtica (FEA) and the Falange Española de las Juntas de Ofensiva Nacional-Sindicalista – sector Diego Marquez (FE de las JONS sector DM), which was founded in 1995 as a split from the FE de las JONS (Ellwood, 1995). As pointed out in the notes to Table 1.1, all these groups have extremely similar ideologies, and together they can be referred to as the Spanish Falangistas.

8 This is not to say that there is no racism at all in Spain. On the contrary, an organization that adhered to classical racism – the Círculo Español de Amigos de Europa (CEDADE) – did exist until 1994. It espoused both anti-Semitic and white supremacist beliefs. However, CEDADE never contested any elections. Instead, it remained confined to the extra-parliamentary arena. For details of CEDADE see Rodríguez (1995).

9 No hard and fast rules exist as to which category of a variable should be chosen as a reference group. The choice, on statistical grounds, is arbitrary, and no choice can be 'wrong'. Some researchers prefer to choose a reference group at the upper or lower boundary, whereas others prefer to select a category that is roughly mid-range. Whichever approach is chosen, however, the reference group should be well defined and should contain a sufficient number of cases to allow for a reasonably precise estimate of the sub-group mean. For further details on regression analysis with dummy variables, see Hardy (1993).

10 Taking the electoral result of each party at each election as a unit of analysis means that it is possible to control for the number of times each particular party has stood for election. In this way, a party that has only competed in elections once or twice but that has recorded high electoral scores (like the AN, for example, which competed in only three elections in the observed period but which recorded high scores) has less of a distorting effect on the mean electoral score of that type of party than if the number of elections were not controlled for.

3

Party organization and leadership

In addition to being influenced by ideology and policies, the electoral fortunes of the parties of the extreme right are also likely to be affected by the parties' internal organization and leadership, and by the consequences of these internal dynamics. In fact, a general consensus in the literature on right-wing extremist parties suggests that 'one of the most important determinants of success is party organization' (Betz, 1998a: 9). In the light of this, this chapter turns its attention to examining the internal structure of the West European parties of the extreme right and seeks to assess how organization and leadership impact on the parties' ability to win votes come election time. In exploring the influence of these factors on the electoral fortunes of the parties of the extreme right, the chapter investigates the extent to which party organization may help account for why the right-wing extremist parties in Western Europe have experienced such diverging levels of electoral success since the late 1970s.

The chapter begins by explaining the ways in which organization and leadership may influence the success of parties at the polls, and it puts forward a number of hypotheses as to the expected effects of party organization and leadership on the electoral fortunes of the different parties. Drawing on the literature on right-wing extremism, the chapter then identifies a number of different groups of extreme right parties on the basis of how well they are organized and how well they are led, and according to the degree of internal dissent and factionalism present within them. Having categorized the parties in such a way, the chapter then examines the link between organization and leadership on the one hand, and electoral success on the other. It concludes with an assessment of the importance of organization in helping to explain the disparity in the electoral fortunes of the West European parties of the extreme right.

The influence of party organization and party leadership

Strong leadership may be assumed to be beneficial to parties of the extreme right, just as it is to all parties. A particular reason why leadership may be even more important to right-wing extremist parties than to others is that these parties have shown themselves to be especially prone to factionalism and infighting. A strong and charismatic figure, capable of uniting the various tendencies or factions, may therefore be invaluable to these organizations. In addition, for the leader to exert the kind of total control that is often essential in parties of the extreme right, a centralized organizational structure with very clear lines of command is likely to be advantageous. Such a structure enables decisions made at the top of the party to be transmitted to the lower echelons in accordance with some set of rules by which party members abide. In turn, if these rules are to be obeyed, they must ideally be backed up by mechanisms that encourage members to conform to the leadership's decisions and expectations. In other words, parties of the extreme right are more likely to experience success if a strong level of internal party discipline exists within them that minimizes dissent, and that fosters internal party cohesion[1] and coherence.[2] With such cohesion and coherence the party is more able to present itself as a unified and credible actor to the electorate, and can thus hope to attract a significant share of the votes at election time.

Another reason why this type of leadership and organizational structure is particularly important to parties of the extreme right – as compared to other political parties – relates to the extent to which they depend on their leaders for direction and legitimacy. In many cases, the right-wing extremist parties are so strongly dependent on their leaders that if the leader were to leave, the party would simply fade into oblivion. In addition, a strong leadership and a well-structured organization enable the party to be more flexible in terms of its programmatic strategy. As Immerfall observes, 'charismatic leadership and tight party organization allow these parties to respond quickly and without too much internal debate to hot issues or shifts in their constituencies . . . As a result, [they] have been able to change ideological course, and discard previously important issues, or change the emphasis of their programs' (1998: 258).

In terms of electoral success, given the perceived importance of these organizational factors, and the way in which they interact, it is reasonable to hypothesize that those parties of the extreme right that have strong and charismatic leaders, a centralized organizational structure, and efficient mechanisms for enforcing party discipline will record higher results at the polls than parties with a weaker and uncharismatic leadership, a less centralized internal structure and weaker party discipline. The former are likely to have lower levels of internal dissent and factionalism, and should therefore exhibit higher levels of internal cohesion than their rivals. The greater programmatic and electoral coherence that is expected to result from this should then, in turn, bring greater party credibility, and hence higher levels of electoral success.

Operationalizing this hypothesis is not without its problems, however. For a start, getting inside the 'black box' of right-wing extremist parties is notoriously difficult, as these parties are particularly renowned for refusing to grant outsiders access to their records and personnel. What is more, even if the official rules and statutes are made available, they tend to shed little light on the real internal dynamics of right-wing extremist parties. Instead, the parties' internal affairs are more likely to depend on the will of the party leader than on party statutes. Bearing these restrictions in mind, this chapter assesses the effect that different party organizational structures have on the fortunes of the parties of the extreme right by drawing on the existing literature on right-wing extremism, in particular on the many single-party case studies. These studies provide rich information on the ways in which the different parties are organized and led, and enable the validity of the hypothesis advanced above to be examined.

Organization, leadership and factionalism: three types of right-wing extremist party

The degree of centralization in a party organization, the strength of the leadership, the level of discipline and the degree of dissent and factionalism within a party are difficult factors to measure or quantify. This said, on the basis of a scrutiny of the existing studies of right-wing extremist political parties, it is nonetheless possible to group the parties of the extreme right broadly according to their leadership, their structure and their internal discipline. More specifically, three different types of parties may be identified: (1) weakly organized, poorly led and divided parties, (2) weakly organized, poorly led but united parties, and (3) strongly organized, well-led but factionalized parties. Each type will be examined in turn.

Weakly organized, poorly led and divided parties

A first group, which contains the majority of the right-wing extremist parties of Western Europe, consists of those parties that have weak organizations and weak leaderships, and that have experienced considerable internal dissent and factionalism. The constituent members of this group are listed in Table 3.1.

The British NF is included in this first group because it has been marred by internal problems since the late 1970s. Following its humiliating defeat in the 1979 general election, when it polled a mere 0.7 percent of the national vote, the NF lost many of its more moderate members and broke down into quarrelling factions. The different groups in the party disagreed strongly over what ideology the NF should adopt, and what strategy the party should embrace if it were to recover from its defeat. As Eatwell explains, one group favoured the party's existing stance, and believed that the reason why the party had not reaped the electoral benefits from its existing policies was that the economic crisis had not yet become severe enough for significant numbers of voters to desert the mainstream parties and turn to the NF. In

Table 3.1   Weakly organized, poorly led and divided right-wing extremist parties

Party	Country
Front National (FN(b))	Belgium (Wallonia)
Front Nouveau de Belgique (FNB)	Belgium (Wallonia)
British National Party (BNP)	Britain
National Front (NF)	Britain
Fremskridtspartiet (FRPd)	Denmark
Nationaldemokratische Partei Deutschlands (NPD)	Germany
Republikaner	Germany
Ethniko Komma (EK)	Greece
Movimento Sociale–Fiamma Tricolore (Ms-Ft)	Italy
Fedrelandspartiet (FLP)	Norway
Ny Demokrati (ND)	Sweden
Sverigedemokraterna (SDk)	Sweden
Falange Española Auténtica (FEA)	Spain
Falange Española de las Juntas de Ofensiva Nacional-Sindicalista (FE de las JONS)	Spain
Falange Española de las Juntas de Ofensiva Nacional-Sindicalista – sector Diego Marquez (FE de las JONS sector DM)	Spain
Falange Española Independiente (FEI)	Spain
[Agir]	Belgium (Wallonia)
[Parti des Forces Nouvelles (PFNb)]	Belgium (Wallonia)
[Ethniki Politiki Enosis (EPEN)]	Greece
[Komma Proodeftikon (KP)]	Greece
[Centrumpartij (CP)]	Netherlands
[Centrumpartij '86 (CP'86)]	Netherlands
[Nederlandse Volksunie (NVU)]	Netherlands
[Partido da Democracia Cristã (PDC)]	Portugal
[Det Nya Partiet (DNP)]	Sweden

Note: Parties in square brackets no longer exist.

strong disagreement, another group maintained that the way forward was to develop an altogether new doctrine, although the precise nature of this doctrine was never made clear, and a whole host of different ideological currents began to emerge, including those that openly advocated the use of political violence (Eatwell, 1998a: 144–5).

The acute ideological and strategic or tactical factionalism that was developing within the NF in turn led to organizational change and leadership factionalism. For Husbands, the defeat in the 1979 election represented 'a major turning point in the organisational development of the NF and marked the beginning of the end of the movement's claim to seek political legitimacy through the ballot box' (1988a: 67). It also precipitated changes of personnel within the party leadership 'as new elements successfully manoeuvred to replace the old guard represented by John Tyndall and Martin Webster' (Husbands, 1988a: 67). Tyndall was forced to resign from the chairmanship in January 1980 and five months later he resigned from the party. A third generation of British fascists moved in to lead the NF on a new path, and Webster was ousted in early 1984 (Thurlow, 1998: 266–7). The ideological, strategic and leadership fragmentation meant that by 'mid-1981, the NF had disintegrated into at least four recognisable groupings, the rump of the old NF and three breakaway groups, and there was a further very small splinter group in East London' (Husbands, 1988a: 67).

Exacerbating this dissent and factionalism, if not causing it in the first place, was a remarkable lack of charisma, authority and expertise in the party leadership. As Eatwell observes, although the senior members of the party displayed differences in terms of background and education, 'the main linking strands at the top seem to have been a distinct lack of charismatic leadership potential, administrative incompetence, and a tendency to ideological schism' (2000b: 178). Tyndall lacked the charisma of other right-wing extremist leaders, even though he thought of himself as an inspirational leader (Eatwell, 1998a: 146). In addition, he displayed none of the political skills necessary to exploit opportunities for the good of the party.

The NF continued to be dogged by severe infighting and instability throughout the 1980s and 1990s. Tyndall and Webster's successors were no more successful in quelling internal party dissent than their predecessors, nor did they display strength or charisma in their leadership. The group that had taken over control of the party from Webster in late 1983, and that was centred on Nick Griffin and Joe Pearce, itself split in 1986. Its two leaders engaged in personal rivalry and were at loggerheads over the party's future strategic direction. The result of this rift was that 'by early 1987 there were essentially two groups calling themselves the National Front' (Husbands, 1988a: 69). The existence of these two rival factions continued throughout the late 1980s, with one wing of the party concentrating more on street battles and on the recruitment of ' "political soldiers", willing to sacrifice all to create a new society', and the other continuing to engage in 'attacks on the ethnic community' but also ensuring that it 'never lost sight of contesting elections and seeking to present a respectable face' (Eatwell, 1992: 178–9).

In January 1990, the 'political soldiers' wing of the party officially closed the NF, and the rival wing, represented by the Flag Group, was able to claim the NF mantle (Silver, 2000). The 'political soldiers' themselves then split and formed two new organizations, the International Third Position and the Third Way. What was left of the NF then also ruptured in 1995. The majority of the party's members decided to form a new organization, the National Democrats. A very small neo-Nazi rump of the NF remains.

The British BNP has been prone to similar infighting. This is not surprising as it was Tyndall who founded the BNP and, as Eatwell argues, the party has been 'in many ways a re-run of the 1970s NF' (2000b: 183). As in the NF, splits in the BNP have centred on groups that, on the one hand, have favoured an electoral path, and groups that, on the other, have been more

prone to pursuing a strategy of street fighting, and that have been quite open
to links with organizations such as Combat 18 and the National Socialist
Alliance (Eatwell, 2000b: 185; Lowles, 2000).

Conflicts within the BNP seemed to diminish a little in the late 1990s,
partly as a result of the slightly stronger leadership that the party acquired
when Nick Griffin took over from John Tyndall as party chairman in 1999.
The BNP's success in the May 2002 local elections further allowed the leadership to strengthen its position within the party and to continue its purge
of dissenters (Lowles, 2002). That said, however, since the summer of 2002
internal disputes have once again become rife within the party. On the one
level divisions have centred on policy and strategy, with many members
threatening to walk out over what they perceive to be a selling out of the
party's core principles. In particular, there has been great anger among hard-
liners (including Tyndall) at the leadership's attempt to present a more moderate party image and to describe the BNP as a 'race-realist' party.

These conflicts over strategy and policy have also led to personal infighting. The expulsion of dissenters has slowly turned organizers across the
country against the party leadership. Opposition to Griffin and to Lecomber,
the party's group development officer and the de facto London leader, has
become fierce in party branches in Scotland, in London and especially in the
northwest of England, where the party has enjoyed its greatest success.
Ordinary party members have also become disillusioned as a result of the
heavy-handed approach of the party leadership (Lowles, 2003a).

While Griffin and Lecomber have become increasingly concerned at this
growing disenchantment among party members towards the leadership,
especially given that the unease has spread to formerly loyal activists, they
have nonetheless continued their attacks on dissenters. In the summer of
2003 the party leadership finally turned on Tyndall and sought to expel him
from the party, together with two of his closest supporters. Tyndall's expulsion may not end infighting within the party, however, as disillusionment is
now widespread. Furthermore, in the short term at least, this is a high-risk
strategy since Tyndall may well become a magnet for anyone inside the party
with a grievance against the leadership (Lowles, 2003b).

Both the NF and the BNP are therefore classic examples of parties that
have experienced high levels of dissent and factionalism. As a result of weak
party organizations and poor leadership, these two right-wing extremist
parties have suffered from schisms throughout their lives, brought about by
disputes over the party ideology and strategy.

Significant internal factionalism and weak leadership have also plagued
the Dutch parties of the extreme right. The NVU suffered from factionalism
from the start. Formed in 1971, the party remained unknown to the electorate until 1974, mainly because it was so preoccupied with internal struggles. When, following an openly racist campaign in the local elections of
1974, the public did become aware of its existence, the bad publicity and

legal action that followed, coupled with the party's radicalization, caused many of its members to leave. They retired from politics altogether or went on to form more moderate parties (Mudde and Van Holsteyn, 2000: 146).

The CP, a successor to the NVU, was also dogged by leadership struggles from very early on in its life. Friction existed between the party leadership, in the form of chairman Konst and vice-chairman De Wijer, and the parliamentary party, which was headed by Hans Janmaat (Mudde and Van Holsteyn, 2000: 147). The frictions were ideological as well as personal: Janmaat represented the 'moderate' wing of the party, while the party leadership stood for the more radical and activist right wing (Lucardie, 1998: 112). This ideological and leadership factionalism intensified at the party congress of May 1984, when the radicals gained the upper hand and assumed control of the executive committee. In this climate Janmaat's position became harder and harder to maintain and in October 1984 he was expelled from the CP along with a number of his followers. Like the British NF and BNP, the Dutch CP thus experienced ideological factionalism, which eventually led to leadership factionalism.

The ousting of Janmaat did not help establish unity within the CP, however. Both Konst and De Wijer left the party as a result of pressure from their employers, and other members deserted the party of their own accord (Mudde and Van Holsteyn, 2000: 147). The party also ran into financial difficulties, partly as a result of losing the subsidies it had received from having gained parliamentary representation. After winning no seats in the elections to the Second Chamber in May 1986, and after being convicted of electoral fraud and ordered to pay compensation to citizens it had deceived while collecting signatures for elections, the party was declared bankrupt (Lucardie, 1998: 113). As a result, the CP was dissolved.

Within days of the CP's collapse, a successor party, the CP'86, was formed. This party was as subject to internal quarrels and factionalism as its predecessor. In fact, it was in such disarray at the end of the 1980s that it failed to contest the parliamentary election of 1989. Ideological, strategic and leadership factionalism continued throughout the early 1990s, mainly revolving around the issue of whether or not to join forces with Janmaat's CD (see below). Disputes reached such a height in May 1996 that the party leader, Henk Ruitenberg, who was in favour of a *rapprochement* with the CD, was removed and replaced by a party veteran, Wim Beaux (Mudde and Van Holsteyn, 2000: 148). However, this change of personnel did not quell the internal problems that beset the CP'86. In November 1996, the neo-Nazi wing of the party was expelled. Following a battle over who should keep the name 'Centrumpartij'86', the 'moderate' wing was left without a party name and most of its members retired from politics altogether. What was left of the CP'86 was banned and dissolved by an Amsterdam court in November 1998.

The German Republikaner is another party that has suffered from internal disputes and that has been weakly led. Almost from the start, the party was beset by struggles between its three founders. The party's chairman, Franz Handlos, accused Franz Schönhuber, the party's speaker and second deputy chairman, of plotting a right-wing takeover and of trying to promote former NPD members within the party. In the light of this, the National Executive Committee decided to expel Schönhuber. The latter pre-empted this move, however, by confronting Handlos with a no-confidence motion (Veen *et al.*, 1993: 23–4). As a result, in 1985, just two years after the party was established, Handlos, along with Ekkehart Voigt (the party's vice-chairman), left the Republikaner, and Schönhuber took over the position of national chairman.

Despite further struggles within the party and criticisms of his leadership, Schönhuber held the chairmanship until 1990. During this time he also managed to build up a broad organizational structure, so that by 1989 the party had a presence in each *Land*. That said, however, the organization was far from strong. In particular, it remained difficult to find enough members to fill organizational positions at regional level (Westle and Niedermayer, 1992: 89).

By 1990 internal struggles within the party were once again rife. On the one hand the infighting centred on Schönhuber's authoritarian style of leadership, as well as the behaviour of the party's general secretary, Harald Neubauer (Backes, 1990: 8). On the other hand, the tensions concerned the party's ideology and its strategy. Traditional right-wing extremists who wanted to move the party further to the right began to distance themselves from members with no previous right-wing extremist history who preferred a more moderate course (Kolinsky, 1992: 69; Backer, 2000: 101). In contrast to the early years of the party, in this conflict Schönhuber represented the 'moderate' faction in the party, and he tried to distance himself from the party's extreme right, which was represented by Neubauer. However, Schönhuber soon found that he was unable to count on broad support within the party and, at the end of May 1990, he resigned as federal chairman, presumably, as Veen and his colleagues argue, so as to pre-empt dismissal by the party's governing board, in which Schönhuber's enemies had meanwhile gained a majority (1993: 24–5).

Schönhuber's departure was short lived. Immediately after his resignation he announced that he would be standing as a candidate for the federal chairmanship of the party at the end of June, thereby, as Backes observes, putting the party to a real test (1990: 8). Schönhuber was duly re-elected as chairman, a development that signalled the apparent defeat of the extreme right wing of the party. This was further underlined when he promptly dismissed all his rivals and replaced almost the entire party executive (Backer, 2000: 101). In particular, he expelled the extreme right Neubauer group and declared the party 'cleansed of all "extremists" ' (Backes and Mudde, 2000: 460).

In spite of these moves, moderates within the party were not convinced of Schönhuber's attempts to distance himself from the more extreme elements of the organization, and of the extreme right in general. By 1994, when Schönhuber met Gerhard Frey, the leader of the extreme right DVU, the dissatisfaction felt by many within the Republikaner over Schönhuber's leadership was growing. In addition to not being able to make-up his mind on the ideological course of the party, Schönhuber was also blamed for electoral losses and declining membership (Backer, 2000: 101). In October 1994, the party executive dismissed him as party chairman and, although he contested the dismissal in court and was later briefly reinstated, he finally stepped down in December 1994 and did not seek re-election.

Schönhuber's final departure and his replacement by Rolf Schlierer, one of the party's former vice-chairmen, at first appeared to suggest a moderating of the party's ideology. Schlierer represents the intellectual side of the Republikaner, and has been able to woo disenchanted conservative voters and attract members with higher levels of income and education (Veen *et al.*, 1993: 27–8). He has also proved to be a good orator, at ease with the media. That said, however, he is not seen as particularly charismatic, and internal disputes have continued under his leadership. He appears caught between trying to steer a more moderate course on the one hand, and acknowledging that competition between the various parties of the extreme right should be avoided on the other, something that would lead to some kind of *rapprochement* with Gerhard Frey's more extreme DVU (Backes and Mudde, 2000: 460).

Throughout their life the Republikaner have thus been plagued by internal dissent centred on disagreements about ideology as well as the strategy or tactics the party should adopt. Ideological and strategic factionalism has also led to leadership factionalism, and Schönhuber showed himself too weak to withstand such dissent.

The Danish FRPd is another right-wing extremist party that can be seen as belonging to this first group. Its leadership has been chaotic and the level of dissent and factionalism within the party has been high. As Andersen explains, 'almost from the beginning, the party has been plagued by conflicts between the adherents of Glistrup's provocative and uncompromising style on the one hand and the adherents of a somewhat more conventional bourgeois line on the other' (1992: 194–5). Two factions began to emerge within the party: a fundamentalist group, to which Glistrup belonged, which refused all compromises with other parties, and a pragmatist wing, centred on Pia Kjærsgaard, which showed itself more willing to negotiate with other parties if this was considered politically advantageous (Widfeldt, 2000: 489).

At first Glistrup was able to count on substantial support from within the party and was able to exert considerable control. However, when he was sentenced to three years in prison for tax fraud in 1983, this soon ended. The pragmatist faction assumed de facto control of the party, and by the time Glistrup returned from jail and was re-elected to parliament in 1987, his position was undermined. His disapproval of the situation was such that, in 1990, he entered the election with his own party, the Cosy Party (Widfeldt, 2000: 489).[3]

The pragmatists' effective control over the party and Glistrup's departure did not stop the internal quarrels that had been rumbling on for a decade or so. The struggle between the two factions continued and reached a new peak in 1994–95. Part of the reason for this was that the pragmatists had never managed to capture the chairmanship of the party even though they had been in charge of the party during and after Glistrup's imprisonment. In 1994, their position was further weakened when the fundamentalists gained the balance of power in the parliamentary party. Unable to appoint her candidate to the parliamentary chair, and under severe pressure from the fundamentalists, Kjærsgaard was forced to resign as parliamentary spokesperson. In response, she appealed to the national party organization for support as the pragmatists commanded a majority in the national committee. At the party conference in September 1995, the clash between the two factions culminated in a clear victory for the fundamentalists. Kjærsgaard and her followers (including three other MPs and about one third of the party membership) decided to leave the FRPd and to form a new party, the DF (Bille, 1996: 318–19; Svåsand, 1998: 81; Andersen and Bjørklund, 2000: 197).

Though the split was followed by a period of relative calm – when Kirsten Jacobsen, a respected and long-serving MP, was elected to the leadership – the FRPd's troubles were far from over. Jacobsen gave up formal leadership of the party in 1998 for personal reasons and then announced in 1999 that she would not contest the next elections (Andersen and Bjørklund, 2000: 200). This move renewed tensions within the party, which were then exacerbated when Glistrup was accepted back as a party member in September 1999. There were immediate calls for his expulsion, emanating in particular from the party's leadership, but when these were not answered, all four of the party's MPs defected (Andersen and Bjørklund, 2000: 200; Widfeldt, 2000: 490). As a result of these defections and of Glistrup's return, the FRPd is seen as a more or less spent force.

The organizational structure of the FRPd had done nothing to prevent the ideological, strategic and leadership factionalism which developed within it. Glistrup had resisted attempts to build a traditional party organization, preferring to see himself as the party's spiritual leader (Widfeldt, 2000: 489; Ignazi, 2003: 143). Though the party did gradually develop an organization, his attitude towards organization-building did nothing to instil discipline or create a clear chain of command throughout the party, something that might well have helped curb internal dissent.

The Swedish right-wing extremist party ND has been subject to similar instability. Immediately after its success in the 1991 elections, the party suffered from a number of defections. In addition, discipline within the parliamentary party group was poor, with some members reaching agreements with other parties in committee, only to backtrack on these when the bill came to the chamber. Furthermore, an ideological divide began to emerge within the party, with a market-liberal group rallying behind one of the party's leaders, Ian Wachtmeister, and a more welfare-oriented faction forming around the other leader, Bert Karlsson (Widfeldt, 2000: 495; Ignazi, 2003: 159).

As the divide developed, the relationship between the two leaders became increasingly strained. In the run-up to the 1994 elections Wachtmeister was accused by his opponents of being 'undemocratic' and of managing the party like a business (Svåsand, 1998: 82). Disillusioned by the internal state of the party and the lack of discipline that existed within some of its groups, Wachtmeister announced that he did not intend to run for re-election as head of the parliamentary group. His withdrawal unleashed a fierce internal struggle in which various forces claimed the right to the party leadership (Svåsand, 1998: 79). 'The process to select a new party leader was chaotic, involving disputed choices and a legal battle . . . Wachtmeister failed to endorse the party and his short-lived successor (replaced after a few months) resigned from the party, urging her supporters to vote for the Moderate party' (Widfeldt, 2000: 496). Karlsson also left the party.

The ND failed miserably at the 1994 national elections, and since grass-roots organization within the party was practically non-existent and what local branches there were had been uncoupled from the national party during 1993, 'there was no organisational infrastructure to compensate for the lack of national leadership' (Svåsand and Wørlund, 2001: 13).

The appointment of John Bouvin as party leader in 1997 did nothing to stem the factionalism present within the party either. When, in April 1998, he announced that the ND would enter an electoral coalition with the neo-fascist Konservativa Partiet (Conservative Party), internal disagreements broke out. A month later, after his arrest at a party rally, Bouvin was expelled from the party (AXT, 2001: 9). Thus, for the ND, personal animosity and rivalry, coupled with strategic and ideological factionalism, brought leadership factionalism.

After leaving the ND in 1994, Ian Wachtmeister went on to form the DNP. The party contested the 1998 election but went largely unnoticed. It was unable to rely on any structured organization and Wachtmeister's leadership was clearly not strong enough to entice many voters. The DNP ceased to function after the election and Wachtmeister withdrew from politics altogether (AXT, 2001: 8).

The Swedish SDk have also suffered from internal struggles and defections. Indeed, after the general election of 1994, the party began to experience an internal conflict that saw those who wished to create an image of greater respectability pitted against those who resisted such a move. The result of this conflict was that many of the more radical members of the party defected to more extreme organizations such as the Nationalsocialistisk

Front (National Socialist Front) and, since 1997, the Konservativa Partiet (AXT, 2001: 8).

Similarly, the Norwegian FLP has experienced a number of resignations. Some of the party's key activists left the organization following its poor showing in the 1997 general election, when it polled a mere 0.2 percent of the vote. The party lost further members in 1998 when an argument broke out at its annual general meeting over the far-right magazine *Fritt Forum*, which had become increasingly extremist since the mid-1990s (AXT, 2000: 8).

The German NPD is another party that is weakly led and weakly organized and has suffered internal divisions. The presence within the party of former National Socialists on the one hand, and new members with no right-wing extremist history or previous party commitments on the other, has led to a detachment of the leadership from the rank and file, and a radicalization of many members (Kolinsky, 1992: 69). As the NPD has become increasingly more militant, it has promoted 'direct (and also violent) actions rather than building up a solid partisan organization' (Ignazi, 2003: 71).

The francophone right-wing extremist parties in Belgium have also experienced factionalism, caused by divisions over ideology and strategy. As Fitzmaurice argues:

> the French-speaking extreme right in Belgium has seemed 'groupusculaire', fractious, divided, introverted, insubstantial, amateurish and unable to choose a clear strategy as between forms of 'entryism' on the fringes of the traditional Christian Social and Liberal parties of the right, romantic violence and 'destabilisation' through links with para-military groups and limited infiltration of the security services, ideological debate such as the so-called 'revisionist' or neo-occidentalist philosophies, as against electoralism. (1992: 305–6)

Indeed, the PFNb 'remained virtually without public activities between 1975 and 1980, as a result of internal quarrels' (Deslore, 1995: 252), and in its later years it was unable to accommodate an influx of more moderate members. Likewise, Agir, which was set up by these more moderate members, also fell victim to personal quarrels (Ignazi, 2003: 128–9). As for the FN(b), Deslore maintains that it similarly 'cannot avoid conflicts between the so-called moderate-populist-liberal wing and an out-and-out far right component. [Its] membership is extremely heterogenous and has a high turnover' (1995: 253). These conflicts culminated shortly after Deslore made these comments, as the FN(b) experienced internal splits that ended in Marguerite Bastien (one of the party's two MPs) leaving the FN(b) in 1995, and going on to form the rival FNB. Almost all the elected officials in the FN(b) defected to other parties as a result of these splits (Ignazi, 2003: 131).

Although the FN(b) resurfaced in 1997, when its remnants combined with those of Agir, a party which had ceased to contest national elections after 1995 (Ignazi, 2003: 131), dissent and infighting within the party continues. One of the FN(b)'s councillors in the Walloon regional parliament, Alain

Sadune, recently led a breakaway faction, leaving the party president, Daniel Féret, rather isolated (Résistances, 2001).

As for Marguerite Bastien's FNB, between 1995 and 1998 it attracted various groupuscules on the francophone extreme right as well as disenchanted elements of the Liberal and Christian Socialist parties (Résistances, 2001). It therefore brought together a very heterogeneous collection of individuals, which did nothing for its cohesion. Tensions and internal crises soon erupted within its ranks, and Marguerite Bastien quickly found herself able to rely upon the support of only a few of her followers. In December 2001, after a period in exile in the south of France, she resigned as party president, prompting the implosion of the FNB. The rump of the party is now considering a *rapprochement* with other extreme right groups in francophone Belgium, including Féret's FN(b) (Résistances, 2001).

Fragmentation has also been a feature of the Spanish Falangistas. By 1977 there were no fewer than four different groups that claimed to be the legitimate successor to Franco's Falange Española de las Juntas de Ofensiva Nacional-Sindicalista (FE de las JONS) (Ellwood, 1992: 379; Casals, 2001: 328). Furthermore, throughout the 1980s and 1990s these organizations have suffered numerous splits and today they remain concerned with little more than their own survival (AXT, 1996: 6).

The Greek parties of the extreme right have generally been composed of a very eclectic mix of people and it has thus not been uncommon for internal struggles to develop within these parties as well. Kapetanyannis notes that this was the case for Ethniki Paratascis – the predecessor of the KP – which developed 'centrifugal tendencies' and suffered defections, ultimately causing the party to disintegrate (1995: 136). He also argues that 'The difficulties of right-wing groups in consolidating a solid electoral base were exacerbated by the lack of any serious, stable leadership and organisation' (1995: 136). Indeed, poor party leadership and organization contributed greatly to the disintegration of the KP in 1984, and to the dissolution of EPEN in 1989, and continues to characterize what is left of the EK.

The picture is similar in Portugal, where 'the talented leaders, the organizing skills, and the infrastructure which could have enabled [the Portuguese extreme right] to carve out even a modest power-base among discontented Portuguese in the revolutionary aftermath were lacking' (Gallagher, 1992: 244). Instead the Portuguese extreme right, including the PDC, displayed 'weakness and fragility', showed itself unable to hold on to its cadres, and also fell victim to internal ideological struggles (Costa Pinto, 1995: 120–1).

A final party that may be considered as belonging to this first group of right-wing extremist parties is the Italian Ms-Ft, which broke away from the MSI in 1995 when the MSI transformed itself into the AN. Following this, the majority of the resources of the MSI (in terms of both money and personnel) were automatically transferred to the AN. The Ms-Ft thus had few organizational resources at its disposal. In addition, in 1998–99 Pino Rauti was challenged for the leadership of the party. The challengers eventually left the party to set up the Movimento Sociale Europeo in 1999 (Baldini, 2001: 2).

These various examples therefore illustrate that for many of the extreme right parties in Western Europe weak leadership and weak party organization have led to factionalism, be it of an ideological, a strategic or a personal variety.

Weakly organized, poorly led but united parties

Not all right-wing extremist parties with weak leadership and weak organization have suffered from as much internal dissent and factionalism as the parties just discussed. A relatively small number of extreme right-wing parties have experienced a reasonably calm internal life and an absence of internal struggles even though they have not benefited from having a charismatic leader or a strong party organization. These parties constitute a second group of right-wing extremist parties, which are listed in Table 3.2.

The Dutch CD is one party that remained unified despite being relatively weakly led and poorly organized. Two months after his expulsion from the CP, Janmaat joined the CD, which had been formed in November 1984 by some of his allies, and became its leader. In spite of some initial internal conflicts and attacks on his leadership, Janmaat was able to weather the storm in the CD, something that he had not been able to do in the CP (Lucardie, 1998: 115). By the late 1980s internal disputes had been suppressed.

In 1994, on the back of a relatively good showing in both local and parliamentary elections and in the wake of a number of defections from the party, Janmaat began to strengthen his position. One means of doing this was by accumulating a number of different positions within the apparatus, a common tactic by which right-wing extremist leaders have attempted to exert control within their party. Not only did he become an MP and the party's parliamentary leader in 1994, but he was also elected party president in the same year. In addition, he was in charge of the party's research office and was secretary of the regional branch of The Hague. Janmaat also extended his control within the party by making sure that all those in a

Table 3.2   Weakly organized, poorly led but united right-wing extremist parties

Party	Country
Deutsche Volksunion (DVU)	Germany
Freiheitspartei der Schweiz (FPS)	Switzerland
Schweizer Demokraten (SD)	Switzerland
[Centrumdemocraten (CD)]	Netherlands
[Frente Nacional]	Spain
[Fuerza Nueva]	Spain

Note: Parties in square brackets no longer exist.

position of power were loyal to him. His wife, Wil Schuurman, who was elected to parliament in 1994, assumed the position of party secretary. She was also a member of the municipal council of The Hague, and a member of the executive committee of the same regional branch. In addition, Schuurman's son took up a prominent position in the party, managing the party office (Lucardie, 1998: 116).

As a result of his presence in all domains of the party, Janmaat was able to exert his control and authority throughout the party apparatus. This also enabled him to be aware of all internal party activities, including the development of any potential rival power-bases. In this way, the likelihood of severe ideological and leadership factionalism within the CD was minimized.

Although he showed himself adept enough to make sure that no one put a claim on the party's leadership, Janmaat did not prove himself to be a popular or charismatic leader. Within his party, 'his character – tormenting and resentful – and his authoritarian style of leadership [were] always a source of frustration for many ambitious or talented party members' (Mudde and Van Holsteyn, 2000: 150). Furthermore, outside the party, he was incapable of exploiting political opportunities or of launching successful populist appeals that might have benefited the party electorally. The CD only appealed to a very narrow section of the Dutch electorate. As Mudde and Van Holsteyn argue, Janmaat simply lacked 'the political skills (of a Dewinter or a Haider) necessary to build a good organization and fully exploit the grievances of the electorate' (2000: 163).

Janmaat left politics in 1998 after the CD lost all its seats in the elections of May of that year. He maintained that a comeback was hopeless since the media and the Dutch security service were working against him. The CD did not contest the elections of 2002, and Janmaat died in June 2002, one month after the elections. The party did not take part in the 2003 elections and became to all intents and purposes extinct.

In a similar fashion, the Swiss SD and FPS have not suffered greatly from internal quarrels, but nor have they enjoyed the strong and charismatic leadership that is characteristic of some of the other West European right-wing extremist parties. The SD have never had a leader as charismatic as their founder James Schwarzenbach, who left the party in 1971 (Gentile and Kriesi, 1998: 134), and their current president, Rudolf Keller, showed a lack of political skill when he stirred up controversy in 1998 by calling for a boycott on all American and Jewish goods and services (Anti-Semitism Worldwide, 1999/2000). He failed to be re-elected to the National Council in 1999. The FPS also lacks a strong helmsman. Having won no seats in either the 1999 or 2003 electoral contests, the FPS currently faces obliteration (Husbands, 2000: 507).

In addition to not having a strong leadership, the SD and the FPS have also lacked a well-developed and structured party organization. Indeed, the Swiss parties of the extreme right are not represented in every canton, and where they are, there are often only a handful of activists. Furthermore, there is no permanent staff at local or regional level; only at national level are there a few permanent employees (Gentile and Kriesi, 1998: 132).[4]

The German DVU may also be considered to belong to this second group of right-wing extremist parties as it too is a weak yet united party. It has not suffered from the kind of internal dissent and leadership factionalism that has beset the Republikaner or the NPD, for example, and control has instead rested firmly in the hands of its leader, Gerhard Frey, mainly as a result of the financial backing and press coverage he has lent the party. As Winkler and Schumann observe, 'he considers himself the owner of the party' (1998: 100). In spite of his dominance, however, it would be inaccurate to describe Frey's leadership as strong and authoritative. What is more, his hold over the party is not accompanied by a centralized, structured party organization. Instead, the DVU's organizational structure is much looser, leading some observers to term it a 'movement' rather than a political party.

The Spanish Fuerza Nueva and Frente Nacional – both led by Blas Piñar – may also be considered as belonging to this second group of right-wing extremist parties. Both parties were weakly organized, and though Piñar displayed a certain charisma, he did not possess the political skills necessary to lead the parties to success. The leadership therefore was far from strong. However, unlike the parties in the first group, both Fuerza Nueva and Frente Nacional remained united.

Fuerza Nueva's party organization was never efficient or modern even though it was fairly extensive. Although the party set up a youth movement, a party magazine, and even a limited number of foreign delegations, the party organization was never developed into a structured, bureaucratic party machine. Instead, the organization assumed a hierarchical, almost presidential structure, with everything revolving around Piñar (Rodríguez, 1990: 91–2; Gilmour, 1992: 214). Fuerza Nueva was also characterized by improvisation and amateurism, and by an absence of tactics and political strategies, so much so that the party never even developed a political programme (Casals, 2001: 327–8). The party was dissolved in November 1982.

Frente Nacional – the second of Piñar's parties – did not benefit from the same type of infrastructure that Fuerza Nueva had had. It was constrained by the fact that it severely lacked resources, so much so that in the late 1980s the party decided to concentrate on European elections only. It did not contest the general elections of 1989 (Gilmour, 1992: 216), and was eventually dissolved in 1994 (Casals, 2001: 331).

Piñar's leadership enabled the two parties to remain united even though a number of figures on the Spanish extreme right tried to displace him from his position of leadership (Rodríguez, 1990: 91). However, despite having a degree of magnetism and being a good orator (Rodríguez, 1990: 89), Piñar did not possess the political skills of a Le Pen or a Haider. This became particularly clear when the attempt to create a Spanish National Front that would unite the various groups failed because of a lack of communication between the main representatives (Rodríguez, 1990: 93).

Strongly organized, well-led but factionalized parties

In contrast to the parties discussed so far, other right-wing extremist parties have been led by strong, more able and more charismatic leaders. In addition, unlike the parties examined above, these parties have developed well-structured party organizations. At the same time, however, these better-led and better-organized parties of the extreme right have experienced significant factionalism. Sometimes the disputes have been over ideology, on other occasions they have centred on strategy. There have also been instances where the struggles have been of a personal kind. More often than not this factionalism has resulted in defections or even in party splits. However, in contrast to the parties of the first group discussed above, which also experienced factionalism, these better-organized and better-led parties have come through their internal struggles unharmed. These parties, which form a third group of right-wing extremist parties, are listed in Table 3.3.

Included in this third group is the Norwegian FRPn. This party has experienced fewer internal wrangles than its Danish namesake, and one important reason for this is that the leadership of the FRPn has been significantly stronger than that of the Danish party. According to Widfeldt:

> Carl I. Hagen displays many of the attributes that have been conducive to the success of Jörg Haider in Austria. He is an effective media performer. Photogenic and articulate, he communicates directly to the 'common man' with a 'common sense' message. He has a strong and loyal personal following and has so far been able to control splits and outbreaks of discontent in the party. (2000: 490–1)

This does not mean that the FRPn has been free of all internal quarrels, however. On the contrary, Svåsand notes that 'the lower echelons of the

Table 3.3   Strongly organized, well-led but factionalized right-wing extremist parties

Party	Country
Freiheitliche Partei Österreichs (FPÖ)	Austria
Vlaams Blok (VB)	Belgium (Flanders)
Dansk Folkeparti (DF)	Denmark
Front National (FN)	France
Mouvement National Républicain (MNR)	France
Alleanza Nazionale (AN)	Italy
Lega Nord (LN)	Italy
Fremskrittspartiet (FRPn)	Norway
Lega dei Ticinesi (LdT)	Switzerland
[Movimento Sociale Italiano (MSI)]	Italy

Note: Party in square brackets no longer exists.

party were characterized by a high degree of turbulence and conflicts, in which the central party leadership had to, or tried to, intervene' (1998: 81). In the wake of the party's electoral success of 1989, these struggles spread to the parliamentary party and, as Bjørklund (2001) explains, fuelled a conflict between the party's 'extreme liberalists' and the 'populists'. These wrangles came to a head at the 1994 party convention, when the 'liberalists' lost out. The parliamentary group split and four of the party's ten MPs broke away. They were accompanied by the party's youth organization, itself dominated by liberals (Svåsand, 1998: 81).

In contrast to events in Denmark, where the exit of the liberal wing marked the beginning of the party's disintegration, the split in the FRPn was not overly damaging (Ignazi, 2003: 152). In fact, as the party's results in the local elections of 1995 (in which it won 10.5 percent of the vote) suggest, the departure of the liberals served the party well, as it meant that it could now concentrate on the theme of immigration without having to engage in damaging internal battles. Throughout the struggles Hagen had remained in firm control of his party, partly because he had ensured that the parliamentary party was subordinated to the party organization, which he, as party chairman, and his populist faction dominated. In addition, the parliamentary party's room for manoeuvre was limited in view of the fact that Hagen was also parliamentary chair (Svåsand, 1998: 81).

Hagen's grip on power has continued, even though internal conflicts continue to surface within the FRPn from time to time. Divisions began to emerge within the party once again in the aftermath of the 1999 local elections, for example, when two factions within the party began to emerge, one centred on Hagen, the other on Øystein Hedstrøm and Vidar Kleppe, two of the party's more extremist MPs. However, the exclusion of a local party branch leader for making extremist comments demonstrates that Hagen can be quite ruthless in dealing with any potential rivals or troublemakers within the party, or with those who may bring the organization bad publicity (AXT, 2000). A number of other party members were expelled from the party in early 2001 after they disobeyed the party leadership over the nomination of candidates. 'Others, MPs as well as members, left in protest over what was seen as an extreme form of centralisation and personal dominance by Carl I. Hagen . . . and the end result was that the parliamentary group was reduced from 25 to 20.' Nonetheless, the party quickly recovered from these departures and by the summer of 2001, 'Carl I. Hagen . . . emerged as a winner in spite of the turmoil' (Svåsand, 2003: 13–14).

Struggles therefore do exist within the FRPn, but Hagen appears to be in control of them, and none of the quarrels or the defections has seriously threatened his position (Andersen and Bjørklund, 2000: 197). Thus, when Svåsand compares the two Progress Parties (FRPn and FRPd) and argues that 'conflicts within the parties had been endemic from the start, with several defections among members of parliament and party members [and that] in the end, conflicts between the hard-liners and the moderates have led to organizational splits in both parties' (1998: 79), it is important to appreciate that the Norwegian party and its leader have managed to withstand these divisions, whereas the Danish party has not.

Another party that has suffered from internal struggles but that ultimately has been able to overcome them is the Italian MSI, re-formed and renamed AN in 1995. As in many of the other parties discussed so far, within the MSI/AN there has been an on-going conflict between the more hard-line wing of the party and the more moderate one. Within the MSI this took the form of struggles between 'radical populists unafraid of embracing the fascist heritage, and moderates prepared to be part of the respectable right' (Gallagher, 2000: 66). It led to a large number of defections by party moderates in the latter half of the 1970s. About half the party's senators and almost half its deputies left the MSI, accusing the party of being involved in right-wing terrorism and of being incapable of building a parliamentary strategy that could bring them out of isolation (Sidoti, 1992: 158). There was thus both ideological and strategic factionalism present in the party, as well as high levels of defection.

Despite the departure of the moderates, the internal disputes rumbled on within the MSI throughout the 1980s. The subject of disagreement remained the same: 'should [the party] accommodate itself to a system based on liberal democracy or instead act as a radical alternative for those sections of society which felt excluded or let down by the system?' (Gallagher, 2000: 66). Internal differences were such that, as Sidoti explains, 'by 1990, the MSI was a party divided into a multiplicity of groups [and the] new leader, Gianfranco Fini, was elected in 1987 by a majority which was split into six factions' (1992: 158). The factionalism that beset the party was further confirmed when Pino Rauti, a somewhat radical figure within the party, briefly replaced Fini as leader in 1990–91. Fini returned as leader in 1991, however, and for the first time in a number of years, under his leadership the party gradually began to find some strategic and ideological direction. As Gallagher observes, in Fini the party had found 'a capable helmsman who has grown in stature since being appointed head of the MSI youth in 1977' (2000: 70).

Three years after his return, Fini led the MSI into the elections of 1994 as part of a broader and more moderate right-wing movement known as the AN. The party gained enormously from such a tactic and Fini decided to adopt this more moderate strategy for his party. In January 1995 the MSI was dissolved and replaced with the AN. The party's transformation precipitated the departure of a number of party members, including Rauti. The defections were not very numerous, however, and all in all Fini has proved adept at keeping the party largely united behind his new venture (Gallagher, 2000: 83). The split also enabled Fini and his followers to declare that the AN has undergone a genuine transformation. As Newell puts it, the departure of the radicals 'was welcomed by the National Alliance's leaders as providing a "certificate of authenticity" of the MSI's transformation' (2000: 482).

Fini has therefore shown himself to be a successful leader since his return to the top in 1991. He has proved to be an authoritative and charismatic figure and has displayed considerable political skill. As a result he has become popular and respected, so much so that in the winter of 1995–96 he topped the polls as most popular politician in Italy (Gallagher, 2000: 80). In addition, he has managed to strengthen his control over the party through a series of organizational changes, and by nominating newcomers to the party hierarchy (Ignazi, 2003: 50). As Ignazi explains, following its transformation:

> the party is expected to abandon the traditional mass-party type of organisation (local branches, bottom–top chain of election, elected local party leaders, collective bodies of decision-making) in favour of a more flexible structure in which local members are organised into 'circles'. The new constitution of the AN has reversed the traditional democratic internal organisation in favour of a rather 'bonapartistic' structure: the chairman (formerly, the secretary) has full control of the party as he/she is no longer responsible to the national executive *which is appointed by the same chairman*. Moreover, the chairman appoints almost half the members of the central committee. (1996a: 709, italics in original)

Fini and the MSI/AN have clearly benefited from a number of other developments in Italian politics, most notably the near collapse of the party system following the *Tangentopoli* scandals that rocked the entire political system in the first half of the 1990s.[5] Even so, it remains doubtful whether, without Fini's leadership, the party would have survived except on the fringes of the Italian political system.

Like the AN, the French FN is a well-organized and well-led political party. Following its success in the 1984 European elections, the party began to build a national organization with permanent offices and a whole host of support associations, including a strong party press, a youth wing, and policy groups (Hainsworth, 1992b: 42). The party also concentrated on attracting more and more members.

Though there is a small element of democracy within the party, with regional and departmental sections able to elect some of the delegates who attend the national conference (Hainsworth, 1992b: 42), the power in the party clearly lies in the hands of the president, a post that, since the foundation of the party, has been filled by Jean-Marie Le Pen. As Mayer observes, 'triumphantly reelected at every congress, he has total control over the party and tolerates no opposition' (1998: 15).

The control Le Pen exerts over his party stems in part from his charisma and personal leadership style. As Hainsworth observes, up until the early 1980s the French extreme right was fragmented and disunited, but under Le Pen's leadership the multitude of groups with very disparate ideological tendencies were rallied together. 'Clearly the movement depends upon his charismatic, oratorical and populist attributes' (1992b: 53; see also Hainsworth, 2000b).

Le Pen also keeps control within his party by packing the upper echelons with his supporters and generally trying to balance or play off potential rivals (Hainsworth, 2000b: 29). In 1995, for example, he secured the election of Bruno Gollnisch to the post of general secretary, partly so as to contain the influence of Bruno Mégret, the party's general delegate and a key actor in policy formulation, who was gradually strengthening his power-base within the party. All in all, Le Pen's authoritarian style of leadership and his strategy of 'divide and rule' proved successful until the late 1990s, even though, as Mayer argues, a number of his lieutenants were clearly preparing for the 'post-Le Pen era' (1998: 22–3), and even though the 1980s and 1990s saw a number of resignations from the party (Hainsworth, 2000b: 29).

By the late 1990s, however, tensions between Mégret and Le Pen, and their respective followers, began to worsen. The struggles were, above all, of a personal kind (Swyngedouw and Ivaldi, 2001: 3), though they also concerned the party's future strategy. Mégret, who, it is useful to remember, originally joined the FN from the mainstream Rassemblement pour la République (RPR), clashed with Le Pen and the old guard over the future direction of the party. He favoured 'refashioning the FN along the line of the Italian ex-Movimento sociale italiano (MSI) and forming an alliance with the moderate right' (Mayer, 1998: 23) as a means of escaping the '15 percent ghetto' into which he felt Le Pen had pushed the party (Hainsworth, 2000b: 30). However, the party leadership was in no way prepared to entertain such a strategy, and the tensions between Le Pen and Mégret erupted into full-scale war in the spring of 1999. Mégret left the party and formed a rival organization, known first as the Front National–Mouvement National, and then, following legal battles over the name 'Front National', as the MNR (Mouvement National Républicain).

Writing in 1999, Hainsworth commented that 'the Le Pen–Mégret split now threatened to return the French extreme right to the more familiar patterns of the past' (2000b: 31). While it is certainly true that the extreme right is more fragmented today than in the early and mid-1990s, and while the FN lost an able policy-maker and a number of its members when Mégret departed (including one of Le Pen's own daughters), the election results of 2002, in which the FN won 11.3 percent of the vote, nonetheless suggest that the FN has not yet really suffered as a result of the split. Le Pen and his party remain able to attract large sections of the vote.

Whether the party will be able to continue to gather such votes in the future is of course open to debate. While the split with Mégret and his followers does not seem to have harmed the FN, the question of where the party goes when Le Pen eventually steps down is more serious. In the regional elections of March 2004 Le Pen threw his support behind his daughter, Marine, who stood in the Ile-de-France region, but there is little evidence to suggest that she has the charisma and leadership required to keep the FN's different tribes together.

Mégret's MNR, like the FN, is also generally viewed as well organized and well led. The party adopted the FN's structural blueprint before deciding to reform these statutes quite significantly so as to introduce more internal democracy into the organization. As a result, party representatives and party members have more say in the internal affairs of the MNR than they did in the FN (Bastow, 2000: 11). As for the party's leadership, while Mégret may not have the charisma of Le Pen, he has shown himself to be a skilled politician. He is 'an arch-technocrat' (Bastow, 2000: 3) and, perhaps acknowledging his lack of magnetism, he has ensured that the party can rely on a strong collective leadership, and has made some important appointments to the party cabinet.

The Austrian FPÖ is another party that belongs to this third group. Like the parties just discussed, the FPÖ has been subject to internal dissent and factionalism, but has managed to remain unaffected by such events. At the root of this factionalism is an ideological conflict that has characterized the Austrian extreme right for most of the post-war period, and that is most often described as one between nationalists and liberals. As Knight explains, the internal dissent that led to the decline and breakup of the League of Independents – the predecessor of the FPÖ – in the early 1950s is seen as 'the revolt of a (generally provincial) "national" (that is German nationalist) grass-roots against a Vienna-based "liberal" leadership' (1992: 290). After the nationalist dominance of the late 1950s and early 1960s, the late 1960s then gave way to what Luther (2000) calls a 'normalization' process in which the liberal wing of the party assumed control of the leadership and determined the direction of the party. This period of liberal domination continued until the mid-1980s, culminating in the FPÖ becoming the junior partner in a coalition with the Sozialdemokratische Partei Österreichs between 1983 and 1986.

The party's participation in government did nothing to quell the internal dissent that existed within the FPÖ. On the contrary, intra-party factionalism continued to grow and in 1986, at the party congress, the 'national' wing of the party launched a coup against the liberal leadership. Although a number of specific events can be identified as precipitating the revolt, the impetus for the coup, as with the breakup of the League of Independents, was that the rank and file felt ignored by the liberal leadership (Knight, 1992: 290).[6] Jörg Haider replaced the more liberally minded Norbert Steger, who was then still Austrian vice-chancellor, as party leader.

Following a skilful manipulation of events, and helped by his close allies within the party, Haider thus emerged from the 1986 congress as 'the undisputed spokesman for the right-wing FPÖ grassroots' (Morrow, 2000: 47). As Morrow observes, 'Haider's lack of support among the previous elite in the FPÖ actually ensured his personal domination over the new party apparatus' (2000: 47). In addition, he has shown himself to be an able, skilful leader, 'quick-witted enough to keep on the offensive' (Knight, 1992: 296). He has also displayed immense charisma.

As well as being able to rely on these attributes, Haider has built up a strong party organization in which he exerts control and on which he can depend. Furthermore, from the early 1990s, power within the organization has been increasingly centralized. Riedlsperger explains that the real leadership has been assumed by the executive committee and that the role of the convention has gradually been downgraded. In addition, he argues that the deferral of authority to the chairman has been so extreme that the party is 'now unflatteringly referred to as a *Führerpartei*' (1998: 30). In the late 1990s the national leadership also began to intervene more and more in the affairs of provincial branches, including in the selection of candidates (Luther, 2000: 434).

In addition to centralizing decision-making within the party, Haider has made sure that those in key posts are loyal to him personally. Ever since 1986 he has ensured party members and representatives are dependent on him for advancement (Morrow: 2000: 49). In more recent years, Luther also notes that Haider has increasingly 'intervened in recruiting party outsiders with little or no ideological commitment [thereby increasing] the number of those in key posts whose loyalty was oriented less to the party than to the leader, while their lack of an organisational foothold within the party also made them more dependent upon him' (2000: 434). In addition, the party central office has 'increasingly sought the support of professional political experts, who . . . are often employed on a short-term or contract-specific basis [and who thus] do not constitute an intra-party factor that might wish (let alone be able) to form an oppositional group' (Luther, 2003: 209).

Even with these mechanisms in place, dissent has occasionally surfaced within the post-1986 FPÖ. As well as the long-standing tensions between liberals and nationals, other internal struggles have persisted, many of which 'were based on political rivalries and regional party interests, while others arose from the inherent contradictions of all-out populist protest at the national level and the exigencies of coalition governments at the provincial level' (Luther, 2000: 434–5). On top of this, Haider's selection and promotion of party outsiders or newcomers has sometimes caused resentment from long-serving public functionaries (Luther, 2000: 435). Haider has shown no patience with dissenters, however, and has rigidly enforced party discipline, ruthlessly driving his rivals to the margins one by one, and making sure that no serious rival power-base developed within the organization that could challenge his dominance (Morrow, 2000: 49). One consequence of this was that in February 1993 the liberal wing of the party finally departed, led by the party's former general secretary, Heide Schmidt.

Haider's dominance over the party took a new turn in 2000, however. In May of that year, three months after the FPÖ entered into coalition with the

Österreichische Volkspartei (ÖVP), Haider resigned the leadership of the party, and left Susanne Riess-Passer in charge. Faced with the realities of government and seemingly unsure of how his party might fare in office, he appeared to have made provisions to ensure that he would not be blamed for any unpopular policies the FPÖ would possibly be party to. He thus lived up to his reputation as a 'Teflon politician', to borrow Müller's term (2000: 198), and manoeuvred himself into a position in which he could escape blame, but from which he could nonetheless continue effectively to control the party.

Although his decision to step down as party leader may still turn out to be advantageous for him personally, it did nothing to stop the severe crises that soon beset the FPÖ. As Luther (2003) explains, the root cause of these problems was incumbency. Incumbency meant that, on the one hand, the party had insufficient manpower to staff and support the governmental team and maintain 'effective communication between the party in public office and the party on the ground'. On the other hand, 'the broader leadership team predominantly comprised persons of a more pragmatic or "careerist" orientation [and] while the under-representation of the more ideological group of "believers" enhanced the party's capacity to cooperate with its coalition partner . . . it exacerbated internal party divisions' (Luther, 2003: 214).

Conflicts broke out over the selection of candidates, and over the party's policy priorities, and personal rivalries intensified (Luther, 2003: 214). Faced with the pressures of coalitional government, and weakened by Haider's constant attacks on its policies, the party leadership was unable to control the conflicts. These reached a peak in the summer of 2002, when the fundamentalist wing of the party, along with Haider, eventually forced the resignation of Susanne Riess-Passer as party leader (Luther, 2003: 215). Shortly afterwards the FPÖ-ÖVP coalition was dissolved and new elections were called.

The party was seriously damaged by this episode, and lost much of the credibility it had started to gain under Riess-Passer's leadership (Luther, 2003: 215). This became evident when the FPÖ polled only 10.0 percent of the vote in the elections of November 2002. Though Haider flirted with the idea of regaining the leadership of the party in the autumn of 2002, he soon decided against such a move, and retreated to his stronghold of Carinthia. There he gradually began to reassert his influence and control over the party. In March 2004 he won back the governorship of Carinthia, polling 42.4 percent of the vote in the province. He also ensured that his supporters headed the party list for the elections to the European Parliament in June 2004. He thus once again manoeuvred himself into a position of influence within the party, and his eventual return to the leadership should not be discounted.

Despite a series of internal crises, the FPÖ remains a party that is well organized and that has, on the whole, benefited from strong leadership. The organization of the party has enabled it to withstand conflicts. As Luther concludes, the FPÖ 'is a fully institutionalized party that retains a sizeable membership and strong local structures, and enjoys state funding at the provincial level. Though things could yet deteriorate, at present the likelihood is that the FPÖ will persist as an organization, albeit in a much weakened form' (2003: 216).

The Belgian VB is another party that belongs to this third group, as it is well led and well organized but has nonetheless suffered from factionalism. Although the VB had only a few leading members and no serious party organization in the very early years, by the beginning of the 1980s things began to change (Mudde, 1995b: 14). From 1983 new members began to enter the party and mechanisms were gradually put in place that promoted discipline within the organization. The leadership was also strengthened. Karel Dillen, the party founder and its chairman until 1996, promoted a number of young members to the party council, including Filip Dewinter and Frank Vanhecke (Mudde, 1995b: 11).

This transformation was not entirely seamless, however. A number of veterans left or were expelled from the organization in the early 1980s and then, in December 1988, the first major split occurred when a group of long-standing, prominent members – including some rather senior figures – left the VB. They had attempted to sideline the new young party leaders whom Dillen had promoted on the grounds that they were too extreme and too preoccupied with the immigration issue rather than the Flemish question. In this conflict, Dillen sided with Dewinter and his colleagues (Mudde, 1995b: 11–12).

This factionalism did not harm the VB in the long run. On the contrary, it appeared to act as an impetus to improve the party's organization. In 1989, Dillen – who had just been elected to the European Parliament – handed the political leadership of the party to the charismatic Dewinter. Upon assuming this position, Dewinter began skilfully to build up the party organization until it became well structured and efficient.

Above all, power is centralized within the VB. The party executive assumes tight overall control and the party chairman has an unofficial right of veto over the executive (Mudde, 1995b: 15; Swyngedouw, 1998: 61). In addition, the development of local, active party groups has been encouraged, as have specialized branches dedicated to such tasks as propaganda, research and communications. Since the running of these groups and branches is overseen by the party executive, the party structure takes on a rather Stalinist profile (Swyngedouw, 2000: 135). Internal party democracy is thus very limited within the VB. As Mudde observes, 'the party divisions do not have the right to appoint their own heads or preferred candidates. They can only put forward nominations, which the party council then has to approve.' In addition, 'the various cadres, at the upper and middle management levels, receive their ideological and political training from one central organization, [which] comes under the jurisdiction of the party executive' (1995b: 15). The party's structure, as Swyngedouw concludes, therefore 'stresses the unity of the leadership, ensures control and encourages effective action' (1998: 61).

Dillen's skills and expertise have also been key in explaining how discipline and leadership control have been secured within the party. Although he does not have the charisma of Jörg Haider or of Jean-Marie Le Pen, he has proved to be a shrewd leader and has acted 'as a bridge between the different factions within the VB' (Mudde, 1995b: 25). In particular, he has ensured that a balance exists between Dewinter, who represents the party's hard-line on immigration, and Gerolf Annemans, who is more concerned with the party's nationalist policies and its focus on the reform of the state (Swyngedouw, 1998: 61–2). This balance was further secured when Dillen chose a third person to takeover the chairmanship of the party when he stepped down in 1996. By appointing Frank Vanhecke as his successor, Dillen avoided having to choose between Dewinter and Annemans.

Since the mid-1980s, therefore, the VB has built up an extremely efficient and well-structured party organization. It has also benefited from having a number of intelligent and well-qualified people within its ranks, most notably Dillen and Dewinter (Husbands, 1992b: 138). These attributes did not stop infighting and defections occurring in the late 1980s, but the party's strong organization and leadership ensured that the VB survived the struggles relatively unscathed.

The Italian LN is a further party that displays a structured organization and a strong leadership. It too has nonetheless experienced a number of defections. The LN's organization is tightly structured and centralized. Formally, the party is divided into twelve national (i.e. regional) sections that are, in turn, subdivided into provincial, district and local sections (Betz, 1998b: 49–50). In practice, however, the regional sections have little power and 'the real decision-making power is largely concentrated in a small circle of party officials who hold membership of the federal council and the federal political secretariat. The most important position is the office of the Federal Secretary, which has been held by Umberto Bossi since the foundation of Lega Nord' (Betz, 1998b: 50). The federal secretary is the most important actor in determining the general political direction of the party. Along with his secretariat he decides how the ideas generated within the party are put into practice, and if there is any disagreement within the federal political secretariat, it is the federal secretary who takes the final decision. The party's structure is thus clearly pyramidal, so much so that Bossi himself has characterized its decision-making process as one of democratic centralism (Betz, 1998b: 50). For him, this 'tight control over the party was necessary to prevent the establishment of internal factions that would have weakened the movement in its struggle against the established parties' (Betz, 1998b: 50).

In addition to this organizational structure, mechanisms are in place to check the party's recruitment. New recruits are carefully screened to protect the movement from opportunism and subversion, and all new members go through a trial period of party activism in which they are granted limited voting rights only (Betz, 1998b: 50). In addition, anyone already inside the party who is found deviating from the party line or who challenges Bossi's leadership has been forced to resign, or has resigned of his or her own accord.

Although these mechanisms have minimized the dissent within the LN, they have not ensured a total absence of internal disagreement. On the contrary, in the wake of the 1994 general election a significant number of deputies and senators (including Bossi's sister) defected from the party. Defections and splits continued until the late 1990s as a result of the party losing the mayorship of Milan in 1997, and following poor results in the administrative elections of 1998 and in the European elections of 1999 (Ignazi, 2003: 57). Nonetheless, the party's organizational structure, the selection of its members and the discipline that is enforced throughout the organization allowed the LN to come through these defections largely unscathed. Bossi's charismatic and authoritarian leadership has also acted as a unifying force for the party. He continues to dominate the party entirely, and is able to impose his will upon the organization (Ignazi, 2003: 57–8).

The Swiss LdT is another party that may be seen as belonging to this third group of right-wing extremist parties. The LdT was founded in 1991 by two charismatic and popular figures, Flavio Maspoli and Giuliano Bignasca. Their strong leadership did not prevent the development of two distinct wings within the party, however, both engaged in a more or less permanent battle for domination of the party organization. This became obvious in the run-up to the 1995 elections to the Council of States (the upper chamber of the Swiss parliament), when considerable competition broke out between Maspoli – who represented the more pragmatist wing of the party, and who was attempting to curb Bignasca's influence within the organization – and Marco Borradori, one of the LdT's other candidates, who appeared to appeal more to the voters. This rivalry continued into the cantonal elections of 1999 (Mazzoleni, 1999: 86–7).

On-going though they may be, these battles have not harmed the LdT, however. The party has been strengthened by the gradual development of a middle-level elite that, as well as helping to ease the tensions between the factions, has allowed the LdT to exercise its function in its many elective offices at communal, cantonal and federal level (Mazzoleni, 1999: 89). Tensions between the two wings of the party have also lessened since 2002 or so as a result of Flavio Maspoli's withdrawal from the party. In November 2002 he was found guilty of fraudulent bankruptcy, disloyal management, accountancy violations and the forging of documents (swisspolitics.org, 2002). Then, in May 2003, he was convicted of electoral fraud, having been found guilty of forging hundreds of signatures in a bid to bring about a referendum in Ticino. Following this second conviction, Bignasca, the party's life-president, excluded Maspoli from the LdT's list for the October 2003 elections (swisspolitics.org, 2003).

The Danish DF has also benefited from strong leadership and a well-structured organization and it too, therefore, belongs to this third group of parties. Indeed, Pia Kjærsgaard has shown herself to be a very able and talented leader (Widfeldt, 2000: 490). She has displayed a considerable amount of political acumen and has been responsive to changes in the electorate's demands. She has also been ruthless in dealing with any potential rivals within the party, which, as Widfeldt observes, has meant that life within the DF has not always been calm (2002: 7). She showed no hesitation, for example, in expelling from the party a number of MPs who had exhibited dissent in the legislature during the 1998–2001 period (Ignazi, 2003: 221). Her treatment of opponents has ensured that the party has not suffered as a result of internal battles.

Having examined the strength of the organization and leadership of the different West European right-wing extremist parties, as well as the degree of factionalism that has existed within them, it is now possible to turn to considering the link between the parties' organization and leadership on the one hand and their electoral scores on the other. In this way, the influence of organization and leadership on the electoral fortunes of the parties of the extreme right may be assessed, with a view to examining the extent to which different patterns of organization and leadership may help account for the disparity in the electoral scores of the right-wing extremist parties across Western Europe.

Party organization, party leadership and the right-wing extremist party vote

The hypothesis put forward at the beginning of this chapter predicted that parties of the extreme right with strong and charismatic leaders, centralized organizational structures, and efficient mechanisms for enforcing party discipline would record higher electoral results than parties with weaker and uncharismatic leaderships, less centralized internal structures, and lower levels of party discipline. It was suggested that the former parties were likely to exhibit higher levels of internal cohesion than their rivals, and thus greater programmatic and electoral coherence. It was argued that this, in turn, was expected to result in greater party credibility, and hence higher levels of electoral success.[7]

With this hypothesis in mind, and with reference to the three groups of right-wing extremist parties identified above, it is thus reasonable to expect (1) that parties of the third group will perform better at the polls than parties of the first and second groups, (2) that parties of the second group will record higher electoral results than those of the first group, but lower results than those of the third, and (3) that parties of the first group will register the lowest electoral scores of all three groups.

Figure 3.1 suggests that the first prediction made above is indeed borne out in practice. Taking the mean electoral score of each of the parties for the

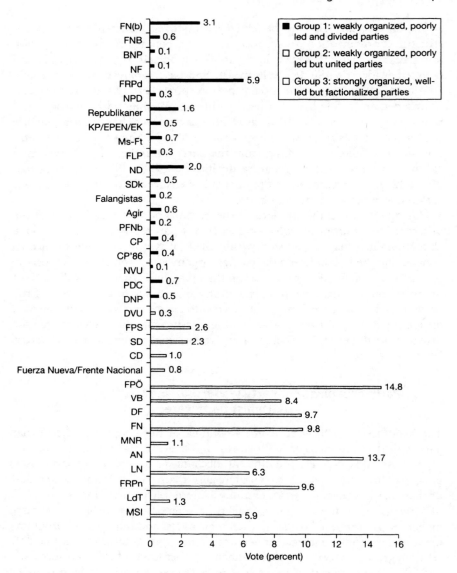

Figure 3.1 Electoral scores of the West European parties of the extreme right, 1979–2003: by type of party organization and leadership, and level of factionalism.

Notes: For full right-wing extremist party names, see Abbreviations (pp. xiii–xiv). The figure illustrates the mean electoral scores of each party in the period 1979–2003. The mean score is calculated by summing the electoral scores of each party at all elections in which it competed and then dividing this total by the number of elections the party constested.

Sources: Mackie and Rose (1991, 1997); Cheles *et al.* (1995); Betz and Immerfall (1998); Hainsworth (2000a); Elections around the World; Parties and Elections in Europe.

entire period under observation, the bar chart illustrates that the parties of the third group – that is, those that are strongly organized and well led – have, in general, performed better at the polls than the other two groups of parties. This said, the average electoral scores of the LdT (1.3 percent) and the MNR (1.1 percent) immediately stand out as being noticeably lower than the scores of the other parties in this third group.[8] Therefore, while it is possible to conclude that, when they are viewed *as a group*, the parties of the third group have recorded higher results than the other two groups of parties, it is important to acknowledge that if they are considered individually this has not always been the case.

As concerns the second proposition made above, Figure 3.1 demonstrates that the right-wing extremist parties that belong to the second group – that is, those that are weakly organized, poorly led but united – have not tended to outperform the parties of the first group consistently. While some of the parties of the second group have recorded scores that have been higher than those of the parties in the first group, others have not. For example, the Swiss FPS has secured an average of 2.6 percent of the vote since it began contesting elections in 1987, which is a better result than those of many of the parties in the first group. However, the Dutch CD, the German DVU and the Spanish Fuerza Nueva/Frente Nacional – also in this second group of parties – recorded averages of 1 percent of the vote or less. Such scores are worse than those of the Belgian FN(b), the Swedish ND, the Danish FRPd and the German Republikaner – all parties which belong to the first group. The expectation that parties of the second group would record higher electoral results than those of the first group but lower results than those of the third group is thus only partly borne out in reality. Parties of the second group have secured lower vote shares than parties of the third group (as anticipated), but they have not always performed better than parties of the first group.

As for the third prediction made above, Figure 3.1 demonstrates that there is some evidence to suggest that parties of the first group – that is, those that are weakly organized, poorly led and divided – register the lowest electoral scores of all three groups of parties. Again, this is the case if these parties are considered as a group, rather than as individual parties. However, it is immediately apparent that a number of parties in this first group stand out as having performed rather better than anticipated, given their weak organization, their poor leadership and their factionalism. Particularly noticeable is the Danish FRPd, which recorded an average of 5.9 percent of the vote over the period under observation even though it suffered from severe factionalism.[9] The Swedish ND, the German Republikaner and the Belgian FN(b) also recorded higher electoral scores than many of the other members of this group.

The patterns apparent in Figure 3.1 may be further examined by way of some simple statistical tests. More specifically, the relationship between the electoral scores of the right-wing extremist parties and their organization, leadership and factionalism may be investigated by a one-way analysis of variance (or ANOVA) test. This test is appropriate because it assesses the relationship between a single nominal independent variable with three or more categories, and a dependent variable measured on an interval or ratio scale.[10] The categorization of the right-wing extremist parties into three groups (based on organization, leadership and factionalism) carried out above means that this is exactly the type of independent variable that is in question. The dependent variable (electoral score) is clearly a ratio variable as it is measured in percent.

As in Chapter 2, it is appropriate at this stage to take the electoral result of each party at each election as a unit of analysis. This is preferable to using the average electoral score of each party over the entire period under observation (as reported in Figure 3.1) because it allows the number of times each particular party has stood for election to be controlled for. A party that has competed in only a few elections but that has recorded extreme electoral scores (either very high or very low) may have a distorting effect on the mean electoral score of that type of party. Using the score of each party at each election removes this distorting effect. In addition, this approach increases the number of cases quite significantly – from 35, if each party represents a unit of analysis as in Figure 3.1, to 146, if the score of each party at each election is taken as a unit of analysis.

Table 3.4 reports the results of the one-way ANOVA test. The table suggests that the differences in the electoral results of the three groups of parties are very unlikely to have occurred by chance. Instead, the results indicate that the groups are significantly different as regards the vote shares they have recorded. These conclusions are reached because the obtained F score (57.354) is larger than the critical F score, which at a 0.01 level of significance is $F_{(0.01, 2, 143)} = 4.79$.[11] Furthermore, the magnitude of the F score as reported in Table 3.4 indicates that the variance between group means is substantial compared to the variance within the various groups. This suggests that there will be only a few exceptions to the rule that, on average,

Table 3.4   Effects of organization, leadership and factionalism on the right-wing extremist party vote: one-way analysis of variance (ANOVA)

	Sum of squares	df	Mean square	F
Between groups	1819.524	2	909.762	57.354***
Within groups	2268.295	143	15.862	
Total	4087.819	145		

n = 146

Notes: The sum of squares between groups reflects the variation in the electoral scores between the different groups of party. In contrast, the sum of squares within groups reflects the pattern of variation in the electoral scores within each of the three groups of party. The respective sum of squares is then divided by the degrees of freedom (df) to obtain the mean square estimates. *** significant at 0.01 level.

parties from one group have higher (or lower) electoral score than parties from another group. Thus, going back to the three predictions made earlier, the results of the ANOVA test imply that it is possible to speak of certain groups of parties performing better than others even though a number of outliers (such as the Danish FRPd) may exist.

Before any further conclusions are drawn, it is important to recognize that while the ANOVA test indicates that at least one of the group means is significantly different from another, the test does not identify which group this is. Thus, it could be that all three groups of parties are significantly different from each other, or, alternatively, it may be the case that only one group of parties is significantly different from the other two, and that these other two resemble each other. Unfortunately, with the ANOVA test there is no way of knowing which of these two possibilities is the correct one. Instead, in order to ascertain which groups of parties differ from others, a means test is required.

A means test compares the mean of an interval or ratio variable between the various categories of a nominal variable (Kleinnijenhuis, 1999: 139). In other words, in the present case, the mean electoral scores of the different types of parties are compared to each other, and the magnitude of the difference between these means is assessed. When the difference between the means is large, as compared to the standard deviation of the dependent variable (electoral score) within the groups, then the means differ substantially from each other. However, if the difference between the means is smaller than the standard deviation of the dependent variable within the different groups, then the groups cannot be said to differ significantly from each other.

Table 3.5 reports the mean electoral score of each of the three groups of right-wing extremist parties. Parties of the first group (with weak organizations, poor leadership and significant levels of factionalism) record a mean of 1.34 percent of the vote, parties of the second group (with weak organizations and poor leadership, but without significant factionalism) register a mean of 1.80 percent of the vote, and parties of the third group (which are

Table 3.5 Effects of organization, leadership and factionalism on the right-wing extremist party vote: means test

	Number of cases	Mean	Std deviation
Group 1	80	1.343	2.335
Group 2	20	1.795	1.425
Group 3	46	9.026	6.322
Total	146	3.826	5.310

Notes: Group 1: weakly organized, poorly led and divided parties. Group 2: weakly organized, poorly led but united parties. Group 3: strongly organized, well-led but factionalized parties.

well-organized and well-led despite having experienced factionalism) report a mean of 9.03 percent of the vote. If these means are simply compared, they suggest that parties of the first group experience lower electoral scores than parties of the second and third groups, that parties of the second group record higher results than parties of the first group but lower scores than parties of the third group, and that parties of the third group outperform parties of the first and second groups.

However, comparing the means in this way fails to determine the degree to which differences between groups hold for all cases within the groups. To take account of this it is necessary to compare the differences between the means of the groups with the variance (or standard deviations) within the groups. If the differences between the means of the groups are *greater* than the standard deviations within the groups, then it is safe to conclude that not many exceptions exist to the hypothesis put forward in the preceding paragraph. However, if the differences between the means of the groups are *smaller* than the standard deviations within the groups, then the different groups cannot be considered significantly different to each other (Kleinnijenhuis, 1999: 140).

From Table 3.5 the difference between the mean of Group 1 and the mean of Group 2 may be calculated to be 0.452 (1.795 − 1.343). At first sight this suggests that the mean electoral score of parties of the first group is some 0.5 percent lower than that of parties of the second group. However, since 0.452 is *not* larger than 2.335, 1.425 or 6.322 (the standard deviations of the electoral scores within each group of parties), this suggests that many exceptions exist to the proposition that parties of the second group perform better than those of the first group. In other words, these results suggest that Groups 1 and 2 do not differ significantly from each other.

The difference between the means of Group 1 and Group 3 may be examined in a similar way. Unlike the last case, however, this figure, namely 7.683 (9.026 − 1.343), is larger than the standard deviations of the electoral scores within each group of parties. This suggests that not many exceptions exist to the proposition that parties of the third group perform better than parties of the first group. It is possible to conclude, therefore, that significant differences exist between these two groups of parties. More specifically, the figures suggest that the mean electoral score of parties of the first group is some 7.7 percent lower than that for parties of the third group.

Finally, the difference between the means of Group 2 and Group 3 can be calculated as being 7.231 (9.026 − 1.795). As with the differences between Group 1 and Group 3, this figure is greater than the standard deviations of the electoral scores within each group of parties. Thus, here too, it is appropriate to draw the conclusion that not many exceptions exist to the proposition that parties of the third group perform better than parties of the second group. The two groups of parties display significant differences, and the mean electoral score of the parties of the second group is some 7.2 percent lower than that for parties of the third group.

The comparison of means therefore indicates that while the first and the second group of parties are significantly different from the third, these first two groups are not significantly different from each other. This result confirms what was already hinted at in Figure 3.1 when the observation was made that some of the parties of the second group performed less well than a number of parties of the first group. The conclusion that the first two groups of right-wing extremist parties do not differ significantly is therefore not overly surprising. However, confirmation that these two groups of parties are not significantly different from each other suggests that it is the strength of the party organization and the skill of the party leadership that are the most important factors in influencing how well the parties of the extreme right perform at the polls. The degree of factionalism that exists within the parties is not the decisive element in explaining their success.

In view of these conclusions, it becomes more appropriate to distinguish simply between two types of right-wing extremist parties: weakly organized and poorly led parties on the one hand, and strongly organized and well-led parties on the other hand. This distinction makes all the more sense because all right-wing extremist parties with strong organizations have benefited from having able leaders, whereas all right-wing extremist parties with weak organizations have been led by weak figures.

This dichotomy also allows for organization and leadership to be represented by a dummy variable. All parties of the extreme right that do have a strong organization and an able leadership may be assigned a code of 1, while those parties which do not have a strong organization or an able leadership may receive a code of 0. The electoral scores of the parties of the extreme right can then be regressed on this dummy so that the effect of organization and leadership on a party's electoral score may be determined.

Table 3.6 reports the results of this bivariate regression analysis. The table indicates that when the independent variable (the organization and

Table 3.6 Effects of organization and leadership on the right-wing extremist party vote (OLS dummy regression)

	Unstandardized coefficients	
	B	Std error
Constant	1.434***	0.397
Organization and leadership	7.593***	0.708
Adjusted R^2	0.440	
n = 146		

Notes: Dependent variable: electoral score (percent). Independent dummy variable (organization and leadership): 0 if the party is weakly organized and poorly led, 1 if the party is strongly organized and well led. *** significant at the 0.01 level.

leadership dummy) is equal to 1, the predicted value of the dependent variable (electoral score) is 9.027 percent (1.434 + 7.593).[12] In contrast, when the organization and leadership dummy equals 0, the predicted electoral score is 1.434 percent. Thus, strongly organized and well-led parties are predicted to record an electoral result that is, on average, 7.593 percentage points greater than the scores of weakly organized and poorly led parties. Furthermore, the coefficients reported in Table 3.6 are both statistically significant at the 0.01 level, suggesting that it is very unlikely that these results have been arrived at by chance alone.

From Table 3.6 it is also possible to ascertain the proportion of variance in the electoral score of the right-wing extremist parties that is explained by party organization and leadership when all other independent variables are discounted. The table suggests that, when no other independent variables are taken into consideration, the strength of party organization and the ability of the party leadership explain some 44 percent of the variance in the right-wing extremist party vote.

Concluding remarks

This chapter has examined the extent to which the electoral scores of the West European parties of the extreme right have been influenced by the parties' internal organizational structures and leaderships. In so doing, it has shed light on a further set of explanations for why right-wing extremist parties across Western Europe have experienced such varying levels of electoral success since the late 1970s.

It was suggested at the outset that right-wing extremist parties with strong, charismatic leaders, centralized organizational structures and efficient mechanisms for enforcing party discipline would perform better at the polls than parties with weaker and uncharismatic leaderships, less centralized internal structures and lower levels of party discipline. The former parties were expected to exhibit greater internal cohesion, and thus greater levels of programmatic and electoral coherence. In turn, these attributes were expected to enhance the parties' credibility and result in higher levels of electoral success.

To test this hypothesis, and to examine the link between party organization and leadership on the one hand, and electoral success on the other, the parties of the extreme right were categorized according to the strength of their organization, the strength of their leadership and the level of dissent and factionalism present within them. On the basis of an in-depth review of the internal structures and the leaderships of the different parties, three types of right-wing extremist party were identified: (1) weakly organized, poorly led and divided parties, (2) weakly organized, poorly led but united parties, and (3) strongly organized, well-led but factionalized parties.

The electoral scores of the three types of party were then compared in a series of analyses. The results show that, as expected, the third group of parties – the strongly organized, well-led but factionalized ones – have performed significantly better in elections than the two other groups. By contrast, however, the electoral fortunes of the other two groups are not markedly different from each other. In some instances the weakly organized, poorly led and divided parties have performed better than their united counterparts. On other occasions, however, they have recorded lower electoral scores than the united parties.

The facts that (1) the most successful right-wing extremist parties have experienced internal conflict and divisions, and (2) no significant difference exists between the electoral scores of the weakly organized, poorly led and divided parties and the electoral scores of the weakly organized, poorly led but united parties, suggest that the degree of party factionalism is not an important factor in determining whether parties of the extreme right encounter success or failure at the polls. The strength of the party organization and the party leadership appears far more decisive in explaining why parties of the extreme right have recorded high or low electoral results. This, in turn, implies that in terms of the parties' internal organization and leadership it is most useful to distinguish between two types of right-wing extremist party, rather than three: (1) well-organized and well-led parties, and (2) badly organized and badly led parties.

The final analysis undertaken in this chapter indicated that, as expected, the well-organized and well-led right-wing extremist parties in Western Europe have tended to record electoral scores that are significantly higher than those of their badly organized and badly led counterparts. Moreover, this regression analysis suggested that party organization and leadership (as an explanatory variable) has considerable power in helping to account for the varying level of electoral success of the right-wing extremist parties across Western Europe in the period under observation. When no other explanatory factors are considered, some 44 percent of the variance in the electoral scores of the right-wing extremist parties is explained by party organization and leadership. Betz's assertion that 'one of the most important determinants of success is party organization' therefore appears to have considerable validity (1998a: 9).

It should be remembered that party organization and party leadership form only one set of explanations that help account for the disparity in the electoral fortunes of the right-wing extremist parties across Western Europe. Therefore, although the conclusions reached in this chapter constitute a firm basis from which to assess the effect of party organization and leadership on the electoral scores of the parties of the extreme right, the exact impact of organization and leadership on the right-wing extremist party vote can only be established when other explanatory factors are also taken into consideration.

In the light of this, the next chapter turns its attention to another set of explanatory factors. It moves to consider the influence of other political actors in the party system, and analyses the patterns of party competition at work in the different countries under observation, so as to investigate whether these patterns may help explain why the parties of the extreme right recorded such varying electoral scores across Western Europe in the period 1979–2003.

Notes

1 Cohesion, according to Ozbudun's definition, refers to 'the extent to which . . . group members can be observed to work together for the group's goals' (1970: 305). In the majority of studies cohesion is taken to mean legislative cohesion – that is, the extent to which parties vote together in the legislature. Here, however, what is of interest is electoral cohesion. The distinction between these two types of cohesion is important, as the demands involved in fighting and winning elections are very different from those involved in winning legislative battles (Bowler *et al.*, 1999: 5).

2 Party coherence may be defined as 'the degree of congruence in the attitudes and *behaviour* of party members' (Janda, 1980: 118, italics in original). As Janda argues, cohesion can be perceived to be the source of coherence, whereas factionalism is a consequence of coherence. Coherence may be operationalized in a number of different ways. Janda makes use of six different variables in order to operationalize this concept: legislative cohesion, ideological factionalism, issue factionalism, leadership factionalism, strategic or tactical factionalism, and party purges. For more details, see Janda (1980: 118–25).

3 There have been various English translations of 'Trivselpartiet'. In addition to its being called the 'Cosy Party' by Widfeldt (2000), Andersen and Bjørklund (2000) have referred to it as the 'Party of Wellbeing', and Arter (1992) has called it the 'Prosperity Party'.

4 The Swiss LdT (Lega dei Ticinesi), as its name implies, only competes in the canton of Ticino. Its party organization therefore only operates in this canton.

5 *Tangentopoli* (which translates as 'bribe-city' or 'Bribesville') is the name given to the rash of corruption scandals that surfaced in Italy in the first part of the 1990s. Numerous politicians and businessmen were alleged to have taken bribes, often on a huge scale, and in the end eight former prime ministers and some 5,000 businessmen and politicians were charged as a result of the police investigation. The scandals led to the demise of the so-called First Republic and to the collapse of the Christian Democrats.

6 The split between the national and the liberal wings of the party surfaced over the 'Reder affair' and the 'Waldheim affair'. The former saw a divide develop within the FPÖ when, in 1985, the party's defence minister, Friedhelm Frischenschlager, organized an official welcome for the convicted war criminal Walter Reder on his release from jail in Italy. The rift worsened the next year as the two wings of the party clashed over their responses to the allegations surrounding Kurt Waldheim's past. Waldheim, who was standing as the Volkspartei's (ÖVP's) presidential candidate, was accused of having lied about his war record, and the controversy

brought the entire question of Austria's role in World War II to the fore. For more details on these two affairs, see Morrow (2000).

7 Clearly, the causal link between organization and leadership on the one hand and party electoral success on the other may not run in only one direction. It is also likely that electoral success spurs a party to develop programmatic coherence and internal cohesion. Success at the polls may also strengthen a party's leadership.

8 The main reason why the electoral score of the LdT is so low is that this party competes in the canton of Ticino only. A national score of 1.3 percent actually equates to about 20 percent of the vote in the Ticino region.

9 Svåsand argues that one reason why the FRPd continued to experience electoral success even though it suffered from severe factionalism is that the internal struggles within the party tended to take place between elections rather than in the run-up to elections. This was in marked contrast to the struggles within the Swedish ND, which broke out just before the election of 1994 (1998: 90).

10 The test is called a *one-way* analysis of variance test because it is assessing the effect of a single variable on another.

11 Critical F scores are obtained from the statistical tables in any textbook or statistics manual. The scores depend on the degrees of freedom for the numerator and denumerator (in this case the degrees of freedom of the variance between groups, and the degrees of freedom of the variance within groups), and also on the significance level that is set.

12 It may be remembered that 9.027 is also the mean electoral score of the parties of the original third group, as was reported above in Table 3.5. This makes sense since all parties of this third group (and no others) were coded 1 on the dummy variable for organization and leadership.

4

Party competition

In its bid to account for the varying levels of electoral success of the parties of the extreme right across Western Europe, this book has so far examined the influence of party-centric factors. It has considered the impact of different types of extreme right party ideology on the right-wing extremist party vote and has also investigated the effects of party organization and leadership. In this chapter, the book turns to exploring the influence of contextual factors on the success of the right-wing extremist parties, and introduces another potential explanation for the disparity in the electoral fortunes of the West European parties of the extreme right: it proposes that different patterns of party competition contribute to the variation in the right-wing extremist party vote.

To assess the validity of this proposition, the chapter follows a four-pronged approach. First, in reflection of the fact that *intra*-cleavage volatility by far outweighs *inter*-cleavage volatility (Bartolini and Mair, 1990), the chapter examines the patterns of party competition on the right side of the political spectrum. It investigates the ideological proximity of the parties of the mainstream right, which are the extreme right parties' nearest competitors, and in so doing, it establishes how much political space is available to the right-wing extremist parties. It then goes on to explore whether the political space available to the parties of the extreme right is in any way related to how well these parties perform at the polls.

The chapter suggests that the electoral fortunes of the right-wing extremist parties, in addition to being influenced by the size of the political space available on the extreme right of the political spectrum are also likely to depend on the positions that these parties choose to adopt for themselves. Therefore, in a second section of the analysis, the chapter examines the location of the right-wing extremist parties within the political space, and investigates whether their electoral scores are in any way affected by their ideological positions.

Having established the ideological positions of both the parties of the mainstream right and the parties of the extreme right, the chapter moves on to consider how these two sets of parties interact, and how this interaction influences the electoral scores of the right-wing extremist parties. More specifically, the chapter examines the effect on the right-wing extremist party vote of (1) an ideological moderation of both the mainstream right and the extreme right, (2) an ideological radicalization of both sets of parties, and (3) a moderation of one set of parties but a radicalization of the other.

The chapter then broadens its outlook. From having considered patterns of party competition on the right side of the political spectrum only, it moves to examine other patterns of party competition at work in the party system. Specifically, it investigates the degree of ideological convergence in the centre of the spectrum (that is, between the mainstream right and the mainstream left), and assesses how these patterns influence the right-wing extremist party vote. The chapter concludes by considering the relative importance of patterns of party competition in an overall explanation of the disparity in the electoral fortunes of right-wing extremist parties across Western Europe.

Before embarking on this analysis, however, the chapter engages in a certain amount of groundwork. First, it explores the concepts of political space and party competition, which are so central to this section of the book. Then, having established the nature and content of the political space within which parties compete, the chapter presents a detailed overview of the different ways in which the political space can be mapped and in which the parties can be located within that space. From this review, one approach to mapping the political space is chosen over the others. Then, in a last step before the analysis begins, the chapter presents details of the data that are employed and discusses the methodological implications of using these data.

The concept of political space and the space of party competition

When political scientists speak of the 'political space' of a system, they are clearly not alluding to a physical area in which electors exist and in which political parties interact. Rather, they are referring to an imagery that, by convention, is used to describe the structure of electoral preferences and of party competition. Although, as Laver and Hunt explain, '[t]here is no particularly deep theoretical reason for the use of the spatial analogy, [and it is instead] a consequence of historical accident, ease of visualization and, by now, convention' (1992: 11), the metaphor is an extremely powerful one. Indeed, 'spatial metaphors have become the *lingua franca* of theorists of party competition' (1992: 7, italics in original).

The tendency to use the term 'political space' and to make use of spatial imageries when referring both to the structure of electoral preferences and to the structure of party competition can be misleading, however. It is, in fact, of crucial importance to distinguish between the two structures, because while electoral preferences are most often described with reference to a multitude of dimensions, each usually depicting a different policy area, party competition is, in contrast, generally considered to be played out along one single, overarching dimension.

To identify the nature and content of the dominant dimensions around which electoral preferences are structured, it is useful to turn to the empirical studies of policy and party competition. Perhaps the most detailed description of these dimensions is to be found in the work of the Manifesto Research Group (which is discussed in further detail below). This project characterizes the political space, and locates the parties within this space, with the use of 54 different 'concept categories', which are then collapsed into seven 'domains', each of which refers to a 'broad area of political debate' (Budge *et al.*, 1987: 457–8). Similarly, Laver and Hunt (1992) identify a wide range of different policy dimensions as being salient. Though they use a very different method- ology to that of the Manifesto Research Group to map the political space (as is also illustrated below), parties are located on at least eight (and in one case ten) different policy dimensions (1992: 43–55).

In contrast to policy competition, party competition is most often depicted as being distinctly unidimensional, organized along an absorptive, over- arching, left–right dimension. The explanation for this unidimensionality can be found in the fundamental nature of party competition. As Sartori observes, '[c]ompetition presupposes a common ground on which *two* parties (at least) speak to the same voters. Therefore, just *one* single-claim party . . . supported by identified voters does not add another dimension of competi- tion' (1976: 340, italics in original). Only when two or more parties compete along this other dimension – be it ethnic, linguistic or religious – does party competition become two-dimensional. Budge and Robertson reach similar conclusions. Like Sartori, they argue that one single dimension 'dominates competition at the level of the parties', and they maintain that it is only in situations where there is an 'overriding preoccupation with national identity or security' that party competition assumes a multidimensional character (1987: 394).

The overarching left–right dimension along which party competition has traditionally been seen to be organized has been defined by the Manifesto Research Group as principally referring to 'classic economic policy- conflicts – government regulation of the economy through direct controls or takeover . . . as opposed to free enterprise, individual freedom, and econ- omic orthodoxy' (Budge and Robertson, 1987: 394–5). In some instances, associated conflicts between internationalism and isolationism or between traditional and progressive moral attitudes may also be absorbed into the left–right divide (Budge and Robertson, 1987: 395). Similarly, Huber and Inglehart (who employ a methodology similar to that of Laver and Hunt, as is illustrated below) conclude that the dominant left–right dimension of party competition is principally made up of the economic or class conflict. They also cite 'traditional versus new culture', 'authoritarianism versus democracy' and 'isolationism versus internationalism' as secondary dimen- sions of conflict that have been absorbed into the overarching left–right dimension (1995: 83).

This dimension is therefore not simply a figurative or symbolic space (Sartori, 1976: 334). Instead, it is an overarching dimension that assumes specific meanings by being 'capable of incorporating a variety of political issues and conflicts' (Knutsen, 1998: 64). By virtue of these qualities, it serves to order objects side by side and thus provides electors with some sense of orientation and communication (Sartori, 1976: 334; Fuchs and Klingemann, 1989: 232).

Having briefly discussed the nature and content of both the political space and the space of party competition, it is now appropriate to turn to examining the different ways in which political parties may be located within these spaces. The following discussion illustrates that there is no single approach to doing this. Instead, the political space and the patterns of party competition of a system may be defined and mapped in a number of different ways. However, as will become clear, some of these approaches are more suitable to the task at hand than others.

Mapping the political space and estimating party positions: five approaches

There are five main ways in which the political space of a system may be mapped. As will become clear, while some approaches are informed by the parties themselves (be it by their programmes, the behaviour of their elites, or the values of their activists or members), other approaches make use of the attitudes and behaviour of voters. Others still take their cues from sources that are altogether exogenous to the electoral process.

Government expenditure flows

A first way in which the positions of parties on particular policy dimensions may be estimated is to examine what parties actually do when elected into office. The flow of public expenditure into particular policy areas can be traced and used as an indicator of government policy in these areas. From this, the positions of parties along the main dimensions of political competition can be identified.

The public expenditure flow approach to mapping the political space of a system has the clear benefit of locating parties within dimensions according to what the parties actually do. In this way, it is based on a 'hard' source of data (Laver and Hunt, 1992: 33). However, this approach has a number of limitations that are particularly pertinent to this study. First, it is limited to locating governmental parties only. This obviously excludes the vast majority of right-wing extremist parties with which this study is concerned. Second, public expenditure flows can only be used as a reliable indicator of a party's location when the party is in office alone. Therefore, even in those cases where right-wing extremist parties are, or have been, in power (Italy and Austria), it is impossible to locate them within the political space of their respective systems using this approach, given their status as junior members of governmental coalitions. In these instances, the expenditure approach is restricted to estimating the nature of governmental outputs only; this is altogether different from the structure of the political space of a system with which this study is concerned. The government expenditure approach to locating parties in their political space is therefore of little use to this study.

Elite studies

A second way in which the political space may be mapped is by the use of elite studies. Some such studies draw on interviews with parliamentary elites or on surveys of middle-level elites or party activists. Responses to these interviews or surveys are subjected to content analysis, and the policy orientations of the parliamentary elites or party activists are first used to identify the main policy dimensions and are then taken as indirect indicators of the positions of the parties along these dimensions (e.g. Daalder and Rusk, 1972; De Swaan, 1973; Sinnott, 1986). Other studies estimate the positions of parties by observing the behaviour of parliamentary elites (e.g. Pedersen *et al.*, 1971; Damgaard and Rusk, 1976).

The practice of using elite studies to map the political space has come in for a number of criticisms, however. First, doubts have long been expressed over whether the attitudes or behaviour of party elites on the one hand, and party activists on the other, are truly representative of the party as a whole. Ever since May's 'law of curvilinear disparity' (1973), it has been argued that party leaders, party activists and ordinary party voters occupy different ideological positions.[1] Therefore, as Mair suggests, the attitudes or behaviour of a party's elites (be they middle-level elites or parliamentary elites) may not be representative of the party's 'externally-directed competitive position' (2001: 15).

A second limitation of elite studies is that they are relatively rare because they are costly to conduct, in terms of both time and money. Although a new technique that examines legislative speeches by making use of computerized text analysis may help solve this problem in due course (see Laver and Benoit, 2002), at present, elite studies remain expensive and time-consuming. These drawbacks mean that elite studies that cover more than one country are particularly rare.

Finally, right-wing extremist parties tend not to be included in most elite studies. Since many of these parties do not have representation in their national legislatures, they do not feature in the studies that examine the attitudes or behaviour of parliamentarians. As for those studies that concentrate on the views of middle-party elites, while it has been possible to interview party activists in some right-wing extremist parties (e.g. Ignazi and Ysmal, 1992, on the MSI and the FN; DeClair, 1999, on the FN), access to party members in other parties is more problematic. In the light of these methodological concerns and because no existing comparative elite studies exist on which this present study is able to draw, the elite study approach to mapping the political space is not adopted in this chapter.

Voter attitudes

The structure of the political space of a system, and the location of different parties within that space, may also be mapped with reference to voter attitudes. One way in which this can be done is by simply asking voters who exhibit a party preference to indicate their own position on a general left–right scale. The mean scores of different sets of party identifiers can then be used to position the party on a left–right dimension (e.g. Inglehart and Klingemann, 1976; Sani and Sartori, 1983).[2]

A second approach to using voter attitudes to map the political space is to question voters about a variety of issues. The positions of the respondents on these issues are taken as indirect indicators of the strategic appeals of party leaders. In contrast to the simple left–right positioning of voters, this more complex approach means that not only can the parties be located in the political space according to the voters' responses, but the nature of the political space can be also ascertained from the issue positions of the party sympathizers. For example, by drawing on data from the *World Values Survey* of 1990, Kitschelt (1995) distinguishes 20 issue items from which possible political issue dimensions may be derived. He then identifies an interpretable two-dimensional political space for each of the countries under observation, and locates the parties within this space.

The practice of mapping the political space of a system by means of voter attitudes has been subject to significant debate (see Kitschelt, 1989). The first approach outlined above – that of asking attached voters to position themselves on a general left–right scale, and of deriving the location of parties from the location of their sympathizers – comes in for criticism on the grounds that it contains some element of tautology. After all, by their very nature, party sympathizers (as opposed to pure 'issue voters', for example) identify with their chosen party in some way; that is, they exhibit some degree of partisan identification. To some extent, then, party sympathizers take their cues from their party. Thus, the position of the party in the political space and the position of the party sympathizers are not independent of each other.

Mapping the political space from the attitudes of party sympathizers towards a variety of issues is certainly a more robust approach than simply making use of their self-placement on a left–right scale. This said, however, the approach is not without its drawbacks. While it is wholly legitimate to identify the dominant axes of political competition from the attitudes of the electors, the practice of locating the parties along these dimensions according to the attitudes of their identifiers is problematic, since it assumes that electors agree wholeheartedly with the party for which they have voted. In other words, the approach rests on the assumption that the structure of the electorate reflects the structure of the party system.

This assumption has been widely questioned, however. As was noted above, it has long been suggested that party leaders, party activists and ordinary party voters occupy different ideological positions (May, 1973; Norris, 1995). Indeed, Budge and Robertson observe that '[s]ubstantial numbers of electors may have preoccupations different from those which parties would ideally like to emphasize [suggesting that] the space of competition may well differ between parties and electors' (1987: 393). Even voters who exhibit a sense of party identification may not hold the same attitudes as those that their party seeks to represent. Hinich and Munger note that 'voters may strongly identify with a party . . . but their perception of the ideology that the party embraces may be quite inaccurate. More subtly, the emphases of the party and the focus of interest of the voter may well differ sharply' (1994: 97). Furthermore, this lack of congruence between party ideology and voter attitudes may be particularly acute in the case of extremist party supporters (Huber, 1989: 616–18).[3]

In addition to the differences that may exist between voter attitudes and party ideologies, the structure of the electorate fails to reflect the space of competition for the reason that, as was argued above, the electorate is distributed along multiple dimensions, but the space of competition is likely to be a single space, regardless of the number of cleavages. While voters may be divided by a whole host of orientations (such as religion, ethnicity and language), parties do not necessarily compete on all these issues. Instead, they compete only along dimensions that are seen as rewarding in terms of capturing floating voters. In addition, the number of dimensions that make-up the political space is further reduced by the way in which parties systematically link issues on independent dimensions, thereby collapsing two dimensions of voter identification (or more) into one single competitive dimension (Kitschelt, 1995: 80). For these reasons, 'the overall perceptions of politics of the *citizen* cannot be automatically transferred to the actual ballot of the *voter*' (Sartori, 1976: 339, emphasis in original).

Put together, these arguments therefore cast doubt on the theoretical accuracy of a political space mapped by voter attitudes, and of the location of individual parties within that space. While voter attitudes certainly shed light on the profile of the electorate, they do not describe the space of competition, nor do they illustrate the patterns of competition at work between the various political parties. The decision not to use voter attitudes to map the political space of the systems under investigation in this book is informed by these theoretical drawbacks, and also by a number of practical considerations.

First, there are doubts over the extent to which the various surveys can be compared. It goes almost without saying that, across different types of survey, there is a lack of uniformity in the questions asked. After all, the different surveys were often designed for very different reasons. However, even within the same type of survey (such as the biannual *Eurobarometer* surveys, which do deal with a unified set of issues) there is often a lack of consistency in the questions posed. Questions are sometimes simply dropped from the survey over the years, thus making temporal comparisons difficult. In other cases, questions are not asked in all countries, or if they are, they sometimes do not have the same meaning everywhere. Cross-national comparisons using survey data are therefore often far from straightforward (see Niemi *et al.*, 1980; Sinnott, 1998).

Another reason for not using these surveys to examine the political space is that they often do not extend to looking at a number of the countries under investigation in this book. For example, Austria, Greece, Portugal and Switzerland were not included in the first wave (1981–83) of the *World Values Surveys*; Greece is not included in the second wave (1990–91); and Austria, Belgium, Denmark, France, Greece, Italy, the Netherlands and Portugal were excluded from the third wave of surveys (1995–97).

Finally, the number of respondents in each survey who identify themselves as right-wing extremist party sympathizers is very limited. In the *World Values Surveys* right-wing extremist voters have typically represented no more than 4 to 9 percent of the national sample, and in one case (Germany) they have accounted for less than 2 percent of respondents (Kitschelt, 1995: 73). The situation is similar for the *Eurobarometer* surveys. This small number of cases implies that the results of any analysis conducted from such survey data would have to be treated with great caution.

For all these reasons – theoretical, methodological and practical – this chapter will not make use of the self-placement of party sympathizers or of the attitudes of voters to map the political space of the systems under investigation and to locate the parties within this space.

Internal analysis of party election programmes

A fourth approach to mapping the political space, already alluded to above, was pioneered in the late 1970s by David Robertson and Ian Budge and their collaborators in the Manifesto Research Group. This research identifies the dominant dimensions of political competition by drawing on the content of party manifestos. Each sentence (or quasi-sentence) of the manifesto is placed into one (and only one) of a number of categories. The coding categories, which are designed to be comparable both across countries and over time, are then organized into seven different 'domains'. Once all the sentences of the manifesto have been allocated to one category, the percentage of sentences that refer to each category (out of the total number of sentences in the whole manifesto) is calculated. The two leading factors within each of the seven domains are identified. These are then fed into a second-stage factor analysis, from which the two leading dimensions of political competition in each country are distinguished and spatially represented, and each party manifesto is located within this multidimensional space.

The methodology employed by the Manifesto Research Group emphasizes the point that the multidimensional policy space and the unidimensional space of party competition are inextricably linked. Although the identification of policy spaces is firmly at the centre of the Manifesto Research Group's work, the practice of isolating the dominant dimensions of political competition allows for the space and the structure of party competition to be discerned.

The internal analysis of election programmes is held by many (not least those involved in the Manifesto Research Group itself) to be the most accurate and authoritative method of identifying the main dimensions of political competition within a system and of locating individual parties along those dimensions. This is because manifestos are seen as the 'only direct and clear statement of party policy available to the electorate and directly attributable to the party as such' (Robertson, 1976: 72). Moreover, rather than mere bargaining chips, with which to 'bribe' electors, manifestos are judged to be 'genuine statements of preference' on the part of parties (Budge, 1987: 15).[4]

The work of the Manifesto Research Group has, nonetheless, been subject to some criticism. Most notably, questions have been raised about the coding scheme used. Laver and Hunt, for example, maintain that the coding scheme is 'ambiguous', and that its design 'strongly conditions the precise empirical description of the manifesto' (1992: 31). Gabel and Huber similarly take issue with the precision of the methodology, and argue that 'there exists no rigorous analysis of whether or under what conditions the various methods for extracting left–right positions from Manifesto Research Group data provide reasonable estimates of these left–right positions' (2000: 95). Janda *et al.* concur with this, and claim that 'while the manifesto data can tell us something about one aspect of a party's identity [they] are not very useful for establishing the party's actual position on any of the issues that constitute its issue profile' (1995: 177).

In addition to these methodological concerns there is the practical issue of data availability. Since analysing the contents of electoral programmes is a large and extremely time-consuming undertaking that demands the input of an international team of scholars, each familiar with the coding scheme of the project, this study would be restricted to the work already carried out by the Manifesto Research Group if it chose to adopt this approach to mapping the political space. Unfortunately, the Manifesto Research Group's work has not included the electoral programmes of many of the right-wing extremist parties under investigation in this book.

More specifically, although the Manifesto Research Group has greatly extended its scope since its launch in 1979, and has now collected and coded the programmes of over 600 parties in more than 50 different countries (Volkens, 2001: 95), many of the smaller right-wing extremist parties with which this book is concerned remain excluded from the data sets. In particular, no data exist on the right-wing extremist parties of Germany, the Netherlands, Britain, Greece, Portugal and Spain. In these cases it is only the mainstream political parties that are examined by the Manifesto Research

Group, and while the political space of these systems can be mapped to some extent, it is not possible to locate the right-wing extremist parties within this space.

Expert judgements

A final way in which the political space of a system may be mapped – and the one employed in this chapter – is by using expert judgements. This approach, pioneered by Castles and Mair (1984), asks country experts (drawn from the political science community) to locate the political parties of their respective systems on one or more scales.[5] The original question-naires designed by Castles and Mair simply asked experts to locate the parties in their political system on a straightforward, single, left–right dimension. Later work by Laver and Hunt (1992) asked experts to locate both party leaders and party voters on eight (and in one case ten) different scales, each representing a different policy dimension. Experts were then instructed to rate the importance attached by the leaders of each party to each policy dimension. Finally, they were asked to locate party leaders, legislators and activists on a further three scales, party leaders on a further two scales and the party in general on one final scale. In all, Laver and Hunt made use of 16 different scales. The subsequent expert judgement studies have all been informed by the works of Castles and Mair, and Laver and Hunt.

Like the other approaches to mapping the political space of different systems, the practice of using expert judgements has come in for some criticism. This has mainly emanated from those who favour the internal analysis of manifestos as a tool with which to identify the main dimensions of competition within political systems (e.g. Budge *et al.*, 1987; Budge, 2000). A first concern of the critics relates to whether experts are locating parties according to the views of party leaders, party activists or party voters. As was discussed above, there is evidence that these various groups within the party occupy different ideological positions. While the questionnaires devised by Laver and Hunt (1992) asked respondents to differentiate between these groups when locating the parties on the scales, other studies have not. Instead, they simply ask experts to locate 'the party'.

Second, there has been some uncertainty over whether the terms 'left' and 'right' – on which most of the scales are based – have the same meaning to different experts, or to the same experts at different times. Budge (2000), in particular, is sceptical about the comparability of these terms. Such draw-backs should not be overstated, however, as the format of the questionnaires sent to country experts has evolved significantly since the pioneering study by Castles and Mair, perhaps in direct response to these kinds of criticism. Many methodological problems have been overcome and the expert surveys have generally become more amenable to cross-national comparisons. In par-ticular, all the studies undertaken since the survey by Castles and Mair have asked respondents to locate parties on a number of different dimensions, rather than on just a single left–right scale. The terms 'left' and 'right' are thus less central in the studies today. Furthermore, in a number of the comparative studies, experts have been either asked or at least given the opportunity to describe the main dimensions of competition present in their own political system, rather than being restricted to an imposed, simple, left–right divide (Laver and Hunt, 1992; Huber and Inglehart, 1995).

While expert judgements are clearly not the perfect tool with which to map the political space (after all, if there were a perfect method, there would not be five contrasting approaches to performing the same task), they nonetheless stand up reasonably successfully to criticism. As the brief discussion above has illustrated, one of their strengths lies in the fact that questionnaire design is always improving. On top of this, expert judgements are also judged to be authoritative, and are easily accessible and interpretable – characteristics which account for their increasing popularity.

In addition to these benefits, expert judgements are particularly attractive in this instance because of their comprehensive nature. Even though, as Laver argues, they might provide 'soft data' in comparison to the manifesto data (1995: 4), they include many of the smaller parties not covered by the Manifesto Research Group work. Due to their scope, therefore, expert judgements represent the preferred, and in some cases the only, way in which to locate parties of the extreme right in the political space of their respective systems. The alternative approaches are, for various reasons, simply less appropriate to the task at hand. On the grounds of data availability, as well as for reasons of methodological accuracy, this chapter will employ expert judgement data to map the political space of the 15 systems under investigation and to locate the parties within this space.

Data and methodology

The chapter makes use of four comprehensive expert judgement studies and four single-country case studies, as follows:

Comprehensive studies:
- Castles and Mair (1984) – questionnaires sent out 1982;
- Laver and Hunt (1992) – questionnaires sent out 1989;
- Huber and Inglehart (1995) – questionnaires sent out 1993;
- Lubbers (2000) – questionnaires sent out 2000.

Single-country case studies:
- Laver (1995) on the Netherlands – questionnaires sent out 1994;
- Laver (1998) on Britain – questionnaires sent out 1997;
- Laver and Mair (1999) on the Netherlands – questionnaires sent out 1998;
- Ray and Narud (2000) on Norway – questionnaires sent out 1998.

The political space in the majority of the countries under investigation can be mapped at four different time points, as defined by the dates at which the comprehensive expert judgement studies were carried out – 1982, 1989, 1993 and 2000. However, in a limited number of cases not all countries are covered in all four comprehensive expert judgement studies and in these instances the political space can be mapped at only two or three time points.[6] In contrast, for Britain, the Netherlands and Norway, the existence of additional single-country case studies allows the political space to be mapped at more than four time points.

As well as exhibiting some variation in their country coverage, the expert judgement studies listed above differ in two other important respects. First, as was mentioned earlier, there are differences in the number of scales included in each study. While the Castles and Mair analysis asked experts to locate parties on a single left–right dimension only, the other studies invited respondents to place parties on a variety of policy dimensions.[7] Huber and Inglehart gave experts the opportunity to replace the labels 'left' and 'right' with their own labels if they so desired. Respondents were also asked to list the key issues that they thought divided left and right (or the other terms which they mentioned). Finally, respondents were asked if they thought that there was some other important dimension that divided the political parties in their countries.

In all other studies experts were specifically asked (rather than simply given the opportunity) to locate the parties in their respective countries on a number of different policy scales. In the survey carried out by Lubbers, as well as placing parties on the left–right dimension, respondents were invited to locate parties on two different scales, each referring to their policy on immigration. In the studies by Laver and Hunt, Laver, Laver and Mair, and Ray and Narud, experts were asked to locate parties on as many as ten different policy scales. In two of these surveys (those by Laver and Mair and by Ray and Narud) respondents were also asked to locate parties on the overarching left–right dimension.

This use of different policy scales in the various expert judgement surveys makes comparisons between the various studies problematic. Thus, if the studies are to be used to map the political space of different systems over time, the various scales must be rendered comparable. One means of achieving this is to draw on the left–right dimension in those instances where it is included in the studies (i.e. in the surveys by Castles and Mair, Huber and Inglehart, Laver and Mair, Ray and Narud, and Lubbers), and to select the most salient or important policy dimensions from those studies in which this overarching dimension does not feature. In this latter case (i.e. in the work by Laver and Hunt and in the two studies by Laver), the dimensions considered most important are those referring to socio-economic policy and to social policy. The positions of the parties on these two dimensions have been added and then averaged so that a new, more general dimension emerges, which is deemed to be comparable to the overarching left–right dimension employed by the other expert judgement studies.[8]

The second way in which the expert judgement studies differ is in the magnitude of the scales that they employ. The questionnaires sent out by Castles and Mair and by Lubbers asked respondents to place political parties on a left–right scale which ranged from 0 to 10, with 0 representing an extreme left position and 10 signalling an extreme right one.[9] In contrast, Laver and Hunt, Laver, Laver and Mair, and Ray and Narud invited experts to locate parties on scales that ran from 1 to 20. The questionnaires devised by Huber and Inglehart were different again, asking respondents to position parties on a scale that ranged from 1 to 10.[10] This variety in the magnitude of the scales makes comparison across expert judgement studies problematic in much the same way as did the use of different policy dimensions, and in order for the position of the political parties to be charted over time, the scores attributed to each party in the different expert judgement studies must be translated onto a common scale. This is done by a process of normalization, which transforms all readings onto a scale that runs from 0 (extreme left) to 1 (extreme right).[11]

Having taken these steps to make the different expert judgement studies comparable, it is now possible to plot the positions of the parties in their respective party systems at the various time points. The political space of each system may thus be mapped over time. This, in turn, means that it is now possible to return to the suggestions first made at the beginning of this chapter, namely that the disparity in the electoral success of right-wing extremist parties might be explained, in part, by the patterns of party competition at work in the various countries.

More specifically, in the introduction to this chapter it was suggested that the right-wing extremist party vote is likely to be influenced by (1) the ideological positions of the parties of the mainstream right, (2) the ideological positions of the right-wing extremist parties themselves, (3) the ideological positions of the parties of the mainstream right and the ideological positions of the parties of the extreme right relative to each other, and (4) the degree of convergence between the mainstream right and the mainstream left. These predictions will now be examined in turn.

Patterns of party competition: the mainstream right and the right-wing extremist party vote

It was first suggested at the beginning of this chapter that right-wing extremist parties are likely to be influenced by the proximity of their mainstream right competitors. This is because the parties of the mainstream right define how much political space is available at the extreme right of the political spectrum. Regardless of the distribution of voters along the left–right continuum, the greater the political space to the right of the mainstream right party, the greater the number of (potential) voters available to the parties of the extreme right. A more centrist mainstream right party will therefore leave more voters available to the parties of the extreme right than will a mainstream right party with a more right-wing agenda.

The proximity of the parties of the mainstream right is particularly important to the right-wing extremist parties because, in general, as Bartolini and Mair (1990) have illustrated, electoral interchange occurs *within* ideological blocs rather than *between* ideological blocs. This suggests that right-wing extremist parties are most likely to gain voters from, and to lose voters to, the parties of the mainstream right. Indeed, Evans (2001) has presented evidence that confirms that the majority of right-wing extremist voters originate from within the right bloc, even though a minority have, in the past, voted for left-wing parties.

Given the way in which the parties of the mainstream right are expected to influence the parties of the extreme right, a first hypothesis may be advanced as follows:

Hypothesis 1: The more moderate the ideology of the party of the mainstream right, the greater the right-wing extremist party vote.

An examination of the ideological positions of the parties of the mainstream right in the countries under observation (as derived from the expert judgement studies) suggests that there is considerable evidence to support this first hypothesis. In a number of instances, parties of the extreme right have experienced increased electoral success when those of the mainstream right have moderated their ideological appeals. Elsewhere, right-wing extremist parties have suffered at the polls as the parties of the mainstream right have radicalized. The following paragraphs will examine this evidence on a case-by-case basis, starting with the example of France, a first country in which this hypothesis is borne out in practice.

Figure 4.1 illustrates the political space in France in the period 1982–2000.[12] It shows that the mainstream right Rassemblement pour la République (RPR) moderated its ideology from 1982 to 1989, and again from 1993 to 2000. In both periods the FN experienced electoral gains, suggesting that, in this instance, the hypothesis holds true.

The RPR's move towards the centre in the early 1980s can be interpreted, in the first instance, as a response to the left winning both the presidential and legislative elections of 1981. The right hoped that by moving towards the centre and widening its electoral appeal it might recapture some voters in time for the next parliamentary election, which was scheduled for 1986 (Wright, 1989: 195-6). Furthermore, some degree of ideological moderation appeared electorally advantageous to the mainstream right in the early 1980s, as the initial programme of the socialists (who were in coalition with the PCF until 1984) was distinctly left-wing (Bell and Criddle, 1984).

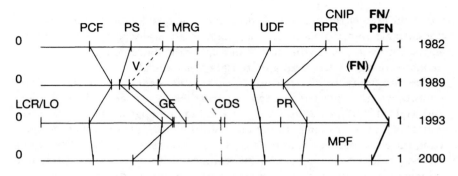

Figure 4.1 Political space in France, 1982–2000

Notes: For the full names of the parties see Appendix A. The heavy, dashed grey line represents the ideological mean of the party system. It is calculated by multiplying the score of each party on the left–right scale (as reported in Appendix A) by the party's share of the vote in the nearest election, expressed as a proportion (i.e. divided by 100). The figures for all the parties are then summed to produce the ideological mean of the system (see Kuntsen, 1998). The dashed line running from 'E' to 'V' indicates a degree of ideological continuity between the various ecological movements which existed at the time of the 1982 expert judgement study (as represented by the letter 'E') and the subsequent Green party 'Les Verts' (V), established in 1984, which features in the 1989 expert judgement survey. The right-wing extremist parties are shown in bold type. The PFN (founded in 1974) did not appear in the later expert judgement studies, as the party atrophied in the early 1980s. The ideological movement of the FN is represented by the heavy black line.

The moderation of the RPR in the 1980s is also explained by the on-going need to enter into electoral agreements with the more moderate, non-Gaullist UDF. This was particularly evident in 1984 during the campaign for the European Parliament elections, when the bulk of the RPR joined forces with the UDF. The two parties presented a joint list under the leadership of the centrist UDF politician Simone Veil (Kitschelt, 1995: 97-101; Marcus, 1995: 136). Although these elections were held under proportional representation rather than under the majority-plurality electoral system, the parties of the right stuck with previously formed alliances in anticipation of the next parliamentary elections: they had no idea at this time that President Mitterrand would alter the electoral system to proportional representation for the 1986 parliamentary contest. The parties of the mainstream right thus decided to engage in some form of electoral catch-allism even though the electoral system in operation for the European Parliament elections of 1984 did not demand it. The moderation continued throughout the next year too, with centrist figures like Veil and Raymond Barre playing important roles in the campaign for the cantonal elections of 1985 (Marcus, 1995: 137).

From 1986 until 1989 some in the mainstream right (particularly those in the RPR) advocated a policy of winning back the voters who had defected to the FN by pursuing tough policies on immigration. Charles Pasqua, the RPR interior minister from 1986 to 1988, was one such person. In May 1988, just weeks before the parliamentary elections, he famously declared that the FN and the mainstream right shared many of the same values (Marcus, 1995: 141). At first sight this might suggest a radicalization of the mainstream right, which the expert judgement studies did not pick up. However, on closer examination, it becomes evident that what radicalization there was was largely limited to rhetoric (Weil, 2001). Chirac himself appeared unwilling to make a firm decision on how best to deal with Le Pen, and continued to issue contradictory statements on race and immigration (Goldey and Johnson, 1988: 197). Moreover, the right-wing government of 1986–88 had failed to deliver on the issue of immigration and was unable to bring forward a new nationality bill it had been promising in advance of the 1988 legislative elections. As a result, the strategy of winning back voters from the FN through tough immigration policies was altogether unsuccessful (Marcus, 1995: 141–2). During this time, the FN's fortunes at the polls did nothing but increase. Having scored a mere 0.2 percent of the vote in the 1981 election, the party won 9.8 percent of the vote in the 1986 contest. Two years later it recorded the same electoral score.

A similar moderation in the ideological stance of the French mainstream right occurred in the period 1993 to 2000 (see Figure 4.1). This time, however, the moderation was much less significant than that of 1982–89, and was mainly due to attempts in the second half of the 1990s to reconcile the different tendencies within the RPR camp. For example, compromise became necessary from the mainstream right between europhiles and euro-phobes, *dirigistes* and economic liberals, and social traditionalists and modernizers (Knapp, 2003). The moderation is also attributable to the departure in the late 1990s of a number of right-wing personalities from the RPR, most notably Charles Pasqua, who broke from the party and set up the Rassemblement pour la France with Philippe de Villiers in September 1999.

In addition to these internal wranglings, ideological moderation in the 1990s may be explained by what Ivaldi has referred to as the end of the 'conciliatory phase' in which 'formal links between the mainstream right and the Front National became much less likely, as it was evident that Le Pen's party was the only beneficiary from such a strategy' (Ivaldi, 2002; see also Dézé, 2001). Finally, as in the early 1980s, the right's moderation in the latter part of the 1990s may also be explained by the left's re-entry into government in 1997.

What is important in terms of the hypothesis put forward above is that, in the period from 1993 to 2000, as the mainstream right moderated its ideological appeal a little, the FN increased its score at the polls, winning 12.7 percent of the vote in the legislative contest of 1993, and securing 14.9 percent of the ballots four years later. Thus, the first hypothesis advanced above is confirmed in this period.

Denmark is another example of the hypothesis being borne out in practice. As in France, the electoral fortunes of the right-wing extremist party

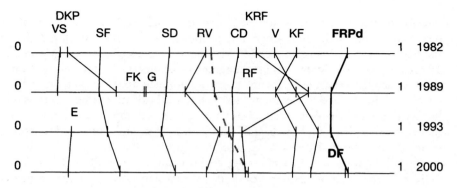

Figure 4.2   Political space in Denmark, 1982–2000

Notes: For the full names of the parties see Appendix A. The heavy, dashed grey line
represents the ideological mean of the party system. For details on how this is
calculated, see notes to Figure 4.1. The ideological movement of the right-wing
extremist FRPd is represented by the heavy black line. The DF (which was formed in
1995 when some members split from the FRPd) is also right-wing extremist. The
right-wing extremist parties are shown in bold type.

have risen and fallen as the parties of the mainstream right have engaged in
ideological moderation and radicalization. It should be noted, however, that
ideological change undertaken by the parties in Denmark has been less
evident than that undertaken by the parties in France, mainly as a result of
the fact that the Danish party system is much more crowded than the French,
and that party competition is more complex. Unlike in France, where politics tends to be played out between polarized party blocs, governmental
composition in Denmark requires the agreement of the centre. Though most
governments are minority coalitions, they nonetheless tend to consist of at
least three different partners, if not more. As a result, shifts in party ideology, when they do occur, must be viewed in conjunction with the obligations
that coalitions bring and thus tend to be less marked than in some other
countries. Hence, while some of the ideological shifts undertaken by the
Danish parties are detected in Figure 4.2, other, more subtle changes are not.

In spite of the complexity of the competition within the Danish mainstream right, it remains the case that the electoral fortunes of the right-wing
extremist party in Denmark (the FRPd) have tended to follow the ideological movements of the parties of the mainstream right. Starting in the
early 1980s, the party began to suffer at the polls just as the parties of
the moderate right (the Konservative Folkeparti – KF; Venstre – V; and the
Kristeligt Folkeparti – KRF) undertook an ideological radicalization.
Though the shift by the moderate right was only slight, the polarization of
the conventional conservative parties against the social democrats constituted the first real departure from the status quo in Danish politics, and the
bourgeois government which came to power in 1982 (which included the

Centrumdemokraterne [CD] and the Radikale Venstre [RV] as well as the three parties mentioned above) attempted for the first time to modify the social democratic welfare state by proposing a number of neo-liberal free market economic policies (Kitschelt, 1995: 126). In this period the FRPd saw its electoral score fall from 11.0 percent in the election of 1979, to 8.9 percent in the election of 1981, to 3.6 percent in the 1984 election.

By late 1986, however, it was clear that the radicalization undertaken by the bourgeois government was beginning to wane and that the economically liberal policies promised were not going to materialize. As Borre notes, going into the 1987 general election, 'the government had to a large extent continued social democratic policies rather than attempting to carry out a radically different policy of free enterprise. Far from dismantling the welfare state, the government had increased the public sector' (1988: 78). At the same time, the FRPd began to recover at the polls, first securing 4.8 percent of the vote in the 1987 contest and then winning 9.0 percent in the following election, held just one year later. Thus, the recovery of the FRPd is best understood by taking into account the behaviour and policies of the conservative parties. As Kitschelt points out, the FRPd's revival in the late 1980s 'came on the heels of lengthy episodes of bourgeois government incumbency gravitating toward increasingly moderate, centrist policies and the seeking of compromises with the opposition social democrats' (1995: 156).

The FRPd's revival was soon to be checked, however. In the 1990 election, the party once again experienced losses at the polls, securing only 6.4 percent of the vote. At the same time, the KF and V entered a new phase in which they exhibited a modicum of radicalization, mainly because their former coalition partners – the CD and the RV (both centrist parties) – indicated that they would not form part of any future coalition. From 1990, the two parties of the moderate right, as sole members of the governmental coalition, were therefore no longer as obliged to co-operate with these centrist parties as before and were able to shift slightly rightwards (see Figure 4.2).

The radicalization of the moderate right continued in the early 1990s, even though the KF–V government proved short-lived and fell in January 1993. Indeed, in the run-up to the 1994 election, the KF and V welcomed a suggestion made by the FRPd's then-leader Pia Kjærsgaard that the three parties should try and create a majority in parliament (Thomsen, 1995: 317–18). Though this apparent accommodation with the FRPd turned out to be a mistake for the KF in particular, the radicalization of the moderate right nonetheless kept the FRPd's fortunes in check. In 1994 the FRPd recorded exactly the same result as it had done four years earlier, securing just 6.4 percent of the vote.

The heavy losses experienced by the KF in 1994 and again in 1998, as well as significant party infighting, led to the resignation in late 1998 of the party's leader, Dr Per Stig Møller. A reassessment of the party's policies began after the 1998 election, and a slight yet visible moderation in the party's ideology took place after this date. Similarly, V replaced their leader in 1998 and the new man in charge, Arne Fogh Rasmussen (now prime minister), immediately showed himself keen to move towards the centre and to embrace a 'more accommodating and co-operative style' (Elklit, 1999: 141). The moderation of both parties in the mid- and late 1990s is evident in Figure 4.2.

The ideological moderation of the Danish moderate right since the mid-1990s has coincided with a revival of the fortunes of the extreme right. Though the FRPd split into two in October 1995, the combined electoral score of the FRPd and the newly formed DF in the 1998 election was 9.8 percent (2.4 and 7.4 percent respectively). In the 2001 contest, the two parties together polled 12.6 percent of the vote (0.6 and 12.0 percent respectively). Thus, the increased electoral success of the Danish extreme right in the mid- and late 1990s, which coincided with an ideological moderation by the mainstream right, lends further support to the first hypothesis put forward above.

The hypothesis is also borne out to some extent in Flanders, in Italy and in Switzerland (see Appendix B for figures illustrating the political space in these systems). There are, however, a number of instances in which the hypothesis is not confirmed in practice. For example, in Austria in the period between 1982 and 1989 the extreme right's (FPÖ) electoral fortunes increased in spite of the fact that the mainstream right (Österreichische Volkspartei – ÖVP) moved to the right (see Figure 4.3). The ÖVP moved rightwards once more after 1993, and the FPÖ again continued to record higher and higher electoral scores. Similarly, in France, in the period between 1989 and 1993, the hypothesis advanced above does not hold true. During this time the French FN's electoral results improved despite the fact that the RPR radicalized (see Figure 4.1 above).

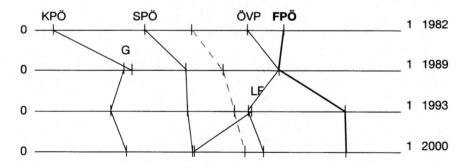

Figure 4.3   Political space in Austria, 1982–2000

Notes: For the full names of the parties see Appendix A. The heavy, dashed grey line represents the ideological mean of the party system. For details on how this is calculated, see notes to Figure 4.1. The ideological movement of the party of the extreme right (FPÖ) is represented by the heavy black line.

One possible explanation for why the Austrian and French parties of the extreme right continued to experience electoral success even though the mainstream right in each of the countries had radicalized is that both the FPÖ and the FN had, by this time, attained a certain level of 'importance' or 'relevance' in their respective party systems. Indeed, from the late 1970s, the Austrian FPÖ began to exhibit what Sartori (1976) has termed 'coalition potential', a potential that was first realized in 1983 when the party joined forces with the Sozialdemokratische Partei Österreichs (SPÖ) and became the junior partner in the governmental coalition. In 1999, and again in 2002, the FPÖ once more formed part of the governmental coalition, this time as the junior partner to the ÖVP. In France, the FN did not display coalition potential, but the party became relevant nonetheless by assuming 'blackmail potential'. From the mid-1980s onwards the FN began to affect both the tactics of party competition and the direction of party competition – the two features which, according to Sartori, qualify a party as having blackmail potential (1976: 121-3). The French parties of the mainstream right found that they had to fight electoral battles on two fronts – in the centre and on the right of the political spectrum. The examples of the Austrian FPÖ and the French FN suggest, therefore, that once a right-wing extremist party has passed what Pedersen (1982) has referred to as 'the threshold of relevance', its electoral fortunes may depend less on the behaviour and ideology of its mainstream right opponents.[13]

The case of Italy in the years 1993-2000 lends further weight to this suggestion. Here too, the two main parties of the extreme right (the MSI, which transformed itself into the AN in 1995, and the LN) experienced increased electoral success in spite of the fact that the mainstream right radicalized ideologically in this period (see Figure 4.4).[14] In 1992 the MSI had polled just 5.4 percent of the vote, but by 1994 the party secured 13.5 percent of the ballots. Two years later, it increased its score again, winning 15.7 percent of the vote. The vote share of the LN also increased by the end of this period, although the party did experience a minor downturn in its fortunes at the 1994 election. In 1992 the LN obtained 8.7 percent of the vote. Two years later, its vote share had fallen a little to 8.4 percent. By 1996, however, the party had not only recovered from this slight decline but had gone on to improve on its 1992 result. In this election the LN won 10.1 percent of the vote.

Like their Austrian and French counterparts, these two political parties have clearly passed the 'threshold of relevance'. With the birth of the Second Republic, and indeed partly due to the events that precipitated the new Republic, both the MSI/AN and the LN assumed coalition potential. Their new-found acceptability as coalition partners was immediately apparent as, following the 1994 election, both parties entered into government as members of the Polo della Libertà coalition, which was led by Berlusconi's Forza Italia (FI).

The examples of Austria, France and Italy thus imply that, provided they have attained political relevance, right-wing extremist parties may continue

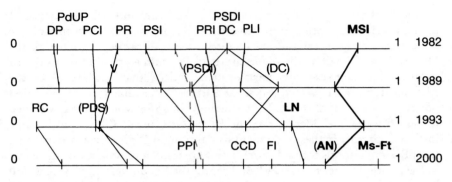

Figure 4.4 Political space in Italy, 1982–2000

Notes: For the full names of the parties see Appendix A. The heavy, dashed grey line represents the ideological mean of the party system. For details on how this is calculated, see notes to Figure 4.1. The ideological movement of the right-wing extremist MSI/AN and LN are represented by heavy black lines. The Ms-Ft (which split from the MSI in 1995) is also a right-wing extremist party. The right-wing extremist parties are shown in bold type.

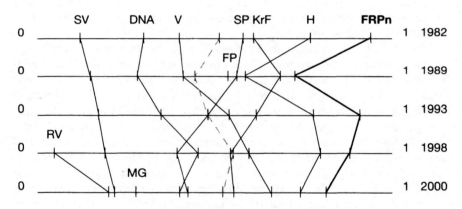

Figure 4.5 Political space in Norway, 1982–2000

Notes: For the full names of the parties see Appendix A. The heavy, dashed grey line represents the ideological mean of the party system. For details on how this is calculated, see notes to Figure 4.1. The ideological movement of the party of the extreme right (FRPn) is represented by the heavy black line.

to experience success at the polls even if their mainstream right opponents undergo ideological radicalization. In contrast, the fortunes of right-wing extremist parties that have not passed the 'threshold of relevance' appear to be much more sensitive to the behaviour and policies of the parties of the mainstream right.

In addition to the Austrian, French and Italian cases, a number of other instances exist in which the first hypothesis advanced above is not confirmed in practice. Here, however, it is not a matter of right-wing extremist parties experiencing electoral gains in seemingly unfavourable circumstances as happened in Austria, France and Italy. Instead, it is the opposite: the hypothesis is not borne out because right-wing extremist parties have suffered at the polls despite being in situations in which the parties of the mainstream right have moderated their ideology.

In Norway, for example, the FRPn suffered losses at the polls in the early and mid-1980s even though the Høyre (H) moderated its ideology in this period (see Figure 4.5). Similarly, in Spain the extreme right has experienced a continuous electoral decline since the early 1980s despite the fact that the mainstream right Partido Popular (PP) has become increasingly moderate (see Figure 4.6). These two cases therefore question the validity of the first hypothesis put forward above.

On closer examination, however, it is possible to explain why the Norwegian and the Spanish right-wing extremist parties suffered electoral losses in the 1980s even though the mainstream right-wing parties in the two respective party systems moderated their ideologies. Recalling the Austrian, French and Italian examples discussed earlier, it was argued that right-wing

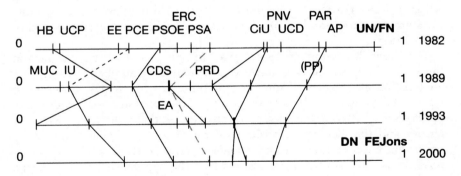

Figure 4.6   Political space in Spain, 1982–2000

Notes: For the full names of the parties see Appendix A. The heavy, dashed grey line represents the ideological mean of the party system. For details on how this is calculated, see notes to Figure 4.1. The dashed line running from the PCE to the IU indicates a degree of ideological continuity between the PCE, which featured in the 1982 expert judgement study, and the IU electoral alliance, featured in the 1989 survey, which was created in 1986 and which was composed of the PCE along with a number of marginal extreme left groups (see Mackie and Rose, 1991: 392). The right-wing extremist parties are shown in bold type. UN was an electoral coalition that existed from 1979 to 1982, and which included Fuerza Nueva (FN), the Falangistas (including the Falange Española de las JONS – FEJons), and other very small groups. No heavy black line links the right-wing extremist parties, as the parties were not included in every successive expert judgement survey.

extremist parties that have reached a certain 'threshold' appear able to continue to experience electoral success even though their mainstream right opponents have undergone radicalization – a phenomenon that would normally result in electoral losses for the parties of the extreme right. In a similar fashion, the Norwegian and Spanish cases suggest that, if right-wing extremist parties have *not* reached this 'threshold of relevance', then they may still experience electoral losses even though the competitive environment appears favourable to them; that is, even though the parties of the mainstream right moderate their stances. In both the Norwegian and the Spanish cases, the parties of the extreme right did not attain the 'threshold of relevance' in the early and mid-1980s – the Norwegian FRPn had to wait until 1989 for this – and both sets of parties were unable to profit from the moderation of the mainstream right that occurred in the two party systems.

Clearly, the existence of an explanation for why the Norwegian and Spanish right-wing extremist parties did not experience electoral success even though their mainstream right opponents moderated their ideologies should not obscure the fact that these cases do not fit the hypothesis advanced above. Equally, just because it is possible to account for why the French, Austrian and Italian parties of the extreme right have continued to encounter electoral success in otherwise unfavourable situations, this does not mean that these cases conform to the hypothesis. This said, examining whether or not parties have attained the 'threshold of relevance' does allow for a greater understanding of why certain cases have not corresponded to expectations.

The above discussion has shown that the first hypothesis put forward in this chapter appears to be confirmed in a significant number of cases. The analysis has also suggested some potential reasons for the few instances in which the hypothesis was not borne out in practice. Thus far, however, the relationship between the electoral fortunes of the right-wing extremist parties and the ideological position of their respective mainstream right opponents has been examined only qualitatively. Therefore, while it has been possible to ascertain the instances in which the hypothesis has been borne out in practice and those in which it has not, it has so far not been possible to determine the nature of the relationship between the electoral scores of the right-wing extremist parties and the ideological position of the parties of the mainstream right in any detail.

The nature of this relationship may be examined more closely by means of a simple correlation. More specifically, the electoral scores of the right-wing extremist parties may be correlated with the positions of the parties of the mainstream right on the left–right spectrum as derived from the expert judgement studies and as reported in Appendix A. Given that, in the discussion above, the hypothesis appeared to be confirmed in practice in the majority of cases, it is reasonable to anticipate a negative correlation between the two variables. That is, it is reasonable to expect that as the scores of the parties of the mainstream right on the left–right spectrum increase (that is, the more right-wing they become), so the right-wing extremist party vote will decrease.[15]

In practice the correlation does indeed yield a negative score: the Pearson correlation coefficient is −.378 (significant at the 0.01 level).[16] This confirms the negative relationship that was anticipated and that was suggested by the qualitative discussion above.[17] From this correlation and from the detailed qualitative discussion presented above, it is thus possible to conclude that a negative association exists between the electoral scores of the right-wing extremist parties on the one hand and the ideological positions of the parties of the mainstream right on the other. The first hypothesis advanced above can therefore be confirmed and the following conclusion can be reached: in general, and with the exception of those cases where the right-wing extremist parties have crossed the 'threshold of relevance', the less successful right-wing extremist parties tend to be located in systems where the parties of the mainstream right are ideologically more radical, whereas the more successful right-wing extremist parties are more likely to be found in systems in which the mainstream right parties are more moderate.

Patterns of party competition: the extreme right and the right-wing extremist party vote

In addition to being influenced by the size of the political space available to the right of the mainstream right party, the electoral fortunes of right-wing extremist parties are also likely to depend on the ideological position these parties choose to adopt for themselves. More specifically, it is reasonable to predict that, all other things being equal, less extreme right-wing extremist parties will perform better at the polls than more extreme right-wing extremist parties. The reasons for this are twofold.

First, it can be logically assumed that voters positioned to the right of the right-wing extremist party (that is, voters who are ideologically more extreme than the party of the extreme right) will vote for this party (that is, if they vote at all) because no alternatives exist which are any more extreme. Therefore, presuming a 'normal' voter distribution, the less extreme the party of the extreme right, the greater the number of voters who are located to the party's right, and hence the greater the number of voters whose support may, in effect, be 'guaranteed'. The second reason for expecting a more moderate right-wing extremist party to perform better than a more extreme one is that the former will be able to attract more centrist voters than its more extreme counterpart. In the light of this, a second hypothesis may thus be advanced:

Hypothesis 2: The more extreme the ideology of the right-wing extremist party, the lower its electoral score.

As with the previous one, this second hypothesis is borne out in practice in a number of cases. In Austria, for example, the FPÖ moderated its ideology in the early 1980s (albeit only very slightly) and, at the same time, the party experienced increased electoral success (see Figure 4.3 above). Until 1986 the FPÖ was very much a liberal party. First under the leadership of Friedrich Peter in the late 1960s and 1970s, and then under the stewardship of Norbert Steger in the early 1980s, the party moderated and began a move to the centre ground. It espoused economically liberal policies and in 1979 it even joined the Liberal International. The party was also brought towards the centre in the 1980s due to coalition obligations: as was noted above, in 1983 it entered into a coalition with the SPÖ. During this time, the party's share of the vote rose from 5.0 percent in 1983 to 9.7 percent in 1986.

The FPÖ started to radicalize only when Jörg Haider assumed the leadership of the party in 1986. Even then, however, the significant shift to the right that the party was to undertake began only three or four years later. In the immediate period after Haider became leader, the party stressed its populist, anti-establishment credentials more than its xenophobic or nationalist side. 'Between 1986 and the election of 1990 . . . the FPÖ campaigns primarily focused on problems that could be laid at the door of the federal government: unemployment, waste of tax monies, corruption and excessive political patronage and scandals' (Riedlsperger, 1998: 29).

The second hypothesis is also upheld in Italy in the period 1993–2000. During these years the MSI became ideologically more moderate (see Figure 4.4 above) and, like the Austrian FPÖ, saw its vote share increase at the same time. The moderation came about with the transformation of the party into the AN. The party first adopted the label 'Movimento Sociale Italiano-Alleanza Nazionale' in mid-1993 in a bid to recruit some independent candidates outside of the MSI (Gallagher, 2000; Baldini, 2001). Then, the following year it entered into a coalition led by Forza Italia (FI), a move that further pushed the party in the direction of the centre. The transformation was completed the next year, 1995, when at the Fiuggi Congress the party changed its name to 'Alleanza Nazionale' and shed its more extreme elements. The departure of hard-liners from the party and the subsequent establishment of the Ms-Ft under the leadership of Pino Rauti further pushed the AN away from the right pole of the political spectrum. Ideological moderation was emphasized again at the Verona conference in the spring of 1998, when party leader Fini publicly condemned a number of past acts that had been carried out in the name of fascism (Baldini, 2001; Ignazi, 2003: 50). During this period of ideological moderation the party experienced increasing electoral success. Having scored only 5.4 percent of the vote in the 1992 election, the party recorded 13.5 percent of the vote in the election of 1994, and then polled 15.7 percent in the 1996 contest. The AN's score did fall slightly in the election of 2001, to 12.0 percent of the vote, but if the 1993–2000 moderation period is examined as a whole, it is characterized by electoral success rather than decline.

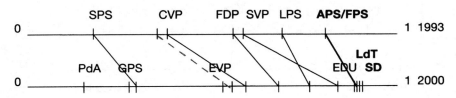

Figure 4.7 Political space in Switzerland, 1993–2000

Notes: For the full names of the parties see Appendix A. The heavy, dashed grey line represents the ideological mean of the party system. For details on how this is calculated, see notes to Figure 4.1. The right-wing extremist parties are shown in bold type. The ideological movement of the right-wing extremist APS/FPS is represented by the heavy black line. The SD and the LdT are also right-wing extremist parties.

The second hypothesis is also confirmed in instances where a radicalization on the part of a right-wing extremist party has coincided with the party suffering at the polls. In Switzerland, for instance, the APS gradually renounced its bourgeois, anti-environment, pro-motorist stance from the early 1990s onwards, renaming itself the FPS in 1992 and embracing increasingly xenophobic policies (Husbands, 2000: 507). As a result, the party shifted markedly towards the right (see Figure 4.7). During this period the electoral score of the APS/FPS fell from 5.1 percent in 1991, to 4.0 percent in 1995, to 0.9 percent in 1999, and finally to 0.2 percent in 2003.

The same pattern is evident in Norway in the period from 1989 to 1993 (see Figure 4.2 above). Here the FRPn moved significantly towards the right in an attempt to continue to differentiate itself from the mainstream parties that had also moved towards the right in this period. Unable to champion the issue of immigration to the same extent as before, because of the passing of a tough new law in 1988 that greatly reduced the number of immigrants entering Norway, the FRPn turned its attention to the related issues of law and order (Arter, 1992: 364). The move was obviously unpopular with the electorate, however, as the party's vote fell from 13.0 percent in 1989 to 6.3 percent in 1993. Similar patterns were at work in Denmark in the period 1993–2000 (see Figure 4.2 above), and in the Netherlands between 1994 and 2000 (see Appendix B). In both instances, the right-wing extremist party's move to the right coincided with it losing votes.

However, as with the first hypothesis, a number of instances exist which contradict the proposition that right-wing extremist parties perform better at the polls when they are more moderate than when they are more extreme. For example, in France, in the period from 1989 to 1993, the FN moved markedly to the right, partly because the mainstream parties also moved rightwards (see Figure 4.1 above). Despite this, the party still experienced increased electoral fortunes, with its vote share rising from 9.8 percent in 1988 to 12.7 percent in 1993. Similarly, in Austria, the FPÖ continued to secure an ever-increasing number of votes between 1989 and 1994 even

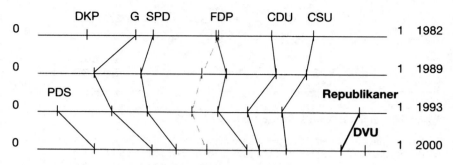

Figure 4.8 Political space in Germany, 1982–2000

Notes: For the full names of the parties see Appendix A. The heavy, dashed grey line represents the ideological mean of the party system. For details on how this is calculated, see notes to Figure 4.1. The ideological movement of the right-wing extremist Republikaner is represented by the heavy black line. The DVU is also a right-wing extremist party. The right-wing extremist parties are shown in bold type.

though the party's ideology was becoming increasingly radical in this period (see Figure 3.4 above).

Elsewhere, right-wing extremist parties have experienced declining electoral scores even though they have moderated their ideologies. In Italy, for example, in the period from 1982 to 1989, the MSI recorded electoral losses despite the fact that the party moderated its ideological appeals during this time (see Figure 4.4 above). Similarly, in Germany, the Republikaner moderated their ideology in the period from 1993 to 2000 (see Figure 4.8), but the party did not experience any increase in its electoral score.

Since the change in the Republikaner leadership in 1995, when former vice-chairman Rolf Schlierer took over from Franz Schönhuber, the party has gradually attempted to turn away from open extremism, in terms of both its ideology and the alliances it makes with other right-wing extremist organizations (AXT, 1998; Backes and Mudde, 2000). However, in spite of this moderation, the Republikaner's vote share has decreased at every election since 1990.

As before, however, it is possible to account for why these cases do not conform to the hypothesis. The 'relevance' explanation put forward above, which helped account for why the first hypothesis was not borne out in a number of instances, also has some bearing on this second hypothesis. Here too, the few cases just described that contradict the hypothesis may be explained with reference to whether or not the right-wing extremist parties in question have attained the 'threshold of relevance' (Pedersen, 1982). Thus, the fact that the French and Austrian parties of the extreme right have continued to enjoy increasing electoral success in spite of their significant ideological radicalization in the early 1990s may, once again, be viewed as a result of the two parties assuming political relevance. Having passed the 'threshold of relevance', the two parties' ideological appeals appear less crucial to their electoral success than before. Conversely, in the cases of Italy in the period 1982–89 and of Germany, even a moderation in the parties' ideology failed to result in increased electoral success because neither party had passed the 'threshold of relevance' at this time – the Italian parties of the extreme right assumed relevance only in the 1990s.

As with the first hypothesis, this second hypothesis can be tested more systematically by means of a correlation. The electoral scores of the right-wing extremist parties can be correlated with the parties' positions on the left–right spectrum, as reported in Appendix A. As with the last hypothesis, a negative relationship is expected between the two variables. As the parties' score on the left–right scale increases (that is, as they become more extreme), so their electoral scores are expected to be lower.

As anticipated, the correlation does reveal a negative score: the Pearson correlation coefficient is −.291, and is significant at the 0.01 level.[18] From this, and from the preceding discussion, it can therefore be confirmed that the second hypothesis advanced above holds true in the majority of cases. It is thus possible to conclude that, in general, the right-wing extremist parties that embrace the most extreme ideology have tended to be the ones that experience lower electoral scores, whereas the more moderate right-wing extremist parties have tended to secure higher vote shares.

Patterns of party competition: the interaction of the mainstream right and the extreme right, and the right-wing extremist party vote

The two hypotheses examined and tested above do not simply operate independently of each other, however. They also combine, meaning that it is necessary to view the ideological positions of the parties of the mainstream right in conjunction with the ideological positions of the parties of the extreme right. The positions of the mainstream right party may interact with the positions of the extreme right party in several different ways. More specifically, four potential scenarios present themselves. The first two scenarios can be discussed with reference to Figures 4.9 and 4.10 below, in which the party of the mainstream right is represented by point C, and the party of the extreme right by point D. Point B represents a party of the mainstream left. From these scenarios two further hypotheses may be advanced.

Scenario 1: Both the party of the mainstream right and the party of the extreme right are ideologically moderate. Since ideological moderation is a relative concept only, this scenario must be compared to a situation in which both the party of the mainstream right and the party of the extreme right are ideologically less moderate. Therefore, with reference to Figure 4.9, this scenario can be illustrated by the party of the mainstream right (represented by point C) moving towards the centre of the political spectrum (to point C_1)

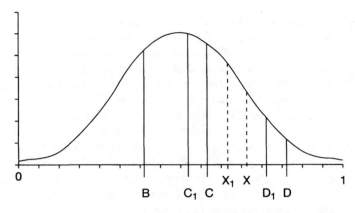

Figure 4.9   Ideological moderation and the right-wing extremist party vote

at the same time as the party of the extreme right moves towards the centre (from point D to point D_1). As a result of this shift, the point at which voters start turning away from the party of the mainstream right and towards the party of the extreme right also moves to the centre (that is, this point moves from x to x_1). In this new situation, the extreme right party is able to attract more voters than before, because it can now attract all voters positioned to the right of point x_1, rather than only voters positioned to the right of point x.

Therefore, if the party of the mainstream right moves towards the centre of the political spectrum at the same time as the party of the extreme right moves towards the centre, it is reasonable to predict that the party of the extreme right will encounter increased electoral success.[19] A third hypothesis can thus be formulated:

Hypothesis 3: The more ideologically moderate the mainstream right party <u>and</u> the more ideologically moderate the right-wing extremist party, the higher the right-wing extremist party vote.

Scenario 2: Both the party of the mainstream right and the party of the extreme right are ideologically extreme. This scenario is illustrated in Figure 4.10, which shows the party of the mainstream right moving towards the right at the same time as the party of the extreme right moves towards the right. The party of the mainstream right moves from point C to point C_2, and the party of the extreme right moves from point D to point D_2. In this instance, the point at which voters start turning away from the party of the mainstream right and towards the party of the extreme right moves to the right, from point x to point x_2. As a result, the party of the extreme right finds itself unable to attract as many voters as before, because instead of being able to capture all voters positioned to the right of point x, it can now only attract voters positioned to the right of point x_2.

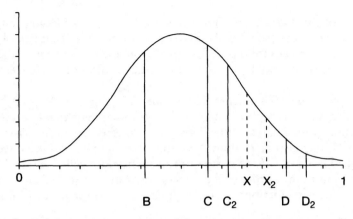

Figure 4.10 Ideological radicalization and the right-wing extremist party vote

Therefore, if the party of the mainstream right and the party of the extreme right both move rightwards at the same time, it is reasonable to expect the party of the extreme right to suffer at the polls. A fourth hypothesis can therefore be put forward:

Hypothesis 4: The more ideologically extreme the mainstream right party <u>and</u> the more ideologically extreme the right-wing extremist party, the lower the right-wing extremist party vote.

Scenario 3: The party of the mainstream right is ideologically more extreme than it was, while the party of the extreme right is ideologically more moderate than it was. Unlike in the two scenarios presented above, it is impossible to predict whether the party of the extreme right will experience electoral gains or suffer electoral losses in this situation, because its fortunes depend on the degree to which these parties move. If the party of the mainstream right moves only slightly to the right, but the party of the extreme right moves markedly to the centre, it is possible that the party of the extreme right may still benefit at the polls. However, a more significant shift to the right by the party of the mainstream right may offset any benefit derived from the extreme right party's ideological moderation.

Scenario 4: The party of the mainstream right is ideologically more moderate than it was, while the party of the extreme right is ideologically more extreme than it was. As with the last scenario, it is impossible to predict whether the party of the extreme right will benefit or will suffer in this situation. Once again, its fortunes depend on the extent to which both parties move along the ideological spectrum. If the party of the mainstream right moves significantly towards the centre but the party of the extreme right moves only slightly towards the right, then it is possible that the party of the extreme right may still increase the number of voters it attracts. However, if the party of the mainstream right becomes only slightly ideologically more moderate while the party of the extreme right becomes significantly more extreme, then any electoral benefit derived from the moderation of the mainstream right party may be offset by the radicalization of the extreme right party.

Recalling some of the earlier discussions of Hypotheses 1 and 2, the evidence in support of the third and fourth hypotheses may now be considered. In addition, the situations that have been referred to as Scenario 3 and Scenario 4 may also be examined. In this way, the interaction between the ideological positions of the parties of the mainstream right and the ideological positions of the parties of the extreme right may be investigated, and the effect of these interactions on the right-wing extremist party vote may be assessed.

The first two instances in which this third hypothesis is borne out in practice are in France in the periods 1982–89 and 1993–2000. As was noted when the first hypothesis was examined, the French mainstream right party (RPR) moderated its ideology in both these periods. At the same time, the right-wing extremist FN also embarked on ideological moderation (see Figure 4.1 above). In both periods, the vote share of the FN increased, as predicted by Hypothesis 3. Having polled a mere 0.2 percent in the 1981 legislative elections, the FN secured 9.8 percent of the vote in the 1986 and 1988 contests. In the 1990s, the party's fortunes improved further, with a score rising from 12.7 percent in 1993 to 14.9 percent in the elections of 1997. After this period, the FN's score fell slightly to 11.3 percent of the vote, but since the expert judgement studies do not include the placements of parties after 2000, it is impossible to determine whether this slight decline may be linked to patterns of competition within the French party system.

This third hypothesis is also confirmed in Italy between 1993 and 2000. As in the French example above, this period saw the right-wing extremist MSI/AN moderate its ideology at the same time as the mainstream right embarked on a course of ideological moderation (see Figure 4.4 above). During this time, the electoral scores of the MSI/AN increased from 5.4 percent in 1992, to 13.5 percent in 1994, to 15.7 percent in 1996.

Another case in which similar dynamics are at work is Norway in the period 1982–89. Here too both the right-wing extremist FRPn and the largest party of the mainstream right – the H – moderated their ideologies at the same time (see Figure 4.5 above). In contrast to the cases of France and Italy, however, the hypothesis is not fully borne out in Norway because, in the first instance at least, the FRPn experienced losses at the polls. While the party had won 4.5 percent of the vote in the 1981 election, in 1985 it secured only 3.7 percent of the ballots. However, by the 1989 election the party recovered, scoring 13.0 percent of the vote. Thus, although the hypothesis is not confirmed in Norway in the early 1980s, it is borne out in the latter part of the decade.

Hypothesis 3 therefore holds true in three of the four cases in which both the mainstream right and the extreme right have undergone simultaneous ideological moderation. Furthermore, it has been seen that in the fourth case (Norway), the hypothesis cannot be fully rejected since, by the latter part of the period in question (1982–89), the right-wing extremist party experienced increased electoral success. Therefore, although there are only a limited number of instances in which it may be assessed (and so insufficient cases for statistical testing), there is reason to believe that this third hypothesis has significant predictive power. This allows the conclusion to be drawn that right-wing extremist parties are more likely to secure high vote shares in situations where they themselves *and* their mainstream right-wing opponents are ideologically more moderate than in situations where they *and* their mainstream right-wing competitors are more extreme.

Evidence in support of Hypothesis 4 also exists in a number of countries. In Norway, for example, in the period 1989–93 both the mainstream right (H) and the FRPn embarked on a process of ideological radicalization (see Figure 4.5 above), and during this time the FRPn experienced a downturn in its electoral score. In the 1989 election the party had polled 13.0 percent of the vote, but by the 1993 contest it managed to secure only 6.3 percent of the ballots.

In Switzerland too, in the period 1993–2000, the extreme right radicalized its ideology as the mainstream right also became more right-wing (see Figure 4.7 above). As predicted, within this period, the extreme right experienced a decline in its electoral fortunes. Whereas the FPS had won 5.1 percent of the votes in 1991, in 1995 it polled only 4.0 percent. Then, in 1999 its electoral score slumped to 0.9 percent (and in 2003 it declined still further, to 0.2 percent). The SD also experienced losses in these years. In 1991 the party had polled 3.3 percent of the vote whereas four years later its score had fallen to 3.1 percent. Then in 1999 it recorded only 1.8 percent of all ballots (and in 2003 it won only 1.0 percent of the vote).[20]

The fourth hypothesis is therefore clearly borne out in two cases. However, two further cases exist in which both the parties of the extreme right and those of the moderate right have radicalized their ideology but in which the vote share of the right-wing extremist party has risen rather than fallen. As such, in these two further cases Hypothesis 4 is not confirmed.

The first of these is France, where between 1989 and 1993 the FN continued to enjoy increasing electoral success despite the fact that both it and the mainstream right RPR radicalized in these years (see Figure 4.1 above). Contrary to the predictions of the hypothesis, the FN saw its electoral score rise from 9.8 percent in 1988 to 12.7 percent in 1993. Similarly, in Austria in the period 1993–2000, even though the mainstream ÖVP and the extremist FPÖ both moved rightwards (see Figure 4.3 above), the electoral score of the FPÖ did not decrease in the period as a whole. The party did experience a very slight dip in its electoral fortunes in 1995 (its vote share fell from

22.5 percent in 1994 to 21.9 percent in 1995), but by the 1999 contest it won a massive 26.9 percent of the vote. Thus, in contrast to the Norwegian and Swiss cases, the fourth hypothesis does not hold true in France in the period between 1989 and 1993, or in Austria in the 1993–2000 period. It may well be the case that the hypothesis holds true in Austria in the period after 2000, since the FPÖ went on to experience a substantial decline at the polls in 2002, when it won only 10.0 percent of the vote. However, since the expert judgement studies do not cover the post-2000 period, it is not possible to test the hypotheses in the period after 2000.

There is thus mixed evidence for Hypothesis 4. While it holds true in two of the four cases where both the mainstream right and the extreme right have radicalized their ideologies at the same time (Norway 1989–93 and Switzerland 1993–2000), it is not confirmed in the two other instances (Austria 1993–2000 and France 1989–93). As was the case with the other hypotheses, however, the political 'relevance' explanation may once again help account for why this fourth hypothesis is not borne out in Austria and France. The fact that the FPÖ and the FN have continued to experience increasing electoral success even though they themselves have radicalized and even though their mainstream right opponents have moved to the right may be explained by their size and influence in their respective party systems. Thus, while smaller right-wing extremist parties appear to suffer in such situations, both the FPÖ and the FN have assumed the political relevance necessary to be able to continue winning ever more votes despite circumstances which would normally be detrimental to right-wing extremist parties.

In addition to situations in which both the mainstream right and the extreme right moderate, and situations in which both the mainstream right and the extreme right radicalize – two scenarios which have just been discussed with reference to Hypothesis 3 and Hypothesis 4 respectively – it was suggested above that the position of the mainstream right parties and those of the right-wing extremist parties may interact in two further possible ways. First, it might be the case that the mainstream right radicalizes as the extreme right moderates.

This scenario – which was referred to earlier as Scenario 3 – has indeed occurred in a number of countries at various time points. In Austria, for example, between 1982 and 1989 the mainstream ÖVP radicalized while the extremist FPÖ moderated – albeit only slightly (see Figure 4.3 above). Similarly, in Germany in the period 1993–2000, the extremist Republikaner moved away from the right pole of the political spectrum at a time when the mainstream CDU radicalized its ideology (see Figure 4.8 above), partly as a result of the greater debate on asylum (Minkenberg, 1997: 81–2). The same dynamics were also evident in Italy between 1982 and 1989 and again (in the case of the MSI/AN) from 1993 to 2000, and in Norway in the years 1993–98 (see Figures 4.4 and 4.5 above).

As was established earlier in the chapter when the different scenarios were discussed, unlike situations in which both the mainstream right and the extreme right moderate (Scenario 1), or situations in which both sets of parties radicalize (Scenario 2), in Scenario 3 it is impossible to predict whether right-wing extremist parties will experience increased electoral success or whether they will suffer at the polls. Indeed, looking at the cases just identified in which Scenario 3 does occur, the right-wing extremist parties have enjoyed rising electoral scores on some occasions, but have recorded electoral losses on others. While the Austrian FPÖ and the Norwegian FRPn saw their vote shares increase in such situations, the German Republikaner experienced falling electoral results. As for the Italian MSI, the party first increased its electoral score in the period 1982–89 and then suffered a slight setback. In contrast, from 1993 to 2000, the MSI/AN recorded an ever-increasing percentage of the vote (though shortly after this period the party's vote fell slightly, to 12.0 percent in 2001). The picture is therefore mixed, and the lack of any trend in the fortunes of the parties of the extreme right underlines the difficulty in predicting whether their electoral scores will increase or decrease in this situation.

The fourth and final scenario identified above saw the parties of the mainstream right moderate while those of the extreme right radicalized. As with Scenario 3, it was argued that in this situation it is impossible to predict whether the parties of the extreme right will enjoy increased electoral success or whether they will experience losses at the polls. Instead, their electoral fortunes are expected to depend on the degree to which both parties move along the left–right spectrum.

This is reflected in those instances in which Scenario 4 occurs in practice. In Austria, for example, in the period 1989–93, when the extremist FPÖ radicalized its ideology and the mainstream ÖVP moderated its appeal (see Figure 4.3 above), the FPÖ saw its electoral score increase. In 1990 the party polled 16.6 percent of the vote, whereas in 1994 it secured 22.5 percent of the ballots. Similarly, in Denmark in the years 1993–2000, where the extreme right also radicalized as the mainstream right moderated (see Figure 4.2 above), the vote share going to the parties of the extreme right increased. In 1994 the FRPd recorded 6.4 percent of the vote, but by 1998 the combined results of the parties of the extreme right (FRPd and DF) had risen to 9.8 percent. They continued to rise in the period after 2000 too, when the DF recorded 12.0 percent of the vote. In Italy, however, where Scenario 4 was also played out, the right-wing extremist MSI did not see its electoral score increase. Instead, in the period 1989–93, when the MSI radicalized and the mainstream right DC moderated (see Figure 4.4 above), the MSI's vote share fell slightly, from 5.9 percent in 1987 to 5.4 percent in 1992. As in Scenario 3, no obvious trend in the electoral scores of the parties of the extreme right is therefore discernible in situations where the mainstream right parties moderate and the right-wing extremist ones radicalize.

Patterns of party competition:
convergence of the mainstream parties

In addition to being influenced by patterns of party competition on the right of the political spectrum, right-wing extremist parties are also likely to be affected by competition at the centre of the political spectrum. More specifically, it is reasonable to expect right-wing extremist parties to benefit when the parties of the mainstream left and the parties of the mainstream right converge ideologically. As Hainsworth has argued, the 'more favourable terrain for the extreme right has often been situations where the ideological distance between the major parties was reduced, thereby creating a vacuum on the right conducive to extreme right success' (1992a: 11). Similarly, Kitschelt maintains that:

> the opportunities for extreme-rightist mobilization depend on the convergence between left and moderate right parties. If the distance between these parties is relatively small, political entrepreneurs have a chance to create a successful electoral coalition with a right-authoritarian agenda. Where 'partocracy' in a country's political economy system prevails, such entrepreneurs should be able to broaden their electorate beyond the right-authoritarian core through populist anti-statist messages and actually build a very strong 'cross-class' alliance against the established parties. (1995: 53)[21]

This chapter has already gone some way towards exploring the situations in which the mainstream right and the mainstream left converge in that, in an earlier section, it examined a number of instances in which the parties of the mainstream right moderated their ideology – a necessary condition for convergence to occur. The conclusion reached from that discussion and analysis – namely that moderation of the mainstream right is related to high right-wing extremist electoral scores – suggests that there is reason to expect that the convergence between the mainstream right and the mainstream left will also be linked to right-wing extremist party success. Given this prediction, and in the light of the comments made by Hainsworth and Kitschelt, the following hypothesis can be formulated:

Hypothesis 5: The greater the ideological convergence between the parties of the mainstream left and the parties of the mainstream right, the higher the right-wing extremist party vote.

In contrast to Kitschelt's examination of this hypothesis, the comprehensive data set that this chapter has employed allows for this hypothesis to be tested across time and across countries. Whereas Kitschelt investigated the convergence between the mainstream left and the mainstream right at one time point only, with the present data it is possible to examine this convergence at four different time points in the case of most countries. The present data set also has the benefit of containing data on countries and parties that were not included in Kitschelt's study.

Referring back to Figures 4.1–4.8 above, which illustrated the political space of the different countries under observation, convergence between the mainstream right and the mainstream left can be seen to have occurred in a number of instances. In fact, the figures suggest that convergence occurred at some time point in 11 of the 15 political systems under investigation. Only in France, Greece, Norway and Switzerland did the parties of the mainstream left and the parties of the mainstream right not converge ideologically in the period 1982–2000.[22]

To take one example, convergence between the mainstream left and the mainstream right occurred in Britain in the period 1989–97. As Figure 4.11 illustrates, during this time both the Labour Party (L) and the Conservative Party (C) moderated their ideologies. For Labour, ideological moderation came about mainly as a result of the party changing its stance on economic issues. In 1989, in a document entitled *Meet the Challenge, Make the Change*, the party argued that the task of a Labour government would be restricted to stimulating the market economy, and that intervention in the economy by the state would be limited to situations in which market forces proved incapable of guaranteeing growth or distributing resources efficiently. This policy was pursued into the 1990s, when the party adopted what it called the 'responsible social market model' (Maor, 1997: 226). The party also changed its attitudes towards privatized industries, and announced that it would not reverse many of the privatizations pushed through by successive Thatcher governments. Then, in 1995 the Labour Party dropped

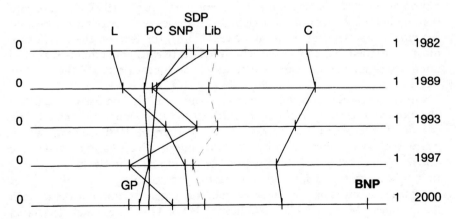

Figure 4.11   Political space in Britain, 1982–2000

Notes: For the full names of the parties see Appendix A. The heavy, dashed grey line represents the ideological mean of the party system. For details on how this is calculated, see notes to Figure 4.1. The right-wing extremist BNP is shown in bold type. No heavy black line links the right-wing extremist parties from year to year, as the parties were not included in every successive expert judgement survey.

Clause IV of its constitution, thereby renouncing its claim to secure 'common ownership of the means of production, distribution and exchange' (Maor, 1997: 227).

The Conservatives' ideological moderation was also partly a result of changes in the party's policies on economic issues. Indeed, after John Major replaced Margaret Thatcher as Conservative leader and prime minister in 1990, the party became less strident in its pursuit of a laissez-faire economic model. The party's approach to privatization was toned down, for example, and the high rates of unemployment in the early 1990s demanded a certain level of state intervention in the economy. The party also engaged in a policy switch over Europe when Major took over the leadership. Like the Labour Party and the Liberal Party, Major favoured a more active role for Britain in Europe, and wanted to 'put Britain at the heart of Europe' (Maor, 1997: 224–34). The convergence between the Labour Party and the Conservative Party came to an end at the 1997 election, when, after a disastrous election defeat, the Conservative Party once again moved to the right, this time under the leadership of William Hague.

If the fifth hypothesis advanced above is correct, and if convergence between the mainstream right and the mainstream left is indeed linked with greater electoral scores for the parties of the extreme right, then both the British NF and BNP should have recorded increased electoral results in the period 1989–97. An examination of the parties' electoral scores shows that there is little evidence to support this expectation, however. The NF continued to secure less than 0.1 percent of the vote from 1987 onwards, and although the BNP passed the 0.1 percent mark at the 1997 election, and then polled 0.2 percent of the vote in 2001, these results may hardly be considered as representing electoral success. Thus, for Britain, the conclusion must be reached that convergence between the parties of the mainstream has not led to significant increased electoral success for the parties of the extreme right.

Convergence between the mainstream right and the mainstream left has also occurred in Spain in the period since 1989 (see Figure 4.6 above). The socialist PSOE began to moderate its stance after the 1989 election (which it won with an absolute majority), and the conservative PP also moved to the centre (Vallès, 1994: 87). One reason for the moderation of the PSOE was that, in the early 1990s, the government began pursuing economic policies designed to ensure Spain would meet the 'convergence criteria' for entry into the European Monetary Union (Gillespie, 1996: 427). These included harsh measures to combat both inflation and unemployment, which were hardly in line with traditional socialist economic policy.

On the right, the PP remained rather vague as to its policies on the economy, preferring to concentrate on criticizing the government. On social matters, however, the party did display some moderation. For example, in the campaign for the 1993 election, it accepted 'the non-criminality of abortion' (Vallès, 1994: 88). As a result of this moderation by both main parties, and also of the lack of firm policy commitments from either side, by the mid-1990s there were few fundamental policy differences between the parties (Gillespie, 1996: 427).

In spite of this convergence between the mainstream parties, the Spanish right-wing extremist parties have not encountered electoral success in the period since 1989, however. Frente Nacional did not even compete in the general elections of 1989 and 1993, and in 1994 the party was dissolved. As for the Falangistas, they recorded 0.15 percent of the vote in 1989, secured a mere 0.04 percent of the vote in 1993, won only 0.06 percent of the ballots in 1996, and gathered only 0.09 percent of the votes in 2000. Thus, in Spain as in Britain, the convergence of the parties of the mainstream left and the mainstream right has not resulted in higher vote shares for the parties of the extreme right.

Denmark is a third country in which the parties of the mainstream right and the parties of the mainstream left have recently converged. Although the convergence is less marked than in Britain and in Spain, as Figure 4.2 above illustrates, the Socialdemokratiet (SD) have moderated their ideology since 1993, and Venstre (V) and the Konservative Folkeparti (KF) have also undergone ideological moderation.

As was explained earlier, the losses that the KF suffered in both the 1994 and 1998 elections led to a reassessment of the party's policies, and to the resignation of the party's leader. V also replaced their leader in 1998, and the new helmsman, Arne Fogh Rasmussen, at once showed himself keen to move towards the centre and to adopt a 'more accommodating and co-operative style' (Elklit, 1999: 141). The moderation of the Danish right therefore came about in large part because of electoral and governmental failure.

On the left, the SD had to contend with the politics of coalition. In 1993, following the collapse of the conservative-liberal government, the SD entered into a coalition with the Radikale Venstre (RV), the Centrum-demokraterne (CD) and the Kristeligt Folkeparti (KRF) (Thomsen, 1995: 316). Centripetal competition then continued after the 1994 election, when the SD entered into coalition with the RV and the CD, and after the election of 1998, when they joined forces with just the RV. Throughout this period compromise with their more centrist coalition partners became necessary. In 1997, for example, the government adopted a tougher line on immigration, and replaced the minister of the interior with someone 'considered more strict on foreigners' (Elklit, 1999: 140). Thus, for the SD, ideological moderation in the period since 1993 was very much a result of the pressure of compromise between coalition partners.

In contrast to the British and Spanish cases just discussed, the vote share of the Danish right-wing extremist parties did increase as the parties of the mainstream left and mainstream right converged. In 1994 the Danish FRPd secured 6.4 percent of the vote – a result that equalled its score of 1990. At the 1998 election, the share of the vote going to parties of the extreme right had risen to 9.8 percent, with the DF recording 7.4 percent of the vote and the FRPd polling 2.4 percent. In 2001, the DF increased its score again, this time winning 12.0 percent of the vote. Unlike in Britain and in Spain, in the case of Denmark, therefore, the hypothesis that convergence of the main-stream parties will lead to greater electoral scores for the parties of the extreme right is borne out in practice.

In view of the mixed evidence that has emerged from the discussion of Britain, Spain and Denmark, the fifth hypothesis advanced above requires greater examination. As with the previous hypotheses, it can be tested more systematically by means of a correlation. The electoral scores of the parties of the extreme right can be correlated with the degree of convergence that exists between the mainstream right party (MR) and the mainstream left party (ML). The convergence scores are calculated as follows:

1 – (MR party score on left–right scale – ML party score on left–right scale)

This 'convergence index' runs from a maximum of 1 to a minimum of 0. High scores indicate a significant degree of convergence between the parties of the mainstream right and the parties of the mainstream left, and low scores denote a low degree of convergence between the two main-stream parties (for the scores of the parties on the left–right scale see Appendix A). If the hypothesis advanced above is correct, then a positive correlation between the two variables should be observed. That is, as the parties of the mainstream right and the parties of the mainstream left con-verge, so the electoral scores of the parties of the extreme right should increase.

In practice the correlation does indeed result in a positive score. When the degree of convergence between the most moderate mainstream parties of the left and the most moderate mainstream parties of the right is correlated with the electoral scores of the right-wing extremist parties, the Pearson correlation coefficient is .377. When the convergence between the largest parties of the mainstream left and the largest parties of the mainstream right is correlated with the electoral scores of the parties of the extreme right, the Pearson correlation coefficient is .340. Both correlation coefficients are statistically significant at the 0.01 level.[23]

The correlation coefficients thus suggest that convergence between the mainstream left and the mainstream right is indeed linked to higher electoral scores for the parties of the extreme right. As such, the suggestions made by Hainsworth and Kitschelt have been substantiated, if only at a bivariate level. These results also imply that patterns of party competition at the centre of the political spectrum go some way to explaining why the West European parties of the extreme right have experienced such differing levels of elect-oral success in the period since 1979.

Concluding remarks

By mapping the political space of the different countries under observation, and by locating the parties of the extreme right within that space, this chapter has been able to draw a number of conclusions about the influence that party competition has on the right-wing extremist party vote. In so doing, it has helped shed further light on why parties of the extreme right have experienced such varying levels of electoral success across Western Europe in the period 1979–2003.

In the first section of the analysis, the chapter examined the relationship between the ideological positions of the parties of the mainstream right and the right-wing extremist party vote. The findings of this investigation suggest that, in general, right-wing extremist parties perform better at the polls when their mainstream right-wing opponents are more moderate than they do when these competitors are more right-wing. In other words, the greater the political space available to the right of the parties of the mainstream right, the more successful the parties of the extreme right tend to be.

Having established how much political space is available on the extreme right of the political spectrum, the chapter then turned its attention to examining where the parties of the extreme are located within this space, and it explored the link between the ideological positions of the right-wing extremist parties and their electoral scores. The conclusions of this analysis suggest that right-wing extremist parties have tended to enjoy greater levels of electoral success when they themselves are more moderate than when they are ideologically more extreme. Their own ideological positions are therefore related to the level of success they experience at the polls.

As well as examining the positions of the parties of the mainstream right and the positions of the parties of the extreme right separately, the chapter also investigated the ways in which these two sets of parties interact. It found evidence that right-wing extremist parties are more likely to be successful when they themselves are more moderate *and* when their mainstream right opponents are more moderate. By contrast, right-wing extremist parties have tended to encounter lower electoral success when *both* they *and* their mainstream right competitors are more right-wing.

In a final section, the chapter considered the influence of patterns of party competition at the centre of the political spectrum. It investigated the relationship between the convergence of the mainstream parties and the right-wing extremist party vote. As was anticipated, the findings from this analysis suggest that high levels of ideological convergence between the parties of the mainstream left and the parties of the mainstream right are associated with high right-wing extremist party scores. In contrast, low levels of ideological convergence between the mainstream parties are linked with lower right-wing extremist party scores.

Throughout the analysis undertaken in this chapter, it has also become apparent that some parties of the extreme right are more likely to experience electoral success in unfavourable situations than other parties. Parties that have passed the 'threshold of relevance', or that have gained what may be described as a 'critical mass' within their respective political system, appear better able to withstand pressures from their mainstream right opponents. In addition, these parties seem more capable of retaining their electoral support when they radicalize – a shift which, in other instances, leads to the loss of votes. By contrast, smaller, less politically relevant right-wing extremist parties appear more sensitive to the pressures of party competition.

This chapter has thus clearly shown that the electoral scores of the parties of the extreme right are linked to the different patterns of competition at work in the political systems under investigation. More specifically, the proximity of the mainstream right competitors, the ideological positions of the right-wing extremist parties themselves, and the degree of convergence that exists between the parties of the mainstream left and the mainstream right are all factors that add to an overall explanation of why some right-wing extremist parties have encountered success at the polls when others have not. This said, the same warnings as were made at the end of Chapter 2 and Chapter 3 should be made here: patterns of party competition are only one set of explanations for the varying electoral success of the parties of the extreme right across Western Europe, and to assess their influence accurately in an overall account of the disparity in the right-wing extremist party vote, they must be considered in conjunction with other explanatory factors.

Before the different explanatory factors are examined together in a series of multivariate analyses in Chapter 6, a further set of explanations for the variation in the electoral fortunes of the parties of the extreme right will first be considered in depth. The next chapter turns its attention to the institutional frameworks that exist in the different countries in which the right-wing extremist parties compete, and assesses the extent to which the variation in the scores of the right-wing extremist parties may be explained by the presence of different institutional structures.

Notes

1 More specifically, May argued that party activists were more ideologically radical than national leaders or ordinary sympathizers, that ordinary party voters assumed more moderate positions, and that national party leaders were more extreme than voters, but less radical than activists. More recent work, based on survey data, has cast some doubt on May's proposition. Norris (1995), for example, has argued that it is national party leaders who embrace the most radical opinions.

2 In addition to examining the self-placement of party sympathizers on a left–right scale, Sani and Sartori (1983) also consider the attitudes of voters towards a variety of issues.

3 Huber argues that partisanship causes extremist party supporters to perceive their left–right location as more extreme than would be expected given their issue attitudes. This is because the partisanship component of left–right orientations is larger for partisans of extremist parties (1989: 616–18).

4 Finer questions this assumption, maintaining instead that party programmes that contain a vast number of policy pledges are often without meaning. He argues that the longer the manifestos, 'the less meaningful the choice between parties and the more nebulous the claim to have a mandate to execute the manifestos' (1975: 379–80).

5 Strictly speaking, expert judgements were first used by Michael John Morgan in a dissertation entitled 'The Modelling of Governmental Coalition Formations: A Policy-Based Approach with Internal Measurement' (University of Michigan PhD, 1976). This dissertation and the results of its survey were never published, however. Eight years later, Castles and Mair more or less replicated Morgan's research design, without even knowing it. Their study, and the new approach that they were credited with having developed, were to become very influential. For a retrospective review of the importance of this work see Pedersen (1997) and Mair and Castles (1997).

6 Greece does not feature in the studies by Castles and Mair or Huber and Inglehart; Portugal is not included in the analysis by Castles and Mair; and Switzerland is omitted from the works by Castles and Mair and Laver and Hunt. The Portuguese political space is thus mapped at only three time points, and the Greek and Swiss political spaces at only two.

7 In addition to locating parties on different policy dimensions, in two of the studies (Laver and Hunt, and Lubbers) experts were asked to consider different facets of the internal organization of the parties.

8 The dimensions that refer to socio-economic policy and social policy feature in all three of the studies that do not contain an overarching left–right scale. These dimensions have been selected because they concern policy areas that are central to the left–right ideological divide. The decision to make use of the average positions of the parties on these two different dimensions was further influenced by helpful comments on the subject by Michael Laver (personal communication).

9 While the left–right scale in Lubbers's survey ran from 0 to 10, the scales that referred to the organizational characteristics of the parties ran from 1 to 10.

10 In contrast to other studies that employ continuous scales on which parties may be located at any point, Huber and Inglehart make use of a scale that is made up of ten 'boxes' or 'spaces'. Experts were asked to write down the parties' name in one of the ten spaces. If they so wished, they could locate two or more parties within the same space.

11 Normalization allows any score to be mapped to the relevant point between 0 and 1, reflecting the location of that score between the minimum possible score and the maximum possible score. Normalized scores are calculated as follows: (score − minimum possible score) / (maximum possible score − minimum possible score).

12 To assist in the comparison across the countries, Figures 4.1–4.8 and 4.11 – that is, all the figures that illustrate the political space of the systems under investigation in this book – are replicated in Appendix B.

13 Pedersen identifies four different thresholds that parties pass or strive to pass. The first of these is the 'threshold of declaration', which is described as 'the point in time when a political group declares its intention to participate in elections' (1982: 6). Next follows the 'threshold of authorization', which parties pass once they have fulfilled all legal obligations required to stand in elections. The third threshold is the 'threshold of representation' (a concept originally introduced by Stein Rokkan), which refers to the 'barrier which parties have to cross in order to obtain seats in the legislature' (1982: 7). The final threshold – and the one which is of importance here – is the 'threshold of relevance', which is derived from Sartori's concept of relevance (1976). To pass this threshold parties must assume either 'coalition potential' or 'blackmail potential'.

14 It should be noted that there was a lack of continuity within the Italian mainstream right in this period because the Democrazia Cristiana (DC) fell apart after 1992. As the First Republic collapsed due to countless revelations of corruption and bribery, and the Second Republic was established, the DC was succeeded by various smaller parties including the Centro Cristiano Democratico (CCD) and the Partito Popolare Italiano (PPI). Since 1994 the largest party on the right of the political spectrum in Italy is Forza Italia (FI).

15 The vote of each right-wing extremist party at each election is correlated with the position of the mainstream right party as reported in the expert judgement study carried out closest to that election. For example, the electoral score of the Austrian FPÖ in the 1983 election is correlated with the position of the ÖVP as reported in the survey carried out in 1982 by Castles and Mair. In some instances, the expert judgement study was carried out after the election, while in others it was undertaken before the election (as in the Austrian example just given). In instances where the time interval between the election and the previous expert judgement study is the same as the interval between the election and the subsequent expert judgement study, the subsequent expert judgement study is used. For example, the electoral scores of the Swedish extreme right parties in the 1991 election are correlated with the positions of the party of the mainstream right in the Huber and Inglehart survey (carried out in 1993), rather than with the positions of the party of the mainstream right in the Laver and Hunt study (carried out in 1989).

16 The Pearson correlation was used because the data in question are ratio scale data, and the relationship between the electoral scores of the right-wing extremist parties and the ideological positions of the parties of the mainstream right is assumed to be a linear one. A one-tailed test was carried out, as the direction of the relationship between the two variables was already hypothesized: a negative relationship was predicted. A significance test was used because, even though the book has adopted an inclusive approach as to which right-wing extremist parties are incorporated in the analysis, strictly speaking, the parties under observation constitute a sample rather than a population. This is because the book examines a limited time period only, and also because some very minor right-wing extremist parties are omitted from the investigation. The parties that are included in the analysis therefore form a sub-set of the greater population of right-wing extremist parties, and a significance test is thus appropriate.

17 The correlation coefficient is $-.378$ when the electoral scores of the right-wing extremist parties are correlated with the positions of the most right-wing

mainstream right parties. If the electoral scores of the right-wing extremist parties are correlated with the position of the largest mainstream right parties then the correlation coefficient is $-.262$ (significant at the 0.01 level).

18 See note 16.

19 This scenario, and indeed all the hypotheses advanced in this chapter, are informed by the spatial theory of voting, first advanced in the work of Anthony Downs (1957). It is therefore assumed throughout this chapter that, since citizens act rationally, each 'citizen casts his vote for the party he believes will provide him with more benefits than any other' (Downs, 1957: 36). Thus, 'each voter votes for the party whose ideology is at the position closest to his or her preferred position' (Laver, 1997: 91).

20 Unfortunately the SD were not included in the Huber and Inglehart expert judgement study. It is therefore impossible to ascertain whether they became more extreme in the period 1993–2000 or whether they moderated their ideology.

21 Kitschelt sees the degree of convergence between the mainstream right and the mainstream left as a factor that shapes the *type* of right-wing extremist party likely to prosper in each country. He argues that where convergence is high and where 'partocracy' holds sway, as in Austria and Italy, for example, the most likely type of right-wing extremist party to emerge is the populist anti-statist one. Kitschelt concentrates more on discussing these different types of party than on directly examining their electoral success. However, given that some types are considered more successful at the polls than others (such as New Radical Right and populist anti-statist parties), the parties' electoral success is considered in an indirect way.

22 It should be noted that the political space in Greece and in Switzerland was mapped at only two time points rather than at four. Thus, in the case of Greece, it is not possible to detect whether there was convergence between the mainstream left and the mainstream right in the period before 1989. In the case of Switzerland, no information is available on the patterns of party competition before 1993.

23 See note 16.

5

The institutional environment

Having examined the influence of party ideology and the effects of party organization and leadership on the right-wing extremist party vote, and having also investigated the impact of different patterns of party competition on the fortunes of the parties of the extreme right, the analysis now turns its attention to the institutional frameworks present in the different countries in which the parties compete. After all, political parties do not exist in a vacuum; they are instead conditioned to a greater or lesser extent by the 'rules of the game' of the political system in which they operate. Any attempt to explain why certain West European right-wing extremist parties have performed better at the polls than others would therefore be incomplete without an in-depth examination of the institutional environment in which these parties exist.

This chapter focuses on two broad sets of institutional features that are considered potentially relevant to an overall explanation of why some right-wing extremist parties have experienced greater electoral success than others. First, the chapter examines the impact electoral systems have on parties of the extreme right. It begins by concentrating on the two main dimensions of electoral systems – the district magnitude and the electoral formula – and it investigates the ways in which these features may influence how well right-wing extremist parties perform at the polls. Then, by examining their disproportionality profiles, it considers the overall effect that electoral systems have on the West European parties of the extreme right.

Since electoral systems form only a part of the electoral laws of a country, in a second section, the chapter turns its attention to other components of the electoral law. In a three-pronged approach it considers (1) the rules governing how parties and candidates may gain access to the ballot; (2) the laws relating to how they may access the broadcast media; and (3) the regulations regarding qualification for state subventions. It examines these three laws both separately and together, and it investigates whether differences in these electoral institutions may help account for the variety in the electoral scores of the right-wing extremist parties. The chapter concludes with a discussion of the relative importance of the different institutional determinants in an overall explanation of the disparity in the electoral fortunes of the right-wing extremist parties across Western Europe.

Electoral systems

The electoral system is an institutional feature that is considered key in explaining the success of parties at the polls. Indeed, ever since Maurice Duverger's seminal book *Political Parties* (1954), electoral systems have been commonly assumed to affect not only the size of parties' representation in parliament, but also the vote shares they receive at the polls. This is because the way in which votes are translated into seats (that is, the mechanical effect of the electoral system) induces a psychological effect on both voters and party elites. This psychological effect comes into being when voters realize that, due to the mechanical workings of the electoral system, small parties may be underrepresented. A vote for a small party may thus become a wasted one and, rather than support this small party, voters may choose instead to favour the least unacceptable of the larger parties. In addition, party leaders may anticipate the mechanical workings of the electoral system and may decide not to compete in certain elections where representation cannot be guaranteed (Duverger, 1954; Taagepera and Shugart, 1989: 65, 118; Blais and Carty, 1991: 80–1).

In view of the relationship between the mechanical and the psychological effects of electoral systems, it is reasonable to predict that the stronger the mechanical effect of the electoral system the stronger its psychological effect on both voters and party elites.[1] In other words, the more an electoral system favours larger parties and discriminates against smaller ones, the more likely it will be that voters will choose to favour a larger party rather than waste their votes on the smaller competitor. Therefore, a strong mechanical effect may, in theory, lead to small parties experiencing low electoral scores.

In one of the very few comparative studies that examines the impact of electoral systems on smaller competitors, Peter Mair discusses the psychological effect of electoral systems. He argues that:

> It goes almost without saying that, *ceteris paribus*, restrictive electoral systems which impose high thresholds and which offer major bonuses to large parties will be most unlikely to provide incentives for small party support. It can therefore be suggested that more proportional electoral systems will be more likely to favour small parties, and hence we can formally hypothesize that *the small party vote will be greater in more proportional electoral systems*. (1991: 54, italics in original)

In light of such assumptions and such arguments, and given that, in the main, right-wing extremist parties continue to be small competitors, it is reasonable to suggest that one possible explanation for why certain parties of the extreme right perform better at the polls than others is that the different parties compete under different electoral systems.[2] As such, the disparity in the electoral fortunes of the parties of the extreme right across Western

Europe may be explained, in part at least, by the presence of different electoral systems. More specifically, in a similar vein to Mair's predictions noted above, it can be hypothesized that the more proportional the electoral system, the more successful the parties of the extreme right will be.

In order to test this hypothesis, and to empirically examine the influence of electoral systems on the West European parties of the extreme right, the next two sections of this chapter focus on the effect of the different determinants of electoral systems: the district magnitude and the electoral formula. Each of these two dimensions has important consequences for the proportionality of the electoral outcome.

District magnitude and legal thresholds

The district magnitude of an electoral system refers to the number of representatives elected in a district. Whereas majoritarian electoral systems usually have a district magnitude of 1, proportional systems always have multi-member districts.[3] Their magnitude normally varies in line with population, with more populous districts returning more representatives to parliament than less populous ones.[4]

Ever since Douglas W. Rae's influential study *The Political Consequences of Electoral Laws* (1967), the district magnitude has been considered crucially important in determining the proportionality of the electoral result. In fact, when majoritarian and proportional electoral systems are considered separately, the district magnitude of the system has since been shown to be the most important determinant of proportionality. If all electoral systems are taken together, however, the electoral formula becomes more important than the district magnitude in determining the proportionality of the electoral outcome (Taagepera and Shugart, 1989: 112; Lijphart, 1994: 98–100; Katz, 1997: 137–8).

Determining the district magnitude of an electoral system is often not as straightforward as might first appear, however. In the simplest cases of proportional representation, a system of single-tier districting is used in which the country is divided into a number of districts each of which elects a number of representatives to the legislature. Single-tier districting is in operation in the Netherlands, Portugal, Spain and Switzerland and was also employed in the 1986 French legislative election, when each *département* constituted an electoral district. Norway used this system up to and including the 1985 parliamentary election too. In the majority of proportional systems, however, a multi-tiered districting system is employed in which a certain number of seats are allocated at a higher tier, such as the region or the country as a whole. All votes that are not needed for seat allocation at the lower tier are pooled and used to determine the seats allocated at the higher tier. Belgium, Denmark, Germany, Italy, Norway (since 1989) and Sweden all use a two-tiered districting system. Austria (since 1994), by contrast, has a districting system that incorporates three tiers.[5] Table 5.1

Table 5.1 Dimensions of electoral systems in Western Europe, 1979–2003

Country	Date	Tier[a]	Formula[b]	Average district magnitude[c]	Number of districts	Assembly size	Legal threshold[d]	Effective threshold[e] (%)
Austria	1979–90	H	d'Hondt	91.50	2	183	1 const. seat	2.6[f]
		L	LR-Hare	20.33	9			
	1994–2002	N	d'Hondt	183	1	183	1 const. seat or 4% (N)	4
		H	d'Hondt	20.33	9			
		L	LR-Hare	4.26	43			
Belgium	1981–91	H	H-B	23.56	9	212	0.66 of a Hare quota	4.8[f]
		L	LR-Hare	7.07	30			
	1995–2003	H	H-B	15.00	10	150	0.33 of a Hare quota	2.8
		L	LR-Hare	7.50	20			
Britain	1979–87		Plurality	1	650	650	–	37.5[g]
	1992		Plurality	1	651	651	–	37.5[g]
	1997–2001		Plurality	1	659	659	–	37.5[g]
Denmark	1979–2001	H	LR-Hare	179	1	179	Special rules[i]	2
		L	MSL	7.32[h]	19			
France[j]	1981		Maj-Plur	1	474	474	–	37.5[g]
	1986		d'Hondt	5.79	96	556	5% (D)	11.0
	1988–2002		Maj-Plur	1	555	555	–	37.5[g]
Germany	1980–83	H	d'Hondt	496	1	496[k]	5% (N) or 3 const. seats	5
		L	Plurality	1	248			
	1987	H	LR-Hare	496	1	496[k]	5% (N) or 3 const. seats	5
		L	Plurality	1	248			
	1990–98	H	LR-Hare	656	1	656[k]	5% (N) or 3 const. seats	5
		L	Plurality	1	328			
	1998–2002	H	LR-Hare	598	1	598[k]	5% (N) or 3 const. seats	5
		L	Plurality	1	299			

Table 5.1 (continued)

Country	Date	Tier[a]	Formula[b]	Average district magnitude[c]	Number of districts	Assembly size	Legal threshold[d] (%)	Effective threshold[e] (%)
Greece[l]	1981	S	LR-Hare	12	1	12	17 (N)	17
		H	d'Hondt[j]	18	1	18	17 (N)	17
		M	d'Hondt[j]	4.22	9	38	17 (N)	17
		L	d'Hondt[j]	4.14	56	232	–	14.6
weighted mean			d'Hondt[j]	5.30		184.77	–	16.1
	1985	S	d'Hondt	12	1	12	–	5.8
		H	d'Hondt[j]	18	1	18	–	3.9
		M	d'Hondt[j]	4.22	9	38	–	14.4
		L	d'Hondt[j]	4.14	56	232	–	14.6
weighted mean			d'Hondt[j]	5.30		184.77	–	14.7
	1989–90	S	d'Hondt	12	1	12	–	3.3
		H	LR-Hare	22.15	13	288	–	
		L	LR-Droop	5.14	56		–	
	1993–2000	S	d'Hondt	12	1	12	3	3
		H	d'Hondt[j]		1		3	
		M	LR-Hare[i]		13		3	
		L	d'Hondt[j]		56	288	3	
Italy	1979–92	H	LR-Hare	630	1	630	1 const. seat and 300,000 votes	2.0[m]
		L	LR-Imp	19.69	32			
	1994–2001	H	LR-Hare	155	1	630	4% (N) for higher tier allocation only	4
		L	Plurality	1	475			
Netherlands	1981–2003		d'Hondt	150	1	150	0.67% (N)	0.67
Norway	1981		MSL	7.75	20	155	–	8.6
	1985		MSL	7.85	20	157	–	8.5
	1989–2001	H	MSL	165	1	165	4% (N)	4
		L	MSL	8.26[n]	19			

Country	Years	Tier	Formula	Magnitude	Districts	Seats	Threshold	Eff. threshold
Portugal	1979–87		d'Hondt	12.50	20	250	–	5.6
	1991–2002		d'Hondt	11.50	20	230	–	6.0
Spain	1979–2000		d'Hondt	6.73	52	350	3% (D)	9.7
Sweden	1979–2002	H	MSL	349	1	349	4% (N)[p]	4
		L	MSL	11.07[o]	28		4% (N) or 12% in one const.	
Switzerland	1979–2003		H-B	7.69	26	200	–	8.6

Notes: [a] H: higher; L: lower; M: medium; N: national; S: state. [b] H-B: Hagenbach-Bischoff formula; LR-Droop: largest remainder Droop formula; LR-Hare: largest remainder Hare formula; LR-Imp: largest remainder Imperiali formula; Maj-Plur: majority-plurality two-ballot formula; MSL: Modified Sainte-Laguë formula. In the case of multi-tiered electoral systems, the table shows which tier is decisive by the use of italics. In remainder-transfer systems this is the formula used at the lower tier, while in adjustment-seat systems this is the formula used at the higher tier. [c] The average district magnitude is calculated by dividing the number of seats in the legislature by the number of districts. [d] Const.: constituency; D: legal threshold applied at the district level; N: legal threshold imposed at the national level. [e] The effective threshold is either determined by the legal threshold of the electoral system, or inferred from the district magnitude, whichever value is higher. If inferred from the district magnitude, the effective threshold is calculated by taking the mean of the upper threshold and the lower threshold: $75/(M + 1)$, where M is the average district magnitude. [f] See Lijphart (1994: 38–9). [g] Approximation (see text for details). [h] In Denmark only 139 seats are distributed among the constituencies. [i] To receive seats at the higher level, Danish parties must either (1) have won at least one constituency seat, (2) have obtained at least as many votes as on average were cast per constituency in at least two of the three regions, or (3) have obtained at least 2 percent of all valid votes in the country as a whole. [j] Metropolitan France only. [k] Not including *Überhangmandate*. [l] The Greek electoral system is extremely complex. From 1981 to 1985 and again from 1993 to 2000, it had four separate tiers (L, M, H and S), and, rather than have a decisive tier, it has taken the form of four separate and parallel elections to four mini-assemblies. Although the electoral formula used in these two periods has been the LR-Hare formula, it actually operates like the d'Hondt formula. By contrast, the electoral system employed in the period 1989–90 was a remainder-transfer system with three separate tiers (L, H, and S). For further details on the Greek electoral systems see Lijphart (1994: 33–45). [m] See Lijphart (1994: 38). [n] In Norway only 157 seats are distributed among the constituencies. [o] In Sweden only 310 seats are distributed among the constituencies. [p] Swedish parties that have obtained seats at the lower level through the 12 percent rule *only* are excluded from representation at the higher tier.

Source: Lijphart (1994); Gallagher *et al.* (1995); LeDuc *et al.* (1996); Inter-Parliamentary Union Parline Database; Lijphart Election Archive.

illustrates which electoral systems have single-tier districting and which have multi-tiered districting.

A notable feature of multi-tier districting is that different tiers may have different district magnitudes and may employ different electoral formulae. In such instances, it becomes important to determine which tier is the decisive one for the proportionality of the electoral outcome. This, as Lijphart explains, depends on how seats are allocated. In so-called remainder-transfer systems all votes not needed in seat allocation at the lower tier are transferred to the higher district(s). This implies that whatever the district magnitude and formula used at the higher tier, large parties cannot be systematically favoured since the parties with the highest number of remaining votes are not necessarily the largest ones. In remainder-transfer systems the decisive tier for the proportionality of the electoral outcome is therefore the *lower* tier (Lijphart, 1994: 32). By contrast, in adjustment-seat systems, although seats are initially allocated in the lower-level districts, the final allocation occurs at the higher tier and depends on all the votes cast in all of the lower-tier districts, which together make-up the higher-tier district. In adjustment-seat systems this *higher* tier thus becomes the crucial one as regards the proportionality of the electoral result (Lijphart, 1994: 32–6). In Table 5.1 the decisive tiers of the electoral systems under observation are reported in italics.

Identifying the decisive tier of an electoral system allows for the relationship between the district magnitude and the right-wing extremist party vote to be properly examined. Since it has been widely demonstrated that, in proportional systems, the proportionality of the electoral outcome improves as the district magnitude increases, it is quite reasonable to expect right-wing extremist parties to perform better where the district magnitude (at the decisive level) is high than where it is low (Taagepera and Shugart, 1989: 112; Lijphart, 1994: 20 and 1999: 150–2; Katz, 1997: 134).[6] In systems with high district magnitude a much smaller share of the vote is required to win a seat than in systems with low district magnitude, and voters are assumed to be aware of this increased chance of representation and to appreciate that their vote might not be 'wasted' even though they are casting it in favour of a small party.

Yet before the influence of district magnitude may be fully investigated, it is important to observe that in some instances, as illustrated in Table 5.1, the effect of district magnitude is overridden by the imposition of legal thresholds. Such thresholds are introduced in cases where the district magnitude is so large that, left unchecked, parties would be able to gain parliamentary representation with only a very small share of the vote. Since situations such as these are usually considered undesirable, as they bring with them the danger of party system fragmentation and governmental instability, legal thresholds have been introduced in many democracies.

Legal thresholds can take a number of forms. In some countries parties are required to win a minimum percentage of the vote to secure parliamentary representation. In the French election of 1986, for example, parties were required to win 5 percent of the vote at the district level if they were to enter the Assemblée nationale (Lijphart, 1994: 22). Similarly, under the Norwegian electoral system introduced in 1989 parties may only secure parliamentary representation if they win 4 percent of the vote at the national level (Lijphart, 1994: 34–5; Gallagher *et al.*, 2001: 310). Elsewhere parties may be required to win a certain number of seats in lower-level districts if they are to gain representation in the legislature. Under the electoral system that was in operation in Austria until 1990, for example, parties were required to win one constituency seat if they were to be represented in the Nationalrat (Lijphart, 1994: 38–9). It is sometimes the case that these two forms of legal threshold are combined. In Germany, for instance, parties may gain parliamentary representations *either* by winning 5 percent of the vote at the national level *or* by securing at least three constituency seats (Farrell, 2001: 97–111; Inter-Parliamentary Union Parline Database). In Italy, under the pre-1993 electoral system, parties were required to win 300,000 votes *and* one constituency seat if they were to gain parliamentary representation (Lijphart, 1994: 38; Lijphart Election Archive).

When legal thresholds exist, the district magnitude may no longer determine the share of the vote a party must win in order to gain parliamentary representation. To take account of this fact, and to enable the comparison of electoral systems across countries with and without legal thresholds, Taagepera and Shugart calculate an 'effective magnitude' (1989: 135–41, 266–9). Lijphart, by contrast, estimates an 'effective threshold', expressed as a percentage of the vote a party must win if it is to secure parliamentary representation (1994: 25–30). Though different in nature, both approaches reflect the real constraints that electoral systems impose on political parties. They thus allow for the influence of district magnitude on the right-wing extremist party vote to be finally examined.

In this chapter Lijphart's 'effective threshold' is adopted in preference to Taagepera and Shugart's 'effective magnitude'. The reason for this is twofold. First, since the nature of the relationship between the district magnitude and the proportionality of the electoral outcome depends on the type of electoral formula employed (that is, increases in district magnitude lead to lower levels of proportionality under majoritarian formulae but bring higher levels of proportionality under proportional formulae), majoritarian and proportional systems must be examined separately if the effective magnitude approach is adopted. However, if the effective threshold approach is used, both types of system may be analysed together. Second, as Lijphart himself argues, since the effective threshold is expressed in terms of a percentage of the vote a party must win in order to gain representation, it is clearer and more meaningful in reflecting the constraints electoral systems impose on small parties than the effective magnitude (1994: 26, 182).

The effective threshold of an electoral system may either be clearly determined by the legal threshold (if such a threshold exists), or be inferred by the
district magnitude. In the latter case, the *average* district magnitude is used,
because in systems with multi-member districts the district magnitude tends
to vary from district to district. The average district magnitude is calculated
by simply dividing the total number of seats in the legislature by the number
of districts. The effective threshold is then worked out by taking the mean
of the upper threshold (the vote share with which a party is guaranteed to
win a seat) and the lower threshold (the minimum percentage with which it
is possible for a party to gain representation). After some discussion, the
effective magnitude of an electoral system, when inferred from the average
district magnitude, has been agreed to be $75 / (M + 1)$, where M is the
average district magnitude (Lijphart, 1994: 26–30 and 1997; Penadés, 1997;
Taagepera, 1998).

Strictly speaking, when inferred from the average district magnitude, the
effective threshold of an electoral system is not a specific percentage of the
vote but a range of possibilities between the upper threshold and the lower
threshold. This range is particularly apparent in majoritarian electoral
systems. Here the upper threshold is 50 percent (plus one vote), since with
this score a party is guaranteed representation even under the most
unfavourable conditions. The lower threshold, in contrast, is more variable
and may be as low as 20 percent if votes are split relatively evenly between
competitors. In majoritarian systems (with single-member districts) the
effective threshold may thus be estimated to be approximately 37.5 percent
(see Taagepera, 1998: 394). Despite its slightly imprecise nature, the effective threshold remains a useful tool with which to assess the extent to which
parties are constrained by the electoral system. The effective thresholds of
the electoral systems under observation in this study are reported in the last
column of Table 5.1.

Having identified the decisive tier of the different electoral systems, and
having taken into account the impact of legal thresholds, it is now finally
possible to examine the effect of district magnitude on the vote share of the
right-wing extremist parties. Since the influence of the district magnitude is
reflected in the effective threshold, and since the district magnitude is considered a very important determinant of proportionality, it is reasonable to
expect right-wing extremist parties to perform better in systems with low
effective thresholds than in systems where the effective threshold is high.
The correlation between the right-wing extremist party vote (as reported in
Table 1.1 in Chapter 1) and the effective threshold should therefore be a negative one.

The correlation does indeed yield a negative score. When all electoral
systems are considered together, the Pearson correlation coefficient is -0.103,
and when proportional electoral systems are considered on their own, the
correlation coefficient is -0.203.[7] The first of these correlation coefficients is

not statistically significant, however.[8] Therefore, when all electoral systems are taken together, the conclusion must be drawn that the right-wing extremist party vote is *not* influenced by the effective threshold of the electoral system. When proportional electoral systems are considered on their own, however, the story is rather different.[9] The second correlation coefficient (-0.203) is statistically significant at the 0.05 level, suggesting that, when proportional electoral systems are taken on their own, high effective thresholds do appear to be associated with low right-wing extremist party scores.[10] These findings thus suggest that district magnitude and legal thresholds are important in helping to account for the disparity in the electoral scores of the right-wing extremist parties in proportional electoral systems. However, these two dimensions of electoral systems cease to have such explanatory power if all electoral systems are considered together.

The finding that high district magnitudes and low legal thresholds are linked with high right-wing extremist electoral scores when proportional electoral systems are considered on their own, but not when all electoral systems are taken together, is perhaps a little puzzling at first sight. It makes sense, however, given that, as was observed above, the district magnitude is the most important determinant of proportionality when majoritarian and proportional electoral systems are considered separately. It ceases to be so when all systems are examined together.

It remains premature to draw any conclusions about the influence of electoral systems on the right-wing extremist party vote at this stage of the discussion, however, because the district magnitude, it should be remembered, is not the only determinant of proportionality of the electoral outcome. The electoral formula also affects the proportionality with which votes are translated into seats. An examination of the impact of the electoral formula on the right-wing extremist party vote will therefore enable further conclusions to be reached.

Electoral formulae

The formula of an electoral system refers to the method used to translate votes into seats. Two main types of electoral formula exist: majoritarian formulae and proportional formulae, and within each of these categories, a number of sub-groups can be found. Majoritarian electoral formulae, which allocate seats in such a fashion that 'the winner takes all', aim to discourage multipartism and promote the construction of parliamentary majorities. They thus reflect a concern for the stability of the political system rather than for the proportionality with which votes are translated into seats (Duverger, 1954; Rae, 1967). By contrast, proportional formulae distribute seats in some proportion to the votes cast for individual parties and/or candidates.

Of the 14 countries under observation in this study, France (with the notable exception of 1986) and Britain employ majoritarian formulae, whereas all other countries make use of proportional formulae – see Table 5.1, which reports which formulae are used in which countries. In Britain the plurality formula is used and candidates must simply win the largest share of the vote in order to gain parliamentary representation. By contrast, in France the double-ballot majority-plurality formula is employed. Here candidates may be elected after a first round of voting if they have gained an absolute majority of the votes cast. Most of the time, however, no candidate secures such a majority in the first round and a second round of voting takes place, in which all candidates with a share of the vote equivalent to 12.5 percent of the electorate (rather than 12.5 percent of the valid vote) on the first ballot compete. In the second round a candidate may win representation with a simple plurality of the vote. In practice, the second round of the French legislative elections is usually contested between two candidates only, although in recent years there has been a growing number of *triangulaires*, where three candidates have progressed to the second ballot.

As was the case with district magnitude, it has long been agreed in the literature on electoral systems that the formula affects the proportionality of the electoral outcome. When majoritarian and proportional electoral systems are considered together, the formula is judged to be an even more important determinant of proportionality than the district magnitude (Taagepera and Shugart, 1989: 112; Lijphart, 1994: 98–100; Katz, 1997: 137–8). Majoritarian formulae give rise to much greater disproportionality than proportional formulae as they tend to systematically favour larger parties. Small parties find it difficult to gain representation – unless their support is geographically concentrated – because they have little chance of winning the plurality or majority of the votes in an electoral district necessary to win a seat.

In the light of this, it is reasonable to assume that right-wing extremist parties should perform less well under majoritarian formulae than under proportional formulae. However, as Figure 5.1 illustrates, this has not been the case. When all types of electoral formula are considered together, there exists no clear relationship between the type of formula used and the electoral scores of the parties of the extreme right. Instead, while right-wing extremist parties have sometimes performed poorly under majoritarian formulae (as in Britain), as was hypothesized, they have also recorded low electoral scores in countries that employ proportional formulae (as in Germany, Greece, the Netherlands, Portugal and Spain). Equally, although extremist parties have sometimes fared well at the polls under proportional formulae (in Austria, France 1986, Italy and Norway, for example), they have also experienced considerable electoral success under majoritarian formulae (as in France).

The absence of a clear relationship between the type of electoral formula and the right-wing extremist party vote is further illustrated if proportional formulae are considered on their own. The countries under observation in this study make use of a number of different proportional formulae and,

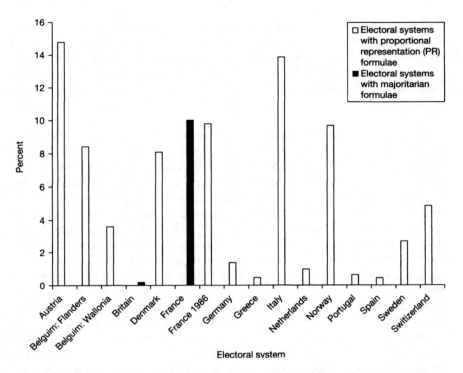

Figure 5.1 Electoral formula and mean votes for extreme right parties, 1979–2003

Notes: The mean vote is calculated as follows: the vote share obtained by all right-wing extremist parties in a given country for each election is summed. This total is then divided by the number of elections in which right-wing extremist parties competed. In the case of multi-tiered electoral systems the graph reports the formula used at the decisive tier. In remainder-transfer systems this is the formula used at the lower tier, while in adjustment-seat systems this is the formula used at the higher tier (see also Table 5.1).
Sources: Mackie and Rose (1991, 1997); Cheles *et al.* (1995); Betz and Immerfall (1998); Hainsworth (2000a); Elections around the World; Parties and Elections in Europe.

although the differences are fairly small, the various formulae can be ranked according to their proportionality.

Two main types of proportional formula are employed in the countries under investigation: highest-average formulae and largest-remainder formulae. Highest-average formulae allocate seats to parties by dividing their votes by a series of divisors. At each stage of the process, the party with the highest average vote is awarded a seat, and the process continues until all the seats have been filled. The d'Hondt formula, the Sainte-Laguë formula and the Modified Sainte-Laguë formula are all examples of highest-average formulae.[11] By contrast, largest-remainder formulae employ electoral quotas to allocate seats. Parties are awarded seats according to the number of quotas they have won, and any remaining seats are allocated to parties with the largest remainder of votes. Common quotas include the Hare quota, the Droop quota and the Imperiali quota, which all lend their names to various electoral formulae.[12] Also relevant to this study is the Hagenbach-Bischoff formula, which combines the highest-average method with a quota.[13] Table 5.1 above illustrates which formulae are used in the different countries under observation in this study.

There is a broad consensus in the literature on electoral systems that the d'Hondt and the Imperiali formulae are the least proportional of the proportional formulae, that the Modified Sainte-Laguë and the Droop formulae form an intermediate category, and that the Hare formula is the most proportional of the proportional formula (Lijphart, 1994: 24, 159; Farrell, 2001: 156).[14] Since the results of the Hagenbach-Bischoff electoral formula are always identical to those of the d'Hondt formula, the Hagenbach-Bischoff formula can be included in the group of least proportional formulae (Lijphart, 1994: 192). From these rankings, it is reasonable to expect right-wing extremist parties to perform best in countries which employ the Hare electoral formula, less well in countries which use the Modified Sainte-Laguë formula or the Droop formula, and least well in countries which employ the d'Hondt, the Imperiali or the Hagenbach-Bischoff formula.

As is illustrated in Table 5.2, no such pattern emerges, however. Although right-wing extremist parties have encountered electoral success in Italy, where, in the period since 1993, the Hare formula is used at the decisive tier, they have also performed well under the less proportional d'Hondt formula, as in France in 1986.[15] Equally, certain parties of the extreme right have recorded low electoral scores in spite of the fact that they have competed under the most proportional type of proportional formula. The German right-wing extremist parties, for example, have not fared well at the polls even though they have competed under the Hare formula since 1987.

The lack of a clear relationship between the electoral formula used and the right-wing extremist party vote is somewhat surprising. Especially remarkable is the fact that, in terms of right-wing extremist party success, no difference emerges between countries which employ majoritarian formulae and those that make use of proportional ones, even though, as was noted above, when all electoral systems are considered together, the formula is deemed to be the most important determinant of proportionality. This finding questions the workings of the psychological effects of electoral systems, as there is little evidence here to suggest that majoritarian electoral systems have consistently discouraged voters from favouring smaller parties such as those of the extreme right. It also raises serious doubts over the validity of the common assumption made by proponents of majoritarian electoral systems that proportional electoral systems promote extremism (Carter, 2002, 2004).

Before any final conclusions are drawn about the influence of electoral systems on the extremist party vote, however, it is useful to investigate the

Table 5.2 Electoral formulae and the mean right-wing extremist party vote, 1979–2003

Country	Period	Number of elections[a]	Formula[b]	Mean right-wing extremist party vote (%)[c]
Italy	1994–2001	3	Largest remainder Hare	21.6
Austria	1979–2002	8	Largest remainder Hare	14.8
Denmark	1979–2001	9	Largest remainder Hare	8.1
Germany	1987–2002	5	Largest remainder Hare	1.9
Norway	1981–2001	6	Modified Sainte-Laguë	9.7
Sweden	1979–2002	8 (4)	Modified Sainte-Laguë	2.7
France	1986	1	d'Hondt	9.8
Flanders	1981–2003	7	Hagenbach-Bischoff	8.4
Italy	1979–92	4	Largest Remainder Imperiali	8.2
Switzerland	1979–2003	7	Hagenbach-Bischoff	4.9
Wallonia	1981–2003	7 (6)	Hagenbach-Bischoff	3.6
Netherlands	1981–2003	8	d'Hondt	1.0
Portugal	1979–2002	9 (5)	d'Hondt	0.7
Spain	1979–2000	7	d'Hondt	0.5
Germany	1980–83	2	d'Hondt	0.2
France	1981 and 1988–2002	5	Majority-plurality	10.0
Britain	1979–2001	6	Plurality	0.2

Notes: The cases are ranked from most to least proportional electoral formula. [a]Figures in parentheses indicate the number of elections in the period 1979–2003 in which right-wing extremist parties competed. [b]In the case of multi-tiered electoral systems the table reports the formula used at the decisive tier. In remainder-transfer systems this is the formula used at the lower tier, while in adjustment-seat systems this is the formula used at the higher tier (see also Table 5.1). [c]The mean right-wing extremist party vote is calculated as in Figure 5.1. Greece is not included in the table because of the sheer complexity of the Greek electoral system. Not only did elections take the form of four separate and parallel elections to four mini-assemblies in the periods 1981–85 and 1993–2000, but the formula employed (largest remainder Hare) in practice operates like the d'Hondt formula (see note [1] to Table 5.1). For these reasons it is extremely difficult to rank the Greek system in terms of its proportionality.
Sources: Mackie and Rose (1991, 1997); Lijphart (1994); Cheles et al. (1995); LeDuc et al. (1996); Betz and Immerfall (1998); Hainsworth (2000a); Elections around the World; Inter-Parliamentary Union Parline Database; Lijphart Election Archive; Parties and Elections in Europe.

overall mechanical effect of each of the different systems under observation in this study. Although the chapter has just examined the impact of the two main determinants of proportionality, the two dimensions have been considered separately rather than together. Establishing the overall mechanical effect of each system and exploring its influence on the extremist party vote allows for the joint influence of district magnitude and electoral formula (as well as the effect of other more minor determinants of proportionality such as assembly size) to be examined. Analysing the impact of the overall mechanical effect of each electoral system therefore enables more complete conclusions to be reached.

The overall mechanical effect of electoral systems: measuring disproportionality

The strength of the mechanical effect of an electoral system can be measured quite easily by calculating the deviation of the seat shares of the parties from their vote shares. Various measures of this deviation – otherwise known as the disproportionality of the electoral system – exist, but perhaps the most favoured is the Gallagher index (1991).[16] High values on this index indicate strong mechanical effects, with larger parties winning a greater percentage of the seats than they did of the vote, and with smaller parties obtaining a smaller share of the seats than of the vote. By contrast, low values on this index suggest that there exists little deviation between the seat shares of the parties and their vote shares. Appendix C reports the disproportionality score of every national election in Western Europe in the period 1979–2003.

As was discussed at the beginning of the chapter, strong mechanical effects are believed to induce strong psychological effects on voters, and this, in turn, is expected to lead to lower scores for smaller parties because these parties stand little chance of securing parliamentary representation. Logically, therefore, the relationship between the disproportionality measure of an electoral system and the right-wing extremist party vote should be a negative one. That is, the more disproportional an electoral system, the lower the electoral scores of the parties of the extreme right are expected to be.

The correlation does indeed reveal a negative relationship between the measure of disproportionality and the right-wing extremist party vote. If all electoral systems are considered together, the Pearson correlation coefficient is -0.047. If proportional systems are taken on their own, the correlation coefficient is -0.057.[17] However, neither correlation is statistically significant.[18] This therefore implies that strong mechanical effects (as reflected by high levels of disproportionality) do not appear to translate into low electoral scores for parties of the extreme right. Equally, weak mechanical effects do not seem to lead to right-wing extremist parties experiencing greater levels of electoral success.

The finding that there exists no significant relationship between the disproportionality of the electoral system and the right-wing extremist party vote when all electoral systems are considered together is not wholly surprising. After all, no significant relationship was found between the right-wing extremist party vote and the district magnitude when all systems were examined together, and no significant relationship existed between the right-wing extremist party vote and the electoral formula. Since these two dimensions of electoral systems make-up the main determinants of proportionality, it is therefore not unexpected that the relationship between the disproportionality of the electoral system and the right-wing extremist party vote is not significant.

However, the finding that no significant association exists between the right-wing extremist party vote and the disproportionality of the electoral system when proportional electoral systems are considered on their own is a little unexpected. When the influence of district magnitudes and legal thresholds was examined above, a significant relationship was found to exist between these two dimensions (as represented by the effective threshold) and the right-wing extremist party vote when proportional systems were considered on their own. Yet it now appears that when the effects of district magnitude and legal thresholds are examined with other factors that contribute to the disproportionality of the electoral system (such as the electoral formula), the association between the electoral system and the right-wing extremist party vote is no longer significant.

These results are also surprising and even almost paradoxical in view of the fact that there exists widespread agreement in the literature that '[t]he disproportionality characteristic of all electoral systems tends to favour the larger parties and to discriminate against the smaller ones' (Lijphart, 1988: 165). Furthermore, they contrast with the results of Peter Mair's comparative study of small parties, in which a much stronger relationship between the disproportionality of electoral systems and the small party vote is uncovered (1991: 54).[19] Whereas Mair is able to conclude that 'a large proportion of the variance in the electoral support for small parties can be explained by reference to the relative degree of constraint imposed by the electoral system' (1991: 55), from the evidence presented above, the same cannot be said about the variance in electoral support for right-wing extremist parties. Instead, the above analysis has shown that, although there is no doubt that proportional systems make life easier for small parties such as those of the extreme right, when all electoral systems are considered together neither the district magnitude, nor the electoral formula, nor even the proportionality profile of the different systems as a whole helps account for the differing levels of success the West European right-wing extremist parties have experienced in the period since 1979. Rather, the share of the vote won by right-wing extremist parties in this period appears unrelated to the type of electoral system employed.

These findings also raise potential questions about the strength and nature of the psychological effects of electoral systems on right-wing extremist party supporters. Given the significant relationship between the right-wing extremist vote and the effective threshold when proportional systems were considered on their own, these results suggest either that, at an aggregate level, voters in countries with proportional electoral systems are more aware of the effects of district magnitude and legal thresholds than are voters in countries with non-proportional systems, or that if voters in non-proportional systems are aware of the impact of district magnitude and legal thresholds, then this awareness that appears overshadowed by other concerns. That said, the findings also suggest that any awareness that voters in proportional electoral systems have of the effects of district magnitude and legal thresholds should not be overstated, as there exists no significant relationship between the overall disproportionality of the electoral system and the right-wing extremist party vote.

The electoral system forms only part of the electoral laws that operate in each of the countries under investigation, however. Thus, it is not the only institutional feature that may affect how well parties perform at the polls. Other electoral laws, including rules relating to ballot access, media access and the receipt of state subventions, also influence the ability of parties to run campaigns and to compete in elections. Therefore, in the search to explain why some parties of the extreme right have experienced success at the polls while others have not, these other electoral laws merit consideration. It is to these that the chapter now turns its attention.

Other electoral laws

While the electoral system is without doubt a core component of the electoral law, a number of other laws exist which may affect the outcome of the election.[20] The importance of these other laws is frequently noted in the literature on electoral systems, and a number of these (such as the rules relating to the financing of elections) have been examined at quite some length. Despite this, however, a precise definition of what constitutes these other laws has not been forthcoming in the literature. Typical is Rae's distinction between electoral systems (which he rather confusingly refers to as 'electoral laws') and electoral laws (which he terms 'election laws'). While he makes clear the need to differentiate between the two, he does not describe what 'election laws' are. Instead he simply states that 'election laws' are the 'broader class of laws which govern elections' or 'those authoritative rules which pertain to the conduct of elections' (1967: 13–14).

More helpful to forming a definition of electoral laws is the list of criteria drawn up by Grofman and Lijphart (1986). Recalling Fishburn's work (1983), as well as the different dimensions of electoral systems, they list a total of 13 sets of features which they consider 'relevant concerns' to a proper analysis of electoral laws and their consequences (1986: 2–3). Included in this list are a number of elements that are particularly relevant to this analysis, since they may possibly assist in helping to form an explanation for why the right-wing extremist party vote has varied so considerably across Western Europe. Of specific interest are the rules regulating the access of parties and/or candidates to the political process, the laws governing access to the media, and those referring to campaign and party financing. All of these rules affect the ability of parties and candidates to enter the race and run an effective campaign. They therefore potentially influence the number of votes a party might win. These three sets of rules will now be examined in turn.

Party/candidate access to the electoral process

Being able to access the ballot dictates whether parties and candidates may take part in the election. In this sense, it is the first hurdle parties or candidates must pass if they are to compete in elections and experience success at the polls. Strictly speaking, ballot access is a matter for party elites rather than voters, since, after weighing up the chances of recovering any deposits or of collecting the required number of signatures, it is the party elite that decides whether and where candidates will stand. In this sense, voters will only be affected by ballot access rules in that there might not be a candidate of their chosen party standing in their constituency.

This said, however, it is fair to assume that the right-wing extremist party vote at the national level will be influenced by ballot access rules, even if these rules are of no direct concern to the individual voter. After all, if voters cannot cast their vote for a right-wing extremist party because no candidate of that party is standing in their constituency, then the party has, in effect, lost any potential votes it might have won in that constituency. Across a whole country such 'lost' votes may add up. Differences in the ballot access rules across the countries under observation therefore matter in that, by encouraging or dissuading parties to present candidates in all districts, they impact on the overall ring-wing extremist party vote.

Table 5.3 shows that the requirements for ballot access vary quite considerably from country to country. Of the countries under observation, it is easiest for candidates and parties to access the ballot in Norway, Portugal, Spain and Sweden. In the first three of these four countries, to stand for election candidates must simply be nominated by political parties. Although the parties must be recognized legal entities, and must therefore collect a number of signatures at the national level, this obligation is not too constraining since, once recognized, registration is continuous. In Sweden, there are simply no requirements to participate in the ballot, although parties do incur a penalty if they fail to record 1 percent of the vote – in such cases they must cover the costs of the production of the ballot papers. In contrast, in all other countries under investigation, candidates or parties must either gather a statutory number of signatures in the run-up to each election if they are to compete, or must pay a deposit. In a limited number of cases they are required to collect signatures *and* pay a deposit.

In spite of the considerable variety in the ballot access laws that exist in the different countries under observation, it is possible to group the countries into categories according to the difficulty of their respective ballot access requirements. More specifically, three different groups of countries are discernible: those with 'easy' requirements (where simple nomination by a political party is sufficient for a candidate to stand for election, or where there are no requirements at all); those with 'medium' requirements (where up to

Table 5.3   Requirements for ballot access

Country	Requirements	Level of difficulty[a]
Austria	Candidates are nominated by political parties and must be supported by 200–500 petitions per electoral district according to size of population, or by three outgoing members of the National Council. Since 1971 a deposit of ATS6,000 (now €435) must be paid by each party in each constituency. This deposit is not reimbursed. (In 1979 ATS6,000 was equal to approx. US$450, which is worth approx. US$1,140 or £630 today. €435 today is equivalent to approx. US$525 or £290.)	Hard (1)
Belgium	Candidates must be supported by at least 500 voters in the constituency of Brussels, at least 400 in Gent, Charleroi, Antwerp and Liege, and at least 200 in other constituencies. Alternatively, they may be supported by three outgoing members of parliament.	Medium (2)
Britain	*Until 1985:* candidates had to be supported by at least 10 signatures and had to pay a deposit of £150, which was refunded if they won 12.5% of the vote. (In 1979 £150 was worth approx. £466 by today's standards, or US$845. In 1985 £150 was worth approx. £280 by today's standards, or US$500.) *Since 1985:* candidates must be supported by at least 10 signatures and must pay a deposit of £500, which is refunded if they secure 5% of the vote. (In 1985 £500 was worth approx. £930 by today's standards, or US$1,690. Today £500 is equal to approx. US$910.)	Hard (1)
Denmark	Parties represented in parliament do not need petitions. Parties not represented in parliament need a number of signatures equal to 1/175 of total valid votes in the last general election (approx. 20,000). Independents need the backing of 150–200 electors from their districts.	Hard (1)
France	Candidates must draw up a signed declaration giving their personal details and those of their substitutes. These are lodged with the prefect. Every candidate is also required to pay a deposit to the chief treasurer and paymaster of the relevant department. This deposit is returned if the candidate obtains at least 5% of the votes cast. As of end 2001 this deposit was FFr1,000 (equal to approx. US$235 in 1979, which in turn is worth approx. US$600 or £330 today, and which at the end 2001 was equal to approx. US$185 or £100 or €150). Candidates do not have to be supported officially by a political party.	Medium (2)
Germany	Parties that have been represented in the Bundestag or in a *Land* parliament by at least 5 members are	Medium (2)

Table 5.3 (continued)

Country	Requirements	Level of difficulty[a]
Germany (cont.)	automatically eligible. Others must prove that they have a democratically elected leadership, a written programme and a written statute, and must have their *Land* lists signed by 1/1,000 voters in the respective *Land,* to a maximum of 2,000 voters. Individual candidatures for constituencies, or candidatures for constituencies submitted by political parties which do not have 5 seats in the *Bundestag* or any *Land* parliament, must be supported by at least 200 electors of the same constituency.	
Greece	Candidates must be supported by 12 signatures, and are required to pay a deposit. From 1981 to 1990 this deposit was Dr. 8,000. (In 1982 Dr. 8,000 was equal to approx. US$120, which is worth approx. US$230 or £125 today. In 1990 Dr. 8,000 was equal to approx. US$50, which is worth approx. US$70 or £40 today.) Since 1993 this deposit has been Dr. 50,000. (In 1993 Dr. 50,000 equaled approx. US$220, which is worth approx. US$280 today or £150.) Since the introduction of the euro, the sum is calculated according to the euro equivalent of Dr. 50,000 (equal to approx. US$180 or £100 or €150 today.) This deposit is not returned. Parties do not need to pay a deposit.	Medium (2)
Italy	*Until 1993:* the symbol and name of a party had to be submitted to the Ministry of the Interior. At constituency level, lists of candidates had to be promoted by at least 300 electors in each constituency. Parties with one seat in either house did not need signatures. *Since 1993:* candidates standing in single-member constituencies require the support of at least 500 electors. Party lists must be supported by between 1,500 and 4,000 signatures.	Medium (2)
Netherlands	*Until 1989:* to present a list in an electoral sub-district a party had to gather at least 25 signatures and had to pay a deposit of Dfl. 1,000, that was reimbursed if the party won three-quarters of an electoral quotient (approx. 0.5 percent of the vote). Parties already represented in parliament did not need to pay this deposit. (In 1979 Dfl. 1,000 was equal to approx. US$500, which is worth approx. US$1,270 or £700 today. In 1989 Dfl. 1,000 was equal to approx. US$470, which is worth approx. US$700 or £390 today.) *Since 1989:* 30 signatures are required to present a list in a sub-district. A deposit of Dfl. 25,000 (now €11,250) must be paid to present a list in one or more sub-districts.	Hard (1)

Table 5.3   (continued)

Country	Requirements	Level of difficulty[a]
Netherlands (cont.)	This is reimbursed if the party wins three-quarters of an electoral quotient (approx. 0.5 percent of the vote). (In 1989 Dfl. 25,000 was equal to approx. US$11,800, which is worth approx. US$17,500 or £9,630 today. €11,250 today is equal to approx. US$13,700 or £7,560.) Parties already represented in either the First or the Second Chamber are exempt from both requirements. Parties must be fully recognized legal entities, and must pay €450 to register their name. This is reimbursed if the party presents a valid list at the election.	
Norway	Lists of candidates must be supported by 500 registered voters in the constituency or must be submitted by a registered party. To register a party, 5,000 signatures are required. Registration is continuous unless the party fails to nominate any candidate in any constituency in two consecutive elections.	Easy (3)
Portugal	Candidates are nominated by political parties. To be recognized, each party must collect 5,000 signatures (nationally) and submit these to the Supreme Court of Justice. Once recognized, parties need not go through this process again. No deposit is required. Independent candidates can only stand by being integrated into party lists.	Easy (3)
Spain	Candidates are nominated by registered political associations, federations or coalitions, or by at least 0.1% (and no fewer than 500) of the constituency's registered electorate.	Easy (3)
Sweden	There are no requirements to participate in ballot, although parties polling less than 1% of the vote must pay for ballot paper production. Parties may register to protect their name with 1,500 members who are eligible to vote.	Easy (3)
Switzerland	*Until 1994:* in each canton with 2 or more seats in the National Council, electoral lists had to be accompanied by 50 signatures. No signatures were required in single-seat cantons. *Since 1994:* the number of signatures that must accompany each electoral list varies by canton and depends on the number of seats the canton has in the National Council (which in turn depends on its population). In cantons with 2–10 seats (14 cantons) 100 signatures are needed; in cantons with 11–20 seats (5 cantons) 200 signatures are needed; in cantons with more than 20 seats (Zurich and Bern) 400 signatures are	Medium (2)

Table 5.3   (continued)

Country	Requirements	Level of difficulty[a]
Switzerland (cont.)	needed. No signatures are required in the 5 single-seat cantons. These requirements concern electoral lists, not parties, which means that parties may present several lists in the same canton if they so wish as long as they collect the required number of signatures per list. The same person may not sign more than one list. No deposit is required. No registration is required.	

Notes: Exchange rates as of mid-2004 unless otherwise stated. [a]The requirements for accessing the ballot are coded according to their level of difficulty. The coding categories are as follows: Easy: minimum requirements such as the need for candidates to be put forward by parties, or parties to incur the cost of ballot paper production if they poll less than a minimum vote (score = 3); Medium: deposit of US$300 or less per district, or up to 500 signatures required (score = 2): Hard: deposit of more than US$300 per district, or large number of signatures required (score = 1).
Sources: Hand *et al.* (1979); Katz and Mair (1992); Katz (1997); ACE Project; Constitution of the Portuguese Republic; Economic History Services (a, b); Inter-Parliamentary Union Parline Database; XE.Com. Personal communication with Hans Hirter; Aphrodite Kassiari; Romain Lachat; Andreas Ladner; Paul Lucardie; Georg Lutz; José Magone; Gerassimos Moschonas; Wolfgang C. Müller; Pascal Sciarini.

a maximum of 500 signatures must be collected at each election and/or where a deposit no larger than US$300 must be paid); and those with 'hard' requirements (where the deposit is more than US$300, or where the number of signatures to be collected is very large, as in the case of Denmark).[21] Table 5.3 indicates to which of these categories the countries under observation belong.

It is reasonable to assume that high ballot access requirements will be detrimental to small or new parties. Almost by definition, such parties command little popular support and will thus find it harder to muster the necessary number of signatures to access the ballot than will a larger, more popular party. Equally, it is more likely that a small or new competitor will be reticent about paying a high electoral deposit, especially if the party or candidate stands only a remote chance of attracting enough votes to be eligible for a reimbursement of the deposit. Therefore, bearing in mind that right-wing extremist parties are still, in the main, small political parties, it is logical to expect these parties to present fewer candidates for election in countries where ballot access requirements are high than in countries where the requirements are lower. If this is so, the extreme right party vote should, in theory, be lower in countries where the ballot requirements are high than in countries where the requirements are low.

In practice, however, the evidence in support of this hypothesis is rather mixed. A number of examples exist in which the hypothesis is confirmed. In

Norway, for instance, where ballot access requirements are low, the FRPn has performed well at the polls, securing as much as 15.3 percent of the vote in 1997. Equally, in Britain and in the Netherlands, where requirements to access the ballot are high, the right-wing extremist parties have recorded low electoral scores. However, there have also been a number of instances in which the hypothesis is not borne out in practice. The right-wing extremist parties in Portugal and Spain, for example, have remained unsuccessful despite the low requirements for accessing the ballot. Conversely, in Austria and Denmark, the parties of the extreme right have recorded high electoral results in spite of the fact that, in both cases, the requirements to access the ballot are high.

The lack of any clear relationship between ballot access requirements and the right-wing extremist party vote can be further illustrated by means of a correlation. The categories of ballot access requirements devised above can be assigned codings, with 'easy' ballot access laws coded 3, 'medium' ballot access laws coded 2, and 'hard' ballot access laws coded 1.[22] If right-wing extremist parties consistently record higher electoral scores in countries where ballot access requirements are easy and lower electoral scores in countries where ballot access requirements are hard (as was hypothesized above), given these codings, a positive correlation coefficient should be observed. The higher the rank of the ballot access category (that is, the easier it is for parties to access the ballot), the higher the right-wing extremist party vote should be.

In the event, the Spearman correlation coefficient is negative (-0.075), rather than positive.[23] However, it is not statistically significant.[24] In the light of this result, therefore, and consistent with the discussion above, the conclusion must be reached that there seems to be little evidence of a clear relationship between the laws governing ballot access and the electoral scores of the parties of the extreme right. Instead, the fortunes of the right-wing extremist parties appear unrelated to the ballot access requirements in place in the respective countries.

It should be emphasized that this finding does not imply that ballot access laws do not matter to political parties. On the contrary, the ballot access requirements may turnout to be critical for a political party, especially in the early part of its life. For example, if the requirements are too high for the party to access the ballot, it might find itself unable to take advantage of a potentially profitable situation. This could be so critical that it could determine whether the party breaks through onto the political scene or whether, instead, the party fades into oblivion. This said, however, in terms of helping to account for the differences in the electoral fortunes of the right-wing extremist parties across Western Europe, ballot access requirements in the countries under observation appear to have little explanatory power.

Access to the broadcast media

The rules governing how parties or candidates may access the ballot are just one of a number of electoral laws. Also worthy of consideration are those requirements that relate to how parties or candidates may gain access to the broadcast media and receive free air time. After all, in view of the amount of time today's typical voter spends listening to the radio or watching television, it is fair to argue that the broadcast media have now become the major channel of political communication and the key campaigning instrument, surpassing more traditional and locally based campaign techniques such as door-to-door canvassing or community meetings (Holtz-Bacha and Kaid, 1995a; Farrell, 1996; Semetko, 1996).

Given the increased reach and influence of radio and television, access to the broadcast media may be critical to how well parties perform at the polls, and parties with access to the media may be expected to perform much better in elections than parties that do not have such access. Therefore, as far as the West European parties of the extreme right are concerned, the disparity in their electoral fortunes may, in part, be explained by the presence of different media access laws. More specifically, it is reasonable to expect parties of the extreme right that have experienced electoral success to be located in systems where media access requirements are low. Conversely, right-wing extremist parties that have recorded low results at the polls are more likely to be found in systems where requirements are high.

Table 5.4 illustrates the requirements that must be met in order for parties and/or candidates to gain access to the media in the different countries under observation. Immediately apparent is the considerable degree of variation that exists from country to country. In Denmark, for example, the requirements are very low. All parties that participate in the ballot are entitled to an equal amount of air time (Siune, 1991; Bille, 1992). By contrast, in Austria and Greece, for instance, the requirements are much higher. In these countries media access is available only to those parties already represented in parliament, or only to parties that fulfil very high requirements (Nassmacher, 1989; Papademetriou, 1991; Müller, 1992).

If, as was suggested above, the relationship between the media access laws and the right-wing extremist vote is such that the lower the media access requirements, the higher the right-wing extremist party vote, then, from the examples just cited, it is reasonable to expect the right-wing extremist party vote to be high in Denmark, but low in Austria and Greece. Furthermore, drawing on the data in Table 5.4, it is also reasonable to predict relatively high vote shares for the parties of the extreme right in Belgium, Germany, Norway, Portugal, Spain and Sweden, as the requirements for ballot access are reasonably low in these countries, but to anticipate low vote scores for right-wing extremist parties in Britain, France and Switzerland, as in these countries the requirements are fairly high.

No such clear pattern emerges in practice, however. While parties of the extreme right have indeed enjoyed electoral success in Denmark, Belgium and Norway, where media access requirements are low, they have also recorded high electoral scores in Austria and France, where requirements are high.

Table 5.4   Requirements for media access

Country	Requirements	Level of difficulty[a]
Austria	Free media time is allotted to parties in and between election campaigns. Representation in the National Council is required for media access. Shares are according to party strength. Parties not in parliament are not entitled to media time. Paid political advertising has been permitted since the early 1980s on private channels only.	Very hard (1)
Belgium	*Access to French-speaking media:* political 'tribunes' of 8 minutes each are allocated proportionally according to are number of seats groups have in the Conseil Culturel. This means 1 programme every year for a group with 2–5% of the seats, 2 programmes for groups with 5–10% of the seats, 4 programmes for groups with 10–15% of the seats, 6 programmes for those with 15–20% of the seats, 8 programmes for groups with 20–30% of the seats, 10 programmes for groups with 30–40% of the seats, and 12 programmes for groups with 40% or more of the seats. *Access to Dutch-speaking media:* every group represented by at least 10 members of the Nederlandse Culturaad can create an organization that has the right to make programmes on radio and television. Half the time is allocated equally, half is allocated proportionally. Groups with at least two members in the Culturaad can also be recognized, in which case broadcasting time is set by the government. Since 1982 every Fraktion (three members) in the Vlaamse Raad (Dutch-speaking council) can create a broadcasting organization.	Medium (3)
Britain	A limited amount of free media access is granted to the major parties according to mutually agreed definition of 'balance', decided partly according to the parties' vote share in the previous election. From 1974 to 1982 the ratio for Conservative: Labour: Liberal was 2:2:1. From 1982 until 1986 the ratio was 5:5:4. Since 1987 the ratio is 1:1:1. This ratio applies to both 'party election broadcasts' (i.e. during election campaigns) and 'party political broadcasts' (i.e. inter-election broadcasts). At election time other parties may also qualify for media time if they have 50 or more candidates in the field on nomination day. Paid access to broadcast media is strictly forbidden.	Hard (2)
Denmark	Equal shares of free media time are awarded to any party participating in the ballot. Governing parties are not favoured in terms of time allocated, though they usually choose their TV spots first (they normally choose an	Easy (4)

Table 5.4   (continued)

Country	Requirements	Level of difficulty[a]
	evening close to the election). All parties participate in a public forum in the form of a 10-minute programme, followed by a 30-minute question session. Party representatives have the opportunity to make a 3-minute statement following this questioning. Paid political advertising is forbidden.	
France	In periods between elections 20 minutes of free time is available every month for parties represented in the National Assembly. During election campaigns parties represented in parliament receive additional free air time. Until 1986 this was approx. 3 hours, which was distributed equally among the parties prior to first ballot. Since 1986 this air time is no longer distributed equally among the parliamentary parties, but according to the number of seats each party holds in parliament. Parties not represented in parliament are given 7 minutes of free air time for the first ballot and another 5 minutes for the second ballot if they nominate at least 75 candidates for the first ballot. Paid political advertising has been forbidden since the early 1990s.	Hard (2)
Germany	Free media time is allocated in campaign periods in proportion to parties' previous percentage of the vote. New or previously unsuccessful parties are allotted a minimum amount of air time. Paid political advertising has been permitted since the early 1980s on private channels. These channels must offer equal opportunities to all parties, and are not allowed to discriminate against parties not in parliament. This said, smaller parties tend to be given fewer spots than larger parties.	Medium (3)
Greece	*Until 1990:* the amount of television coverage parliamentary parties received was decided by the government. *Since 1990:* regulations have been codified. Political parties or candidates can transmit advertising spots in the pre-election period. These spots must be short (max. 1 minute), limited to one-third of the total weekly time allocated to each party, and transmitted only between programmes. These spots are free of charge. The basis for the allocation of time is the strength of the party in the previously dissolved parliament. The three largest parties in the previous parliament are each entitled to 38 minutes of air time per week. The transfer of time from one week to another is permitted, as long as the total time does not exceed 50 minutes. Smaller parties with members in the previous parliament are each	Very hard (1)

Table 5.4   (continued)

Country	Requirements	Level of difficulty[a]
Greece (cont.)	entitled to 8 minutes per week. Parties with no representation in parliament but with a list of candidates in 75% of the electoral districts are entitled to 5 minutes per week. In addition to the above time, each large party is entitled to one 45-minute broadcast. Private broadcasting stations are obliged to invite politicians from all the largest parties for interviews (on an equal basis) and are obliged to transmit the same number of spots per party as the public station, free of charge. These spots must be transmitted at the same time of the day for each party.	
Italy	*Until 1993:* all parties had media access. The Parliamentary Address and Surveillance Commission for Radio and Television Services oversaw the allocation and scheduling of broadcasts. It sought to guarantee equal space and equal conditions for all entities that participated in elections. Paid political advertising on private channels began in 1979. *1993:* in the light of previous regulations not being adhered to, a new law (No. 515) was passed which sought to guarantee equal media coverage (in terms of both space and conditions) for all lists and groups of candidates at regional level, and for all parties and political movements at national level. *1995–99:* after the 1994 election campaign, in which it was felt that all parties did not receive equal coverage on private channels, the very restrictive Gambino Law was passed, which ruled that all networks must provide equal coverage and equal time for all parties and movements participating in the election, their leaders and their propaganda. Paid political advertising was still permitted on private channels but private broadcasters had to guarantee equal treatment too. *2000 –:* Law No. 28 (known as the 'par condicio' law) rules that any 'political body' (parties, coalitions and candidates) should have equal access to and equal treatment in the media, in both election and non-election periods. This includes political broadcasts, debates etc. as well as other programmes in which political opinions are expressed.	Easy (4)
Netherlands	*Until 1982:* during campaign periods, free media time was allocated in equal shares to any party that presented a list in at least one electoral sub-district. During the inter-campaign period, parties represented in the Second Chamber received free air time in equal shares.	Until (and incl.) 1982: Easy (4)

Table 5.4 (continued)

Country	Requirements	Level of difficulty[a]
	Since 1982: free media access during the election period is now limited to parties that participate in all 19 electoral sub-districts. Time is distributed equally among these parties. During the inter-campaign period, parties represented in the Second Chamber receive free air time in equal shares. Paid political advertising is forbidden on public channels. Since 1994 a minor amount of paid political advertising takes place on private channels.	Since 1982: Very hard (1)
Norway	There are no official rules, but the national broadcasting corporation (NRK) requires parties to have been represented in parliament in at least one of the last two parliamentary periods, to nominate candidates in a majority of the constituencies, and to have a national organization if they are to be entitled to 'equal treatment'. If these criteria are met, the same number of participants and the same amount of time are allowed to all parties. Programmes take the form of questions from journalists or a panel of voters rather than parties presenting their own platforms. At the end of this series of programmes, a debate is held in which all party leaders and the prime minister take part. Parties which do not meet the criteria for 'equal treatment' but which are acknowledged as running in the election are accorded shorter programmes combining information and questioning. To participate in local programmes, parties must nominate candidates in at least a quarter of the municipalities. Paid political advertising is forbidden.	Medium (3)
Portugal	During electoral campaigns, all competing parties (including those not represented in parliament) have equal free time on national television and radio. In inter-election periods, only parties represented in the Assembly have a right to free air time on radio and television. This is distributed in proportion to their electoral strength. Paid political advertising is permitted on private channels.	Easy (4)
Spain	*For the 1977, 1979 and 1982 elections* parties received free media time on public channels as follows: if they presented candidates in 25 or more electoral districts they received 3 slots of 10 minutes on nationwide channels; if they presented candidates in fewer than 25 electoral districts they received 2 slots of 10 minutes in regional programming; and if they presented candidates in 4 or more districts that together accounted for at least 25% of the national electorate, they also received 1 slot of 10 minutes on nationwide channels.	Medium (3)

Table 5.4   (continued)

Country	Requirements	Level of difficulty[a]
Spain (cont.)	*Since 1985:* all parties receive free media time on public channels, with a minimum allocation of one 10-minute slot. Parties fielding candidates in at least 75% of electoral districts receive additional broadcasting time in proportion to their share of the vote in previous elections. The two largest parties may receive up to 40 minutes each. Purely regional parties are also given 15 minutes of free air time if they have won over 20% of the vote within their respective regions. Paid political advertising is not permitted on television, although it is allowed on private radio.	
Sweden	The allocation of free media time is decided upon by the television and radio companies. In election campaigns, interviews and debates are the main form of election broadcast, rather than the parties making their own films. These have been generally restricted to parties represented in parliament (and these parties have been given equal coverage), although exceptions have occurred on a very few occasions when smaller parties have been included. In other cases smaller parties have been given short spots and/or interviews, which, though smaller than those of the major parties, have been equal among themselves. They have not tended to be included in the specially arranged issue-oriented debates or in the final debate. No paid political advertising is allowed on terrestrial television or radio. Paid political advertising has been allowed on satellite channels since the early 1980s.	Medium (3)
Switzerland	Parties receive some coverage on television before elections. However, since the early 1980s these spots are not produced by the parties themselves, but by the media companies (public and private), which decide how much coverage they wish to accord to which parties. The media companies provide fairly equal coverage of the four largest parties (which together amass about 80% of the vote), as they are required to do by law. Smaller parties (with representation in parliament) also receive coverage, though they are accorded less air time. Smaller parties with no representation in parliament are accorded coverage if they have had success in previous cantonal elections. The smallest groups tend not to be covered. In view of linguistic divisions, decisions over how much coverage to accord a party are made according to the regional (rather than national) strength of the parties. In general, broadcasts take the form of debates or	Hard (2)

Table 5.4 (continued)

Country	Requirements	Level of difficulty[a]
	discussions in which two or more parties are present, so as to maximize viewers' interest. Paid political advertisements on the radio or on television are not allowed.	

Notes: [a] The requirements for accessing the media are coded according to their level of difficulty. The coding categories are as follows: Easy: equal shares to all parties (score = 4); Medium: small parties receive some minimum time (score = 3); Hard: small parties receive minimum time if certain requirements are met (score = 2); Very hard: media time is reserved for parties in parliament only, or very high requirements must be met before access is granted (score = 1). Countries may change categories if the media access laws are altered. The change in the media access laws in 1982 in the Netherlands, for example, meant that the media laws went from being easy to very hard.
Sources: Smith (1981); Borre (1988); Gunlicks (1988); del Castillo (1989, 1994); Nassmacher (1989); Papademetriou (1991); Siune (1991); Katz and Mair (1992); Drysch (1993); Avril (1994); Gamaleri (1995); Holtz-Bacha and Kaid (1995a, 1995b); LeDuc *et al.* (1996); Ricolfi (1997); Lange (1999); Farrell and Webb (2000); Gunther *et al.* (2000); Legge 28/00 (2000); Marletti and Roncarolo (2000); Pujas (2000); Van Biezen (2000); ACE Project; Constitution of the Portuguese Republic. Personal communication with Luciano Bardi; Hans Hirter; Romain Lachat; Andreas Ladner; Georg Lutz; José Magone; José Ramón Montero; Wolfgang C. Müller; Pascal Sciarini; Lars Svåsand.

Similarly, although the right-wing extremist parties in Britain have been unsuccessful at the polls, as was hypothesized, so too have their German and Spanish counterparts, even though the media access requirements in Germany and Spain are relatively low. Thus, just as was the case with the ballot access laws, it appears that, at first sight at least, the differences in the media access requirements across the countries under investigation do not contribute in any way to explaining why the right-wing extremist party vote has varied so much from country to country.

Before the explanatory power of media access requirements is dismissed completely, however, it is useful to run a simple correlation, as was done when ballot access requirements were examined. The countries may be placed into one of four categories depending on the ease with which parties may gain access to the media: 'easy', where all candidates and/or parties receive equal time as long as they have gained access to the ballot; 'medium', where smaller competitors receive some minimum air time; 'hard', where small parties receive some limited air time if they meet certain requirements; and 'very hard', where access to broadcasting is reserved for parliamentary parties only, or where the requirements to be met before access is granted are very high.[25] As with the ballot access laws, these categories may be coded, with 'easy' requirements assigned a score of 4, 'medium' requirements coded as 3, 'hard' requirements coded as 2, and 'very hard' requirements coded as 1. These scores may then be correlated with the electoral results of the right-wing extremist parties. If the hypothesis advanced above is correct, a positive correlation coefficient is expected. Given the codings, the higher the media access category (that is, the easier it is to access the media), the higher the electoral scores of the parties of the extreme right are expected to be.

The Spearman correlation coefficient is positive (.153), as anticipated, and is significant at the 0.05 level.[26] This suggests that the fortunes of the West European right-wing extremist parties are indeed related to the media access laws present in the various countries, and more specifically that, overall, parties of the extreme right tend to perform better in systems where access to the media is relatively easy than they do where access to the media is relatively difficult. The hypothesis advanced above is therefore borne out in practice.

Access to state subventions

A third dimension of electoral laws relates to the financing of political parties. These rules deserve examination in this chapter because, as with the requirements regarding access to the ballot and the regulations governing access to the media, the laws relating to the financing of parties potentially influence how well parties of the extreme right perform at the polls. Clearly, parties with greater financial resources are expected to perform better in elections than parties with more meagre funds, since, as Fisher argues, 'increased spending capacity provides parties with greater opportunity to promote themselves to voters' (1999: 520). Substantial resources enable parties to field more candidates, buy more advertising space in the press or more time on television, print more campaign literature and, generally, reach a greater number of voters. Alexander has even maintained that since money 'buys what cannot be volunteered', finance is the most important source of political power, dominating what he calls 'the electoral and organizational constituencies' of power (1989: 10–12).

Given the perceived importance of political money and given its potential influence on the electoral success of political parties, it is reasonable to suggest that one explanation for the differing fortunes of the right-wing extremist parties across Western Europe might lie in the varying levels of wealth of the parties. In other words, the disparity in the electoral scores of the parties of the extreme right may potentially be explained, in part, by the fact that some parties are richer than others.

Comparing the wealth of the different parties across different countries is easier said than done, however. The study of political finance in the comparative perspective is beset by a number of obstacles, the most notable of which is the chronic lack of data on the subject. As Nassmacher points out, 'data covering all aspects of party activity are presently not available for one country, let alone several' (1993: 236). Even where parties are obliged by law to provide reports of their main sources of income and their main items of expenditure, the systems of reporting differ significantly from country to county. In Austria and Sweden, for example, parties need only report their headquarters' finances, meaning that financial transactions carried out by local or provincial party organizations remain undisclosed (Nassmacher, 1989, 1993; Klee, 1993). In Germany, parties need not disclose the finances of their parliamentary groups or of their political foundations, although these are audited separately (von Arnim, 1993; Nassmacher, 1993). Obtaining a complete picture of the finances of the different parties in these countries therefore remains extremely difficult.

In other countries, information on the income and expenditure of parties is even harder to come by than it is in Austria, Sweden and Germany. In some instances, even where disclosure of revenue and expenditure is obligatory by law, public access to the parties' reports is not always guaranteed. In Spain, for instance, access to the information presented by parties remains rather restricted to non-politicians (del Castillo, 1989: 182). Elsewhere, the lack of data is a result of an absence of reporting requirements altogether. Drysch explains that in France, prior to the introduction of a new system of political finance in 1988, 'it was impossible to receive even somewhat reliable figures concerning the revenues and expenditures of the parties, since they were not required to account for their revenues and expenditures' (1993: 155–6).

The situation as regards data on the finances of parties is therefore worse in some countries than in others. In addition, the availability of data varies from party to party, with data on the finances of smaller competitors (including most of the parties of the extreme right) being particularly hard to come by. When, in the absence of official reports, researchers have had to delve into internal party documents and rely on interviews with party officials to gather data on the finances of the parties, they have been inclined to focus on gathering information on the larger, established parties only, a practice which has invariably meant that smaller parties have been excluded from the majority of studies. Analyses of the finances of small parties have therefore tended to suffer more than others from the problem of insufficient data.

Attempting to ascertain the wealth of the parties of the extreme right is therefore problematic because of the fact that the majority of these parties are small and have thus been overlooked by most analyses. On top of this, gathering information on the finances of the parties of the extreme right is particularly difficult because of the closeness with which party accounts are guarded and the reticence with which information is divulged. Whether justified or not, parties of the extreme right have earned themselves somewhat of a reputation for having rather murky finances, something which Hennion (1993), for instance, has observed in her investigation into the finances of the French FN.

An alternative way of measuring the wealth of the different parties of the extreme right, which to some extent overcomes the problem of data shortage, is to examine whether the parties have access to state funding. Although this is clearly not the same as determining the wealth of the parties, it nonetheless sheds some light on the level of their resources. A generous system of public funding with low access requirements may be taken as a reasonable indicator of well-funded parties, while an absence of public money can be taken to suggest that parties are, on the whole, less affluent. In addition to overcoming the problem of data shortage, this approach to examining the resources available to the parties of the extreme right also makes sense in the context of this chapter, because, by investigating state subventions which are considered part of a country's electoral law, the focus remains squarely on electoral institutions and on their impact on the right-wing extremist party vote.

Table 5.5 reports the requirements that must be met if parties are to receive state subventions. It also indicates whether subventions are generous or

Table 5.5   Requirements for state subventions

Country	Requirements	Level of difficulty[a]
Austria	*Subsidies to parliamentary Fraktions:* 5 MPs are required to form a Fraktion. Base amount and supplementary amount are awarded according to the number of seats held by the party (awarded yearly). Base amount is reasonably high, so small parties benefit more. *Direct subsidies to central party organizations:* fixed sum for parties with at least 5 MPs; yearly funds for parties represented in the National Council, awarded according to share of vote won in previous election; yearly funds for public relations for parties represented in National Council, awarded according to the share of the vote won in previous election. *Campaign subsidies:* since 1989 each party represented in the National Council receives a campaign contribution in election years. This is calculated on the basis of an amount per eligible voter, and the sum of this amount is then shared out according to the parties' vote share at the previous election. As of 2003 this amount was €1.94 per eligible voter (approx. US$2.458 or £1.34). Since 1975 parties polling a minimum of votes (1%) without gaining representation in the National Council receive limited subsidies in election years. Subsidy based on share of the vote. *Grants to party academies/educational institutions:* base amount and amount per parliamentary seat held. One institution per party, funded if party has at least 5MPs. *Level of state subvention: generous*	Easy (4)

Table 5.5 (continued)

Country	Requirements	Level of difficulty[a]
Belgium	*Subsidy to parliamentary Fraktions:* 3 MPs are required to form a Fraktion. Base amount and supplementary amount are awarded according to the number of seats held by the party (awarded yearly and adjusted for inflation yearly).	Until 1991: hard (2)
	Subsidies to central party organization since 1989: parties with at least 1 MP receive a fixed amount and an amount per valid vote cast at the last election on its House list, and an amount per valid vote cast on its Senate list. Sums are paid yearly (adjusted for inflation at regular intervals).	From 1995: medium (3)
	Level of state subvention: until 1989, modest; since 1989, generous	
Britain	State subvention has been available to opposition parliamentary parties in the House of Commons since 1975 – known as 'Short Money'. It takes the form of an annual payment to help cover costs incurred in performing the opposition parties' parliamentary functions. The amount payable is worked out according to the number of seats held and the vote share won in the last general election. The sums for the House of Commons for the year 2001–02 were £11,012 (approx. US$16,180 as of 2002) per year per seat won plus £21.99 (approx. US$32 as of 2002) per 200 votes won, with no maximum limit. In order to qualify a party must win a minimum of 2 seats in the House of Commons, or 1 seat and 150,000 votes.	Very hard (1)
	Level of state subvention: modest	
Denmark	*Subsidies to parliamentary party:* 1 MP is required to form a parliamentary group. The amount is awarded according to the number of seats held. Grants for 'expert' assistance are also paid to parliamentary groups.	Until 1987: medium (3)
	Subsidies to central party: 1987–94, Dkr.5 per vote (equal to approx. US$0.73 in 1987, worth approx. US$1.18 or £0.65 today; equal to approx. US$0.79 in 1994, worth approx. US$0.98 or £0.54 today) in general elections if minimum of 1,000 votes won. Received annually. From 1995, amount raised to Dkr.19.50 per vote (approx. US$3.17 or £1.75 today) in general elections.	From 1987: easy (4)
	Level of state subvention: until 1987, modest; since 1987, generous	
France	*Pre-1988:* no substantial subsidies. Candidates who received more than 5% of the vote on the first ballot were reimbursed costs of campaign letter, flyers and	Until 1988: no state subvention

Table 5.5   (continued)

Country	Requirements	Level of difficulty[a]
France (cont.)	posters. They also were reimbursed their deposit of FFr1,000 (equal to approx. US$235 in 1979, worth approx. US$596 or £330 today; equal to approx. US$168 in 1988, worth approx. US$260 or £145 today). This was lost for candidates with less than 5%.	1988: very hard (1)
	Since 1988: candidates who win less than 5% of the vote are reimbursed for the printing and mailing of programmes, posters and ballots only. As of end 2001, candidates winning more than 5% were reimbursed FFr50,000 (approx. US$9,200 or £5,100 or €7,620 today).	From 1993: Medium (3)
	Public funding to parties has existed since 1988 and is distributed in two equal parts: (1) funds are allocated to parties that have presented candidates in at least 75 districts, and are distributed in proportion to the number of votes won by candidates on the first ballot (in force from the 1993 election); (2) funds are allocated to parties on the basis of their parliamentary representation.	
	Level of state subvention: until 1988, no state subventions; since 1988, generous	
Germany	*Subsidies to parliamentary Fraktions:* since 1969, 26 MPs are required to form a Fraktion, which is approx. 5% of the Bundestag. Opposition Fraktions receive bonus grants.	Easy (4)
	Public funding to parties:	
	Until the end of 1993, a set sum per eligible voter was shared out proportionally among the parties according to their vote percentage. From 1969 parties had to win 0.5% of second (list) votes if they were to receive this reimbursement, and from 1979 independent candidates are also entitled to this reimbursement if they win 10% of the vote in their constituency. From 1974 to 1983 this reimbursement was 3.50 DM per eligible voter (equal to approx.US$1.91 in 1979, worth approx. US$4.84 or £2.66 today; equal to approx. US$1.37 in 1983, worth approx. US$2.53 or £1.39 today). From 1983 to end 1993 it was raised to 5.00 DM per eligible voter (equal to approx. US$1.96 in 1983, worth approx. US$3.62 or £2.00 today; equal to approx. US$3.01 in 1993, worth approx. US$3.83 or £2.10 today). Only 50% of parties' income was allowed to come from state sources.	
	Since 1994 the system has been changed so that each party annually receives (1) €0.70 for each valid vote cast for its list, or (2) €0.70 for each valid vote cast for it in a constituency or polling district in a Land where its list was not approved, and (3) €0.38 for each euro obtained	

Table 5.5   (continued)

Country	Requirements	Level of difficulty[a]
	through membership fees, deputy fees or rightfully obtained donations. Notwithstanding (1) and (2), the amount a party annually receives for the first 4 million valid votes it wins is €0.85 (rather than €0.70). Parties are eligible for this money if they win 0.5% of the valid votes cast for lists at the last election, or if they have obtained 10% of the valid votes cast in a constituency or polling district. *Campaign subsidies:* from 1989 until 1993 parties winning at least 2% of the votes in the prior elections were eligible for very modest reimbursement of campaign costs (Sockelbetrag). However, this was declared unconstitutional in 1992 with effect from 1994. *Funds for educational activities* since 1959. *Grants to party foundations* since 1962. *Level of state subvention: generous*	
Greece	1975–84: no state subventions to political parties. *From 1984:* introduction of subsidies to cover the operational costs of parties and their campaign expenditures. A set amount of money is allocated for this purpose (0.001% of the total state budget). All parties that participated in the last parliamentary elections either (1) on their own and received 3% of the total valid votes and presented a list of candidates in at least two-thirds of the electoral districts, or (2) in a coalition with other parties and presented a list of candidates in two-thirds of the electoral districts, and received at least 5% of the total valid votes in the case of a coalition of two parties, or 6% for a coalition of three or more parties are eligible for public subsidies. 10% of the subsidy is distributed equally among all parties that participated in the elections; the remainder is shared among the parties in proportion to the number of votes received at the election. *Level of state subvention: until 1984, no state subventions; since 1984, generous*	Until 1984: no state subvention From 1984: medium (3)
Italy	*Until 1993:* *Subsidies to parliamentary Fraktion:* from 1974 parliamentary groups received an annual contribution from the state (normally 20 MPs required for a group in the Chamber of Deputies, although smaller groups were allowed if parties participated in at least 20 constituencies and qualified for seat allocation at the national level). Of this money, 2% was shared equally among all parliamentary groups, 75% was allocated	Medium (3)

Table 5.5   (continued)

Country	Requirements	Level of difficulty[a]
Italy (cont.)	proportionally to groups on the basis of their membership, and the remainder was allocated according to a mixed system. The vast majority of this money was ploughed back into the central party.	

Campaign subsidies: parties that contested seats in at least two-thirds of the constituencies and won either at least 1 quotient and at least 300,000 votes, or at least 2% of the valid vote were eligible for campaign subsidies. 20% of the funds set aside for campaign subsidies were distributed in equal shares to all parties with candidates in two-thirds of the constituencies, 80% were distributed in proportion to the vote share won.

Since 1993:

After a referendum on party finance in April 1993 the public funding of parties was abolished. A new law passed in December 1993 (No. 515) introduced a system based on the direct reimbursement of electoral expenses to candidates rather than on subventions to parties. Reimbursement was in proportion to the vote won by candidates. Expenses were reimbursed to parties or groups with more than 4% of the vote or with at least 1 elected candidate and 3% of the vote. Candidates received reimbursement through their agents. There was a ceiling per candidate (80 million lire (US$50,000 or £27,500), plus 100 lire [US$0.06, or £0.03] per citizen in a single-seat constituency or 10 lire per citizen in a multi-seat constituency) and there were also limits on the expenditure of parties.

   In January 1997, in view of the financial crisis of parties, a new form of public support was proposed whereby taxpayers could allocate 4 lire of every 1,000 of their income tax to their chosen party. This provision turned out to be unsuccessful as so few people took advantage of it. It was abolished in 1999.

   In March 1999 a new law (No. 157) was passed which modified the reimbursement system and provided for a sum of 4,000 lire per eligible voter to be shared out proportionally among the parties according to their vote. Of this money, 40% is distributed in the first year after the election, and 15% is distributed in each of the following four years. Parties are entitled to this reimbursement subsidy if either they have won 4% of the votes or one of their candidates has won a direct mandate and the party has won 1% of the vote. Since the introduction of the euro, this sum is calculated according to the euro equivalent of 4,000 lire (equal to €2.07 or US$2.61 or £1.43 today).

Level of state subvention: generous

Table 5.5   (continued)

Country	Requirements	Level of difficulty[a]
Netherlands	*Subvention to parliamentary parties:* fixed amount per parliamentary group (1 MP is required to form group) plus an amount per seat held in the Second Chamber. *Subvention for research institutes:* for parties in the Second Chamber only, a fixed amount per party plus an additional amount on the basis of the number of seats. This grant must be matched with an equal amount of private resources. One institute per party. *Subvention for educational institutes:* a fixed amount per party plus an additional amount on the basis of the number of seats. Private resources must make-up at least 30% of funds of educational institutes. For parties in the Second Chamber only. *Subvention for parties' youth organizations:* the grant depends on the size of the parliamentary group. No matching funds are required. *Level of state subvention: modest*	Easy (4)
Norway	*Subsidy to parliamentary party:* all MPs of the same party belong to the same group, so if a party has only 1 MP, he or she can constitute a group on his or her own. Since 1983 the three smallest parties receive increased support. The basic support for small party groups is about double that of large party groups, e.g. in 1991 small parties received a basic support sum of Nkr.432,136 (equal to approx. US$66,600 in 1991, worth approx. US$90,000 or £49,500 today), whereas he basic support sum for large parties was Nkr.216,279 (equal to approx. US$33,300 in 1991, worth approx. US$45,000 or £24,800 today). Parties also receive support per MP (in 1991 this was Nkr.30,856, equal to approx. US$4,750 in 1991, worth approx. US$6,420 or £3,540 today), with extra support for MPs from small party groups since 1991. *Subsidy to central party organization:* since 1970 parties are entitled to a per vote subsidy. Parties must have presented candidates in at least half the constituencies and have won at least 2.5% of the votes to be eligible for this per vote subsidy. In 1991 this per vote subsidy was Nkr.22.10 (equal to approx. US$3.41 in 1991, worth approx. US$4.61 or £2.54 today). Sums are adjusted annually. *Subsidies to youth and educational organizations* since 1978. *Level of state subvention: generous*	Medium (3)
Portugal	*Subsidies to parliamentary groups:* each group receives an equal amount of money, and in addition a fixed	Until 1993: hard (2)

Table 5.5   (continued)

Country	Requirements	Level of difficulty[a]
Portugal (cont.)	amount is allocated for each seat in the legislature. No minimum number of MPs is required to form a group.	
	Subsidies to central party organization: paid annually for routine (i.e. non-electoral) activities and allocated on the basis of the votes won. Until 1993 this subsidy was restricted to parties with at least one parliamentary seat. Since 1993 the threshold is set at obtaining more than 50,000 votes, thus formally no longer discriminating in favour of parties with parliamentary representation.	From 1993: easy (4)
	Campaign subsidies: introduced in 1993. The sum of state money for legislative elections is a fixed amount, of which 20% is divided equally among the participating parties, and 80% is distributed in proportion to the electoral result obtained. Parties must obtain at least 2% of the votes in order to qualify for reimbursement of their electoral expenditure.	
	Level of state subvention: generous	
Spain	*Subsidies to parliamentary groups:* each group receives an equal base sum, and in addition a fixed amount is allocated per seat in the legislature. 5 MPs are required to form a group.	Hard (2)
	Subsidies to central party: paid annually since 1978. An amount of money is determined by the government and included in the annual budget. By law, one-third of this amount is distributed to the parties according to the number of seats they hold, and two-thirds according to the number of votes that they won in the most recent elections to the lower House. Extra-parliamentary parties do not receive this state subsidy.	
	Campaign subsidies: parties must obtain at least one parliamentary seat (in the Congress of Deputies or the Senate) if they are to receive campaign subsidies. A set sum is awarded to each parliamentary party for each vote gained in electoral districts in which the party obtains at least 1 seat, which means that monetary compensation is awarded only for those votes obtained in districts where the party wins representation. In the 1979 and 1982 campaigns this set sum was 15 pesetas per vote won in the election to the Congress of Deputies (in 1979 15 pesetas was equal to approx. US$0.22, worth approx. US$0.56 or £0.31 today). The sum was increased to 65 pesetas in 1986, 77 pesetas in 1989, 83 pesetas in 1993, 96 pesetas in 1996, and 101 pesetas in 2000. (Today 101 pesetas is equal to approx. US$0.74 or £0.40 or €0.61).	
	Parties also receive a sum for each seat won in each of the two chambers. In the 1979 and 1982 elections this	

Table 5.5 (continued)

Country	Requirements	Level of difficulty[a]
	sum was 1 million pesetas per seat in each House (in 1979 1 million pesetas was equal to approx. US$14,900, worth approx. US$37,750 or £20,800 today). The sum was increased to 1.63 million pesetas in 1986, to 1.915 million pesetas in 1989, to 2.2 million pesetas in 1993, to 2.546 million pesetas in 1996, and to 2.692 million pesetas in 2000. (Today 2.692 million pesetas is equal to approx. US$20,400 or £11,200 or €16,200). *Level of state subvention: generous*	
Sweden	*Subvention to parliamentary Fraktions:* no rule exists as to how many MPs are needed to form a Fraktion. Sums are awarded on a per seat basis, with opposition parties granted more than government parties. As well as the per seat subsidy paid for by the state, parliamentary groups also receive a basic grant from the state, a basic grant from parliament and another per seat subsidy from parliament. The two per seat subsidies favour the opposition party groups, sometimes by more than double the amount for government groups. The basic grants are the same for all parties. A portion of the basic grant from the state is awarded to the parliamentary groups of parties that won 4% or more of the vote in the previous election but less in the present election. This amount is de-escalated over the 3 subsequent years. *Subvention to central party organization:* a per seat subsidy is set and is paid to parties with seats in parliament and with 4% of the vote or more. In addition, for parties with no seats and with less than 4% of the vote, one per seat subsidy is paid for every 0.1% gained above 2.5% of the vote. For parties with seats but with less than 4% of the vote (i.e. those parties which have won over 12% in a constituency), one per seat subsidy is paid per seat, and one per seat subsidy for every 0.1% of the vote gained above 2.5% of the vote. For these parties there is an upper limit of 14 per seat subsidies. Parties that won 4% in the previous election but not in the present election receive a smaller subsidy that is de-escalated over the 3 subsequent years. Subsidies are paid annually. *Subsidies for youth and women's organizations.* *Level of state subvention: generous*	Medium (3)
Switzerland	*Subsidies to parliamentary groups* since 1972. Amounts are based on the number of MPs in each parliamentary group. Each group receives an annual sum and a sum per	Hard (2)

Table 5.5   (continued)

Country	Requirements	Level of difficulty[a]
Switzerland (cont.)	member. In 2000 these were set at SFr90,000 (approx. US$71,000 or £39,000), plus SFr16,500 (approx. US$13,000 or £7,150) per member. Parliamentary groups must have a minimum of 5 members. Group members do not have to come from the same party but in practice, they do tend to, except in the case of the smallest parties, which sometimes come together with each other to form a group. Groups may be (and most are) formed from members of both chambers.	

Level of state subvention: modest

Notes: Exchange rates as of mid-2004 unless otherwise stated. [a] The requirements for accessing state subventions are coded according to their level of difficulty. The coding categories are as follows: Easy: parties receive state subventions with 1% of the vote or less (score = 4); Medium: parties receive state subventions with 1–4% of the vote or are required to nominate a minimum number of candidates as in France (score = 3); Hard: parties receive state subventions with 4–10% of the vote (score = 2); Very hard: parties receive state subventions with more than 10% of the vote (score = 1). Countries may change categories if the state subvention laws are altered. The change in the state subvention laws in 1993 in Portugal, for example, meant that the state subvention laws went from being hard to easy.

Sources: Ewing (1987); Gunlicks (1988); Ciaurro (1989); del Castillo (1989, 1994); Koole (1989, 1994); Nassmacher (1989); Gidlund (1991, 1994); Papademetriou (1991); Svåsand (1991); Katz and Mair (1992); von Arnim (1993); Johnston and Pattie (1993); Klee (1993); Avril (1994); Landfried (1994); Linton (1994); Bille (1996, 1997); Rhodes (1997); Gentile and Kriesi (1998); Swyngedouw (1998); Pujas and Rhodes (1999); Pierre *et al.* (2000); Pujas (2000); Van Biezen (2000); Sear (2001); Parteiengesetz (2002, 2003); ACE Project; Economic History Services (a, b); Inter-Parliamentary Union Parline Database; XE.Com. Personal communications with Luciano Bardi; Hans Hirter; Romain Lachat; Andreas Ladner; Georg Lutz; José Magone; Luis Ramiro; Pascal Sciarini.

modest in each of the countries under observation. As with the rules governing ballot and media access, the regulations vary considerably from country to country. In some countries it is relatively easy for parties to gain access to state subventions. In Austria, for example, parties are entitled to receive state subventions in election years if they have secured 1 percent of the vote (Nassmacher, 1989; Müller, 1992). In Germany, a mere 0.5 percent of list votes is required for parties to be able to claim state funds (Poguntke and Boll, 1992; Linton, 1994), and in Denmark, since the introduction of subsidies to central party organizations in 1987, parties receive subsidies if they gather as little as 1,000 votes (Bille, 1992).

By contrast, elsewhere parties must be represented in parliament or must record a high electoral score before they may be entitled to state funds. In Britain, for instance, state subventions are only available to those parties that make-up the parliamentary opposition. Given the very high effective threshold that operates in Britain (see Table 5.1), state subsidies are therefore restricted to very few parties (Webb, 1992). Parliamentary representation is also necessary in Spain and Switzerland if parties are to be entitled to state money, and although the effective threshold is not as high in these two countries as it is in Britain, it is nonetheless high enough to mean that only a limited number of Spanish and Swiss parties may draw on state funds (del Castillo, 1989, 1994; Gentile and Kriesi, 1998; Van Biezen, 2000).

Just as the different countries under observation were categorized according to how easy it is for parties to gain access to the ballot and to the media, they can also be categorized according to the ease with which parties may gain access to state subventions. As with the media access laws, four distinct groups can be identified: those countries where parties may receive state subventions with 1 percent of the vote or less (which may be labelled 'easy'); those countries where parties are entitled to state subventions if they poll between 1 and 4 percent of the vote, or where there are requirements to nominate a minimum number of candidates (labelled 'medium'); those countries where parties receive state funds when they gather between 4 and 10 percent of the vote (labelled 'hard'); and finally, those countries where more than 10 percent of the vote is required if parties are to be entitled to state money (labelled 'very hard'). Table 5.5 indicates to which of the categories the different countries belong.

Since parties with greater financial resources are expected to perform better at the polls than parties with lesser funds, it is reasonable to hypothesize that the right-wing extremist parties which are located in countries where it is easiest to gain access to state subventions (those countries categorized as 'easy' or 'medium' in Table 5.5) will record higher electoral scores than those parties which compete in systems where accessing state subventions is more difficult (those countries labelled 'hard' or 'very hard').

In practice, this hypothesis is borne out in about half the cases. In Austria and Denmark (since the introduction of subsidies to central party organizations in 1987), where parties have needed to win only a small percentage of the vote before they become entitled to state funds, the parties of the extreme right have recorded high electoral scores, as was anticipated. By contrast, in Britain, in Portugal (in the period before the law on party financing was modified in 1993) and in Spain, where the requirements governing access to state subventions are high, the parties of the extreme right have performed poorly at the polls.

In countries where the requirements for state subventions have been categorized as being of 'medium' difficulty (see Table 5.5), the parties of the extreme right have either tended to perform well at the polls, or at least recorded reasonably high electoral scores, even if their results have not been among the highest in Western Europe. In Norway, for example, the FRPn has won between 3.7 and 15.3 percent of the vote in the period since 1979. In Italy too, the MSI/AN has been relatively successful at the polls. As the MSI, the party won between 5.3 and 6.8 percent of the vote, and since becoming the AN, it has won between 12.0 and 15.7 percent of the vote. Similarly, in Denmark, where in the period before 1987 the requirements for state subventions can also be considered as being of 'medium' difficulty, the FRPd performed relatively well at the polls, recording between 3.6 and 11.0 percent of the vote.

The hypothesis is also confirmed to some extent in Belgium, where, as state subventions have become easier to access, the electoral scores of the parties of the extreme right have increased. The change in the Belgian electoral system in time for the elections of 1995 meant that the effective threshold fell from 4.8 percent to 2.8 percent (see Table 5.1). Therefore, although there was no simultaneous modification of the regulations governing state subsidies, and parliamentary representation is still required for parties to gain access to state subventions, it has effectively become easier to receive state money since 1995, as it has become easier for parties to win a seat in parliament. This change is reflected in Table 5.5, as Belgium is located in the 'hard' category in the period from 1979 to 1991, but is placed in the 'medium' category thereafter. At the same time as it has become easier for the parties to access state subsidies, the parties of the extreme right, both in Flanders and in Wallonia, have, on the whole, experienced growing electoral support. Having recorded electoral scores of between 1.6 percent and 9.5 percent of the vote in the period before 1995, the VB went on to poll 11.9 percent of the vote in 1995, 14.2 percent in 1999 and 16.8 percent in 2003. Similarly, the FN(b) has recorded higher electoral scores in the period since 1995 than it did in the years before then.

These cases appear to confirm the hypothesis that right-wing extremist parties will perform better in systems that have low requirements for state subventions than they will in countries where the requirements are much higher. This said, however, the extent to which the hypothesis is confirmed in practice should not be overestimated. While a pattern does undeniably exist which supports the hypothesis, there are a number of cases that do not conform to expectations.

One such case is Germany, where the right-wing extremist parties have not performed very well at the polls even though the requirements for state subvention access are considered 'easy' (see Table 5.5). Indeed, the Republikaner's score of 2.1 percent of the vote in 1990 constitutes the highest electoral result of all the German right-wing extremist parties in the period 1979–2003. Similarly, the Dutch parties of the extreme right have not experienced electoral success despite the fact that, here too, regulations for state subventions are low. The highest score by a right-wing extremist party in the Netherlands in the period under observation was 2.5 percent, obtained by the CD in the election of 1994.

The case of Switzerland also casts doubt on the strength of the hypothesis, because here the extreme right has experienced considerable fluctuations in its electoral fortunes despite the fact that the rules regarding state subventions have remained unchanged in the period under observation. The requirements to access state subventions in Switzerland are categorized as 'hard' (see Table 5.5), and in some instances the Swiss parties of the extreme right have indeed experienced low electoral scores as predicted by the hypothesis. For example, in 1979 the NA polled only 1.3 percent of the vote. Similarly in the election of 2003 both the SD (the successors to the NA) and the FPS recorded only 1.0 and 0.2 percent of the vote respectively. However, these two parties have also experienced some success at the polls, thereby contradicting the hypothesis. In 1991, for instance, the SD secured 3.3 percent of the vote and the FPS won 5.1 percent of the vote.

The patterns apparent in Germany and the Netherlands, where parties of the extreme right have been electorally unsuccessful even though state subvention access is deemed easy, and the fluctuations in the electoral scores of the Swiss right-wing extremist parties therefore put into question just how influential the regulations governing access to state subventions are, when it comes to explaining how well the parties of the extreme right perform at the polls.

The relationship between state subvention access and the electoral scores of the right-wing extremist parties throughout Western Europe may be further analysed by means of a correlation, similar to that carried out when the impact of the ballot access rules and the influence of the media access rules were examined. Having grouped the state subvention laws which operate in the countries under investigation according to their difficulty, as detailed above and as illustrated in Table 5.5, the different categories can now be coded, with those requirements which are regarded as being 'easy' to meet coded as 4, those which are of 'medium' difficulty coded as 3, those which are perceived as being 'hard' coded as 2, and finally, those which are considered 'very hard' to meet coded as 1.[27] If the relationship between state subvention rules and the extreme right party vote is such that right-wing extremist parties will encounter greater electoral success where state subvention access requirements are low than where they are high, a positive correlation coefficient is anticipated, given these codings. In other words, the higher the rank of the category, and hence the easier the requirements to access state subventions, the higher the electoral scores of the parties of the extreme right are expected to be.

In practice, the correlation coefficient is indeed positive, as anticipated. When the state subvention access laws are correlated with the electoral scores of the right-wing extremist parties the Spearman correlation coefficient is .305, and is statistically significant at the 0.01 level.[28] This finding thus lends weight to the hypothesis put forward above that the easier it is for parties of the extreme right to obtain state subventions, the better they will tend to perform at the polls.

Examining how easy or how difficult it is for parties to gain access to state subventions does not take into account how generous the state subventions are, however. The coding applied above therefore does not differentiate, for example, between a situation in which it is relatively easy for parties to access state subventions but where the funds they receive are modest (as in the Netherlands), and a situation in which it is harder to gain access to state money but where, if such money is secured, the sums are reasonably generous (as in Spain or Sweden).

One way in which it is possible to distinguish between such situations, and to take account of the different levels of state subventions in the countries under observation, is by weighting the scores that have been attributed to the state subventions laws. More specifically, where the funds awarded to the parties are generous, the codings assigned above can be given a double weighting, whereas where funds are rather modest, their original scores can be retained. A system in which state money is easy to obtain and state subventions are generous thus assumes a coding of 8, rather than its previous coding of 4. By contrast, where access to state subsidies is easy but where such funds are modest, the original coding of 4 is retained.

Table 5.5 indicates which systems of state subventions are considered 'generous' and which are judged to be 'modest'. Within the first category are those systems that provide campaign subsidies to political parties and that also grant public money to central party organizations for routine activities. Being 'generous' systems of state subventions, these cases are awarded a double weighting. In the second group are those systems in which only the parliamentary party groups receive state funds. These systems retain their original codings.

Differentiating between these two groups is clearly not an exact science. However, this distinction does provide the state subvention measure which was constructed above with more sensitivity, and it does therefore enable the impact of the different state subvention schemes to be analysed in greater detail. Furthermore, it is interesting to observe that the groupings devised above are very much in line with the categories that Nassmacher alludes to in his comparative study of campaign and party finance (1993: 256–8).

Bearing in mind these different levels of state subvention, it is now reasonable to anticipate that the parties of the extreme right should perform best in Austria, in Denmark (in the period since 1987 when subsidies to central party organizations were introduced) and in Germany, as in all three of these countries, state subsidies are easy to obtain and are also generous. In contrast, the electoral scores of the British and the Swiss right-wing extremist parties are expected to be among the lowest, since here not only are the requirements for access to state subsidies very hard to meet, but the subventions themselves are only limited. Finally, according to this logic, the right-wing extremist parties in all other countries are expected to experience greater electoral success than their British and Swiss counterparts, but to perform less well than their Austrian, Danish and German equivalents.

Right-wing extremist parties have indeed performed well in Austria and Denmark, as expected. The Austrian FPÖ is one of the most successful right-wing extremist parties in Western Europe, and polled over 20 percent of the vote in all elections in the 1990s. The Danish right-wing extremist parties have also performed well at the polls. The FRPd regularly secured between 4 and 11 percent of the vote until the late 1990s, and the DF has since taken on this mantle. In 1998 it recorded 7.4 percent of the vote, and in 2003 it polled 12.0 percent of the vote. The Austrian and Danish examples therefore add weight to the hypothesis that right-wing extremist parties will tend to perform well in systems where the requirements to access state subventions are low, and where the state subventions are generous.

The British case further confirms the hypothesis. The right-wing extremist parties in Britain have recorded low electoral scores, as anticipated given the high requirements to access state subventions and the modesty of the subsidies. Throughout the period 1979–2003 the NF and the BNP experienced electoral failure – the two parties never polled more than 0.7 percent of the vote.

As with previous hypotheses, however, a number of cases exist that do not conform to expectations. For example, the right-wing extremist parties in Germany have not performed well at the polls, even though they have been competing in a system in which state subventions are easy to access and are generous. The Republikaner have never secured more than 2.1 percent of the vote since they began competing in federal elections in 1990, and the DVU and NPD have been even more unsuccessful. The DVU recorded its highest electoral score in 1998, when it polled 1.2 percent of the vote. Prior to that date, it had never won more than 0.6 percent of the vote, and even then, the party was in an electoral coalition with the NPD. The Swiss case also calls into question the validity of the hypothesis. As was discussed above, the Swiss parties of the extreme right have experienced fluctuations in their levels of electoral support even though there has been no change in the regulations that govern access to state subventions in Switzerland. While they have recorded low electoral scores, as anticipated in view of the difficult requirements to access subventions and the modesty of the subsidies, the parties also encountered some success in the early and mid-1990s.

The hypothesis that parties of the extreme right will perform better in systems where it is easy to access state subventions, and where state subventions are generous, than they will in systems where access is difficult, and where state subventions are only modest, can be further examined if the electoral scores of the right-wing extremist parties are correlated with the weighted scores of the state subvention access laws. If the hypothesis is correct, the correlation should yield a positive correlation coefficient. That is, the right-wing extremist party vote should increase as the weighted scores increase, since increased scores indicate that the requirements for state subvention access are easy and that the subventions are generous.

The Spearman correlation coefficient is indeed positive (.379). Furthermore, it is statistically significant at the 0.01 level.[29] Thus, when the size of state subventions is taken into account, the state subvention access laws become even more strongly linked to the right-wing extremist party vote. As was hypothesized, generous levels of state subventions and easy access requirements are associated with high right-wing extremist party scores, whereas modest levels of state subsidies and access requirements that are difficult to satisfy are linked with low right-wing extremist party scores.

Ballot access, media access and state subvention rules: the overall impact of other electoral laws

As well as examining the influence of ballot access laws, media access laws and the laws regulating the access to state subventions separately, it is possible to consider these three laws together. In this way, the overall impact of these other electoral laws on the right-wing extremist party vote can be assessed. Table 5.6 reports the difficulty of the ballot access rules, the media

Table 5.6 Electoral laws and their impact on right-wing extremist parties, 1979–2003

Country	Ballot access	Media access	State subvention access	Extent of state subvention[a]	Overall score[b]
Austria	Hard (1)	Very hard (1)	Easy (4)	Generous	10
Belgium					
until 1989	Medium (2)	Medium (3)	Hard (2)	Modest	7
1989–91	Medium (2)	Medium (3)	Hard (2)	Generous	9
from 1995	Medium (2)	Medium (3)	Medium (3)	Generous	11
Britain	Hard (1)	Hard (2)	Very hard (1)	Modest	4
Denmark					
until 1987	Hard (1)	Easy (4)	Medium (3)	Modest	8
from 1987	Hard (1)	Easy (4)	Easy (4)	Generous	13
France					
until 1988	Medium (2)	Hard (2)	No state subvention	No state subvention	4
1988	Medium (2)	Hard (2)	Very hard (1)	Generous	6
from 1993	Medium (2)	Hard (2)	Medium (3)	Generous	10
Germany	Medium (2)	Medium (3)	Easy (4)	Generous	13
Greece					
until 1984	Medium (2)	Very hard (1)	No state subvention	No state subvention	3
from 1984	Medium (2)	Very hard (1)	Medium (3)	Generous	9
Italy	Medium (2)	Easy (4)	Medium (3)	Generous	12
Netherlands					
until 1982	Hard (1)	Easy (4)	Easy (4)	Modest	9
from 1982	Hard (1)	Very hard (1)	Easy (4)	Modest	6

Table 5.6   (continued)

Country	Ballot access	Media access	State subvention access	Extent of state subvention[a]	Overall score[b]
Norway	Easy (3)	Medium (3)	Medium (3)	Generous	12
Portugal					
until 1993	Easy (3)	Easy (4)	Hard (2)	Generous	11
from 1993	Easy (3)	Easy (4)	Easy (4)	Generous	15
Spain	Easy (3)	Medium (3)	Hard (2)	Generous	10
Sweden	Easy (3)	Medium (3)	Medium (3)	Generous	12
Switzerland	Medium (2)	Hard (2)	Hard (2)	Modest	6

Notes: For details of the coding categories see Tables 5.3–5.5. [a] A distinction is made between those countries which offer generous state subventions and those where state subventions are more modest. See Nassmacher (1993) for details of how large the state subventions are in the various countries. Making this distinction allows a double weighting of the state subvention codes in those countries where they are generous.
[b] Overall scores are calculated by summing the ballot access scores, the media access scores and the state subvention access scores. The overall scores take account of the size of state subventions by double weighting these scores when state subventions are generous.
Sources: Hand *et al.* (1979); Smith (1981); Ewing (1987); Borre (1988); Gunlicks (1988); Ciaurro (1989); del Castillo (1989); Koole (1989); Nassmacher (1989); Gidlund (1991); Papademetriou (1991); Siune (1991); Svåsand (1991); Katz and Mair (1992); von Arnim (1993); Drysch (1993); Johnston and Pattie (1993); Klee (1993); Avril (1994); del Castillo (1994); Gidlund (1994); Koole (1994); Landfried (1994); Linton (1994); Gamaleri (1995); Holtz-Bacha and Kaid (1995a, 1995b); Bille (1996); LeDuc *et al.* (1996); Bille (1997); Katz (1997); Rhodes (1997); Ricolfi (1997); Gentile and Kriesi (1998); Swyngedouw (1998); Lange (1999); Pujas and Rhodes (1999); Farrell and Webb (2000); Gunther *et al.* (2000); Lege 28/00 (2000); Marletti and Roncarolo (2000); Pierre *et al.* (2000); Pujas (2000); Van Biezen (2000); Sear (2001); Parteiengesetz (2002); Parteiengesetz (2003); ACE Project; Constitution of the Portuguese Republic; Economic History Services (a, b); Inter-Parliamentary Union Parline Database; XE.Com. Personal communication with Luciano Bardi; Hans Hirter; Aphrodite Kassiari; Romain Lachat; Andreas Ladner; Paul Lucardie; Georg Lutz; José Magone; José Ramón Montero; Gerassimos Moschonas; Wolfgang C. Müller; Luis Ramiro; Pascal Sciarini; Lars Svåsand.

access rules and the state subventions access requirements in the different countries under observation, as well as the generosity of the state subventions. Taking these three sets of electoral laws together, a number of predictions can be made as to how well the right-wing extremist parties are expected to have performed.

It is reasonable to expect parties of the extreme right to have encountered electoral success in Portugal, for example, both in the period until 1993 (the year the state subvention laws were changed) and in the years after that date. In the first of these periods, two of the three sets of requirements (ballot and media access) were categorized as 'easy' to fulfil. In the second period, all three sets of requirements were categorized as 'easy' to meet. What is more, in both periods the state subventions were considered generous. Equally, it is reasonable to expect parties of the extreme right to have performed well in Denmark in the period since 1987, in Germany, in Italy, in Norway and in Sweden. In all these countries the regulations governing ballot access, media access and state subventions, when considered together, have been relatively easy to meet.

In contrast, the parties of the extreme right may be expected to perform badly at the polls in Britain, in France in the period until 1993, in Greece in the period until 1984, in the Netherlands in the years since 1982 and in Switzerland. In these countries the rules relating to ballot access, media access and state subventions were such that, together, they made for an institutional environment that was restrictive to small parties such as those of the extreme right. Furthermore, in those instances where the right-wing extremist parties in these countries were able to gain access to state subventions, these subsidies were only modest.

As has been the case with all of the hypotheses examined above, these expectations are borne out in some countries, but do not hold true in others. As predicted, the parties of the extreme right have indeed performed well at the polls in Denmark in the period since 1987, in Italy and in Norway. Similarly, right-wing extremist parties have recorded low electoral scores in Britain, in Greece and in the Netherlands, as anticipated. However, the extreme right parties in Portugal and in Germany have not experienced electoral success as was predicted. Equally, the French FN has encountered success at the polls even though the institutional environment in which it has competed has been relatively restrictive.

The combined effect of the three sets of regulations may be further analysed if the scores assigned to each set of laws in each country are summed. For example, in the case of Austria, where the ballot access regulations were assigned a score of 1 (hard), the media access requirements a score of 1 (very hard), and the state subvention requirements a score of 4 (easy), the combined effect of the three sets of laws may be given a score of 6 (1 + 1 + 4) if the generosity of the state subventions is ignored, or a score of 10 (1 + 1 + 8) if the state subvention scores are double weighted in view of the fact that they are generous. These overall scores, which are reported in the last column of Table 5.6, thus reflect just how restrictive the electoral laws are in the different countries under observation. They also allow for the relationship between the three sets of electoral laws and the right-wing extremist party vote to be examined further, as these overall scores can be correlated with the electoral scores of the right-wing extremist parties.

As with the previous correlations, a positive correlation coefficient is anticipated because the higher the overall score of the electoral laws (that is, the less restrictive the electoral environment), the higher the extreme right party vote is expected to be. In practice, the correlation coefficient is indeed positive. When no attention is paid to the size of the state subventions (that is, when the state subvention scores are not double weighted), the Spearman correlation coefficient is .176, and when the size of state subventions is taken into account, the correlation coefficient is 0.270. The first of these coefficients is statistically significant at the 0.05 level, and the second is statistically significant at the 0.01 level.[30]

These findings suggest that, when considered together, the three electoral laws do influence the right-wing extremist party vote. More specifically, they indicate that low ballot access requirements, low media access requirements, and low state subvention access requirements together make for more successful right-wing extremist parties. They also suggest that, if the size of the state subventions is taken into consideration, the relationship between the electoral laws and the right-wing extremist party vote is even stronger, with more generous state subventions being associated with higher right-wing extremist party scores. However, having examined the three sets of electoral laws separately, as well as together, it appears that the significant association that was found to exist between the electoral laws and the right-wing extremist party vote is mostly due to the link that exists between the media access requirements and the right-wing extremist party vote, and to the (even stronger) relationship that exists between the state subvention requirements and the right-wing extremist party vote. After all, when the ballot access rules were examined on their own, no association was found to exist between them and the right-wing extremist party vote.

Concluding remarks

This chapter has examined the relationship between the right-wing extremist party vote and the electoral institutions present in the countries under observation, so as to establish whether the varying levels of electoral success of the West European parties of the extreme right may be attributed in any way to the presence of different electoral institutions. From its analysis of the influence of electoral systems, as well as from its investigation into the impact of three broader sets of electoral laws, the conclusion must be reached that the institutional environment has only limited power in explaining why the right-wing extremist party vote has varied so significantly across Western Europe in the period 1979–2003.

As far as electoral systems are concerned, the above discussions have shown that district magnitude and legal thresholds (as represented by effective thresholds) do help explain some of the variation in the electoral scores of the parties of the extreme right. However, these dimensions of the electoral system assume this explanatory power only when proportional electoral systems are considered on their own. When all electoral systems are examined together, high district magnitudes and low legal thresholds are no longer consistently linked to high right-wing extremist party scores. Furthermore, when other dimensions of electoral systems (such as the electoral formula) are taken into consideration, and when the overall disproportionality of the system is examined, no significant relationship is found to exist between the right-wing extremist party vote and the type of electoral system in operation.

It is important to emphasize that the present findings do not imply that electoral systems have no effect on the parties of the extreme right, however. After all, the political consequences of electoral systems have been well documented throughout the existing literature, and their effect on small parties has been discussed in detail. Nonetheless, this chapter has suggested that the relationship between electoral systems and the right-wing extremist party vote is a somewhat elusive one, since electoral systems are not able to account for the disparity in the electoral scores of the right-wing extremist parties across Western Europe.

The systematic analysis of the relationship between electoral systems and the right-wing extremist party vote that has been undertaken in this chapter sheds light on an area of study that has traditionally been characterized by assumption rather than by empirical research. The findings have challenged the 'conventional wisdom' frequently aired by proponents of majoritarian electoral systems that proportional representation encourages political extremism. In addition, the conclusions reached in this chapter raise important questions about the nature of the psychological effect of electoral systems. Since high levels of electoral proportionality have not been consistently linked with high electoral scores for the parties of the extreme right, it may be the case that the psychological effects of electoral systems are being overshadowed by other concerns. Alternatively, it could be that voters continue to vote for the extreme right, even though they know these parties stand little chance of gaining representation.

With regard to other electoral laws, the chapter has shown that while the ballot access requirements do not help account for why some right-wing extremist parties have performed better than others at the polls, the rules governing the parties' access to the broadcast media and the regulations relating to state subventions do appear important in explaining the disparity in the electoral success of the parties of the extreme right. Where access to the media has been relatively easy to obtain, and where requirements for state subventions have been low and the levels of state subvention have been generous, the right-wing extremist party vote has been high. Conversely, where it has been difficult for parties to gain access to the broadcast media and to state subventions, and where subsidies have been modest, the parties of the extreme right have, on the whole, performed poorly at the polls.

It should be remembered that electoral laws have been considered in isolation only in this chapter, and it may well be that their influence on the right-wing extremist party vote changes when they are examined in conjunction with other explanatory factors. Therefore, while the conclusions reached in this chapter form a very useful base from which to assess the effects of electoral institutions on the parties of the extreme right, the precise impact of the institutional environment can only be determined when the influence of other explanatory factors are also taken into account.

The next chapter turns its attention to precisely this matter. It briefly reviews the conclusions reached so far in the book, and then moves to consider the ways in which the different explanatory variables examined in the last four chapters together help account for the variation in the right-wing extremist party vote across Western Europe.

Notes

1 The prediction that the mechanical effect and the psychological effect of electoral systems are linked in this way is confirmed by Blais and Carty (1991). They measure the impact of the psychological effect of electoral systems and conclude that it is similar in magnitude to their mechanical effect.

2 There is no generally accepted definition of what constitutes a 'small' political party. Instead, a number of different definitions have been put forward which draw on different approaches. In a useful review of these, Smith (1991) suggests that smallness may be thought of either in quantitative terms or in systemic terms. In the former approach, as used by Mair (1991), upper and lower thresholds are set and any party that falls within these limits is considered to be a small party. Mair, for example, includes all parties that have polled more than 1 percent but less than 15 percent of the vote, provided they have contested at least three elections. This approach benefits from simplicity, is open to quantitative testing and is amenable to cross-national comparison. Its main disadvantage, however, is that the thresholds are somewhat arbitrary. In the second approach, smallness is considered a systemic property: the size of individual parties is viewed in relation to the entire party system, and the nature of small parties varies as the format of the party system varies.

3 In some cases, majoritarian electoral formulae are used in multi-member districts. For instance, Thailand, Chile and South Korea employ the plurality formula in multi-member districts, while Mali uses the majority formula in multi-member districts. In these instances, the electoral outcome is even more disproportional than in single-member districts (Taagepera and Shugart, 1989: 23).

4 In some instances the district magnitude varies in line with the total electorate or the turnout rather than with the population. For example, in the German *Land* of Baden-Württemberg the district magnitude is determined by the turnout.

5 The country is first divided into 43 regional districts (the lower tier). Any votes not needed in the allocation of seats at this tier are pooled at the province level. The nine provinces (*Länder*) of the country make-up the second tier (the higher tier). Finally, any votes not used in seat allocations at the provincial level are pooled at the national level (the national tier) (Müller, 1993; Inter-Parliamentary Union Parline Database).

6 Under majoritarian formulae, as the district magnitude increases, the proportionality of the electoral outcome decreases.

7 As in Chapter 4, the Pearson correlation coefficient is used here because the data in question are ratio scale data, and the relationship between the electoral scores

of the right-wing extremist parties and the effective threshold of the electoral systems is assumed to be a linear one. A one-tailed test was carried out because the direction of the relationship between the two variables was already hypothesized: a negative relationship was predicted.

8   Again, as in Chapter 4, a significance test is used here, as even though this analysis has adopted an inclusive approach as to which right-wing extremist parties are incorporated in the investigation, strictly speaking, these parties constitute a sample rather than a population. This is because the study examines a limited time period only and because some very minor right-wing extremist parties may have been omitted from the analysis.

9   The post-1993 Italian electoral system is usually defined in the literature as a 'mixed' electoral system, since it makes use of a combination of different electoral formulae. As Table 5.1 illustrates, it is a multi-tiered system that uses the plurality formula at the lower tier and employs the Hare formula at the upper tier. Three-quarters of the seats are allocated at the lower tier and one-quarter are allocated at the higher tier. The upper tier corrects some of the disproportionality caused by the lower tier (see Katz, 1996a; Farrell, 2001: 119). Classifying mixed electoral systems is a contentious issue, because a judgement must be made as to the relative weight of the majoritarian element on the one hand and the proportional element on the other. Whereas Massicotte and Blais (1999) include the post-1993 Italian system in their 'corrective' category of electoral systems, and hence consider its proportional element sufficient to warrant its being termed a mixed-member-proportional (MMP) system, Shugart and Wattenberg (2001) maintain that its element of correction is only limited, and they therefore include it in the mixed-member-majoritarian (MMM) category of mixed electoral systems. In this analysis, the post-1993 Italian electoral system is included in the proportional representation (PR) category of electoral systems on the grounds that it is the proportional formula that operates at the decisive level, even though the system's corrective capacity may not be as great as it could be.

10   This finding contrasts with the results of earlier work, in which no significant relationship was found to exist between effective thresholds and the right-wing extremist party vote when all electoral systems were considered together *and* when proportional systems were examined on their own (see Carter, 2002). The major difference between this earlier work and the present analysis is that, in the earlier study, Belgium was treated as one political system rather than two as it is here (see Chapter 1).

11   Under the d'Hondt formula, the votes of the parties are first divided by 1, and the party with the highest average vote is awarded a seat. The process continues with the divisors 2, 3, 4, 5, 6 etc. until all the seats are filled. Under the Sainte-Laguë formula the divisors 1, 3, 5, 7 etc. are used. This electoral formula is no longer employed in Europe, however, as the Scandinavian countries chose to replace it with the modified version (which uses the divisors 1.4, 3, 5, 7 etc.) on the grounds that the pure variant was too accommodating to small parties. The raising of the first divisor from 1 to 1.4 now makes it more difficult for small competitors to win their first seat, and hence renders the system less proportional. For parties that have already won their first seat the pure version and the modified version of the formula operate identically (Lijphart, 1994: 23, 157, 181).

12 The Hare quota is calculated by dividing the number of valid votes by the district magnitude. The Droop quota, by contrast, is worked out by dividing the number of valid votes by the district magnitude plus 1. When the Imperiali quota is used, the number of valid votes is divided by the district magnitude plus 2.

13 Under the Hagenbach-Bischoff formula, parties are first awarded seats according to the Droop quota, and then the number of seats already won plus 1 is used as the divisor (Taagepera and Shugart, 1989: 30; Farrell, 2001: 213–14).

14 When ranking the different formulae according to their proportionality, Katz (1997) distinguishes between highest-average formulae and largest-remainder formulae. According to him, the d'Hondt formula is the least proportional of the highest-average formulae, the Modified Sainte-Laguë forms an intermediate category and the pure Sainte-Laguë is the most proportional. As for largest-remainder formulae, he maintains that the Hare formula is the most proportional, followed by the Droop formula and then the Imperiali formula. Importantly, however, Katz argues that the proportionality profiles of the different formulae depend on the number of parties contesting the election (1997: 123).

15 For details of the post-1993 Italian electoral system see note 9.

16 The Gallagher (least-squares) index is calculated by taking the vote–seat share differences for each party, squaring them and then adding them. This total is then divided by 2. Finally the square root of this value is taken as the measure of disproportionality (see Gallagher, 1991). Other measures of disproportionality include the Rae index (1967), which sums the absolute differences between the vote percentages and the seat percentages, and then divides by the number of parties. This measure has come in for criticism, however, as it is overly sensitive to the presence of very small parties, and therefore understates the disproportionality of systems that contain small competitors. Another measure is the Loosemore-Hanby index (1971). Here, the absolute values of all vote–seat share differences are added, as was the case in the Rae index, but then divided by 2 (rather than divided by the number of parties). While the Loosemore-Hanby index avoids the problems that beset the Rae index, it too has its own drawbacks. Most notably, it tends to exaggerate the disproportionality of systems that contain large numbers of parties, and therefore overstates the disproportionality of proportional systems. The advantage of the Gallagher index is that it strikes a balance between the Rae and the Loosemore-Hanby indices. For a discussion of the various indices see Lijphart (1994: 58–67).

17 See note 7.

18 See note 8.

19 The correlation coefficient between the small party vote and the disproportionality of the electoral system in Mair's study is -0.283. In contrast to this present investigation, however, Mair includes all small parties in Western Europe in the post-war period up to 1990, and, rather than using the small party vote at each national election as units of analysis, he employs the mean small party vote in one of two election phases (1947–66 and 1967–87). His methodology is therefore quite different to the one employed here. When he excludes two deviant cases (Austria 1967–87 and West Germany 1967–87) and the two majoritarian systems that have very high disproportionality values (France 1947–66 and 1967–87, and the UK 1967–87), he arrives at even stronger negative correlations (-0.423 and -0.572).

20 A previous, abridged version of the material contained in this section appeared in Bowler *et al.* (2003).
21 This coding scheme is informed by the procedure adopted in Bowler *et al.* (2003).
22 The 'easy' category is coded 3 and the 'hard' category is coded 1 because when the laws relating to state subventions are examined later in the chapter these codings allow for the distinction to be made between generous and modest state subventions.
23 Since the ballot access data are ordinal data, in the form of ranked categories, the Spearman correlation coefficient was used. A one-tailed test was carried out as the direction of the relationship was already anticipated: a positive correlation coefficient was predicted.
24 See note 8.
25 Whereas the ballot access data naturally fell into three categories ('easy', 'medium' and 'hard'), the media access data display greater variety. They are therefore grouped into four different categories ('easy', 'medium', 'hard' and 'very hard').
26 See note 23 and note 8.
27 In view of the fact that state subvention laws have been frequently altered, the level of difficulty of the laws in each country has often changed. This is reflected in Table 5.5.
28 See note 23 and note 8. The very few instances in which there were no state subventions at all (France until 1988 and Greece until 1984) were treated as missing data and were not included in the correlation.
29 See note 8 and note 23.
30 See note 8 and note 23.

Accounting for varying electoral fortunes

Over the course of the last four chapters, this book has proposed, examined and tested four separate sets of political explanations for why the parties of the extreme right in Western Europe have recorded such divergent electoral scores in the period 1979–2003. Throughout this analysis, the fact that these separate explanations do not exist independently of each other has been kept firmly in mind, and each chapter has warned of the dangers of drawing conclusions about the power of each set of explanations when they are considered in isolation only. In light of these concerns, this final chapter brings the four sets of explanations together, and establishes the extent to which they may together account for why right-wing extremist parties in Western Europe have experienced such varying levels of electoral success since the late 1970s.

Before the four different sets of explanations are examined together, in the first instance, it is useful to review the analysis undertaken in the previous chapters, and to recall the conclusions drawn from these investigations. As well as serving as a reminder of what findings have been uncovered in the course of the analysis, this review enables some preliminary predictions to be made about the strength of each set of explanations in an overall account of the disparity in the electoral scores of the parties of the extreme right. With these predictions in mind, it is then possible to construct a series of integrated models that examine how well all the different variables, in combination, explain the uneven electoral success of the parties of the extreme right across Western Europe.

Explanations for the variation in the right-wing extremist party vote: the story so far

Chapter 2 began the analysis by investigating the influence of different types of right-wing extremist party ideology, and examined whether right-wing extremist electoral success has been associated with a specific type of right-wing extremist ideology, or whether, conversely, the nature of a party's ideology has not been related to its electoral fortunes in any way. In the first instance, Chapter 2 suggested that right-wing extremist party ideology is far from uniform. More specifically, five different types of right-wing extremist party ideology were identified: neo-Nazi ideologies; neo-fascist ideologies; authoritarian xenophobic ideologies; neo-liberal xenophobic ideologies; and neo-liberal populist ideologies. In terms of the link between ideology and electoral success, the analysis suggested that two particular types of ideology (namely neo-Nazi and neo-fascist ideologies) are associated with low electoral scores. In contrast, the other three types of party ideology (authoritarian xenophobic, neo-liberal xenophobic and neo-liberal populist ideologies) have tended to be linked with electoral success. At the same time, however, it was observed that these three latter types of ideology do not necessarily guarantee that a party will record high electoral scores.

Chapter 3 then turned its attention to exploring the impact of the parties' organizational structures and leaderships on their electoral performance. From a detailed examination of the parties' internal dynamics, the chapter categorized the parties of the extreme right into two groups: well-organized and well-led parties, and badly organized and badly led parties. An investigation of the relationship between the organization and leadership of the parties and their electoral scores found that, as expected, the parties that are well organized and well led performed markedly better at the polls than their badly organized and badly led counterparts. The analysis also indicated that the degree of factionalism within the parties appears to have little relevance to how well they performed at the polls. Strong organization and leadership seem able to overcome any dissent within the parties, whereas weak organization and leadership appear unable to cope with such rifts.

Having explored the influence of party-centric factors, the analysis then turned its attention to examining the impact of contextual factors on the right-wing extremist party vote. Chapter 4 considered the effects of different patterns of party competition on the electoral fortunes of the parties of the extreme right. In a first section it investigated the ideological proximity of the parties of the mainstream right, and sought to ascertain whether the positions of these mainstream competitors affected the right-wing extremist party vote. Having determined how much political space was available at the extreme right of the political spectrum, the chapter went on to explore whether the location of the right-wing extremist parties within this political space in any way influenced their levels of electoral success. It then examined the interaction between the positions of the parties of the mainstream right and the positions of the parties of the extreme right. Finally, the chapter considered the influence of patterns of party competition at the centre of the political spectrum, and investigated whether ideological convergence between the parties of the mainstream left and the parties of the mainstream right affected the right-wing extremist party vote.

The results of Chapter 4 suggested that, as had been expected, right-wing extremist parties have tended to perform better when their mainstream right opponents are more moderate than when they are more right-wing. That is, the greater the political space available to the parties of the extreme right, the higher their levels of electoral success have tended to be. As far as their own ideological position within this space is concerned, the analysis indicated that the right-wing extremist parties have, on the whole, enjoyed higher electoral scores when they themselves are more moderate than when they are more extreme. These two trends further interacted to suggest that right-wing extremist parties have tended to perform especially well when both they and their mainstream right opponents are ideologically moderate. By contrast, when both the right-wing extremist parties and the mainstream right parties are more right-wing, the electoral scores of the parties of the extreme right have tended to be low. Finally, the last section of the chapter demonstrated that, as anticipated, right-wing extremist parties have tended to record higher vote shares when the parties of the mainstream left and the parties of the mainstream right have converged ideologically than when these two sets of parties have remained ideologically more distinct from each other.

Finally, Chapter 5 examined the impact of electoral institutions on the right-wing extremist party vote. In its first section the chapter investigated the influence of different electoral systems, and focused on the effects of district magnitudes and legal thresholds (as represented by effective thresholds), and electoral formulae. It also considered the impact of the overall proportionality profile of the electoral system. In a second section, the chapter moved on to explore the influence of other electoral laws, namely ballot access requirements, media access requirements and the laws regulating access to state subventions.

The findings from this chapter suggested that different electoral systems across the countries under observation have limited power in helping to explain the variation in the electoral scores of the parties of the extreme right. When proportional electoral systems were examined on their own, a relationship was found to exist between district magnitudes and legal thresholds (as represented by effective thresholds) on the one hand, and the right-wing extremist party vote on the other: high district magnitudes and low legal thresholds (that is, low effective thresholds) were consistently linked with high right-wing extremist party scores. However, when all electoral systems were examined together, effective thresholds no longer assumed such explanatory power. The chapter also suggested that electoral formulae did not help account for the uneven right-wing extremist party vote, and this was the case when all systems were considered together as well as when proportional systems were examined on their own. Finally, the analysis showed that even the overall proportionality profile of the electoral system did not contribute to explaining the variation in the electoral scores of the West European parties of the extreme right. When all electoral systems were examined together and when proportional systems were considered on their own, no significant relationship was found to exist between the right-wing extremist party vote and the proportionality profile of the electoral system.

In terms of other electoral laws, the analysis in Chapter 5 suggested that the rules governing access to the ballot do not seem to influence the right-wing extremist party vote in any consistent way. However, the laws relating to access to the broadcast media, and those concerned with the receipt of state subventions, do appear to have some power in helping to account for the parties' uneven electoral performances. Where access to the broadcast media is relatively easy to obtain, right-wing extremist parties have tended to record high electoral scores. By contrast, where access is relatively difficult, the parties' scores have, on the whole, been lower. Similarly, where state subventions are easy to access and subsidies are generous, parties of the extreme right have tended to record high electoral scores. In contrast, where access is difficult and state subventions are only modest, the parties have tended to poll lower electoral scores.

The findings from the last four chapters therefore suggest that the type of ideology right-wing extremist parties embrace, the organization and leadership of the parties, and the different patterns of party competition at work in the various political systems under investigation are all likely to be important factors in an overall explanation for the variation in the right-wing extremist party vote. By contrast, electoral institutions are expected to play only a limited role in helping to understand why certain right-wing extremist parties have performed better than others in elections, since when they were examined on their own, these variables contributed little to explaining the uneven vote of the parties.

It is important to recognize that these predictions rest on bivariate analyses, however, and that these analyses have their limitations because they only examine the influence of one variable upon another. When the different explanations for the variation in the right-wing extremist party vote are examined together, rather than separately as has been the case up until now, their explanatory power may well change. It is quite possible for a variable that appeared highly significant when considered in isolation to become insignificant when it is considered in conjunction with other explanatory variables. Likewise, factors that assumed no explanatory power when viewed on their own might become important in an overall account of the divergent electoral scores of the parties of the extreme right.

In the following section, all four sets of explanations for the variation in the extreme right party vote are examined together by means of two multiple regression models. Multiple regression not only allows for the overall power of the four different sets of explanations to be assessed, but also means that the relative power of each separate set of explanations can be investigated. In other words, the influence of one set of variables can be examined while taking account of the impact of all others sets of variables.

Explanations for the variation in the right-wing extremist party vote: putting the pieces together

Table 6.1 reports the results of an OLS regression model of the combined effects on the right-wing extremist party vote of the four sets of explanations examined in the previous chapters. The model includes explanatory variables that account for right-wing extremist party ideology, right-wing extremist party organization and leadership, patterns of party competition (measured by the ideological positions of the parties of the mainstream right, the ideological positions of the parties of the extreme right, and the ideological convergence between the parties of the mainstream left and the parties of the mainstream right), and electoral systems (as measured by the effective threshold and the disproportionality scores) and other electoral laws. All cases are included in the model for which data are available (n = 77).[1]

The model presented in Table 6.1 (labelled Model 1) indicates that many of the variables discussed in the previous four chapters are important in an overall explanation for the variation in the right-wing extremist party vote across Western Europe. In the first instance, it suggests that both sets of party-centric factors (party ideology, and party organization and leadership) are particularly powerful in explaining the uneven electoral scores of the parties of the extreme right. As regards party ideology, the results indicate that neo-fascist, authoritarian xenophobic, neo-liberal xenophobic and neo-liberal populist ideologies are all linked with high electoral scores for the parties of the extreme right. This therefore suggests that right-wing extremist parties are more likely to experience electoral failure if they embrace a neo-Nazi type of ideology (the base category) than if they adopt any of the other four types of right-wing extremist party ideology.

These results, to some extent, concur with the conclusions reached in Chapter 2, in which the effects of party ideology on the right-wing extremist party vote were examined in isolation. In Chapter 2 it was suggested that parties that embraced an authoritarian xenophobic, a neo-liberal xenophobic or a neo-liberal populist type of party ideology were more likely to experience electoral success than parties that adopted a neo-Nazi or a neo-fascist type of ideology. The advantages of embracing an authoritarian xenophobic, a neo-liberal xenophobic or a neo-liberal populist type of ideology are confirmed here, but the disadvantages of adopting a neo-fascist type of ideology are not. Instead, in Model 1 a neo-fascist type of party ideology is a significant predictor of party success.[2]

The findings also indicate that party organization and leadership are important factors in explaining why certain parties of the extreme right encounter electoral success while others do not. Right-wing extremist parties that are well organized and well led perform substantially better at the polls than right-wing extremist parties that are badly organized and badly led. Indeed, when all other variables are held constant, well-organized

Table 6.1 Effects of party ideology, party organization and leadership, party competition and electoral institutions on the right-wing extremist party vote (OLS regression): Model 1

Independent variables	Unstandardized coefficients		Standardized coefficients
	B	Std error	Beta
Neo-fascist parties (dummy)	6.654**	2.920	0.413
Authoritarian xenophobic parties (dummy)	7.255***	2.641	0.574
Neo-liberal xenophobic parties (dummy)	9.694***	3.037	0.745
Neo-liberal populist parties (dummy)	7.529**	3.201	0.401
Organization and leadership	6.466***	1.194	0.536
Ideological position of nearest mainstream right party	−16.372*	8.908	−0.228
Ideological position of right-wing extremist party	5.075	8.656	0.068
Convergence between mainstream left and mainstream right	23.592***	7.175	0.388
Effective threshold	−0.033	0.132	−0.050
Disproportionality index	0.208	0.220	0.170
Three electoral laws	−0.156	0.286	−0.068
Constant	−11.110		
Adjusted R²	0.487		
Durbin-Watson	1.268		
n = 77			

Notes: Dependent variable: right-wing extremist party vote (in percent). *Independent variables:* the base category for party ideology is the neo-Nazi category of parties. Organization and leadership: dummy variable: 1 indicates well-organized and well-led parties; 0 indicates badly organized and badly led parties. Ideological position of nearest mainstream right party: as measured on a left–right scale that runs from 0 to 1, with 0 indicating extreme left scores, and 1 indicating extreme right scores (see Chapter 4 for further details). Ideological position of right-wing extremist party: as measured on a left–right scale that runs from 0 to 1, with 0 indicating extreme left scores, and 1 indicating extreme right scores (see Chapter 4 for further details). Convergence between mainstream left and mainstream right: calculated as follows: 1−(mainstream right party score on left-right scale−mainstream left party score on left–right scale). The measure runs from 1 to 0. High scores reflect significant convergence between the mainstream parties; low scores reflect low convergence between the mainstream parties (see Chapter 4 for further details). Effective threshold (in percent). Disproportionality index: Gallagher index (see Chapter 5 for further details). Three electoral laws: this measure reflects ballot access, media access and state subvention access requirements as well as the generosity of state subventions. High scores reflect requirements that are easy to meet and state subventions that are generous; low scores reflect requirements that are difficult to meet and state subventions that are only modest (see Chapter 5 for further details). *** coefficient significant at the 0.01 level; ** coefficient significant at the 0.05 level; * coefficient significant at the 0.1 level.

and well-led parties have recorded an average of 6.5 percent more of the vote than their badly organized, badly led counterparts.

The ideological positions of the parties of the mainstream right also have a significant effect on the right-wing extremist party vote. As expected, the more right-wing the party of the mainstream right, the lower the right-wing extremist party vote has tended to be. Similarly, the degree of ideological convergence between the parties of the mainstream left and the parties of the mainstream right influences the right-wing extremist vote in a significant fashion. As anticipated, as the mainstream parties become ideologically more similar, the right-wing extremist party vote increases.

The other explanatory variables included in the model are not statistically significant (at the 0.1 level or better). Thus, contrary to expectations, the findings indicate that the ideological positions of the parties of the extreme right on the left–right spectrum do not help explain the variance in the right-wing extremist party vote. The association that was found to exist between these ideological positions and the electoral scores of the parties of the extreme right in Chapter 4 thus disappears when all explanatory variables are considered together.

As regards electoral institutions, in line with the predictions made above and consistent with the findings of Chapter 5, the results show that neither the effective threshold nor the overall proportionality profile of the electoral system exerts an effect on the right-wing extremism party vote.[3] Contrary to expectations, however, the electoral laws regulating access to the ballot, to the broadcast media and to state subventions also have no effect on the right-wing extremist party vote when all explanatory variables are considered together, and hence play no part in helping to account for the uneven electoral fortunes of the parties.

The model presented in Table 6.1 explains some 49 percent of the variance in the right-wing extremist party vote. In view of the fact that this analysis has been concerned with political explanations for the disparity in the electoral scores of the right-wing extremist parties only, and has not examined socio-economic, cultural or historical explanations, this is quite substantial.[4] In spite of its explanatory power, however, Model 1 suffers from the major drawback that the number of cases it examines is limited to 77, because of the lack of expert judgement data on the smallest parties of the extreme right. In the light of this, a second, alternative model was constructed (Model 2, illustrated in Table 6.2), from which the ideological positions of the parties of the extreme right were excluded. Excluding this variable does not present a significant problem, since the continued inclusion of dummy variables for the different types of right-wing extremist party ideology means that the model still takes the ideology of the parties of the extreme right into account. Excluding the ideological positions of the parties of the extreme right from this second model results in the number of cases being boosted from 77 to 134.[5]

Table 6.2   Effects of party ideology, party organization and leadership, party competition and electoral institutions on the right-wing extremist party vote (OLS regression): Model 2

Independent variables	Unstandardized coefficients		Standardized coefficients
	B	Std error	Beta
Neo-fascist parties (dummy)	1.552	1.388	0.097
Authoritarian xenophobic parties (dummy)	2.230**	1.088	0.195
Neo-liberal xenophobic parties (dummy)	3.374***	1.264	0.258
Neo-liberal populist parties (dummy)	0.060	1.492	0.003
Organization and leadership	6.802***	0.793	0.592
Ideological position of nearest mainstream right party	−7.765	4.994	−0.122
Convergence between mainstream left and mainstream right	14.249***	4.385	0.247
Effective threshold	−0.046	0.081	−0.094
Disproportionality index	0.114	0.147	0.112
Three electoral laws	−0.067	0.173	−0.036
Constant	−2.687	6.238	
Adjusted R^2	0.540		
Durbin-Watson	1.105		
n = 134			

Notes: Dependent variable: right-wing extremist party vote (in percent). *Independent variables:* the base category for party ideology is the neo-Nazi category of parties. Organization and leadership: dummy variable: 1 indicates well-organized and well-led parties; 0 indicates badly organized and badly led parties. Ideological position of nearest mainstream right party: as measured on a left–right scale that runs from 0 to 1, with 0 indicating extreme left scores, and 1 indicating extreme right scores (see Chapter 4 for further details). Ideological position of right-wing extremist party: as measured on a left–right scale that runs from 0 to 1, with 0 indicating extreme left scores, and 1 indicating extreme right scores (see Chapter 4 for further details). Convergence between mainstream left and mainstream right: calculated as follows: 1−(mainstream right party score on left-right scale−mainstream left party score on left–right scale). The measure runs from 1 to 0. High scores reflect significant convergence between the mainstream parties; low scores reflect low convergence between the mainstream parties (see Chapter 4 for further details). Effective threshold (in percent). Disproportionality index: Gallagher index (see Chapter 5 for further details). Three electoral laws: this measure reflects ballot access, media access and state subvention access requirements as well as the generosity of state subventions. High scores reflect requirements that are easy to meet and state subventions that are generous; low scores reflect requirements that are difficult to meet and state subventions that are only modest (see Chapter 5 for further details). *** coefficient significant at the 0.01 level; ** coefficient significant at the 0.05 level; * coefficient significant at the 0.1 level.

It is immediately apparent that a number of the coefficients that were significant in Model 1 are no longer significant in Model 2, and that the predictive power of others has changed. More specifically, party ideology is considerably less powerful in explaining the variation in the right-wing extremist party vote in Model 2 than it was in Model 1. Furthermore, in Model 2, neither a neo-fascist type of party ideology nor a neo-liberal populist type of party ideology is related to right-wing extremist electoral success. Instead, only authoritarian xenophobic and neo-liberal xenophobic types of party ideology remain linked with high right-wing extremist party vote shares.

In addition, the ideological positions of the nearest parties of the mainstream right no longer exert an effect on the right-wing extremist party vote in Model 2. By contrast, the degree of convergence between the parties of the mainstream left and the parties of the mainstream right remains a significant predictor of the right-wing extremist party vote. High levels of ideological convergence between the mainstream parties continue to be linked with high right-wing extremist electoral scores.

Party organization and party leadership remain important predictors of the right-wing extremist party vote in Model 2. In fact, this variable has slightly more explanatory power in Model 2 than it did in Model 1. Well-organized and well-led parties continue to enjoy consistently higher electoral scores than badly organized and badly led parties. As for the variables that relate to the institutional environment (the effective threshold, the disproportionality of the electoral system, and the laws regulating access to the ballot, the broadcast media and state subventions), they remain unrelated to the right-wing extremist party vote in Model 2, just as they were in Model 1. Despite the weaker predictive power of many of the variables in Model 2, the model explains some 54 percent of the variance in the right-wing extremist party vote across Western Europe.

The fact that the overall explanatory power of party ideology is weaker in Model 2 than it was in Model 1, that the ideological positions of the nearest parties of the mainstream right no longer assume any explanatory power in Model 2, and that the degree of ideological convergence between the mainstream parties has less predictive power in Model 2 than it did in Model 1, comes as no great surprise. After all, the 57 new cases included in Model 2 are the vote scores of very unsuccessful right-wing extremist parties, which were not included in some of the expert judgement studies precisely because they were electorally unsuccessful. The stronger predictive power of party organization and leadership can be explained by the same logic: since the majority of these 57 new cases consist of the electoral scores of parties that are badly organized and badly led, it is not surprising that party organization and leadership assumes greater explanatory power in Model 2 than it did in Model 1.

What is less easy to explain, however, is why the neo-fascist type of party ideology and the neo-liberal populist type of party ideology no longer assume any predictive power in Model 2. These changes cannot be attributed to an overrepresentation of neo-fascist or neo-liberal populist parties among the 57 new cases, because even if the neo-fascist cases for which no expert judgement data exist (that is, the neo-fascist cases among the 57 new cases) are excluded temporarily from the model, the neo-fascist ideology coefficient remains non-significant, and similarly, even if the new neo-liberal populist cases are temporarily excluded from the model, the neo-liberal populist ideology coefficient continues to be non-significant.

The findings that emerge from the two models presented above clearly suggest that party ideology is important in an overall explanation for the variation in the right-wing extremist party vote. In particular, an authoritarian xenophobic or a neo-liberal xenophobic type of party ideology appears to translate into high electoral scores for the parties of the extreme right, whereas a neo-Nazi type of party ideology seems linked with poor electoral fortunes. The most successful forms of right-wing extremist party ideology are therefore ones in which culturism (or new racism) is favoured over classical racism, and in which the fundamental values, procedures and institutions of the democratic constitutional state are not rejected outright. By contrast, the least successful type of right-wing extremist party ideology is one that embraces classical racism and that calls for a wholesale replacement of the existing democratic order.

Without wanting to impute individual-level motivations from aggregate data, this suggests that electorates are put off by parties that adhere to classical racism. Parties that distinguish between groups solely on the grounds of race, rather than culture, that stress the inequality of the races, and that embrace overtly anti-Semitic beliefs appear to be beyond the pale for large sections of the electorate. By contrast, parties that believe differences exist between different groups of people on the basis of culture rather than race, and that stress the incompatibilities of different cultures, seem, at the aggregate level at least, to be more palatable to the electorates of Western Europe. Similarly, parties that reject the existing democratic order completely, including its institutions, its procedures and its norms, also appear to be too extreme for many voters. More appealing to the electorates is a call for some significant reform of the established democratic system.

The analysis also indicates that party organization and leadership are crucial in accounting for the uneven right-wing extremist party vote across Western Europe. In fact, Model 2 suggests that this is the most powerful variable in explaining the varying electoral scores of the parties of the extreme right, confirming Betz's assertion that 'one of the most important determinants of [right-wing extremist party] success is organization' (1998a: 9). Again, remaining aware of the risks of drawing conclusions about individual-level motivations from aggregate-level data, this suggests that electorates are more willing to support parties that exhibit cohesion and coherence, and hence that present themselves as credible actors, than ones that do not. The predictive power of this variable can also be explained by the fact that badly organized and badly led parties are not always able to compete in all constituencies, and so limit their ability to record high electoral scores even before they present themselves to the electorate.

Together, these two sets of party-centric explanations help account for much of the variation in the electoral success of the parties of the extreme right across Western Europe. Moreover, party ideology remains an important predictor of the right-wing extremist party vote even if party organization and leadership is temporarily excluded from Models 1 and 2.[6] Similarly, party organization and leadership continues to have considerable explanatory power even if party ideology is temporarily removed from the two models.[7]

The models also confirm that the degree of ideological convergence between the mainstream parties is important in explaining the variation in the right-wing extremist party vote. This finding is very much in line with the arguments made by Hainsworth (1992a) and Kitschelt (1995), who both suggest that right-wing extremist parties are more likely to experience electoral success in situations in which the mainstream parties converge ideologically than they are when the mainstream parties are more distinct. Convergence between the mainstream parties is likely to result in higher levels of anti-party sentiment within the electorate, and in a greater ability on the part of extreme right parties to play the anti-establishment card and to claim that, if voters really wish to see a change, then only a vote for the extreme right will achieve this, given that the mainstream parties resemble each other so significantly.

In contrast to party ideology, party organization and leadership, and patterns of party competition, the institutional environment in which the parties operate appears to add little to an overall explanation for the disparity in the right-wing extremist party vote. Indeed, in both the models presented above, none of the variables that related to the institutional framework assumed any predictive power.[8] This was also the case if the different types of right-wing extremist party (neo-Nazi; neo-fascist; authoritarian xenophobic; neo-liberal xenophobic; and neo-liberal populist) were considered separately.[9] This implies that, at the aggregate level at least, both party elites and voters are not responding in a strategic fashion to the institutional environment in which they find themselves. Instead, party elites appear to continue to present candidates in elections in systems characterized by high levels of disproportionality, and by ballot access, media access and state subvention access requirements that are difficult to meet. At the same time, party elites seem not to participate in elections in countries that have highly proportional electoral systems, and where it is relatively easy to gain access to the ballot, to the broadcast media and to state subventions. Similarly, voters appear to support extreme right parties in countries in which the institutional setting is such that these parties have little chance of gaining representation. Voters also seem to shy away from backing them in systems that are characterized by high levels of proportionality.

As was argued in Chapter 5, these findings raise important questions about the psychological effects of electoral systems. One explanation for the fact that electoral institutions do not help explain the variation in the right-wing extremist party vote is that voters are simply not aware of the mechanical workings of the electoral system. However, an alternative, and perhaps more convincing, argument for the absence of a relationship between the electoral institutional variables and the right-wing extremist party vote is that voters who support the parties of the extreme right are not as concerned with helping their chosen party into parliament, or even into office, as are other party voters. Indeed, there is evidence to suggest that, although some right-wing extremist party voters are motivated by pragmatic and ideological considerations in the same way as mainstream party voters are, and vote for the parties of the extreme right in an attempt to influence public policies, others vote in an expressive fashion, casting their ballot for parties of the extreme right so as to send a message of discontent to the established, mainstream parties (Van der Brug et al., 2000; Van der Brug and Fennema, 2003). These protest voters are not discouraged by the fact that the parties of the extreme right may stand little chance of gaining parliamentary representation because of the way the electoral system works. Rather, disproportional electoral systems might even encourage them to vote for parties of the extreme right because, since the 'outsider' nature of a right-wing extremist party is likely to be reinforced if the party has little chance of being represented in parliament, disproportional electoral systems might emphasize the protest character of a right-wing extremist vote. Given this strong element of protest voting, it makes sense that the psychological effects of electoral systems are likely to have a weaker impact on right-wing extremist party supporters than on other sections of the electorate.

Concluding remarks

The findings to emerge from the two integrated models presented above, and from the accompanying discussion, confirm many of the conclusions reached in the previous four chapters of this book. They suggest that the variation in the electoral scores of the parties of the extreme right across Western Europe may be explained, in part, by differences in the type of ideology that the parties embrace, by differences in their organization and leadership, and by differences in the degree of ideological convergence that exists between the mainstream parties. They also indicate that differences in the type of electoral system in operation in the various countries add little to an overall account of why some parties of the extreme right have performed better at the polls than others.

Contrary to the conclusions reached in the previous four chapters, and against expectations, the findings suggest that the ideological positions that the extreme right parties choose to adopt in the political space that is available to them are of little importance in an overall explanation of their levels of electoral success. Likewise, the electoral laws governing access to the ballot, the broadcast media and state subventions play no role in an overall account of the uneven electoral fortunes of the West European parties of the extreme right.

The analysis conducted above indicates that just over 50 percent of the variation in the right-wing extremist party vote may be accounted for by the four explanations put forward throughout this book. This is quite substantial given that socio-economic, cultural and historical explanations for why some parties of the extreme right have performed better than others at the polls have not been considered in this study. Clearly, if the variation in the electoral scores of the right-wing extremist parties is to be more fully accounted for, future work would do well to investigate the influence of these other factors. While operationalizing cultural and historical explanations would be particularly challenging, especially in a comparative perspective, an analysis that considered socio-economic, cultural and historical factors in conjunction with the political explanations examined in this book would make for a truly comprehensive account of the uneven electoral fortunes of the parties of the extreme right across Western Europe.

Furthermore, future investigations into the variation in the right-wing extremist party vote would benefit from combining aggregate-level explanations such as those examined throughout this book with individual-level explanations. Notwithstanding issues of data availability, including the attitudes and political preferences of voters in an overall account of the uneven right-wing extremist party vote would be particularly worthwhile. A number of existing studies have already shown these factors to be important in helping to explain why some parties of the extreme right have performed better than others in elections (Van der Brug et al., 2000; Lubbers et al., 2002; Van der Brug and Fennema, 2003).

As well as shedding light on why some parties of the extreme right have performed better in elections than others, the findings of this study also have wider implications. In particular, they suggest that institutional engineering seems to be a much less effective way of trying to prevent the success of challenges from the extreme right than prudent political behaviour by the established political forces may be. Erecting institutional barriers against challenger parties does not seem to prevent their success. In fact, if anything, it may foster a generalized rejection of established politics, particularly if the mainstream parties resemble each other significantly and offer no visible alternatives within the boundaries of established, moderate politics to disaffected voters.

Of course, a substantial factor in the success of extreme right-wing parties success is beyond the influence of established politics. Organization and leadership are by far the strongest supply-side predictors of extreme right party success, and given that a pool of disenchanted voters, susceptible to varying degrees of extreme-right sympathy, exists in all Western democracies, much depends on contingent factors such as the availability of skilful political leaders who are capable of exploiting this potential at a crucial juncture in a country's political history. The political prowess of leaders like Jean-Marie Le Pen and Carl I. Hagen clearly demonstrates the vulnerability of modern party systems.

At the same time, however, the established parties might, to some extent, be able to develop strategies to counter the surge of the extreme right. The rise and decline of the Austrian FPÖ, for instance, shows that bringing these parties in from the cold can result in their weak points being exposed. Alternatively, as the examples of the Norwegian FRPn and the Italian AN suggest, treating these parties as 'normal' parties may lead to them moderating their ideologies. By contrast, erecting a *cordon sanitaire* and thereby institutionalizing the pariah status of the parties of the extreme right, as the established parties in Belgium have done, appears to do little to stop their advance.

That said, the established parties must tread a very fine line: while excluding the extremists may have its costs, because such a strategy may both galvanize the 'outsider' nature of the parties of the extreme right and lead to the established parties becoming too alike, going too far in trying to accommodate and recapture voters who have left the boundaries of democratic politics also has its dangers.

Notes

1 As was explained in Chapter 4, some of the smaller right-wing extremist parties were not included in every expert judgement study. This means that when the ideological positions of the right-wing extremist parties are included in the regression model, the number of cases drops to 77.

2 The neo-fascist type of ideology continues to be significant even if the Italian AN is temporarily excluded from the model, on the basis that the party may be moving out of the extreme right party family (see Chapter 2).

3 To test whether this lack of significance was caused by the strong effect of the French cases (where disproportionality is high but extreme right party success is also high), France was temporarily removed from the regression model. The results changed little, however, and both the effective threshold and the disproportionality remained not significant.

4 The fact that explanatory variables are missing from the model is reflected in the low Durbin-Watson score of 1.268.

5 Since Greece, Portugal and Switzerland did not feature in all the expert judgement studies, data are missing for 12 of the 146 cases that make-up the data set.

6 If party organization and leadership is removed from Model 1, all the coefficients that were previously significant remain significant. If the variable is removed from Model 2, all the coefficients that were previously significant remain significant, and the ideological positions of the mainstream right parties assume explanatory power (as they did in Model 1), as do the neo-fascist and neo-liberal populist types of ideology (again, as they did in Model 1).

7 If party ideology is excluded from Model 1, the ideological positions of the nearest mainstream right party cease to have any explanatory power. The degree of convergence between the mainstream parties continues to assume some predictive power, as does party organization and leadership. When party ideology is removed from Model 2, the coefficients that were previously significant (the degree of convergence between the mainstream parties, and party organization and leadership) remain significant.

8 This was the case even if one of the two electoral system variables (effective threshold and disproportionality) was temporarily excluded from each of the models.

9 It should be noted that, when the different types of party were considered separately, the number of cases was sometimes too small to draw generalizable conclusions. For example, there were only 18 neo-liberal populist cases.

Appendix A

The ideological positions of West European political parties

The tables below report the ideological positions of political parties through-out Western Europe, and are based on data from the following eight expert judgement studies, as listed in Chapter 4:

Comprehensive studies:
- Castles and Mair (1984) – questionnaires sent out 1982;
- Laver and Hunt (1992) – questionnaires sent out 1989;
- Huber and Inglehart (1995) – questionnaires sent out 1993;
- Lubbers (2000) – questionnaires sent out 2000.

Single-country case studies:
- Laver (1995) on the Netherlands – questionnaires sent out 1994;
- Laver (1998) on Britain – questionnaires sent out 1997;
- Laver and Mair (1999) on the Netherlands – questionnaires sent out 1998;
- Ray and Narud (2000) on Norway – questionnaires sent out 1998.

The scores of these parties represent their position on the left–right spectrum, with 0 indicating an extreme left position and 1 indicating an extreme right one (for details on how these scores were calculated see the section on data and methodology in Chapter 4). The scores in **bold** are those of the right-wing extremist parties, and the underlined scores are those of the closest parties of the mainstream right.

Austria

	Castles and Mair	Laver and Hunt	Huber and Inglehart	Lubbers
FPÖ	**0.68**	**0.667**	**0.848**	**0.850**
G	–	0.243	0.207	0.250
KPÖ	0.05	0.265	–	–
LF	–	–	<u>0.592</u>	0.436
ÖVP	<u>0.58</u>	<u>0.667</u>	0.583	<u>0.625</u>
SPÖ	0.30	0.412	0.417	0.431

Notes: FPÖ: *Freiheitliche Partei Österreichs* (Freedom Party); G: *Die Grünen* (Greens); KPÖ: *Kommunistische Partei Österreichs* (Communist Party); LF: *Liberales Forum* (Liberal Forum); ÖVP: *Österreichische Volkspartei* (People's Party); SPÖ: *Sozialdemokratische Partei Österreichs* (Socialist Party).

Belgium

Flanders

	Castles and Mair	Laver and Hunt	Huber and Inglehart	Lubbers
A	0.45	0.363	0.267	0.265
CVP	0.58	<u>0.753</u>	0.556	0.578
PCB/KPB	0.14	–	–	–
PVV/VLD	0.78	0.579	–	<u>0.676</u>
RAD/UDRT	<u>0.92</u>	–	–	–
SP	0.29	0.242	0.356	0.358
VB	**0.98**	**0.842**	–	**0.930**
VU	0.68	0.711	<u>0.611</u>	0.509

Notes: Agalev: *Anders gaan leven* (Live Differently – Flemish Greens); CVP: *Christelijke Volkspartij* (Christian People's Party); PCB/KPB: *Kommunistische Partij van Belgie/Parti Communiste de Belgique* (Communist Party); PVV: *Partij voor Vrijheid en Vooruitgang* (Party of Liberty and Progress); VLD: *Vlaamse Liberalen en Democraten* (Flemish Liberals and Democrats) – successor party to PVV; RAD/UDRT: *Respect voor Arbeit en Democratie/Union Démocratique pour le Respect du Travail* (Democratic Union for the Respect of Labour); SP: *Socialistische Partij* (Flemish Socialist Party); VB: *Vlaams Blok* (Flemish Bloc); VU: *Volksunie* (Flemish People's Union).

Wallonia

	Castles and Mair	Laver and Hunt	Huber and Inglehart	Lubbers
E	0.45	0.363	0.278	0.208
FDF	0.56	0.485	0.667	–
FN(b)	–	–	–	**0.950**
PCB/KPB	0.14	–	–	–
PRL	0.76	0.625	<u>0.699</u>	<u>0.661</u>
PS	0.25	0.237	0.333	0.326
PSC	0.63	<u>0.700</u>	0.523	0.566
RAD/UDRT	<u>0.92</u>	–	–	–
RW	0.26	–	–	–

Notes: E: *Ecolo* (Francophone Greens); FDF: *Front Démocratique des Francophones* (Francophone Democratic Front); FN(b): *Front National Belge* (National Front); PCB/KPB: *Kommunistische Partij van Belgie/Parti Communiste de Belgique* (Communist Party); PRL: *Parti Réformateur Libéral* (Liberal Reform Party); PS: *Parti Socialiste* (Francophone Socialist Party); PSC: *Parti Social Chrétien* (Christian Social Party); RAD/UDRT: *Respect voor Arbeit en Democratie/Union Démocratique pour le Respect du Travail* (Democratic Union for the Respect of Labour); RW: *Rassemblement Wallon* (Walloon Rally).

Britain

	Castles and Mair	Laver and Hunt	Huber and Inglehart	Laver	Lubbers
BNP	–	–	–	–	0.948
C	<u>0.78</u>	<u>0.803</u>	<u>0.746</u>	<u>0.692</u>	<u>0.707</u>
GP	–	–	–	–	0.275
L	0.23	0.260	0.381	0.436	0.443
Lib	0.50	0.344	0.468	0.277	0.398
PC	0.34	0.321	–	0.333	0.305
SDP	0.46	–	–	–	–
SNP	0.44	0.356	–	0.334	0.332

Notes: BNP: *British National Party*; C: *Conservatives*; GP: *Green Party of England and Wales*; L: *Labour*; Lib: *Liberal Party/Liberal Democrats*; PC: *Plaid Cymru* (Party of Wales); SDP: *Social Democratic Party* (in alliance with the *Liberal Party* 1983–1987 as the Alliance, merged with the Liberal Party in 1988 to form *Social and Liberal Democrats*, later renamed *Liberal Democrats*); SNP: *Scottish National Party*.

Denmark

	Castles and Mair	Laver and Hunt	Huber and Inglehart	Lubbers
CD	0.57	0.553	0.556	0.555
DF	–	–	–	0.865
DKP	0.10	0.234	–	–
E	–	–	0.111	0.103
FK	–	0.311	–	–
FRPd	0.87	0.826	0.903	0.873
G	–	0.316	–	–
KF	<u>0.73</u>	0.673	0.729	0.720
KRF	0.62	<u>0.763</u>	0.580	0.590
RF	–	0.602	–	–
RV	0.48	0.424	0.519	0.483
SD	0.38	0.371	0.358	0.397
SF	0.19	0.187	0.210	0.245
V	0.67	0.729	<u>0.790</u>	<u>0.770</u>
VS	0.08	0.073	–	–

Notes: CD: *Centrumdemokraterne* (Centre Democrats); DF: *Dansk Folkeparti* (Danish People's Party); DKP: *Danmarks Kommunistiske Parti* (Communist Party); E: *Enhedslisten – de rød-grønne* (Unity List – The Red Greens); FK: *Faelles Kurs* (Common Course); FRPd: *Fremskridtspartiet* (Progress Party); G: *De Grønne* (The Greens); KF: *Konservative Folkeparti* (Conservative People's Party); KRF: *Kristeligt Folkeparti* (Christian People's Party); RF: *Retsforbundet* (Justice League); RV: *Radikale Venstre* (Social Liberal Party); SD: *Socialdemokratiet* (Social Democrats); SF: *Socialistisk Folkeparti* (Socialist People's Party); V: *Venstre* (Liberals); VS: *Venstresocialisterne* (Left Socialist Party).

France

	Castles and Mair	Laver and Hunt	Huber and Inglehart	Lubbers
CDS	–	–	0.528	–
CNIP	0.86	–	–	–
E	0.35	–	–	–
FN	0.98	0.931	1.000	0.950
GE	–	–	0.378	–
LCR	–	–	0.000	–
LO	–	–	0.000	–
MPF	–	–	–	0.853
MRG	0.38	0.337	0.417	–
PCF	0.14	0.203	0.139	0.150
PFN	0.98	–	–	–
PR	–	–	0.689	–
PS	0.26	0.226	0.348	0.336
RPR	0.82	0.697	0.764	0.750
UDF	0.66	0.608	0.630	0.643
V	–	0.254	0.382	0.264

Notes: CDS: *Centre des Démocrates Sociaux* (Social Democratic Centre); CNIP: *Centre National des Indépendants et Paysans* (Independents and Farmers); E: Ecologists – various disparate tendencies; FN: *Front National* (National Front); GE: *Génération Écologie* (Écologists); LCR: *Ligue Communiste Révolutionnaire* (Revolutionary Communist League); LO: *Lutte Ouvrière* (Workers' Struggle); MPF: *Mouvement pour la France* (Movement for France); MRG: *Mouvement des Radicaux de Gauche* (Left Radicals); PCF: *Parti Communiste Français* (French Communist Party); PFN: *Parti des Forces Nouvelles* (Party of the New Forces); PR: *Parti Républicain* (Republican Party); PS: *Parti Socialiste* (Socialist Party); RPR: *Rassemblement pour la République* (Rally for the Republic); UDF: *Union pour la Démocratie Française* (Union for French Democracy); V: *Les Verts* (The Greens).

Germany

	Castles and Mair	Laver and Hunt	Huber and Inglehart	Lubbers
CDU*	<u>0.67</u>	<u>0.683</u>	<u>0.602</u>	<u>0.636</u>
CSU	0.79	0.770	0.700	0.713
DKP	0.14	–	–	–
DVU	–	–	–	0.939
FDP	0.51	0.540	0.516	0.600
G	0.28	0.161	0.212	0.328
PDS	–	–	0.056	0.163
Republikaner	–	–	0.922	0.870
SPD	0.33	0.295	0.314	0.397

Notes: * The CDU, rather than the CSU, is taken as the closest mainstream party since the CSU is a regional party, only active in Bavaria. CDU: *Christlich Demokratische Union* (Christian Democratic Union); CSU: *Christlich Soziale Union* (Christian Social Union); DKP: *Deutsche Kommunistische Partei* (German Communist Party); DVU: *Deutsche Volksunion* (German People's Union); FDP: *Freie Demokratische Partei* (Free Democrats); G: *Die Grünen* (The Greens); PDS: *Partei des Demokratischen Sozialismus* (Party of Democratic Socialism); Republikaner: *Die Republikaner* (The Republicans); SPD: *Sozialdemokratische Partei Deutschlands* (Social Democrats).

Greece

	Castles and Mair	Laver and Hunt	Huber and Inglehart	Lubbers
DKK	–	–	–	0.420
EM	–	–	–	0.978
KKE	–	0.283	–	0.163
KKKes	–	0.176	–	–
ND	–	<u>0.722</u>	–	0.738
PA	–	–	–	<u>0.788</u>
PASOK	–	0.324	–	0.508
SAP	–	–	–	0.373

Notes: DKK: *Dimokratiki Kinoniku Kinima* (Democratic Social Movement); EM: *Eliniko Metopon* (Greek Front); KKE: *Kommounistiko Komma Ellados* (Communist Party of Greece); KKKes: *Kommounistiko Komma Ellados Esoterikou* (Communist Party of Greece – Interior); ND: *Nea Dimokratia* (New Democracy); PA: *Politiki Anixi* (Political Spring); PASOK: *Panellino Socialistiko Kinima* (Pan-Hellenic Social Movement); SAP: *Sinaspismos tis Aristeras ke ti Proodu* (Coalition of the Left and Progress).

Italy

	Castles and Mair	Laver and Hunt	Huber and Inglehart	Lubbers
AN	–	–	–	0.817
CCD	–	–	–	0.585
DC	0.54	0.684	0.592	–
DP	0.05	0.064	–	–
FI	–	–	–	0.665
LN	–	–	0.722	0.755
Ms-Ft	–	–	–	0.966
MSI	0.91	0.844	0.926	–
PCI	0.16	0.164	–	–
PDS	–	–	0.167	0.300
PdUP	0.06	–	–	–
PLI	0.59	0.577	0.700	–
PPI	–	–	–	0.450
PR	0.23	0.203	–	–
PRI	0.48	0.500	0.511	–
PSDI	0.54	0.440	0.472	–
PSI	0.31	0.352	0.444	–
RC	–	–	0.000	0.071
V	–	0.210	0.178	0.256

Notes: AN: *Alleanza Nazionale* (National Alliance) succeeded MSI in 1995; CCD: *Centro Cristiano Democratico* (Christian Democratic Centre); DC: *Democrazia Cristiana* (Christian Democrats) reformed into PPI in 1994; DP: *Democrazia Proletaria* (Proletarian Democracy) merged with PCI before 1992 election; FI: *Forza Italia* (Forward Italy); LN: *Lega Nord* (Northern League); Ms-Ft: *Movimento Sociale Italiano–Fiamma Tricolore* (Italian Social Movement – Tricolour Flame) broke away from MSI when MSI reformed into AN; MSI: *Movimento Sociale Italiano* (Italian Social Movement) reformed into AN in 1995; PCI: *Partito Comunista Italiano* (Communist Party), became PDS in 1991; PDS: *Partito Democratico della Sinistra* (Democratic Party of the Left) succeeded PCI in 1991; PdUP: *Partito di Unità Proletaria per il Comunismo* (Party of Proletarian Unity for Communism) merged with PCI in 1984; PLI: *Partito Liberale Italiano* (Liberal Party); PPI: *Partito Popolare Italiano* (Popular Party) successor to DC; PR: *Partito Radicale* (Radical Party); PRI: *Partito Repubblicano Italiano* (Republican Party); PSDI: *Partito Socialista Democracio Italiano* (Social Democrats); PSI: *Partito Socialista Italiano* (Socialist Party); RC: *Rifondazione Comunista* (Communist Refoundation) breakaway of PCI in 1991 when PCI became PDS; V: *Federazione dei Verdi* (Greens).

Netherlands

	Castles and Mair	Laver and Hunt	Huber and Inglehart	Laver	Laver and Mair	Lubbers
AOV	–	–	–	0.536	–	–
CD	–	–	0.944	0.760	–	0.897
CDA	0.57	0.694	0.589	0.655	0.547	0.542
CPN	0.08	0.067	–	–	–	–
CU	–	–	–	–	–	0.703
D/66	0.44	0.309	0.422	0.314	0.458	0.446
GL	–	–	0.087	0.142	0.146	0.236
GPV	0.90	0.842	0.873	0.795	0.770	–
PPR	0.16	0.081	–	–	–	–
PSP	0.06	0.043	–	–	–	–
PvdA	0.26	0.205	0.356	0.283	0.378	0.369
RPF	<u>0.92</u>	<u>0.881</u>	<u>0.889</u>	0.809	0.762	–
SGP	<u>0.92</u>	0.879	<u>0.889</u>	<u>0.829</u>	<u>0.886</u>	<u>0.788</u>
SP	–	–	–	0.207	0.108	0.143
Unie 55+	–	–	–	0.523	–	–
VVD	0.74	0.566	0.689	0.551	0.727	0.671

Notes: AOV: *Algemeen Ouderverbond* (United Old Persons' League); CD: *Centrumdemocraten* (Centre Democrats); CDA: *Christen Democratisch Appèl* (Christian Democratic Appeal); CPN: *Communistische Partij Nederland* (Communist Party) became part of GL in 1990; CU: *ChristenUnie* (Christian Union) created January 2000 from merger of GPV and RPF; D '66: *Democraten '66* (Democrats 66); GL: *Groen Links* (Green Left) created in 1990 from CPN, PSP, PPR and Evangelical People's Party; GPV: *Gereformeerd Politiek Verbond* (Reformed Political Union); PPR: *Politieke Partij Radicalen* (Radical Political Party); PSP: *Pacifistisch-Socialistische Partij* (Pacifist Socialist Party) became part of GL in 1990; PvdA: *Partij van de Arbeid* (Labour Party); RPF: *Reformatorische Politieke Federatie* (Reformed Political Federation); SGP: *Staatkundig Gereformeerde Partij* (Political Reformed Party); SP: *Socialistische Partij* (Socialist Party); Unie 55+: *Ouderenpartij Unie 55+* (Pensioners Union 55+); VVD: *Volkspartij voor Vrijheid en Democratie* (People's Party for Freedom and Democracy).

Norway

	Castles and Mair	Laver and Hunt	Huber and Inglehart	Ray and Narud	Lubbers
DNA	0.30	0.282	0.348	0.453	0.400
FP	–	0.537	–	–	–
FRPn	0.94	0.726	0.909	0.881	0.814
H	0.77	0.586	0.778	0.798	0.741
KrF	0.61	0.685	0.617	0.544	0.553
MG	–	–	–	–	0.277
RV	–	–	–	0.047	0.200
SP	0.58	0.562	0.481	0.393	0.424
SV	0.12	0.149	0.172	0.190	0.217
V	0.40	0.411	0.540	0.596	0.660

Notes: DNA: *Det Norske Arbeiderparti* (Labour Party); FP: *Folkepartiet* (Liberal People's Party); FRPn: *Fremskrittspartiet* (Progress Party); H: *Høyre* (Conservatives); KrF: *Kristelig Folkeparti* (Christian People's Party); MG: *Miljøpartiet – De Grønne* (Greens); RV: *Rød Valgallianse* (Red Electoral Alliance); SP: *Senterpartiet* (Centre Party); SV: *Sosialistik Venstreparti* (Socialist Left Party); V: *Venstre* (Liberals).

Portugal

	Castles and Mair	Laver and Hunt	Huber and Inglehart	Lubbers
CDS/PP	–	0.873	0.820	0.820
DI	–	0.184	–	–
MDP	–	0.211	–	–
P.XXI	–	–	–	0.200
PCP	–	0.108	0.292	0.216
PDC	–	0.930	–	–
PEV	–	0.105	–	0.240
PRD	–	0.448	–	–
PSD	–	0.642	0.598	0.598
PSN	–	–	–	0.806
PSP	–	0.388	0.431	0.425
PSR	–	0.123	–	0.094
UDP	–	0.105	–	0.104

Notes: CDS/PP: *Partido do Centro Democrático Social* (Centre Social Democrats) renamed *Partido Popular* (Popular Party) in 1995; DI: *Intervençao Democrática* (Democratic Intervention); MDP: *Movimento Democrático Português* (Democratic Movement); P.XXI: *Politica XXI* (Politics XXI); PCP: *Partido Comunista Português* (Communist Party); PDC: *Partido da Democracia Cristã* (Party of Christian Democracy); PEV: *Partido Ecologista 'Os Verdes'* (Greens); PRD: *Partido Renovador Democrático* (Democratic Renewal Party); PSD: *Partido Social Democráta* (Social Democratic Party); PSN: *Partido de Solidariedade Nacional* (National Solidarity Party); PSP: *Partido Socialista Português* (Socialist Party); PSR: *Partido Socialista Revolucionário* (Revolutionary Socialist Party); UDP: *União Democratico Popular* (Democratic People's Union).

Spain

	Castles and Mair	Laver and Hunt	Huber and Inglehart	Lubbers
AP/PP	0.84	0.784	0.722	0.685
CDS	–	0.384	0.489	–
CiU	0.66	0.511	0.574	0.567
DN	–	–	–	0.920
EA	–	–	0.408	–
EE	0.24	–	–	–
ERC	0.41	–	–	–
FEJons	–	–	–	0.953
HB	0.05	0.217	0.000	–
MUC	–	0.070	–	–
PAR	0.82	–	–	–
PCE/IU	0.27	–	–	–
PNV	0.67	0.621	0.571	0.606
PRD	–	0.447	–	–
PSA	0.45	–	–	–
PSOE	0.36	0.279	0.333	0.396
UCD	0.71	–	–	–
UCP	0.07	0.095	0.153	0.254
UN/FN	0.98	–	–	–

Notes: AP/PP: *Alianza Popular/Partido Popular* (Popular Alliance/Popular Party) AP merged with the Liberal Party in 1989 to become PP; CDS: *Centro Democrático y Social* (Democratic and Social Centre) successor to UCD; CiU: *Convergència y Unió* (Convergence and Unity); DN: *Democracia Nacional* (National Democracy); EA: *Eusko Alkartasuna* (Basque Solidarity); EE: *Euzkadiko Ezkerra* (Basque Left); ERC: *Esquerra Republicana de Catalunya* (Catalan Republican Left); FEJons: *Falange Española de las Juntas de Ofensiva Nacional-Sindicalista* (Spanish Phalanx of Committees for National Syndicalist Attack). HB: *Herri Batasuna* (United People); MUC: *Mesa per la Unididad de los Comunistas* (Communist Unity); PAR: *Partido Aragonés Regionalista* (Aragonese Regionalist Party); PCE/IU: *Partido Comunista de España/Izquierda Unida* (Communist Party/United Left); PNV: *Euzko Alberdi Jeltzalea/Partido Nacionalista Vasco* (Basque Nationalist Party); PRD: *Partido Reformista Democrático* (Democratic Reform Party); PSA: *Partido Socialista Andaluz/Partido Andaluz* (Andalusian Socialist Party); PSOE: *Partido Socialista Obrero Español* (Socialist Party); UCD: *Unión del Centro Democrático* (Union of Democratic Centre) became CDS in 1982; UCP: *Coalición Unión del Pueblo Canario* (Canary People's Union); UN/FN: *Unión Nacional/Fuerza Nueva* (National Union/New Force).

Sweden

	Castles and Mair	Laver and Hunt	Huber and Inglehart	Lubbers
CP	0.59	0.540	0.547	0.602
FP	0.55	0.484	0.547	0.567
G	–	0.302	0.361	0.346
KDS	–	0.714	0.667	0.729
M	0.77	0.716	0.814	0.796
ND	–	–	0.899	0.896
SdAP	0.29	0.323	0.342	0.400
SDk	–	–	–	0.950
VP	0.12	0.147	0.180	0.221

Notes: CP: *Centerpartiet* (Centre Party); FP: *Folkpartiet – Liberalerna* (People's Party – the Liberals); G: *Miljöpartiet de Gröna* (Greens); KDS: *Kristdemokraterna* (Christian Democrats); M: *Moderata Samlingspartiet* (Moderate Unity Party); ND: *Ny Demokrati* (New Democrats); SdAP: *Sveriges Socialdemokratiska Arbetarepartiet* (Social Democrats); SDk: *Sverigedemokraterna* (Sweden Democrats); VPK: *Vänsterpartiet* (Left Party).

Switzerland

	Castles and Mair	Laver and Hunt	Huber and Inglehart	Lubbers
APS/FPS	–	–	0.806	0.891
CVP	–	–	0.378	0.590
EDU	–	–	–	0.884
EVP	–	–	–	0.528
FDP	–	–	0.556	0.679
GPS	–	–	–	0.274
LdT	–	–	–	0.898
LPS	–	–	0.689	0.763
PdA	–	–	–	0.152
SD	–	–	–	0.906
SPS	–	–	0.178	0.293
SVP	–	–	0.583	0.839

Notes: APS/FPS: *Autopartei der Schweiz/Parti Automobiliste Suisse* (Car Party of Switzerland), renamed *Freiheitspartei der Schweiz* (Freedom Party of Switzerland) in 1995; CVP: *Christlich Demokratische Volkspartei der Schweiz/Parti Démocrate-Chrétien Suisse* (Christian Democratic People's Party); EDU: *Eidgenössich-Demokratische Union/Union Démocratique Fédérale* (Federal Democratic Union); EVP: *Evangelische Volkspartei der Schweiz/Parti Populaire Évangelique* (Protestant People's Party); FDP: *Freisinnig Demokratische Partei der Schweiz/Parti Radical Suisse* (Radical Democrats); GPS: *Grüne Partei der Schweiz/Parti Écologiste Suisse* (Green Party); LdT: *Lega dei Ticinesi* (Ticino League); LPS: *Liberale Partei der Schweiz/Parti Libéral Suisse* (Liberal Party); PdA: *Partei der Arbeit der Schweiz/Parti Suisse du Travail* (Labour Party); SD: *Schweizer Demokraten/Démocrates Suisses* (Swiss Democrats); SPS: *Sozialdemokratische Partei der Schweiz/Parti Socialiste Suisse* (Social Democrats); SVP: *Schweizerische Volkspartei/Union Démocratique du Centre* (Swiss People's Party).

Appendix B

The political space in the different countries of Western Europe

The following figures represent the political space in the different countries in Western Europe. They replicate the figures shown in Chapter 4, and also map the political space in Flanders, Wallonia, Greece, the Netherlands, Portugal and Sweden. The heavy, dashed grey line represents the ideological mean of the party system. It is calculated by multiplying the score of each party on the left–right scale (as reported in Appendix A) by the party's share of the vote in the nearest election, expressed as a proportion (i.e. divided by 100). The figures for all the parties are then summed to produce the ideological mean of the system (see Knutsen, 1998). For the full names of the parties see Appendix A. The right-wing extremist parties are shown in **bold** type.

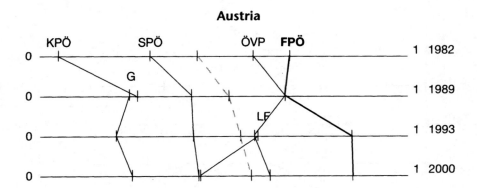

Austria

Belgium

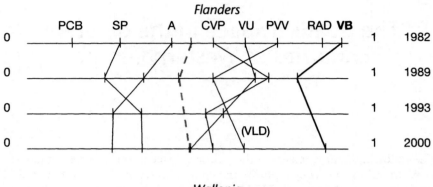

Wallonia

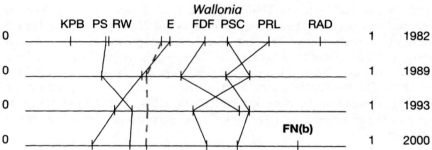

Britain

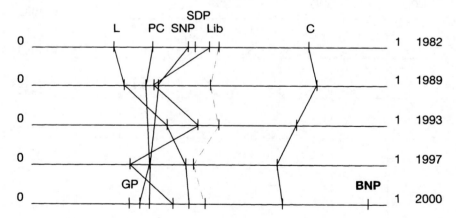

Denmark

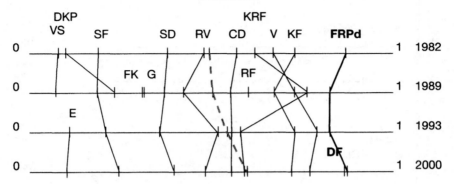

France

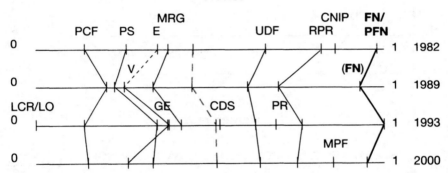

Germany

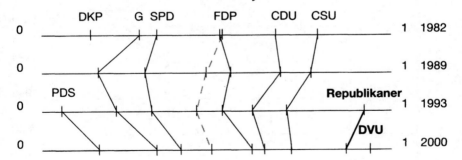

Greece

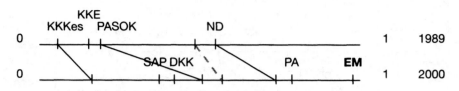

Italy

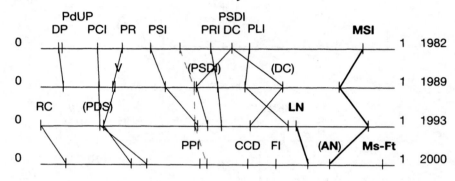

Netherlands

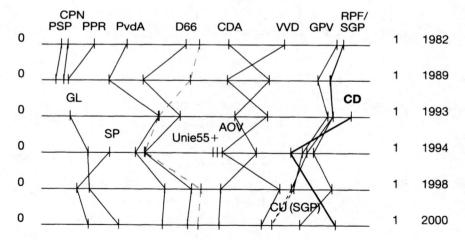

Norway

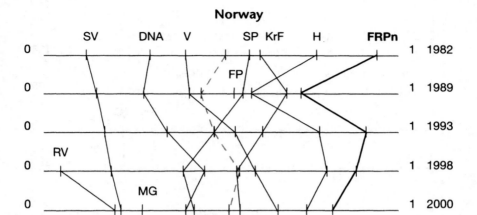

Portugal

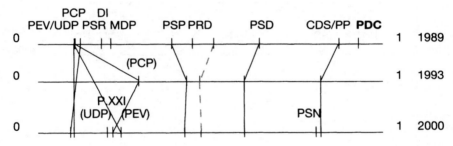

Spain

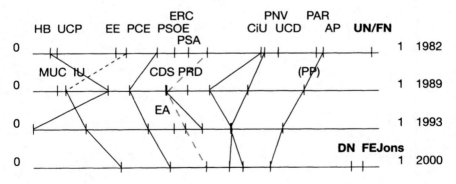

Sweden

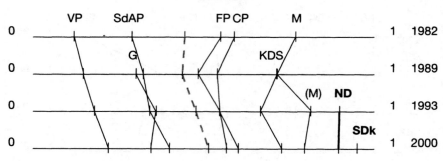

Switzerland

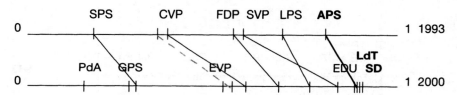

Appendix C

The disproportionality of elections, 1979–2003

	1979	1980	1981	1982	1983	1984	1985	1986	1987	1988	1989	1990
Austria	0.96				2.48			0.91				2.08
Flanders			2.41				3.46		3.77			
Wallonia			6.55				3.56		3.14			
Britain	11.60				20.64				17.74			
Denmark	1.53		1.53			1.40			2.13	2.35		2.61
France			15.95					7.19		11.80		
Germany		1.40			0.49				0.66			4.70
Greece			8.34				7.12				J4.34	3.90
											N3.91	
Italy	2.64				2.59				2.48			
Netherlands			1.25	1.10				1.60			1.17	
Norway			4.92				4.73				3.63	
Portugal	3.99	4.11			2.93		3.74		6.26			
Spain	10.58			8.07				6.71			9.18	
Sweden	1.28			2.43			1.34			2.41		
Switzerland	2.05				3.12				3.74			

Notes: Disproportionality scores calculated using the Gallagher index. The vote–seat differences for each party are squared and then added. This total is then divided by two, and finally the square root of this value is taken as the disproportionality score. The votes and seats of parties described by electoral returns as 'others' (i.e. very small parties) are not included in the calculations (see Lijphart, 1994: 61). Parties with less than 0.5 percent of the vote and with no representation are not included in the

1991	1992	1993	1994	1995	1996	1997	1998	1999	2000	2001	2002	2003
			1.16	1.05				3.33			1.36	
4.13				3.39				2.33				4.43
3.56				8.33				3.80				7.89
	13.50					16.63				17.86		
			1.52				0.32			1.54		
		25.55				18.64					21.86	
			2.18				3.11				11.63	
		7.57			9.43				6.79			
	2.48		9.59		6.74					6.73		
			1.39				1.26				0.92	1.07
		3.95				3.71				3.31		
6.03				4.58				4.96		5.41		
		7.05			5.37				4.82			
2.87			1.56				0.94				1.69	
2.60				4.49				3.06				2.25

calculations either. Parties with less than 0.5 percent of the vote but with representation are included. For Greece, 1989J denotes the election of 18 June 1989, and 1989N refers to the election of 5 November 1989.

Source: Mackie and Rose (1991, 1997); Cheles *et al.* (1995); Betz and Immerfall (1998); Hainsworth (2000a); Elections around the World; Parties and Elections in Europe.

Bibliography

Abedi, Amir (2002), 'Challenges to Established Parties: The Effects of Party System Features on the Electoral Fortunes of Anti-Political-Establishment Parties', *European Journal of Political Research*, 41(4): 551–83.

ACE (Administration and Cost of Election) Project, www.aceproject.org.

Alexander, Herbert E. (1989), 'Money and Politics: Rethinking a Conceptual Framework', in Herbert E. Alexander (ed.), *Comparative Political Finance in the 1980s*, pp. 9–23, Cambridge: Cambridge University Press.

Alexander, Herbert E. and Rei Shiratori (1994), 'Introduction', in Herbert E. Alexander and Rei Shiratori (eds), *Comparative Political Finance Among the Democracies*, pp. 1–11, Boulder CO: Westview.

Andersen, Jørgen Goul (1992), 'Denmark: The Progress Party – Populist Neo-Liberalism and Welfare State Chauvinism', in Paul Hainsworth (ed.), *The Extreme Right in Europe and the USA*, pp. 193–205, London: Pinter.

Andersen, Jørgen Goul and Tor Bjørklund (2000), 'Radical Right-Wing Populism in Scandinavia: From Tax Revolt to Neo-Liberalism and Xenophobia', in Paul Hainsworth (ed.), *The Politics of the Extreme Right: From the Margins to the Mainstream*, pp. 193–223, London: Pinter.

Andeweg, Rudy B. (2001), 'Lijphart versus Lijphart: The Cons of Consensus Democracy in Homogeneous Societies', *Acta Politica*, 36(2): 117–28.

Anti-Semitism Worldwide (1999/2000), *Switzerland*, www.tau.ac.il/Anti-Semitism/asw99-2000/switzerland.htm.

Anti-Semitism Worldwide (2000/1), *Sweden*, www.tau.ac.il/Anti-Semitism/asw2000-1/sweden.htm.

Arnim, Hans Herbert von (1993), 'Campaign and Party Finance in Germany', in Arthur B. Gunlicks (ed.), *Campaign and Party Finance in North America and Western Europe*, pp. 201–18, Boulder CO: Westview.

Arter, David (1992), 'Black Faces in the Blond Crowd: Populist Racialism in Scandinavia', *Parliamentary Affairs*, 45(3): 357–72.

Avril, Pierre (1994), 'Regulation of Political Finance in France', in Herbert E. Alexander and Rei Shiratori (eds), *Comparative Political Finance among the Democracies*, pp. 85–95, Boulder CO: Westview.

AXT (Antisemitism and Xenophobia Today) (1996), *Spain*, www.axt.org.uk/antisem/archive/archive1/spain/index.htm.

AXT (Antisemitism and Xenophobia Today) (1998), *Germany*, www.axt.org.uk/antisem/countries/germany/index.html.

AXT (Antisemitism and Xenophobia Today) (2000), *Norway*, www.axt.org.uk/ antisem/countries/norway/index.html.

AXT (Antisemitism and Xenophobia Today) (2001), *Sweden*, www.axt.org.uk/ antisem/countries/sweden/index.html.

Backer, Susann (2000), 'Right-Wing Extremism in Unified Germany', in Paul Hainsworth (ed.), *The Politics of the Extreme Right: From the Margins to the Mainstream*, pp. 87–120, London: Pinter.

Backes, Uwe (1990), 'The West German Republikaner: Profile of a Nationalist, Populist Party of Protest', *Patterns of Prejudice*, 24(1): 3–18.

Backes, Uwe (2001), 'L'extrême droite: les multiples facettes d'une catégorie d'analyse', in Pascal Perrineau (ed.), *Les croisés de la société fermée: l'Europe des extrêmes droites*, pp. 13–29, La Tour d'Aigues: Editions de l'Aube.

Backes, Uwe and Patrick Moreau (1993), *Die Extreme Rechte in Deutschland. Geschichte – gengenwärtige Gefahren – Ursachen – Gengenmassnahme*, Munich: Akademischer Verlag for B'Nai B'rith, Munich.

Backes, Uwe and Cas Mudde (2000), 'Germany: Extremism without Successful Parties', *Parliamentary Affairs*, 53(3): 457–68.

Baldini, Gianfranco (2001), *Extreme Right Parties in Italy: An Overview*, Extreme Right Electorates and Party Success, http://cidsp.upmf-grenoble.fr/guest/ereps/download/italy_overview.htm.

Bardi, Luciano and Leonardo Morlino (1992), 'Italy', in Richard S. Katz and Peter Mair (eds), *Party Organizations: A Data Handbook*, pp. 458–618, London: Sage.

Barker, Martin (1981), *The New Racism: Conservatives and the Ideology of the Tribe*, London: Junction Books.

Bartolini, Stefano and Peter Mair (1990), *Identity, Competition and Electoral Availability: The Stability of European Electorates 1885–1985*, Cambridge: Cambridge University Press.

Bastow, Steve (2000), 'Le Mouvement National Républicain: Moderate Right-Wing Party or Party of the Extreme Right?', *Patterns of Prejudice*, 34(2): 3–18.

Bell, David S. and Byron Criddle (1984), *The French Socialist Party: Resurgence and Victory*, Oxford: Clarendon.

Betz, Hans-Georg (1993a), 'The New Politics of Resentment: Radical Right-Wing Populist Parties in Western Europe', *Comparative Politics*, 25(4): 413–27.

Betz, Hans-Georg (1993b), 'The Two Faces of Radical Right-Wing Populism in Western Europe', *Review of Politics*, 55(4): 663–85.

Betz, Hans-Georg (1994), *Radical Right-Wing Populism in Western Europe*, Basingstoke: Macmillan.

Betz, Hans-Georg (1998a), 'Introduction', in Hans-Georg Betz and Stefan Immerfall (eds), *The New Politics of the Right: Neo-Populist Parties and Movements in Established Democracies*, pp. 1–10, New York: St Martin's Press.

Betz, Hans-Georg (1998b), 'Against Rome: The Lega Nord', in Hans-Georg Betz and Stefan Immerfall (eds), *The New Politics of the Right: Neo-Populist Parties and Movements in Established Democracies*, pp. 45–57, New York: St Martin's Press.

Betz, Hans-Georg (2003), 'The Growing Threat of the Radical Right', in Peter H. Merkl and Leonard Weinberg (eds), *Right-Wing Extremism in the Twenty-First Century*, pp. 74–93, London: Frank Cass.

Betz, Hans-Georg and Stefan Immerfall (eds) (1998), *The New Politics of the Right: Neo-Populist Parties and Movements in Established Democracies*, New York: St Martin's Press.

Beyme, Klaus von (1988), 'Right-Wing Extremism in Post-War Europe', *West European Politics*, 11(2): 1–18.

Bille, Lars (1992), 'Denmark', in Richard S. Katz and Peter Mair (eds), *Party Organizations: A Data Handbook*, pp. 199–272, London: Sage.

Bille, Lars (1996), 'Denmark', *European Journal of Political Research Political Data Yearbook*, 30(3–4): 315–19.

Bille, Lars (1997), *Partier I Forandring*, Odense: Odense Universitetsforlag.

Billiet, Jaak and Hans De Witte (1995), 'Attitudinal Dispositions to Vote for a "New" Extreme Right-Wing Party: the Case of "Vlaams Blok"', *European Journal of Political Research*, 27(2): 181–202.

Billig, Michael (1989), 'The Extreme Right: Continuities in Anti-Semitic Conspiracy Theory in Post-War Europe', in Roger Eatwell and Noel O'Sullivan (eds), *The Nature of the Right*, pp. 146–66, London: Pinter.

Birenbaum, Guy (1992), *Le Front National en politique*, Paris: Editions Balland.

Bjørklund, Tor (2001), *Extreme Right Parties in Scandinavia: An Overview*, Extreme Right Electorates and Party Success, http://cidsp.upmf-grenoble.fr/guest/ereps/download/scandinavia_overview.pdf.

Blais, André (1988), 'The Classification of Electoral Systems', *European Journal of Political Research*, 16(1): 99–110.

Blais, André (1991), 'The Debate over Electoral Systems', *International Political Science Review*, 12(3): 239–60.

Blais, André and R. Kenneth Carty (1991), 'The Psychological Impact of Electoral Laws: Measuring Duverger's Elusive Factor', *British Journal of Political Science*, 21(1): 79–93.

Blais, André and Louis Massicotte (1996), 'Electoral Systems', in Lawrence LeDuc, Richard G. Niemi and Pippa Norris (eds), *Comparing Democracies: Elections and Voting in Global Perspective*, pp. 49–81, Thousand Oaks CA: Sage.

Blinkhorn, Martin (1990), 'Introduction: Allies, Rivals or Antagonists? Fascists and Conservatives in Modern Europe', in Martin Blinkhorn (ed.), *Fascists and Conservatives: The Radical Right and the Establishment in Twentieth-Century Europe*, pp. 1–13, London: Unwin Hyman.

Bogdanor, Vernon (1982), 'Reflections on British Political Finance', *Parliamentary Affairs*, 35(4): 367–80.

Boix, Carles (1999), 'Setting the Rules of the Game: The Choice of Electoral Systems in Advanced Democracies', *American Political Science Review*, 93(3): 609–24.

Borre, Ole (1988), 'The Danish General Election of 1997', *Electoral Studies*, 7(1): 75–9.

Borre, Ole (1991), 'The Danish General Election of 1990', *Electoral Studies*, 10(2): 133–8.

Bowler, Shaun, Elisabeth Carter and David M. Farrell (2003), 'Changing Party Access to Elections', in Bruce E. Cain, Russell J. Dalton and Susan E. Scarrow (eds), *Democracy Transformed? Expanding Political Opportunities in Advanced Industrial Democracies*, pp. 81–111, Oxford: Oxford University Press.

Bowler, Shaun, David M. Farrell and Richard S. Katz (1999), 'Party Cohesion, Party Discipline, and Parliaments', in Shaun Bowler, David M. Farrell and Richard S.

Katz (eds), *Party Discipline and Parliamentary Government*, pp. 3–22, Columbus OH: Ohio State University Press.

Brants, Kees (1995), 'The Blank Spot: Political Advertising in the Netherlands', in Lynda Lee Kaid and Christina Holtz-Bacha (eds), *Political Advertising in Western Democracies: Parties and Candidates on Television*, pp. 142–60, Thousand Oaks CA: Sage.

Bréchon, Pierre and Subrata Kumar Mitra (1992), 'The National Front in France: The Emergence of an Extreme Right Protest Movement', *Comparative Politics*, 25(1): 63–82.

British National Party (1997a), *Campaign 97 – Policy Issues*, www.webcom.com/bnp/policy.html.

British National Party (1997b), *Party Election Manifesto 1997*, www.webcom.com/bnp/manif.html.

British National Party (2002), *Putting the British First!*, www.bnp.org.uk/policies.html.

Budge, Ian (1987), 'The Internal Analysis of Election Programmes', in Ian Budge, David Robertson and Derek Hearl (eds), *Ideology, Strategy and Party Change: Spatial Analysis of Post-War Election Programmes in 19 Democracies*, pp. 15–38, Cambridge: Cambridge University Press.

Budge, Ian (1993), 'Issues, Dimensions, and Agenda Change in Postwar Democracies: Longterm Trends in Party Election Programs and Newspaper Reports in Twenty-three Democracies', in William H. Riker (ed.), *Agenda Formation*, pp. 41–80, Ann Arbor: University of Michigan Press.

Budge, Ian (1994), 'A New Spatial Theory of Party Competition: Uncertainty, Ideology and Policy Equilibria Viewed Comparatively and Temporally', *British Journal of Political Science*, 24(4): 443–67.

Budge, Ian (2000), 'Expert Judgements of Party Positions: Uses and Limitations in Political Research', *European Journal of Political Research*, 37(1): 103–13.

Budge, Ian (2001), 'Validating Party Policy Placements', *British Journal of Political Science*, 31(1): 210–23.

Budge, Ian and Dennis Farlie (1977), *Voting and Party Competition*, London: Wiley.

Budge, Ian and Michael Laver (1986), 'Policy, Ideology and Party Distance: Analysis of Election Programmes in 19 Democracies', *Legislative Studies Quarterly*, 11(4): 607–17.

Budge, Ian and David Robertson (1987), 'Do Parties Differ, and How? Comparative Discriminant and Factor Analyses', in Ian Budge, David Robertson and Derek Hearl (eds), *Ideology, Strategy and Party Change: Spatial Analysis of Post-War Election Programmes in 19 Democracies*, pp. 388–416, Cambridge: Cambridge University Press.

Budge, Ian, Ivor Crewe and Dennis Farlie (1976), *Party Identification and Beyond: Representations of Voting and Party Competition*, New York: Wiley.

Budge, Ian, David Robertson and Derek Hearl (eds) (1987), *Ideology, Strategy and Party Change: Spatial Analysis of Post-War Election Programmes in 19 Democracies*, Cambridge: Cambridge University Press.

Budge, Ian, Hans-Dieter Klingemann, Andrea Volkens, Judith Bara and Eric Tanenbaum (2001), *Mapping Policy Preferences: Estimates for Parties, Electors and Governments 1945–1998*, Oxford: Oxford University Press.

Bundesamt für Verfassungsschutz (1999), *Rechtsextremistische Parteien in der Bundesrepublik Deutschland – Agitation, Ziele, Wahlen*, Cologne: Bundesamt für Verfassungsschutz.

Butler, David, Howard Penniman and Austin Ranney (eds) (1981), *Democracy at the Polls*, Washington DC: American Enterprise Institute.

Caciagli, Mario (1988), 'The Movimento Sociale Italiano – Destra Nazionale and New-Fascism in Italy', *West European Politics*, 11(2): 19–33.

Cain, Bruce E., Russell J. Dalton and Susan E. Scarrow (eds) (2003), *Democracy Transformed? Expanding Political Opportunities in Advanced Industrial Democracies*, Oxford: Oxford University Press.

Capoccia, Giovanni (2002), 'Anti-System Parties: A Conceptual Reassessment', *Journal of Theoretical Politics*, 14(1): 9–35.

Carter, Elisabeth L. (2002), 'Proportional Representation and the Fortunes of Right-Wing Extremist Parties', *West European Politics*, 25(3): 125–46.

Carter, Elisabeth (2004), 'Does PR Promote Extremism? Evidence from the West European Parties of the Extreme Right', *Representation*, 40(2): 82–100.

Casals, Xavier (2001), 'Le national-populisme en Espagne: les raisons d'une absence', in Pascal Perrineau (ed.), *Les croisés de la société fermée: l'Europe des extrêmes droites*, pp. 323–38, La Tour d'Aigues: Editions de l'Aube.

Castles, Francis G. and Peter Mair (1984), 'Left–Right Political Scales: Some "Expert" Judgements', *European Journal of Political Research*, 12(1): 73–88.

Chapin, Wesley D. (1997), 'Explaining the Electoral Success of the New Right: The German Case', *West European Politics*, 20(2): 53–72.

Cheles, Luciano, Ronnie Ferguson and Michalina Vaughan (eds) (1991), *Neo-Fascism in Europe*, London: Longman.

Cheles, Luciano, Ronnie Ferguson and Michalina Vaughan (eds) (1995), *The Far Right in Western and Eastern Europe*, 2nd edition, London: Longman.

Chiarini, Roberto (1995), 'The Italian Far Right: The Search for Legitimacy', in Luciano Cheles, Ronnie Ferguson and Michalina Vaughan (eds), *The Far Right in Western and Eastern Europe*, 2nd edition, pp. 20–40, London: Longman.

Childs, David (1995), 'The Far Right in Germany since 1945', in Luciano Cheles, Ronnie Ferguson and Michalina Vaughan (eds), *The Far Right in Western and Eastern Europe*, 2nd edition, pp. 290–308, London: Longman.

Ciaurro, Gian Franco (1989), 'Public Financing of Parties in Italy', in Herbert E. Alexander (ed.), *Comparative Political Finance in the 1980s*, pp. 153–71, Cambridge: Cambridge University Press.

Cole, Alistair and Peter Campbell (1989), *French Electoral Systems and Elections since 1789*, Aldershot: Gower.

Constitution of the Portuguese Republic (Fourth Revision 1997), www.parlamento.pt/frames/constituicao_index.htm.

Costa Pinto, António (1995), 'The Radical Right in Contemporary Portugal', in Luciano Cheles, Ronnie Ferguson and Michalina Vaughan (eds), *The Far Right in Western and Eastern Europe*, 2nd edition, pp. 108–28, London: Longman.

Cox, Gary W. (1990), 'Centripetal and Centrifugal Incentives in Electoral Systems', *American Journal of Political Science*, 34(4): 903–35.

Cox, Gary (1997), *Making Votes Count: Strategic Coordination in the World's Electoral Systems*, Cambridge: Cambridge University Press.

Daalder, Hans and Jerrold G. Rusk (1972), 'Perceptions of Party in the Dutch Parliament', in Samuel C. Patterson and John C. Wahlke (eds), *Comparative Legislative Behavior: Frontiers of Research*, pp. 143–98, New York: Wiley.

Dalton, Russell J. and Martin P. Wattenberg (eds) (2000), *Parties Without Partisans: Political Change in Advanced Industrial Democracies*, Oxford: Oxford University Press.

Damgaard, Erik and Jerrold G. Rusk (1976), 'Cleavage Structures and Representational Linkages: A Longitudinal Analysis of Danish Legislative Behaviour', in Ian Budge, Ivor Crewe and Dennis Farlie (eds), *Party Identification and Beyond: Representation of Voting and Party Competition*, pp. 163–88, London: Wiley.

Davis, Thomas C. (1998), 'The Iberian Peninsula and Greece: Retreat from the Radical Right?', in Hans-Georg Betz and Stefan Immerfall (eds), *The New Politics of the Right: Neo-Populist Parties and Movements in Established Democracies*, pp. 157–72, New York: St Martin's Press.

DeClair, Edward G. (1999), *Politics on the Fringe: The People, Policies and Organization of the French Front National*, Durham NC: Duke University Press.

Del Castillo, Pillar (1989), 'Financing of Spanish Political Parties', in Herbert E. Alexander (ed.), *Comparative Political Finance in the 1980s*, pp. 172–96, Cambridge: Cambridge University Press.

Del Castillo, Pillar (1994), 'Problems in Spanish Party Financing', in Herbert E. Alexander and Rei Shiratori (eds), *Comparative Finance Among the Democracies*, pp. 97–104, Boulder CO: Westview.

Deschouwer, Kris (1992), 'Belgium', in Richard S. Katz and Peter Mair (eds), *Party Organizations: A Data Handbook*, pp. 121–98, London: Sage.

Deslore, Guy (1995), 'The Far Right in Belgium: The Double Track', in Luciano Cheles, Ronnie Ferguson and Michalina Vaughan (eds), *The Far Right in Western and Eastern Europe*, 2nd edition, pp. 245–57, London: Longman.

De Swaan, Abram (1973), *Coalition Theories and Cabinet Formation*, Amsterdam: Elsevier.

Deutsche Volksunion (2002), *Partei-Programm*, www.dvu.de.

Dézé, Alexandre (2001), 'Entre adaptation et démarcation: la question du rapport des formations d'extrême droite aux systèmes politiques des démocraties européennes', in Pascal Perrineau (ed.), *Les croisés de la société fermée: l'Europe des extrêmes droites*, pp. 339–65, La Tour d'Aigues: Editions de l'Aube.

Die Republikaner (1998), *Das Parteiprogramm*, www.republikaner.org/wahl98.

Dimitras, Panayote Elias (1992), 'Greece: The Virtual Absence of an Extreme Right', in Paul Hainsworth (ed.), *The Extreme Right in Europe and the USA*, pp. 246–68, London: Pinter.

Dimitras, Panayote Elias (1993), 'The Greek Parliamentary Election of October 1993', *Electoral Studies*, 13(3): 235–39.

Dimitras, Panayote Elias (1994), 'Electoral Systems in Greece', in Stuart S. Nagel and Vladimir Rukavishnikov (eds), *Eastern European Development and Public Policy*, pp. 143–75, New York: St Martin's Press.

Downs, Anthony (1957), *An Economic Theory of Democracy*, New York: Harper and Row.

Drysch, Thomas (1993), 'The New French System of Political Finance', in Arthur B. Gunlicks (ed.), *Campaign and Party Finance in North America and Western Europe*, pp. 155–77, Boulder CO: Westview.

Duverger, Maurice (1954), *Political Parties: Their Organization and Activity in the Modern State*, London: Methuen.

Eatwell, Roger (1992), 'Why has the Extreme Right Failed in Britain?', in Paul Hainsworth (ed.), *The Extreme Right in Europe and the USA*, pp. 175–92, London: Pinter.

Eatwell, Roger (1995), 'How to Revise History (and Influence People!), Neo-Fascist Style', in Luciano Cheles, Ronnie Ferguson and Michalina Vaughan (eds), *The Far Right in Western and Eastern Europe,* 2nd edition, pp. 309–26, London: Longman.

Eatwell, Roger (1998a), 'Britain: The BNP and the Problem of Legitimacy', in Hans-Georg Betz and Stefan Immerfall (eds), *The New Politics of the Right: Neo-Populist Parties and Movements in Established Democracies*, pp. 143–55, New York: St Martin's Press.

Eatwell, Roger (1998b), 'The Dynamics of Right-Wing Electoral Breakthrough', *Patterns of Prejudice*, 32(3): 3–31.

Eatwell, Roger (2000a), 'The Rebirth of the "Extreme Right" in Western Europe', *Parliamentary Affairs*, 53(3): 407–25.

Eatwell, Roger (2000b), 'The Extreme Right and British Exceptionalism: The Primacy of Politics', in Paul Hainsworth (ed.), *The Politics of the Extreme Right: From the Margins to the Mainstream*, pp. 172–92, London: Pinter.

Eatwell, Roger (2003), 'Ten Theories of the Extreme Right', in Peter Merkl and Leonard Weinberg (eds), *Right-Wing Extremism in the Twenty-First Century*, pp. 47–73, London: Frank Cass.

Eatwell, Roger and Cas Mudde (eds) (2004), *Western Democracies and the New Extreme Right Challenge*, London: Routledge.

Eatwell, Roger and Noel O'Sullivan (eds) (1989), *The Nature of the Right: European and American Politics and Political Thought since 1789*, London: Pinter.

Economic History Services (EH.Net) (a), *What was the Exchange Rate Then?*, http://eh.net/hmit/exchangerates.

Economic History Services (EH.Net) (b), *How Much is that Worth Today?*, http://eh.net/hmit/ppowerusd.

Elections around the World, www.electionworld.org.

Elections Belges depuis 1830, www.vub.ac.be/belgianelections.

Eleweb, www.eleweb.net

Elgie, Robert (1997), 'Two-Ballot Majority Electoral Systems', *Representation*, 34(2): 89–94.

Elklit, Jørgen (1999), 'The Danish March 1998 Parliamentary Election', *Electoral Studies*, 18(1): 137–42.

Ellwood, Sheelagh M. (1992), 'The Extreme Right in Post-Francoist Spain', *Parliamentary Affairs*, 45(3): 373–85.

Ellwood, Sheelagh (1995), 'The Extreme Right in Spain: A Dying Species?', in Luciano Cheles, Ronnie Ferguson and Michalian Vaughan (eds), *The Far Right in Western and Eastern Europe*, 2nd edition, pp. 91–107, London: Longman.

Enelow, James and Melvin Hinich (1984), *The Spatial Theory of Voting: An Introduction*, New York: Cambridge University Press.

Enelow, James and Melvin Hinich (eds) (1989), *Advances in the Spatial Theory of Voting*, New York: Cambridge University Press.

Evans, Jocelyn (2001), 'Les bases sociales et psychologiques du passage gauche-extrême droite. Exception française ou mutation européenne?', in Pascal Perrineau (ed.), *Les croisés de la société fermée: l'Europe des extrêmes droites*, pp. 73–101, La Tour d'Aigues: Editions de l'Aube.

Ewing, Keith (1987), *The Funding of Political Parties in Britain*, Cambridge: Cambridge University Press.

Ewing, Keith (1992), *Money, Politics and Law*, Oxford: Clarendon.

Falter, Jürgen and Siegfried Schumann (1988), 'Affinity towards Right-Wing Extremism in Western Europe', *West European Politics*, 11(2): 96–110.

Farrell, David M. (1996), 'Campaign Strategies and Tactics', in Lawrence LeDuc, Richard G. Niemi and Pippa Norris (eds), *Comparing Democracies: Elections and Voting in Global Perspective*, pp. 160–83, Thousand Oaks CA: Sage.

Farrell, David M. (2001), *Electoral Systems: A Comparative Introduction*, Basingstoke: Palgrave.

Farrell, David M. and Paul Webb (2000), 'Political Parties as Campaign Organizations', in Russell J. Dalton and Martin P. Wattenberg (eds), *Parties Without Partisans: Political Change in Advanced Industrial Democracies*, pp. 102–28, Oxford: Oxford University Press.

Fennema, Meindert (1997), 'Some Conceptual Issues and Problems in the Comparison of Anti-Immigrant Parties in Western Europe', *Party Politics*, 3(4): 473–92.

Finer, Samuel E. (1975), 'Manifesto Moonshine', *New Society*, 13 November: 379–80.

Fishburn, Peter C. (1983), 'Dimensions of Election Procedures: Analyses and Comparisons', *Theory and Decision*, 15(4): 371–97.

Fisher, Justin (1994), 'The Institutional Funding of British Political Parties', in David Broughton, Colin Rallings, David M. Farrell and David Denver (eds), *British Elections and Parties Yearbook 1994*, pp. 181–96, London: Frank Cass.

Fisher, Justin (1999), 'Party Expenditure and Electoral Prospects: A National Level Analysis of Britain', *Electoral Studies*, 18(4): 519–32.

Fitzmaurice, John (1992), 'The Extreme Right in Belgium: Recent Developments', *Parliamentary Affairs*, 45(3): 300–8.

FPÖ (Freiheitliche Partei Österreichs) (1997), *Das Programm der Freiheitlichen Partei Österreichs: Das neue Parteiprogramm*, www.fpoe.or.at/bb/programm97/FP-Programm.pdf.

FPÖ (Freiheitliche Partei Österreichs) (1999), *Program of the Austrian Freedom Party*, www.fpoe.at/englisch/Program.htm.

FPÖ (Freiheitliche Partei Österreichs) (2002a), *The Program of the Freedom Party of Austria, Chapter 4: The Right to a Cultural Identity (Heimat)*, www.fpoe.at/fpoe/bundesgst/programm/chapter4.htm.

FPÖ (Freiheitliche Partei Österreichs) (2002b), *The Program of the Freedom Party of Austria, Chapter 8: Reform of Democracy – A Free Republic*, www.fpoe.at/fpoe/bundesgst/programm/chapter8.htm.

Fremskridtspartiet (1998), *The Progress Party*, www.frp.dk/foreign/engelsk.html.

Front National (1997a), *Un programme pour gouverner: 16 axes d'action pour réussir la grande alternance*, www.front-nat.fr/axes.html.

Front National (1997b), *Le programme complet (législatives juin 97): le grand changement*, www.front-nat.fr/progrleg.html.

Fuchs, Dieter and Hans-Dieter Klingemann (1989), 'The Left–Right Schema', in M. Kent Jennings, Jan W. Van Deth, Samuel H. Barnes, Dieter Fuchs, Felix J. Heunks, Ronald Inglehart, Max Kaase, Hans-Dieter Klingemann and Jacques

J. A. Thomassen, *Continuities in Political Action: A Longitudinal Study of Political Orientations in Three Western Democracies*, pp. 203–34, Berlin: de Gruyter.

Furlong, Paul (1992), 'The Extreme Right in Italy: Old Orders and Dangerous Novelties', *Parliamentary Affairs*, 45(3): 345–56.

Fysh, Peter and Jim Wolfreys, (1992), 'Le Pen, the National Front and the Extreme Right in France', *Parliamentary Affairs*, 45(3): 309–26.

Gabel, Matthew J. and John D. Huber (2000), 'Putting Parties in their Place: Inferring Party Left–Right Ideological Positions from Party Manifestos Data', *American Journal of Political Science*, 44(1): 94–103.

Gallagher, Michael (1991), 'Proportionality, Disproportionality and Electoral Systems', *Electoral Studies*, 10(1): 33–51.

Gallagher, Michael, Michael Laver and Peter Mair (1995) *Representative Government in Modern Europe*, 2nd edition, New York: McGraw-Hill.

Gallagher, Michael, Michael Laver and Peter Mair (2001) *Representative Government in Modern Europe*, 3rd edition, New York: McGraw-Hill.

Gallagher, Tom (1992), 'Portugal: The Marginalisation of the Extreme Right', in Paul Hainsworth (ed.), *The Extreme Right in Europe and the USA*, pp. 232–45, London: Pinter.

Gallagher, Tom (1993), 'Regional Nationalism and Party System Change: Italy's Northern League: Review Article', *West European Politics*, 16(4): 616–21.

Gallagher, Tom (2000), 'Exit from the Ghetto: The Italian Far Right in the 1990s', in Paul Hainsworth (ed.), *The Politics of the Extreme Right: From the Margins to the Mainstream*, pp. 64–86, London: Pinter.

Gamaleri, Gianpiero (1995), 'Italy and the 1994 Elections: Media, Politics and the Concentration of Power', in Yasha Lange and Andrew Palmer (eds), *Media and Elections: A Handbook*, pp. 73–89, Düsseldorf: European Institute for the Media.

Gardberg, Annvi (1993), *Against the Stranger, the Gangster, and the Establishment: A Comparative Study of the Ideologies of the Swedish Ny Demokrati, the German Republikaner, the French Front National and the Belgium Vlaams Blok*, Helsingfors: Universitetstryckeriet.

Gellner, Ernest (1983), *Nations and Nationalism*, Oxford: Blackwell.

Gentile, Pierre and Hanspeter Kriesi (1998), 'Contemporary Radical-Right Parties in Switzerland: History of a Divided Family', in Hans-Georg Betz and Stefan Immerfall (eds), *The New Politics of the Right: Neo-Populist Parties and Movements in Established Democracies*, pp. 125–42, New York: St Martin's Press.

Gidlund, Gullan (1991), 'Public Investment in Swedish Democracy: Gambling with Gains and Losses', in Matti Wiberg (ed.), *The Public Purse and Political Parties: Public Financing of Political Parties in Nordic Countries*, pp. 13–54, Jyväskylä: Gummerus.

Gidlund, Gullan M. (1994), 'Regulation of Party Finance in Sweden', in Herbert E. Alexander and Rei Shiratori (eds), *Comparative Political Finance Among the Democracies*, pp. 105–14, Boulder CO: Westview.

Gillespie, Richard (1996), 'The Spanish General Election of 1996', *Electoral Studies*, 15(3): 425–31.

Gilmour, John (1992), 'The Extreme Right in Spain: Blas Piñar and the Spirit of the Nationalist Uprising', in Paul Hainsworth (ed.), *The Extreme Right in Europe and the USA*, pp. 206–31, London: Pinter.

Bibliography

Golder, Matt (2003a), 'Explaining Variation in the Succ[ ] in Western Europe', *Comparative Political Studies*

Golder, Matt (2003b), 'Electoral Institutions, Un[ ] Parties: A Correction', *British Journal of Political Sc.*

Goldey, David B. and R. W. Johnson (1988), 'The French . 24 April–8 May and the General Election of 5–12 June 198ᵇ , 7(3): 195–223.

Griffin, Roger (1993), *The Nature of Fascism*, London: Routledge.

Griffin, Roger (1996), 'The "Post-Fascism" of the Alleanza Nazionale: A Case Stu[ ] in Ideological Morphology', *Journal of Political Ideologies*, 1(2): 123–45.

Grofman, Bernard and Arend Lijphart (1986), 'Introduction', in Bernard Grofman and Arend Lijphart (eds), *Electoral Laws and their Political Consequences*, pp. 1–15, New York: Agathon Press.

Gunlicks, Arthur B. (1988), 'Campaign and Party Finance in the West German "Party State"', *Review of Politics*, 50(1): 30–48.

Gunlicks, Arthur B. (1993), 'Introduction', in Arthur B. Gunlicks (ed.), *Campaign and Party Finance in North America and Western Europe*, pp. 3–14, Boulder CO: Westview.

Gunther, Richard, José Ramon Montero and José Ignacio Wert (2000), 'The Media and Politics in Spain: From Dictatorship to Democracy', in Richard Gunther and Anthony Mughan (eds), *Democracy and the Media: A Comparative Perspective*, pp. 28–84, Cambridge: Cambridge University Press.

Guyomarch, Alain (2001), 'Electoral Politics and Party Competition', in Alain Guyomarch, Howard Machin, Peter A. Hall and Jack Hayward (eds), *Developments in French Politics 2*, pp. 23–49, Basingstoke: Palgrave.

Hain, Peter (1986), *Proportional Misrepresentation: The Case against PR in Britain*, Guilford: Wildwood House.

Hainsworth, Paul (1992a), 'Introduction – The Cutting Edge: The Extreme Right in Post-War Western Europe and the USA', in Paul Hainsworth (ed.), *The Extreme Right in Europe and the USA*, pp. 1–28, London: Pinter.

Hainsworth, Paul (1992b), 'The Extreme Right in Post-War France: The Emergence and Success of the Front National', in Paul Hainsworth (ed.), *The Extreme Right in Europe and the USA*, pp. 29–60, London: Pinter.

Hainsworth, Paul (2000a), 'Introduction: The Extreme Right', in Paul Hainsworth (ed.), *The Politics of the Extreme Right: From the Margins to the Mainstream*, pp. 1–17, London: Pinter.

Hainsworth, Paul (2000b), 'The Front National: From Ascendancy to Fragmentation on the French Extreme Right', in Paul Hainsworth (ed.), *The Politics of the Extreme Right: From the Margins to the Mainstream*, pp. 18–32, London: Pinter.

Hainsworth, Paul and Paul Mitchell (2000), 'France: The Front National from Crossroads to Crossroads?', *Parliamentary Affairs*, 53(3): 443–56.

Hand, Geoffrey, Jacques Georgel and Christoph Sasse (1979), *European Electoral Systems Handbook*, London: Butterworths.

Hardy, Melissa A. (1993), *Regression with Dummy Variables*, Newbury Park CA: Sage.

Harmel, Robert and John D. Robertson (1985), 'Formation and Success of New Parties: A Cross-National Analysis', *International Political Science Review*, 6(4): 501–23.

, Robert and Lars Svåsand (1997), 'The Influence of New Parties on Old
cies' Platforms: The Case of the Progress Parties and Conservative Parties in
enmark and Norway', *Party Politics*, 3(3): 315–40.

.arris, Geoffrey (1990), *The Dark Side of Europe: The Extreme Right Today*,
Edinburgh: Edinburgh University Press.

Harrison, Lisa (1997), 'Maximising Small Party Potential: The Effects of Electoral
System Rules on the Far Right in German Sub-National Elections', *German
Politics*, 6(3): 132–51.

Harrison, Lisa (2000), 'The Impact of German Electoral Systems upon Extremist
Party Representation – A Comparative Analysis', *Representation*, 37(1): 29–38.

Hauss, Charles and David Rayside (1978), 'The Development of New Parties in
Western Democracies since 1945', in Louis Maisel and Joseph Cooper (eds),
Political Parties: Development and Decay, pp. 31–57, Beverly Hills CA: Sage.

Hazan, Reuven Y. (1997), *Centre Parties: Polarization and Competition in European
Parliamentary Democracies*, London: Pinter.

Helms, Ludger (1997), 'Right-Wing Populist Parties in Austria and Switzerland:
A Comparative Analysis of Electoral Support and Conditions of Success', *West
European Politics*, 20(2): 37–52.

Hennion, Blandine (1993), *Le Front National, l'argent et l'establishment 1972–
1993*, Paris: Editions la Découverte.

Hermens, Ferdinand A. (1941), *Democracy or Anarchy? A Study of Proportional
Representation*, Notre Dame IL: University of Notre Dame Press.

Herz, Theodor A. (1975), *Soziale Bedingungen für Rechtsextremismus in der
Bundesrepublik Deutschlands und in den Vereinigten Staaten. Eine vergleichende
Analyse der Anhänger der Nationaldemokratischen Partei Deutschlands und der
Anhänger von George C. Wallace*, Meisenheim am Glan: Hain.

Hinich, Melvin J. and Michael C. Munger (1994), *Ideology and the Theory of
Political Choice*, Ann Arbor: University of Michigan Press.

Hobsbawm, Eric J. (1990), *Nations and Nationalism since 1780: Programme, Myth,
Reality*, Cambridge: Cambridge University Press.

Holtz-Bacha, Christina and Lynda Lee Kaid (1995a), 'A Comparative Perspective
on Political Advertising: Media and Political System Characteristics', in Lynda
Lee Kaid and Christina Holtz-Bacha (eds), *Political Advertising in Western
Democracies: Parties and Candidates on Television*, pp. 8–18, Thousand Oaks
CA: Sage.

Holtz-Bacha, Christina and Lynda Lee Kaid (1995b), 'Television Spots in German
National Elections: Content and Effects', in Lynda Lee Kaid and Christina Holtz-
Bacha (eds), *Political Advertising in Western Democracies: Parties and Candidates
on Television*, pp. 61–88, Thousand Oaks CA: Sage.

Hossay, Patrick (1996), '"Our People First!" Understanding the Resonance of the
Vlaams Blok's Xenophobic Programme', *Social Identities*, 2(3): 343–64.

Hotelling, Harold (1929), 'Stability in Competition', *Economic Journal*, 39: 41–59.

Huber, John D. (1989), 'Values and Partisanship in Left–Right Orientations: Measuring
Ideology', *European Journal of Political Research*, 17(5): 599–621.

Huber, John D. and Ronald Inglehart (1995), 'Expert Interpretations of Party Space
and Party Locations in 42 Societies', *Party Politics*, 1(1): 73–111.

Hug, Simon (2000), 'Studying the Electoral Success of New Political Parties:
A Methodological Note', *Party Politics*, 6(2): 187–97.

Husbands, Christopher T. (1981), 'Contemporary Right-Wing Extremism in Western European Democracies: A Review Article', *European Journal of Political Research*, 9(1): 75–99.

Husbands, Christopher T. (1988a), 'Extreme Right-Wing Politics in Great Britain: The Recent Marginalisation of the National Front', *West European Politics*, 11(2): 65–79.

Husbands, Christopher T. (1988b), 'The Dynamics of Racial Exclusion and Expulsion: Racist Politics in Western Europe', *European Journal of Political Research*, 16(6): 701–20.

Husbands, Christopher T. (1992a), 'The Other Face of 1992: The Extreme-Right Explosion in Western Europe', *Parliamentary Affairs*, 45(3): 267–84.

Husbands, Christopher T. (1992b), 'Belgium: Flemish Legions on the March', in Paul Hainsworth (ed.), *The Extreme Right in Europe and the USA*, pp. 126–50, London: Pinter.

Husbands, Christopher T. (1992c), 'The Netherlands: Irritants on the Body Politic', in Paul Hainsworth (ed.), *The Extreme Right in Europe and the USA*, pp. 95–125, London: Pinter.

Husbands, Christopher T. (2000), 'Switzerland: Right-Wing and Xenophobic Parties, from Margin to Mainstream?', *Parliamentary Affairs*, 53(3): 501–16.

Ignazi, Piero (1992), 'The Silent Counter-Revolution: Hypotheses on the Emergence of Extreme Right-Wing Parties in Europe', *European Journal of Political Research*, 22(1): 3–34.

Ignazi, Piero (1996a), 'From Neo-Fascists to Post-Fascists? The Transformation of the MSI into the AN', *West European Politics*, 19(4): 693–714.

Ignazi, Piero (1996b), 'The Crisis of Parties and the Rise of New Political Parties', *Party Politics*, 2(4): 549–66.

Ignazi, Piero (1996c), 'The Intellectual Basis of Right-Wing Anti-Partyism', *European Journal of Political Research*, 29(3): 279–96.

Ignazi, Piero (1997a), 'New Challenges: Postmaterialism and the Extreme Right', in Martin Rhodes, Paul Heywood and Vincent Wright (eds), *Developments in West European Politics*, pp. 300–19, Basingstoke: Macmillan.

Ignazi, Piero (1997b), 'The Extreme Right in Europe: A Survey', in Peter H. Merkl and Leonard Weinberg (eds), *The Revival of Right-Wing Extremism in the Nineties*, pp. 47–64, London: Frank Cass.

Ignazi, Piero (2003), *Extreme Right Parties in Western Europe*, Oxford: Oxford University Press.

Ignazi, Piero and Colette Ysmal (1992), 'New and Old Extreme Right Parties: The French Front National and the Italian Movimento Sociale', *European Journal of Political Research*, 22(1): 101–21.

Ignazi, Piero and Colette Ysmal (eds) (1998), *The Organization of Political Parties in Southern Europe*, London: Praeger.

Immerfall, Stefan (1998), 'Conclusion: The Neo-Populist Agenda', in Hans-Georg Betz and Stefan Immerfall (eds), *The New Politics of the Right: Neo-Populist Parties and Movements in Established Democracies*, pp. 249–61, New York: St Martin's Press.

Inglehart, Ronald (1977), *The Silent Revolution: Changing Values and Political Styles Among Western Publics*, Princeton NJ: Princeton University Press.

Inglehart, Ronald and Hans-Dieter Klingemann (1976), 'Party Identification, Ideological Preference and the Left–Right Dimension among Western Mass Publics', in Ian Budge,

Ivor Crewe and Dennis Farlie (eds), *Party Identification and Beyond: Representations of Voting and Party Competition*, pp. 243–73, New York: Wiley.

Inter-Parliamentary Union Parline Database, www.ipu.org/parline-e/ parlinesearch.asp.

Irwin, Galen A. (1995), 'The Dutch Parliamentary Election of 1994', *Electoral Studies*, 14(1): 72–7.

Ivaldi, Gilles (2002), *Extreme Right Parties in France: An Overview*, Extreme Right Electorates and Party Success, http://cidsp.upmf-grenoble.fr/guest/ereps/download /france_overview.htm.

Jackman, Robert W. and Karin Volpert (1996), 'Conditions Favouring Parties of the Extreme Right in Western Europe', *British Journal of Political Science*, 26(4): 501–21.

Janda, Kenneth (1980), *Political Parties: A Cross National Survey*, New York: Free Press.

Janda, Kenneth, Robert Harmel, Christine Edens and Patricia Goff (1995), 'Changes in Party Identity: Evidence from Party Manifestos', *Party Politics*, 1(2): 171–96.

Jennings, M. Kent, Jan W. Van Deth, Samuel H. Barnes, Dieter Fuchs, Felix J. Heunks, Ronald Inglehart, Max Kaase, Hans-Dieter Klingemann and Jacques J. A. Thomassen (1990), *Continuities in Political Action: A Longitudinal Study of Political Orientations in Three Western Democracies*, Berlin: de Gruyter.

Johnston, Ron J. and Charles J. Pattie (1993), 'Great Britain: Twentieth Century Parties Operating under Nineteenth Century Regulations', in Arthur B. Gunlicks (ed.), *Campaign and Party Finance in North America and Western Europe*, pp. 123–54, Boulder CO: Westview.

Kapetanyannis, Vassilis (1995), 'Neo-Fascism in Modern Greece', in Luciano Cheles, Ronnie Ferguson and Michalina Vaughan (eds), *The Far Right in Western and Eastern Europe*, 2nd edition, pp. 129–44, London: Longman.

Kaplan, Jeffrey and Leonard Weinberg (1998), *The Emergence of a Euro-American Radical Right*, New Brunswick NJ: Rutgers University Press.

Karvonen, Lauri (1997), 'The New Extreme Right-Wingers in Western Europe: Attitudes, World Views and Social Characteristics', in Peter H. Merkl and Leonard Weinberg (eds), *The Revival of Right-Wing Extremism in the Nineties*, pp. 91–110, London: Frank Cass.

Katz, Richard S. (1996a), 'Electoral Reform and the Transformation of Party Politics in Italy', *Party Politics*, 2(1): 31–53.

Katz, Richard S. (1996b), 'Party Organizations and Finance', in Lawrence LeDuc, Richard G. Niemi and Pippa Norris (eds), *Comparing Democracies: Elections and Voting in Global Perspective*, pp. 107–33, Thousand Oaks CA: Sage.

Katz, Richard S. (1997), *Democracy and Elections*, New York: Oxford University Press.

Katz, Richard S. and Peter Mair (eds) (1992), *Party Organizations: A Data Handbook on Party Organizations in Western Democracies, 1960–90*, London: Sage.

Katz, Richard S. and Peter Mair (1995), 'Changing Models of Party Organization and Party Democracy: The Emergence of the Cartel Party', *Party Politics* 1(1): 5–28.

Kim, Heemin and Richard C. Fording (1998), 'Voter Ideology in Western Democracies, 1946–1989', *European Journal of Political Research*, 33(1): 73–97.

Kirchheimer, Otto (1966), 'The Transformation of the Western European Party Systems', in Joseph LaPalombara and Myron Weiner (eds), *Political Parties and Political Development*, pp. 177–200, Princeton NJ: Princeton University Press.

Kitchen, Martin (1976), *Fascism*, Basingstoke: Macmillan.

Kitschelt, Herbert (1989), 'The Internal Politics of Parties: The Law of Curvilinear Disparity Revisited', *Political Studies*, 37(3): 400–21.

Kitschelt, Herbert (1995), *The Radical Right in Western Europe: A Comparative Analysis*, Ann Arbor: University of Michigan Press.

Kitschelt, Herbert (1997), 'European Party Systems: Continuity and Change', in Martin Rhodes, Paul Heywood and Vincent Wright (eds), *Developments in West European Politics*, pp. 131–50, Basingstoke: Macmillan.

Klee, Gudrun (1993), 'Financing Parties and Elections in Small European Democracies: Austria and Sweden', in Arthur B. Gunlicks (ed.), *Campaign and Party Finance in North America and Western Europe*, pp. 178–200, Boulder CO: Westview.

Kleinnijenhuis, Jan (1999), 'Statistics in Political Science', in Paul Pennings, Hans Keman and Jan Kleinnijenhuis, *Doing Research in Political Science: An Introduction to Comparative Methods and Statistics*, pp. 74–221, London: Sage

Klingemann, Hans-Dieter (1995), 'Party Positions and Voter Orientations', in Hans-Dieter Klingemann and Dieter Fuchs (eds), *Citizens and the State*, pp. 183–205, New York: Oxford University Press.

Klingemann, Hans-Dieter, Richard I. Hofferbert and Ian Budge (1994), *Parties, Policies and Democracy*, Boulder CO: Westview.

Knapp, Andrew (2003), 'From the Gaullist Movement to the President's Party', in Jocelyn A. J. Evans (ed.), *The French Party System*, pp. 121–36, Manchester: Manchester University Press.

Knigge, Pia (1998), 'The Ecological Correlates of Right-Wing Extremism in Western Europe', *European Journal of Political Research*, 34(2): 249–79.

Knight, Robert (1992), 'Haider, the Freedom Party and the Extreme Right in Austria', *Parliamentary Affairs*, 45(3): 285–99.

Knutsen, Oddbjørn (1998), 'Expert Judgements of the Left–Right Location of Political Parties: A Comparative Longitudinal Study', *West European Politics*, 21(2): 63–94.

Koch, Koen (1991), 'Back to Sarajevo or Beyond Trianon? Some Thoughts on the Problem of Nationalism in Eastern Europe', *Netherlands Journal of Social Sciences*, 27(1): 29–42.

Kolinsky, Eva (1992), 'A Future for Right Extremism in Germany?', in Paul Hainsworth (ed.), *The Extreme Right in Europe and the USA*, pp. 61–94, London: Pinter.

Koole, Ruud (1989), 'The "Modesty" of Dutch Party Finance', in Herbert E. Alexander (ed.), *Comparative Political Finance in the 1980s*, pp. 200–19, Cambridge: Cambridge University Press.

Koole, Ruud (1994), 'Dutch Political Parties: Money and the Message', in Herbert E. Alexander and Rei Shiratori (eds), *Comparative Political Finance among the Democracies*, pp. 115–31, Boulder CO: Westview.

Koole, Ruud and Hella Van de Velde (1992), 'The Netherlands', in Richard S. Katz and Peter Mair (eds), *Party Organizations: A Data Handbook*, pp. 619–731, London: Sage.

Krejčí, Jaroslav (1995), 'Neo-Fascism – West and East', in Luciano Cheles, Ronnie Ferguson and Michalina Vaughan (eds), *The Far Right in Western and Eastern Europe*, 2nd edition, pp. 1–12, London: Longman.

Landfried, Christine (1994), 'Political Finance in West Germany', in Herbert Alexander and Rei Shiratori (eds), *Comparative Political Finance among the Democracies*, pp. 133–44, Boulder CO: Westview.

Lange, Yasha (1999), *Media and Elections: Handbook*, Strasbourg: Council of Europe.

Laver, Michael (1981), *The Politics of Private Desires*, Harmondsworth: Penguin.

Laver, Michael (1995), 'Party Policy and Cabinet Portfolios in the Netherlands, 1994', *Acta Politica*, 30(1): 3–28.

Laver, Michael (1997), *Private Desires, Political Action: An Invitation to the Politics of Rational Choice*, London: Sage.

Laver, Michael (1998), 'Party Policy in Britain 1997: Results from an Expert Survey', *Political Studies*, 46(2): 336–47.

Laver, Michael (2001a), 'Why Should we Estimate the Policy Positions of Political Actors?', in Michael Laver (ed.), *Estimating the Policy Position of Political Actors*, pp. 3–9, London: Routledge.

Laver, Michael (2001b), 'How Should we Estimate the Policy Positions of Political Actors?', in Michael Laver (ed.), *Estimating the Policy Position of Political Actors*, pp. 239–44, London: Routledge.

Laver, Michael and Kenneth Benoit (2002), 'Locating TDs in Policy Spaces: The Computational Text Analysis of Dáil Speeches', *Irish Political Studies*, 17(1): 59–73.

Laver, Michael and Ian Budge (eds) (1992), *Party Policy and Government Coalitions*, London: Macmillan.

Laver, Michael and J. Garry (2000), 'Estimating Policy Positions from Political Texts', *American Journal of Political Science*, 44(3): 619–34.

Laver, Michael and W. Ben Hunt (1992), *Policy and Party Competition*, New York: Routledge.

Laver, Michael and Peter Mair (1999), 'Party Policy and Cabinet Portfolios in the Netherlands, 1998: Results from an Expert Survey', *Acta Politica*, 34(1): 49–66.

Laver, Michael and Norman Schofield (1990), *Multiparty Government: The Politics of Coalition in Europe*, Oxford: Oxford University Press.

LeDuc, Lawrence, Richard G. Niemi and Pippa Norris (1996), 'Introduction: The Present and Future of Democratic Elections', in Lawrence LeDuc, Richard G. Niemi and Pippa Norris (eds), *Comparing Democracies: Elections and Voting in Global Perspective*, pp. 1–48, Thousand Oaks CA: Sage.

Legge 28/00 (2000), 'Disposizioni per la parità di accesso ai mezzi di informazione durante le campagne elettorali e referendarie e per la comunicazione politica', Legge del 22. Februar 2000, No. 28, *Gazzetta Ufficiale*, 43.

Levush, Ruth (1991), 'Campaign Financing: A Comparative Study', in Ruth Levush (ed.), *Campaign Financing of National Elections in Foreign Countries*, pp. 1–24, Washington DC: Law Library of Congress.

Lijphart, Arend (1988), *Democracies: Patterns of Majoritarian and Consensus Government in Twenty-One Countries*, New Haven CT: Yale University Press.

Lijphart, Arend (1994), *Electoral Systems and Party Systems: A Study of Twenty-Seven Democracies 1945–1990*, New York: Oxford University Press.

Lijphart, Arend (1997), 'The Difficult Science of Electoral Systems: A Commentary on the Critique by Alberto Penadés', *Electoral Studies*, 16(1): 73–7.

Lijphart, Arend (1999), *Patterns of Democracy: Government Forms and Performance in Thirty-six Countries*, New Haven CT: Yale University Press.

Lijphart, Arend (2001), 'The Pros and Cons – But Mainly Pros – of Consensus Democracy', *Acta Politica*, 36(2): 129–39.

Lijphart, Arend and Bernard Grofman (eds) (1984), *Choosing an Electoral System: Issues and Alternatives*, New York: Praeger.

Lijphart Election Archive, www.dodgson.ucsd.edu/lij.

Linton, Martin (1994), *Money and Votes*, London: Institute for Public Policy Research.

Loosemore, John and Victor J. Hanby (1971), 'The Theoretical Limits of Maximum Distortion: Some Analytic Expressions for Electoral Systems', *British Journal of Political Science*, 1(4): 467–77.

Lowles, Nick (2000), *1990–1999: Ballot Box to Bomb – Fighting on all Fronts*, www.searchlightmagazine.com/stories/century/1990-1999.htm.

Lowles, Nick (2002), *BNP Purge Continues*, www.searchlightmagazine.com/stories/story_index.htm.

Lowles, Nick (2003a), *Walkouts Threatened after BNP Promotes Race-Mixing*, www.searchlightmagazine.com/stories/story_index.htm.

Lowles, Nick (2003b), *Tyndall's Last Stand*, www.searchlightmagazine.com/stories/story_index.htm.

Lubbers, Marcel (2000), *Expert Judgement Survey of Western European Political Parties 2000*, Nijmegen: NOW, Department of Sociology, University of Nijmegen.

Lubbers, Marcel and Peer Scheepers (2000), 'Individual and Contextual Characteristics of the German Extreme Right-Wing Vote in the 1990s: A Test of Complementary Theories', *European Journal of Political Research*, 38(1): 63–94.

Lubbers, Marcel and Peer Scheepers (2002), 'French *Front National* Voting: A Micro and Macro Perspective', *Ethnic and Racial Studies*, 25(1): 120–49.

Lubbers, Marcel, Mérove Gijsberts and Peer Scheepers (2002), 'Extreme Right-Wing Voting in Western Europe', *European Journal of Political Research*, 41(3): 345–78.

Lucardie, Paul (1998), 'The Netherlands: The Extremist Center Parties', in Hans-Georg Betz and Stefan Immerfall (eds), *The New Politics of the Right: Neo-Populist Parties and Movements in Established Democracies*, pp. 111–24, New York: St Martin's Press.

Lucardie, Paul (2000), 'Prophets, Purifiers and Prolocutors: Towards a Theory on the Emergence of New Parties', *Party Politics*, 6(2): 175–85.

Luther, Kurt Richard (2000), 'Austria: A Democracy under Threat from the Freedom Party?', *Parliamentary Affairs*, 53(3): 426–42.

Luther, Kurt Richard (2003), 'The FPÖ: From Populist Protest to Incumbency', in Peter H. Merkl and Leonard Weinberg (eds), *Right-Wing Extremism in the Twenty-First Century*, pp. 191–219, London: Frank Cass.

Machin, Howard (2001), 'Political Leadership', in Alain Guyomarch, Howard Machin, Peter A. Hall and Jack Hayward (eds), *Developments in French Politics 2*, pp. 68–91, Basingstoke: Palgrave.

Mackie, Thomas T. and Richard Rose (1991), *The International Almanac of Electoral History*, 3rd edition, Basingstoke: Macmillan.

Mackie, Tom and Richard Rose (1997), *A Decade of Election Results: Updating the International Almanac*, Glasgow: Centre for the Study of Public Policy, University of Strathclyde.

Mair, Peter (1991), 'The Electoral Universe of Small Parties in Postwar Western Europe', in Ferdinand Müller-Rommel and Geoffrey Pridham (eds), *Small Parties in Western Europe: Comparative and National Perspectives*, pp. 41–70, London: Sage.

Mair, Peter (1996), 'Party Systems and Structures of Competition', in Lawrence
    LeDuc, Richard G. Niemi and Pippa Norris (eds), *Comparing Democracies:
    Elections and Voting in Global Perspective*, pp. 83–106, Thousand Oaks CA:
    Sage.
Mair, Peter (2001), 'Searching for the Positions of Political Actors: A Review of
    Approaches and a Critical Evaluation of Expert Surveys', in Michael Laver (ed.),
    Estimating the Policy Position of Political Actors, pp. 10–30, London: Routledge.
Mair, Peter and Francis G. Castles (1997), 'Reflections: Revisiting Expert Judgements',
    European Journal of Political Research, 31(1–2): 150–7.
Mair, Peter and Cas Mudde (1998), 'The Party Family and its Study', *Annual Review
    of Political Science*, 1: 211–29.
Mannheimer, Renato (1995), 'Questions and Answers about Northern League', in
    Lieven de Winter (ed.), *Non-State Wide Parties in Europe*, pp. 97–116, Barcelona:
    Institut de Ciències Polítiques i Socials.
Maor, Moshe (1997), *Political Parties and Party Systems: Comparative Approaches
    and the British Experience*, London: Routledge.
Marcus, Jonathan (1995), *The National Front and French Politics: The Resistible
    Rise of Jean-Marie Le Pen*, Basingstoke: Macmillan.
Marletti, Carlo and Franca Roncarolo (2000), 'Media Influence in the Italian Tran-
    sition from a Consensual to a Majoritarian Democracy', in Richard Gunther and
    Anthony Mughan (eds), *Democracy and the Media: A Comparative Perspective*, pp.
    195–240, Cambridge: Cambridge University Press.
Marradi, Alberto (1990), 'On Classification', in Anton Bebler and Jim Seroka (eds),
    Contemporary Political Systems: Classifications and Typologies, pp. 11–43, Bouler
    CO: Lynne Rienner.
Massicotte, Louis and André Blais (1999), 'Mixed Electoral Systems: A Conceptual
    and Empirical Survey', *Electoral Studies*, 18(3): 341–66.
May, John D. (1973), 'Opinion Structure of Political Parties: The Special Law of
    Curvilinear Disparity', *Political Studies*, 21(2): 135–51.
Mayer, Nonna (1998), 'The French Front National', in Hans-Georg Betz and Stefan
    Immerfall (eds), *The New Politics of the Right: Neo-Populist Parties and
    Movements in Established Democracies*, pp. 11–25, New York: St Martin's Press.
Mayer, Nonna (1999), *Ces français qui votent Le Pen*, Paris: Flammarion.
Mayer, Nonna and Pascal Perrineau (1992), 'Why Do They Vote for Le Pen?',
    European Journal of Political Research, 22(1): 127–41.
Mazzoleni, Gianpietro and Cynthia S. Roper (1995), 'The Presentation of Italian
    Candidates and Parties in Television Advertising', in Lynda Lee Kaid and Christina
    Holtz-Bacha (eds), *Political Advertising in Western Democracies: Parties and
    Candidates on Television*, pp. 89–108, Thousand Oaks CA: Sage.
Mazzoleni, Oscar (1999), 'La Lega dei Ticinesi: vers l'intégration?', *Swiss Political
    Science Review*, 5(3): 79–95.
McDonald, Michael D. and Silvia M. Mendes (2001), 'The Policy Space of Party
    Manifestos', in Michael Laver (ed.), *Estimating the Policy Position of Political
    Actors*, pp. 90–114, London: Routledge.
Merkl, Peter H. (1997), 'Why are they So Strong Now? Comparative Reflections on
    the Revival of the Radical Right in Europe', in Peter H. Merkl and Leonard
    Weinberg (eds), *The Revival of Right-Wing Extremism in the Nineties*, pp. 17–46,
    London: Frank Cass.

Merkl, Peter H. (2003), 'Stronger than Ever', in Peter H. Merkl and Leonard Weinberg (eds), *Right-Wing Extremism in the Twenty-First Century*, pp. 23–46, London: Frank Cass.

Merkl, Peter and Leonard Weinberg (eds) (1993), *Encounters with the Contemporary Radical Right*, Boulder CO: Westview.

Merkl, Peter and Leonard Weinberg (eds) (1997), *The Revival of Right-Wing Extremism in the Nineties*, London: Frank Cass.

Miles, Robert and Annie Phizacklea (eds) (1979), *Racism and Political Action in Britain*, London: Routledge.

Minkenberg, Michael (1992), 'The New Right in Germany: The Transformation of Conservatism and the Extreme Right', *European Journal of Political Research*, 22(1): 55–81.

Minkenberg, Michael (1997), 'The New Right in France and Germany: Nouvelle Droite, Neue Rechte, and the New Right Radical Parties', in Peter H. Merkl and Leonard Weinberg (eds), *The Revival of Right-Wing Extremism in the Nineties*, pp. 65–90, London: Frank Cass.

Minkenberg, Michael and Martin Schain (2003), 'The National Front in Context: French and European Dimensions', in Peter H. Merkl and Leonard Weinberg (eds), *Right-Wing Extremism in the Twenty-First Century*, pp. 161–90, London: Frank Cass.

Mitra, Subrata (1988), 'The National Front in France – A Single Issue Movement?', *West European Politics*, 11(2): 47–64.

Monzat, René (1992), *Enquêtes sur la droite extrême*, Paris: Le Monde-Éditions.

Morgan, Michael John (1976), 'The Modelling of Governmental Coalition Formations: A Policy-Based Approach with Internal Measurement', Ann Arbor: University of Michigan PhD thesis.

Moring, Tom (1995), 'The North European Exception: Political Advertising on TV in Finland', in Lynda Lee Kaid and Christina Holtz-Bacha (eds), *Political Advertising in Western Democracies: Parties and Candidates on Television*, pp. 161–85, Thousand Oaks CA: Sage.

Morrow, Duncan (2000), 'Jörg Haider and the New FPÖ: Beyond the Democratic Pale?' in Paul Hainsworth (ed.), *The Politics of the Extreme Right: From the Margins to the Mainstream*, pp. 33–63, London: Pinter.

Mudde, Cas (1995a), 'Right-Wing Extremism Analyzed: A Comparative Analysis of the Ideologies of Three Alleged Right-Wing Extremist Parties (NPD, NDP, CP'86)', *European Journal of Political Research*, 27(2): 203–24.

Mudde, Cas (1995b), 'One Against All, All Against One!: A Portrait of the Vlaams Blok', *Patterns of Prejudice*, 29(1): 5–28.

Mudde, Cas (1996a), 'The War of Words Defining the Extreme Right Party Family', *West European Politics*, 19(2); 225–48.

Mudde, Cas (1996b), 'The Paradox of the Anti-Party Party: Insights into the Extreme Right', *Party Politics*, 2(2): 265–76.

Mudde, Cas (1999), 'The Single-Issue Party Thesis: Extreme Right Parties and the Immigration Issue', *West European Politics*, 22(3): 182–97.

Mudde, Cas (2000), *The Ideology of the Extreme Right*, Manchester: Manchester University Press.

Mudde, Cas and Joop Van Holsteyn (2000), 'The Netherlands: Explaining the Limited Success of the Extreme Right', in Paul Hainsworth (ed.), *The Politics of the Extreme Right: From the Margins to the Mainstream*, pp. 144–71, London: Pinter.

Müller, Wolfgang C. (1992), 'Austria (1945–1990)', in Richard S. Katz and Peter Mair (eds), *Party Organizations: A Data Handbook*, pp. 21–120, London: Sage.

Müller, Wolfgang C. (1993), 'Austria', *European Journal of Political Research Data Yearbook*, 24(4), 373–81.

Müller, Wolfgang C. (2000), 'Election Reports: The Austrian Election of October 1999: A Shift to the Right', *West European Politics*, 23(3): 191–200.

Müller-Rommel, Ferdinand (1991), 'Small Parties in Comparative Perspective: The State of the Art', in Ferdinand Müller-Rommel and Geoffrey Pridham (eds), *Small Parties in Western Europe: Comparative and National Perspectives*, pp. 1–22, London: Sage.

Nassmacher, Karl-Heinz (1989), 'Structure and Impact of Public Subsidies to Political Parties in Europe: the Examples of Austria, Italy, Sweden and West Germany', in Herbert E. Alexander (ed.), *Comparative Political Finance in the 1980s*, pp. 236–63, Cambridge: Cambridge University Press.

Nassmacher, Karl-Heinz (1993), 'Comparative Party and Campaign Finance in Western Democracies', in Arthur B. Gunlicks (ed.), *Campaign and Party Finance in North America and Western Europe*, pp. 233–67, Boulder CO: Westview.

Nationaldemokratische Partei Deutschlands (2002), *Parteiprogramm der Nationaldemokratischen Partei Deutschlands*, www.npd.de/npd_startseiten/ programme.html.

Newell, James L. (2000), 'Italy: The Extreme Right Comes in from the Cold', *Parliamentary Affairs*, 53(3): 469–85.

Niemi, Richard G., Richard S. Katz and David Newman (1980), 'Reconstructing Past Partisanship: The Failure of the Party Identification Recall Questions', *American Journal of Political Science*, 24(4): 633–51.

Nohlen, Dieter, Florian Grotz, Michael Krennerich and Bernhard Thibaut (2000), 'Appendix: Electoral Systems in Independent Counties', in Richard Rose (ed.), *International Encyclopedia of Elections*, pp. 353–79, London: Macmillan.

Nolte, Ernst (1965), *The Three Faces of Fascism: Action Française, Italian Fascism, National Socialism*, London: Weidenfeld and Nicolson.

Norris, Pippa (1995), 'May's Law of Curvilinear Disparity Revisited: Leaders, Officers, Members and Voters in British Political Parties', *Party Politics*, 1(1): 29–47.

Nozari, Fariborz (1991), 'Sweden', in Ruth Levush (ed.), *Campaign Financing of National Elections in Foreign Countries*, pp. 147–51, Washington DC: Law Library of Congress.

Ozbudun, Ergun (1970), *Party Cohesion in Western Democracies: A Causal Analysis*, Beverly Hills CA: Sage.

Panebianco, Angelo (1988), *Political Parties: Organization and Power*, Cambridge: Cambridge University Press.

Papademetriou, Theresa (1991), 'Greece', in Ruth Levush (ed.), *Campaign Financing of National Elections in Foreign Countries*, pp. 75–83, Washington DC: Law Library of Congress.

Parteiengesetz (2002), 'Gesetz über die politischen Parteien (Parteiengesetz)', BGBl. I S. 149 and BGBl. I S. 2268.

Parteiengesetz (2003), 'Bundesgesetz über die Aufgaben, Finanzierung und Wahlwerbung politischer Parteien (Parteiengesetz – PartG)', BGBl. Nr. 404/1975 idF BGBl. I Nr. 71/2003.

Parties and Elections in Europe, www.parties-and-elections.de/indexe.html.

Pedersen, Mogens N. (1982), 'Towards a New Typology of Party Lifespans and Minor Parties', *Scandinavian Political Studies*, 5(1): 1–16.

Pedersen, Mogens N. (1991), 'The Birth, Life and Death of Small Parties in Danish Politics', in Ferdinand Müller-Rommel and Geoffrey Pridham (eds), *Small Parties in Western Europe: Comparative and National Perspective*, pp. 95–114, London: Sage.

Pedersen, Mogens N. (1997), 'Nomination: "Some Expert Judgements" Live On', *European Journal of Political Research*, 31(1–2): 147–50.

Pedersen, Mogens N. and Lars Bille (1991), 'Public Financing and Public Control of Political Parties in Denmark', in Matti Wiberg (ed.), *The Public Purse and Political Parties: Public Financing of Political Parties in Nordic Countries*, pp. 147–72, Jyväskylä: Gummerus.

Pedersen, Mogens N., Erik Damgaard and P. Nannestad Olsen (1971), 'Party Distances in the Danish Folketing 1945–1968', *Scandinavian Political Studies*, 6: 87–106.

Penadés, Alberto (1997), 'A Critique of Lijphart's "Electoral Systems and Party Systems"', *Electoral Studies*, 16(1): 58–71.

Perrineau, Pascal (1997), *Le symptôme Le Pen: Radiographie des électeurs du Front National*, Paris: Fayard.

Pierre, Jon and Anders Widfeldt (1992), 'Sweden', in Richard S. Katz and Peter Mair (eds), *Party Organizations: A Data Handbook*, pp. 781–836, London: Sage.

Pierre, Jon, Lars Svåsand and Anders Widfeldt (2000), 'State Subsidies to Political Parties: Confronting Rhetoric with Reality', *West European Politics*, 23(3): 1–24.

Pinto-Duschinsky, Michael (1989), 'Trends in British Political Funding, 1983–87', *Parliamentary Affairs*, 42(2): 197–212.

Pinto-Duschinsky, Michael (1991), 'The Party Foundations and Political Finance in Germany', in F. Leslie Seidle (ed.), *Comparative Issues in Party and Election Finance*, pp. 179–250, Toronto: Dundurn.

Pinto-Duschinsky, Michael (1994), 'British Party Funding, 1983–1988', in Herbert E. Alexander and Rei Shiratori (eds), *Comparative Political Finance among the Democracies*, pp. 13–28, Boulder CO: Westview.

Plenel, Edwy and Alain Rollat (1984), *L'effet Le Pen*, Paris: Editions la Découverte.

Poguntke, Thomas and Bernhard Boll (1992), 'Germany', in Richard S. Katz and Peter Mair (eds), *Party Organizations: A Data Handbook*, pp. 317–88, London: Sage.

Poguntke, Thomas and Susan E. Scarrow (1996), 'The Politics of Anti-Party Sentiment: Introduction', *European Journal of Political Research*, 29(3): 257–62.

Przeworski, Adam and Henry Teune (1970), *The Logic of Comparative Social Inquiry*, New York: Wiley.

Pujas, Véronique (2000), 'The Funding of Political Parties and Control of the Media: Another Italian Anomaly', in Mark Gilbert and Gianfranco Pasquino (eds), *Italian Politics: The Faltering Transformation*, pp. 139–52, New York: Berghahn Books.

Pujas, Véronique and Martin Rhodes (1999), 'Party Finance and Political Scandal in Italy, Spain and France', *West European Politics*, 22(3): 41–63.

Rabinowitz, George and Stuart Elaine Macdonald (1989), 'A Directional Theory of Issue Voting', *American Political Science Review*, 83(1): 93–121.

Rae, Douglas W. (1967), *The Political Consequences of Electoral Laws*, New Haven CT: Yale University Press.

Ray, Leonard and Hanne Marthe Narud (2000), 'Mapping the Norwegian Political Space: Some Findings from an Expert Survey', *Party Politics*, 6(2): 225–39.

Reif, Karlheinz and Hermann Schmitt (1980), 'Nine Second-Order National Elections – A Conceptual Framework for the Analysis of European Election Results', *European Journal of Political Research*, 8(1): 3–44.

Rémond, René (1982), *Les Droites en France*, Paris: Aubier Montaigne.

Résistances (2001), www.resistances.be/bastien.html.

Rhodes, Martin (1997), 'Financing Party Politics in Italy: A Case of Systemic Corruption', *West European Politics*, 20(1): 54–80.

Ricolfi, Luca (1997), 'Politics and the Mass Media in Italy', *West European Politics*, 20(1): 135–56.

Riedlsperger, Max (1998), 'The Freedom Party in Austria: From Protest to Radical Right Populism', in Hans-Georg Betz and Stefan Immerfall (eds), *The New Politics of the Right: Neo-Populist Parties and Movements in Established Democracies*, pp. 27–43, New York: St Martin's Press.

Roberts, Geoffrey K. (1992), 'Right-Wing Radicalism in the New Germany', *Parliamentary Affairs*, 45(3): 327–44.

Roberts, Geoffrey K. (1994), 'Extremism in Germany: Sparrows or Avalanche?', *European Journal of Political Research*, 25(4): 470–89.

Robertson, David (1976), *A Theory of Party Competition*, Chichester: Wiley.

Rodríguez, José Luis (1990), 'The Extreme Right in Spain after Franco', *Patterns of Prejudice*, 24(2–4): 87–96.

Rodríguez, José L. (1995), 'Neo-Nazism in Spain', *Patterns of Prejudice*, 29(1): 53–68.

Rose, Richard (1964), 'Parties, Factions and Tendencies in Britain', *Political Studies*, 12(1): 33–46.

Rose, Richard (ed.) (2000), *International Encyclopedia of Elections*, London: Macmillan.

Roth, Dieter (1993), '*Volksparteien* in Crisis? The Electoral Success of the Extreme Right in Context – The Case of Baden-Württemberg', *German Politics*, 2(1): 1–20.

Saalfeld, Thomas (1993), 'The Politics of National-Populism: Ideology and Politics of the German Republikaner Party', *German Politics*, 2(2): 177–99.

Sani, Giacomo and Giovanni Sartori (1983), 'Polarization, Fragmentation and Competition in Western Democracies', in Hans Daalder and Peter Mair (eds), *Western European Party Systems: Continuity and Change*, pp. 307–40, London: Sage.

Sartori, Giovanni (1970), 'Concept Misinformation in Comparative Politics', *American Political Science Review*, 64(4): 1033–53.

Sartori, Giovanni (1976), *Parties and Party Systems: A Framework for Analysis*, Cambridge: Cambridge University Press.

Sartori, Giovanni (1984), 'Guidelines for Concept Analysis', in Giovanni Sartori (ed.), *Social Science Concepts*, pp. 15–85, Beverly Hills CA: Sage.

Sartori, Giovanni (1994), *Comparative Constitutional Engineering: An Inquiry into Structures, Incentives and Outcomes*, Basingstoke: Macmillan.

Scammell, Margaret and Holli A. Semetko (1995), 'Political Advertising on Television: The British Experience', in Lynda Lee Kaid and Christina Holtz-Bacha (eds), *Political Advertising in Western Democracies: Parties and Candidates on Television*, pp. 19–43, Thousand Oaks CA: Sage.

Schain, Martin A. (1988), 'Immigration and Change in the French Party System', *European Journal of Political Research*, 16(6): 597–621.

Schain, Martin A. (2001), 'L'impact du Front National sur le système politique français', in Pascal Perrineau (ed.), *Les croisés de la société fermée: l'Europe des extrêmes droites*, pp. 287–302, La Tour d'Aigues: Editions de l'Aube.

Schedler, Andreas (1996a), 'Anti-Political-Establishment Parties', *Party Politics*, 2(3): 291–312.

Schedler, Andreas (1996b), *The End of Politics? Explorations into Modern Antipolitics*, London: Macmillan.

Schneider, Hans-Peter (1989), 'The New German System of Party Funding: The Presidential Committee Report of 1983 and its Realization', in Herbert E. Alexander (ed.), *Comparative Political Finance in the 1980s*, pp. 220–35, Boulder CO: Westview.

Sear, Chris (2001), *Parliamentary Pay and Allowances: Current Rates*, Research Paper 01/87, House of Commons Library: Parliament and Constitution Centre, www.parliament.uk/commons/lib/research/rp2001/rp01-087.pdf.

Semetko, Holli A. (1996), 'The Media', in Lawrence LeDuc, Richard G. Niemi and Pippa Norris (eds), *Comparing Democracies: Elections and Voting in Global Perspective*, pp. 254–79, Thousand Oaks CA: Sage.

Shugart, Matthew Soberg and Martin P. Wattenberg (eds) (2001), *Mixed-Member Electoral Systems: The Best of Both Worlds?*, Oxford: Oxford University Press.

Sidoti, Francesco (1992), 'The Extreme Right in Italy: Ideological Orphans and Counter-Mobilization', in Paul Hainsworth (ed.), *The Extreme Right in Europe and the USA*, pp. 151–74, London: Pinter.

Silver, Steve (2000), *1980–1989: Blood and Honour Spawned – Britain's Fascists Split*, www.searchlightmagazine.com/stories/century/1980-1989.htm.

Sinnott, Richard (1986), 'Party Differences and Spatial Representation: The Irish Case', *British Journal of Political Science*, 16(2): 217–41.

Sinnott, Richard (1998), 'Party Attachment in Europe: Methodological Critique and Substantive Implications', *British Journal of Political Science*, 28(4): 627–50.

Siune, Karen (1991), 'Campaign Communication in Scandinavia', in Frederick J. Fletcher (ed.), *Media, Elections and Democracy*, pp. 87–105, Toronto: Dundurn.

Siune, Karen (1995), 'Political Advertising in Denmark', in Lynda Lee Kaid and Christina Holtz-Bacha (eds), *Political Advertising in Western Democracies: Parties and Candidates on Television*, pp. 124–42, Thousand Oaks CA: Sage.

Skenderovic, Damir (2001), 'The Swiss Radical Right in Perspective: A Reevaluation of Success Conditions in Switzerland', paper presented at the Workshop on 'Democracy and the New Extremist Challenge in Europe', ECPR Joint Sessions, Grenoble, 6–11 April.

Smith, Anthony (1981), 'Mass Communications', in David Butler, Howard R. Penniman and Austin Ranney (eds), *Democracy at the Polls: A Comparative Study of Competitive National Elections*, pp. 173–95, Washington DC: American Enterprise Institute for Public Policy Research.

Smith, Anthony D. (1995), 'The Dark Side of Nationalism: The Revival of Nationalism in Late Twentieth Century Europe', in Luciano Cheles, Ronnie Ferguson and Michalina Vaughan (eds), *The Far Right in Western and Eastern Europe*, 2nd edition, pp. 13–19, London: Longman.

Smith, Gordon (1987), 'Party and Protest: The Two Faces of Opposition in Western Europe', in Eva Kolinsky (ed.), *Opposition in Western Europe*, pp. 52–76, London: Croom Helm.

Smith, Gordon (1991), 'In Search of Small Parties: Problems of Definition, Classification and Significance', in Ferdinand Müller-Rommel and Geoffrey Pridham (eds), *Small Parties in Western Europe: Comparative and National Perspectives*, pp. 23–40, London: Sage.

Sternhall, Zev (1987), *Ni droite, ni gauche: l'idéologie fasciste en France*, Paris: Editions Complexe.

Stokes, Donald E. (1963), 'Spatial Models of Party Competition', *American Political Science Review*, 57(2): 368–77.

Stöss, Richard (1988), 'The Problem of Right-Wing Extremism in West Germany', *West European Politics*, 11(2): 34–46.

Svåsand, Lars (1991), 'State Subventions for Political Parties in Norway', in Matti Wiberg (ed.), *The Public Purse and Political Parties: Public Financing of Political Parties in Nordic Countries*, pp. 119–46, Jyväskylä: Gummerus.

Svåsand, Lars (1992), 'Norway', in Richard S. Katz and Peter Mair (eds), *Party Organizations: A Data Handbook*, pp. 732–80, London: Sage.

Svåsand, Lars (1998), 'Scandinavian Right-Wing Radicalism', in Hans-Georg Betz and Stefan Immerfall (eds), *The New Politics of the Right: Neo-Populist Parties and Movements in Established Democracies*, pp. 77–93, New York: St Martin's Press.

Svåsand, Lars (2003), 'The Norwegian Progress Party: A Populist Party?', paper presented at the 'Contemporary Populisms in Historical Perspective' Conference, Liguria Center, Bogliasco, Genoa, 7–10 January.

Svåsand, Lars and Ingemar Wørlund (2001), 'The Rise and Fall of the Swedish Party New Democracy', paper presented at the Annual Meeting of the American Political Science Association, San Fransisco, 30 August–2 September.

swisspolitics.org (2002), *Prison avec sursis pour le ténor de la Lega*, www.swisspolitics.org/fr/wissen/index.php?page=parteien_artikel&story_id=1455447&politiker_partei_id=8.

swisspolitics.org (2003), *Flavio Maspoli se retire de la politique*, www.swisspolitics.org/fr/wissen/index.php?page=parteien_artikel&story_id=1863083&politiker_partei_id=8.

Swyngedouw, Marc (1998), 'The Extreme Right in Belgium: Of a Non-existent Front National and an Omnipresent Vlaams Blok', in Hans-Georg Betz and Stefan Immerfall (eds), *The New Politics of the Right: Neo-Populist Parties and Movements in Established Democracies*, pp. 59–75, New York: St Martin's Press.

Swyngedouw, Marc (2000), 'Belgium: Explaining the Relationship between Vlaams Blok and the City of Antwerp', in Paul Hainsworth (ed.), *The Politics of the Extreme Right: From the Margins to the Mainstream*, pp. 121–43, London: Pinter.

Swyngedouw, Marc and Gilles Ivaldi (2001), 'The Extreme Right Utopia in Belgium and France: The Ideology of the Flemish Vlaams Blok and the French Front National', *West European Politics*, 24(3): 1–22.

Taagepera, Rein (1998), 'Effective Magnitude and Effective Threshold', *Electoral Studies*, 17(4): 393–404.

Taagepera, Rein and Mathew Soberg Shugart (1989), *Seats and Votes: The Effects and Determinants of Electoral Systems*, New Haven CT: Yale University Press.

Taggart, Paul (1995), 'New Populist Parties in Western Europe', *West European Politics*, 18(1): 34–51.

Taguieff, Pierre-André (1984), 'La rhétorique du national-populisme', *Mots*, 9: 113–39.

Taguieff, Pierre-André (1986), 'La doctrine du national-populisme en France', *Etudes*, 1: 27–46.

Taguieff, Pierre-André (1995), 'Political Science Confronts Populism: From a Conceptual Mirage to a Real Problem', *Telos*, 103: 9–36.

Thomsen, Søren Risbjerg (1995), 'The 1994 Parliamentary Election in Denmark', *Electoral Studies*, 14(3): 315–22.

Thränhardt, Dietrich (1995), 'The Political Uses of Xenophobia in England, France and Germany', *Party Politics*, 1(3): 323–45.

Thurlow, Richard (1998), *Fascism in Britain: From Oswald Mosley's Black Shirts to the National Front*, London: I. B. Tauris.

Tillie, Jean and Meindert Fennema (1998), 'A Rational Choice for the Extreme Right', *Acta Politica*, 33(3): 223–49.

Tossutti, Livianna (1996), 'From Communitarian Protest Towards Institutionalisation: The Evolution of "Hybrid" Parties in Canada and Italy', *Party Politics*, 2(4): 435–54.

Vallès, Josep M. (1994), 'The Spanish General Election of 1993', *Electoral Studies*, 13(1): 87–91.

Van Biezen, Ingrid (2000), 'Party Financing in New Democracies', *Party Politics*, 6(3): 329–42.

Van der Brug, Wouter (2003), 'How the LPF Fuelled Discontent: Empirical Tests of Explanations of LPF Support', *Acta Politica*, 38: 89–106.

Van der Brug, Wouter and Meindert Fennema (2003), 'Protest or Mainstream? How the European Anti-Immigrant Parties Developed into Two Separate Groups by 1999', *European Journal of Political Research*, 42(1): 55–76.

Van der Brug, Wouter, Meindert Fennema and Jean Tillie (2000), 'Anti-Immigrant Parties in Europe: Ideological or Protest Vote?', *European Journal of Political Research*, 37(1): 77–102.

Van Deth, Jan W. and Peter A. T. M. Geurts (1989), 'Value Orientation, Left–Right Placement and Voting', *European Journal of Political Research*, 17(1): 17–34.

Vaughan, Michalina (1995), 'The Extreme Right in France: "Lepénisme" or the Politics of Fear', in Luciano Cheles, Ronnie Ferguson and Michalina Vaughan (eds), *The Far Right in Western and Eastern Europe*, 2nd edition, pp. 215–33, London: Longman.

Veen, Hans-Joachim, Norbert Lepszy and Peter Mnich (1993), *The Republikaner Party in Germany: Right-Wing Menace or Protest Catchall?*, Washington DC: Center for Strategic and International Studies.

Voerman, Gerrit and Paul Lucardie (1992), 'The Extreme Right in the Netherlands: The Centrists and their Radical Rivals', *European Journal of Political Research*, 22(1): 35–54.

Volkens, Andrea (2001), 'Quantifying the Election Programmes: Coding Procedures and Controls', in Ian Budge, Hans-Dieter Klingemann, Andrea Volkens, Judith Bara and Eric Tanenbaum, *Mapping Policy Preferences: Estimates for Parties, Electors and Governments 1945–1998*, pp. 93–109, Oxford: Oxford University Press.

Webb, Paul D. (1992), 'The United Kingdom', in Richard S. Katz and Peter Mair (eds), *Party Organizations: A Data Handbook*, pp. 837–70, London: Sage.

Weil, Patrick (2001), 'The Politics of Immigration', in Alain Guyomarch, Howard Machin, Peter A. Hall and Jack Hayward (eds), *Developments in French Politics 2*, pp. 211–26, Basingstoke: Palgrave.

Westle, Bettina and Oskar Niedermayer (1992), 'Contemporary Right-Wing Extremism in West Germany: "The Republicans" and their Electorate', *European Journal of Political Research*, 22(1): 83–100.

Wicha, Barbara (1989), 'Party Funding in Austria', in Anton Pelinka and Fritz Plasser (eds), *The Austrian Party System*, pp. 357–87, Boulder CO: Westview.

Widfeldt, Andreas (2000), 'Scandinavia: Mixed Success for the Populist Right', *Parliamentary Affairs*, 53(3), 486–500.

Widfeldt, Andreas (2002), 'Populist Right Parties in the Nordic Countries: Aberration or a Sign of Crisis?', paper presented to the PSA Specialist Group on Scandinavian Politics Workshop on 'Populism in Scandinavia', University College London, 12 April.

Winkler, Jürgen P. and Siegfried Schumann (1998), 'Radical Right-Wing Parties in Contemporary Germany', in Hans-Georg Betz and Stefan Immerfall (eds), *The New Politics of the Right: Neo-Populist Parties and Movements in Established Democracies*, pp. 95–110, New York: St Martin's Press.

Winock, Michel (1993), *Histoire de l'extrême droite en France*, Paris: Seuil.

Wright, Vincent (1989), *The Government and Politics of France*, 3rd edition, London: Routledge.

XE.Com – The Universal Currency Converter, www.xe.com/ucc.

Zimmermann, Ekkart and Thomas Saalfeld (1993), 'The Three Waves of West German Right-Wing Extremism', in Peter Merkl and Leonard Weinberg (eds), *Encounters with the Contemporary Radical Right*, pp. 50–74, Boulder CO: Westview.

Index

Note: Page numbers in *italics* refer to tables and figures.

Agir
electoral results *4–5*
ideology
democracy, parliamentarism and
pluralism *42*, 47
electoral success *55*, *56*, 59
immigration *30*, 33
racism *36*, 38
type of party *51*
organization and leadership 67,
75
electoral success 92
see also institutional environment
Alleanza Nazionale (AN)
electoral laws 187–8
electoral results 1, 2, *4–5*
ideology
democracy, parliamentarism and
pluralism 41, *42*
electoral success *55*, 56
fit with right-wing extremist party
family 57
immigration *30*, 33–4, 62n.6
racism *36*, 40
type of party *51*
in coalition 1, 121, 126, 214
organization and leadership *80*,
82–3
electoral success 92
party competition 121, *122*, 126,
132, 134–5, *222*, *230*
see also institutional environment;
right-wing extremism

anti-democratic sentiment *see*
democracy, parliamentarism and
pluralism
anti-Semitism 35, 37, 40, 63n.8,
210–11
see also racism
anti-system *see* democracy,
parliamentarism and pluralism
Austria *see* Freiheitliche Partei
Österreichs (FPÖ); institutional
environment; party competition
authoritarian xenophobic type of party
51, *52*, 60, *61*
electoral success 54, *55*, 56–61, *58*,
59, 202, 205, *206*, *208*, 208–11
Autopartei der Schweiz (APS) *see*
Freiheitspartei der Schweiz
(FPS)

Bastien, Marguerite 25, 75–6
Belgium
separate party systems 4n.a, 9, 12n.4
see also Flanders; Wallonia
Bignasca, Giuliano 90
Bossi, Umberto 34, 40, 89–90
Bouvin, John 74
Britain *see* British National Party
(BNP); institutional
environment; National Front
(NF); party competition
British National Party (BNP)
electoral laws 191
electoral results 2, *4–5*

British National Party (BNP) (*cont.*)
  ideology
    democracy, parliamentarism and
      pluralism 42, 43
    electoral success 55
    immigration 30, 33
    racism 35, 36
    type of party 50
  organization and leadership 67, 68–9
    electoral success 92
  party competition 137, 138, 218,
    228
  see also institutional environment

Centrumdemocraten (CD)
  electoral laws 188
  electoral results 2, 4–5
  ideology
    democracy, parliamentarism and
      pluralism 42, 47
    electoral success 55, 56, 59
    immigration 30, 33
    racism 36, 39
    type of party 51
  organization and leadership 77, 77–8
    electoral success 92, 93
  party competition 223, 230
  see also institutional environment
Centrumdemokraterne (CD) 119, 139
Centrumpartij (CP)
  electoral results 4–5
  ideology
    democracy, parliamentarism and
      pluralism 42, 47
    electoral success 55, 56, 59
    immigration 30, 33
    racism 36, 39
    type of party 51
  organization and leadership 67, 70
    electoral success 92
  see also institutional environment
Centrumpartij'86 (CP'86)
  electoral results 4–5
  ideology
    democracy, parliamentarism and
      pluralism 42, 43–4
    electoral success 55, 59
    immigration 30, 33

racism 36, 37
    type of party 50
  organization and leadership 67, 70
    electoral success 92
  see also institutional environment
Christlich Demokratische Union (CDU)
    134
Círculo Español de Amigos de Europe
    (CEDADE) 63n.8
classical racism *see* racism
Conservative Party 137–8
culturism *see* racism

Dansk Folkeparti (DF)
  electoral laws 191
  electoral results 1, 4–5
  ideology
    democracy, parliamentarism and
      pluralism 20, 42, 48
    electoral success 55, 56
    immigration 30, 32
    racism 36, 39
    type of party 51
  organization and leadership 73, 80,
    91
    electoral success 92
  party competition 118, 120, 135,
    140, 219, 229
  supporting governmental coalition
    1
  see also institutional environment
democracy, parliamentarism and
    pluralism 15–20, 27–9, 41, 42,
    47–50, 50–1, 52–4
  see also under individual parties
Democrazia Cristiana (DC) 135,
    144n.14
Denmark *see* Dansk Folkeparti (DF);
    Fremskridtspartiet (FRPd);
    institutional environment; party
    competition
Det Nya Partiet (DNP)
  electoral results 4–5
  ideology
    democracy, parliamentarism and
      pluralism 42, 48
    electoral success 55, 56, 59
    immigration 30, 32

racism 36, 39
type of party 51
organization and leadership 67, 74
    electoral success 92
see also institutional environment
Deutsche Volksunion (DVU)
DVU-Liste D 4n.b
electoral laws 191
electoral results 4–5
ideology
    democracy, parliamentarism and
        pluralism 42, 44
    electoral success 54, 55
    immigration 30, 31
    racism 35, 36, 37
    type of party 50
organization and leadership 77, 79
    electoral success 92, 93
party competition 128, 221, 229
see also institutional environment
Dewinter, Filip 88–9
Dillen, Karel 88–9

Ethniki Paratascis 76
Ethniki Politiki Enosis (EPEN)
electoral results 4–5
ideology
    democracy, parliamentarism and
        pluralism 42, 49
    electoral success 55, 56, 59
    immigration 30, 34
    racism 36, 39–40
    type of party 51
organization and leadership 67, 76
    electoral success 92
see also institutional environment
Ethniko Komma (EK)
electoral results 4–5
ideology
    democracy, parliamentarism and
        pluralism 42, 49
    electoral success 55, 56
    immigration 30, 34
    racism 36, 39–40
    type of party 51
organization and leadership 67, 76
    electoral success 92
see also institutional environment

expert judgements see party
    competition
extreme right see right-wing extremism
extremism 15–20, 53
see also right-wing extremism;
    terminology

factionalism see party organization
Falange Española Auténtica (FEA) see
    Falangistas
Falange Española de las Juntas de
    Ofensiva Nacional-Sindicalista
    (FE de las JONS) see Falangistas
Falange Española de las Juntas de
    Ofensiva Nacional-Sindicalista –
    sector Diego Marquez (FE de las
    JONS sector DM) see
    Falangistas
Falange Española Independiente (FEI)
    see Falangistas
Falangistas
composition 4–5n.i, 62–3n.7
electoral results 4–5
ideology
    democracy, parliamentarism and
        pluralism 42, 43
    electoral success 55, 57, 59
    immigration 30, 33–4
    racism 36, 39–40
    type of party 51
organization and leadership 67, 76
    electoral success 92
party competition 123, 123–4, 139,
    225, 231
Unión Nacional 5n.j
see also institutional environment
far right see terminology
fascism 17, 21, 26, 29, 41–3, 57, 62n.1
see also neo-fascist type of party
Fedrelandspartiet (FLP)
electoral results 4–5
ideology
    democracy, parliamentarism and
        pluralism 42, 48
    electoral success 55, 56
    immigration 30, 32
    racism 36, 39
    type of party 51

264

Index

Fedrelandspartiet (FLP) (*cont.*)
organization and leadership 67, 75
electoral success 92
see also institutional environment
Féret, Daniel 76
Fini, Gianfranco 34, 40, 42, 57, 82–3, 126
Flanders *see* institutional environment; party competition; Vlaams Blok (VB)
Forza Italia 1, 121, 126, 144n.14
France *see* Front National (FN); institutional environment; Mouvement National Républicain (MNR); party competition
Freiheitliche Partei Österreichs (FPÖ)
electoral laws 191
electoral results 1–2, 4–5
ideology
democracy, parliamentarism and pluralism 42, 47
electoral success 55, 56
immigration 30, 31
racism 36, 39
type of party 51
in coalition 1, 86–7, 214
organization and leadership 80, 85–8, 100–1n.6
electoral success 92
party competition 120–1, 120, 126–8, 133–5, 217, 227
see also institutional environment
Freiheitspartei der Schweiz (FPS)
electoral laws 189
electoral results 4–5
ideology
democracy, parliamentarism and pluralism 42, 49
electoral success 55, 56
immigration 30, 33
racism 36, 39
type of party 51
organization and leadership 77, 78–9
electoral success 92, 93
party competition 127, 127, 133, 226, 232
see also institutional environment

Fremskridtspartiet (FRPd)
electoral laws 188, 191
electoral results 1–2, 4–5
ideology
democracy, parliamentarism and pluralism 20, 42, 48, 54
electoral success 55, 56
immigration 30, 31–2, 34
racism 36, 39–41
type of party 51
organization and leadership 67, 72–3, 81–2
electoral success 92, 93, 101n.9
party competition 118, 118–20, 135, 139–40, 219, 229
see also institutional environment
Fremskrittspartiet (FRPn)
electoral laws 167–8, 187
electoral results 1–2, 4–5
ideology
democracy, parliamentarism and pluralism 20, 42, 48
electoral success 55, 56
immigration 30, 31–2, 34
racism 36, 39–41
type of party 51
organization and leadership 80, 80–2
electoral success 92
party competition 122, 123–4, 127, 132–3, 135, 224, 231
supporting governmental coalition 1, 214
see also institutional environment
Frente Nacional
electoral results 4–5
ideology
democracy, parliamentarism and pluralism 42, 43
electoral success 55, 56–7, 59
immigration 27, 30, 33–4
racism 27, 36, 39–40
type of party 51
organization and leadership 77, 79–80
electoral success 92, 93
party competition 139
see also institutional environment
Frey, Gerhard 72, 76

Front National (FN)
  electoral laws 194
  electoral results 1, 4–5
  ideology
    democracy, parliamentarism and
      pluralism 42, 45
    electoral success 55, 56
    immigration 29, 30, 31
    racism 36, 37–8
    type of party 51
  organization and leadership 80, 83–5
    electoral success 92
  party competition 115–17, 116,
      120–1, 127, 132–4, 220, 229
  see also institutional environment
Front National (Belge) (FN(b))
  electoral laws 188
  electoral results 4–5
  ideology
    democracy, parliamentarism and
      pluralism 42, 46–7
    electoral success 55, 56
    immigration 30, 32
    racism 36, 38
    type of party 51
  organization and leadership 67, 75–6
    electoral success 92, 93
  party competition 218, 228
  see also institutional environment
Front Nouveau de Belgique (FNB)
  electoral results 4–5
  ideology
    democracy, parliamentarism and
      pluralism 42, 46–7
    electoral success 55, 56
    immigration 30, 32
    racism 36, 38
    type of party 51
  organization and leadership 67, 75–6
    electoral success 92
  see also institutional environment
Fuerza Nueva
  electoral results 4–5
  ideology
    democracy, parliamentarism and
      pluralism 42, 43
    electoral success 55, 56–7, 59
    immigration 30, 33–4

racism 36, 39–40
    type of party 51
  organization and leadership 77,
      79–80
    electoral success 92, 93
  party competition 123, 123–4, 225,
      231
  Unión Nacional 5n.j
  see also institutional environment
fundamentalist see terminology

Gallagher index 160, 199n.16, 233–5
  see also institutional environment
German Federal Constitutional Court
      and Office for the Protection of
      the Constitution 16, 22, 35, 44
Germany see Deutsche Volksunion
      (DVU); institutional
      environment;
      Nationaldemokratische Partei
      Deutschlands (NPD); party
      competition; Republikaner
Glimmerveen, Joop 37
Glistrup, Mogens 72–3
Greece see Ethniki Politiki Enosis
      (EPEN); Ethniko Komma (EK);
      institutional environment;
      Komma Proodeftikon (KP);
      party competition
Griffin, Nick 33, 35, 68–9

Hagen, Carl I. 80–1, 214
Haider, Jörg 27, 31, 85–7, 126
Høyre (H) 123, 132–3

ideological position of parties see party
      competition
ideology see under individual parties;
      right-wing extremism
  electoral success 54–63, 55, 201–2,
      205, 206, 208, 209–10
  immigration 28–34, 30, 50, 50–1,
      52–3
  see also under individual parties
institutional environment
  electoral system 146–62, 195–6,
      203–4, 206, 207, 208, 209,
      211–13

institutional environment (*cont.*)
electoral system (*cont.*)
Austria 148, *149–51*, 153, 156,
157, *159*, 197n.5, *233–5*
Belgium 148, *149–51*, *157*, *159*,
233–5
Britain *149–51*, 155–6, *157*, *159*,
233–5
Denmark 148, *149–51*, *157*, *159*,
233–5
disproportionality of 160–2,
149–51, *233–5*
district magnitude and legal
thresholds 148–55, *149–51*
electoral formula 155–9, *149–51*,
157, *159*
electoral success of right-wing
extremist parties 146–8, 152–6,
157, 158–62, *159*, 195–6,
198n.10, 199n.19, 203–4, *206*,
207, *208*, 209, 211–13, 214n.3,
215n.8
France 148, *149–51*, 153, 155–6,
157, 158, *159*, *233–5*
Germany 148, *149–51*, 153, 156,
157, 158, *159*, *233–5*
Greece *149–51*, 156, *157*, *233–5*
Italy 148, *149–51*, 153, 156, *157*,
158, *159*, 198n.9, *233–5*
Netherlands 148, *149–51*, 156,
157, *159*, *233–5*
Norway 148, *149–51*, 153, 156,
157, *159*, *233–5*
Portugal 148, *149–51*, 156, *157*,
159, *233–5*
psychological effects of 147, 158,
160–2, 196, 197n.1, 211–12
Spain 148, *149–51*, 156, *157*, *159*,
233–5
Sweden 148, *149–51*, *157*, *159*,
233–5
Switzerland 148, *149–51*, *157*,
159, *233–5*
other electoral laws 162–96, 195–6,
203–4, *206*, 207, *208*, 209,
211–13
all three laws together 192–5,
192–3

Austria *164–7*, 168–9, *170–5*,
177, *178–86*, 186–7, 190–1,
192–3
ballot access rules 163, *164–7*,
167–8
Belgium *164–7*, 169, *170–5*,
178–86, 188, *192–3*
Britain *164–7*, 168–9, *170–5*, 175,
178–86, 186–7, 190–1, *192–3*,
194
Denmark *164–7*, 168–9, *170–5*,
178–86, 186–8, 190–1, *192–3*,
194
electoral success of right-wing
extremist parties 146, 162–3,
167–9, 175–6, 187–96, 203–4,
206, 207, *208*, 209, 211–13
France *164–7*, 169, *170–5*, 177,
178–86, *192–3*, 194
Germany *164–7*, 169, *170–5*, 175,
177, *178–86*, 186, 188–91,
192–3, 194
Greece *164–7*, 169, *170–5*,
178–86, *192–3*, 194
Italy *164–7*, *170–5*, *178–86*, 187,
192–3, 194
media access rules 168–9, *170–5*,
175–6
Netherlands *164–7*, 168, *170–5*,
178–86, 188–90, *192–3*, 194
Norway 163, *164–7*, 167–9,
170–5, *178–86*, 187, *192–3*,
194
Portugal 163, *164–7*, 168–9,
170–5, *178–86*, 187, *192–3*,
193–4
Spain 163, *164–7*, 168–9, *170–5*,
175, 177, *178–86*, 187, 190,
192–3
state subvention access rules
176–8, *178–86*, 186–92
Sweden 163, *164–7*, 169, *170–5*,
177, *178–86*, 187, 190, *192–3*,
194
Switzerland *164–7*, 169, *170–5*,
178–86, 187–91, *192–3*, 194
International Third Position 68
Isänmaallinen Kansallis-Liitto (IKL) 9

Italy *see* Alleanza Nazionale (AN);
  institutional environment; Lega
  Nord (LN); Movimento
  Sociale–Fiamma Tricolore (Ms-
  Ft); Movimento Sociale Italiano
  (MSI); party competition

Jacobsen, Kirsten 73
Janmaat, Hans 70, 77–8

Kjærsgaard, Pia 72–3, 91, 119
Komma Proodeftikon (KP)
  electoral results 4–5
  ideology
    democracy, parliamentarism and
      pluralism 42, 49
    electoral success 55, 56, 59
    immigration 30, 34
    racism 36, 39–40
    type of party 51
  organization and leadership 67, 76
    electoral success 92
  see also institutional environment
Konservative Folkeparti (KF) 118–19,
  139
Kristeligt Folkeparti (KRF) 118, 139

Labour Party 137–8
leadership *see* party organization and
  leadership
Lega dei Ticinesi (LdT)
  electoral results 4–5
  ideology
    democracy, parliamentarism and
      pluralism 42, 49
    electoral success 55, 56
    immigration 30, 34
    racism 36, 40
    type of party 51
  organization and leadership 80, 90
    electoral success 92
  party competition 127, 226, 232
  see also institutional environment
Lega Nord (LN)
  electoral results 1, 4–5
  ideology
    democracy, parliamentarism and
      pluralism 42, 49

    electoral success 55, 56
    immigration 30, 32, 34
    racism 36, 40
    type of party 51
  in coalition 1, 121
  organization and leadership 80, 89–90
    electoral success 92, 93
  party competition 121, 122, 222, 230
  see also institutional environment
Le Pen, Jean-Marie 37, 45, 83–4, 117,
  214
Lijst Pim Fortuyn (LPF) 9

Manifesto Research Group *see* party
  competition
Maspoli, Flavio 90
Mégret, Bruno 31, 38, 84–5
Mouvement National Républicain
  (MNR)
  electoral results 4–5
  ideology
    democracy, parliamentarism and
      pluralism 42, 46
    electoral success 55
    immigration 30, 31
    racism 36, 38
    type of party 51
  organization and leadership 80, 84–5
    electoral success 92, 93
  see also institutional environment
Movimento Independente para a
  Reconstrução Nacional (MIRN)
  4n.h
Movimento Sociale–Fiamma Tricolore
  (Ms-Ft)
  electoral results 4–5
  ideology
    democracy, parliamentarism and
      pluralism 42, 42
    electoral success 55, 56
    immigration 30, 33
    racism 36, 40
    type of party 51
  organization and leadership 67, 76–7
    electoral success 92
  party competition 122, 126, 222,
    230
  see also institutional environment

Movimento Sociale Italiano (MSI)
  electoral laws 187–8
  electoral results 2, 4–5
  ideology
    democracy, parliamentarism and
      pluralism 41, 42
    electoral success 55, 56–7
    immigration 30, 33–4, 62n.6
    racism 36, 40
    type of party 51
  organization and leadership 80, 82–3
    breakaway of Ms-Ft 76
    electoral success 92
  party competition 121, 122, 126,
      128, 132, 134–5, 222, 230
  see also institutional environment

National Democrats 68
Nationaldemokratische Partei
    Deutschlands (NPD)
  electoral laws 191
  electoral results 4–5
  ideology
    democracy, parliamentarism and
      pluralism 42, 44
    electoral success 55
    immigration 30, 31
    racism 35, 36
    type of party 50
  organization and leadership 67, 75
    electoral success 92
  see also institutional environment
Nationale Aktion für Volk und Heimat
    (NA) 62n.4
  see also Schweizer Demokraten (SD)
National Front (NF)
  electoral laws 191
  electoral results 2, 4–5
  ideology
    democracy, parliamentarism and
      pluralism 42, 43
    electoral success 55, 59
    immigration 27, 30, 33
    racism 27, 35, 36
    type of party 50
  organization and leadership 66–9, 67
    electoral success 92
  party competition 138

  see also institutional environment
nationalism 14–15, 17, 62n.2, 62n.3
national populism see terminology
National Socialism 35, 38
Nazi see neo-Nazi type of party;
    terminology
Nederlandse Volksunie (NVU)
  electoral results 4–5
  ideology
    democracy, parliamentarism and
      pluralism 42, 43
    electoral success 55, 59
    immigration 30, 33
    racism 36, 37
    type of party 50
  organization and leadership 67,
      69–70
    electoral success 92
  see also institutional environment
neo-fascist type of party 51, 52, 57, 60,
    61
  electoral success 54, 55, 56–61, 58,
      59, 202, 205, 206, 208, 208–11,
      214n.2
  see also fascism; terminology
neo-liberal populist type of party 51,
    52–4, 60, 61
  electoral success 54, 55, 56–61, 58,
      59, 202, 205, 206, 208, 208–11
neo-liberal xenophobic type of party
    51, 52, 60, 61
  electoral success 54, 55, 56–61, 58,
      59, 202, 205, 206, 208, 208–11
neo-Nazi type of party 50, 50, 52, 60,
    61
  electoral success 54, 55, 57–61, 58,
      59, 61, 202, 205, 206, 208, 208,
      210–11
  see also terminology
neo-populism see terminology
Netherlands see Centrumdemocraten
    (CD); Centrumpartij (CP);
    Centrumpartij'86 (CP'86);
    institutional environment;
    Nederlandse Volksunie (NVU);
    party competition
new populism see terminology
new racism see racism

new radical right *see* terminology
Norway *see* Fedrelandspartiet (FLP);
    Fremskrittspartiet (FRPn);
    institutional environment; party
    competition
Ny Demokrati (ND)
    electoral results 4–5
    ideology
        democracy, parliamentarism and
            pluralism 42, 48
        electoral success 55, 56
        immigration 30, 32
        racism 36, 39
        type of party 51
    organization and leadership 67, 73–4
        electoral success 92, 93, 101n.9
    party competition 226, 232
    see also institutional environment

Österreichische Volkspartei (ÖVP)
    in coalition with the FPÖ 1, 86–7
    party competition 120–1, 133–5

parliamentarism *see* democracy,
    parliamentarism and pluralism
Parti des Forces Nouvelles (PFNb)
    electoral results 4–5
    ideology
        democracy, parliamentarism and
            pluralism 42, 43–4
        electoral success 55, 59
        immigration 30, 33
        racism 36, 37
        type of party 50
    organization and leadership 67, 75
        electoral success 92
    see also institutional environment
Partido da Democracia Cristã (PDC)
    electoral results 4–5
    ideology
        democracy, parliamentarism and
            pluralism 42, 43
        electoral success 55, 57, 59
        immigration 30, 33–4
        racism 36, 39–40
        type of party 51
    organization and leadership 67, 76
        electoral success 92

party competition 224, 231
    see also institutional environment
Partido Popular (PP) 123, 138–9
Partido Socialista Obrero Español
    (PSOE) 138
party competition
    approaches to mapping the political
        space 105–12
        elites studies 106–7
        expert judgements 111–12
        government expenditure flows
            105–6
        internal analysis of party election
            programmes 109–11
        voter attitudes 107–9
    concept of political space and party
        competition 103–5
    convergence of mainstream parties
        and right-wing extremist party
        vote 136–42, 203, 206, 207,
        208, 209, 211–12
    *see also under individual countries;
        under individual parties*
    data used 112–14
    in individual countries
        Austria 120–1, *120*, 126–9, 133–5,
            217, 227
        Britain 137–9, *137*, *218*, 228
        Denmark 117–20, *118*, 127, 135,
            139–40, *219*, 229
        Flanders 120, *217*, 228
        France 115–17, *116*, 120–1,
            127–9, 132–4, *220*, 229
        Germany 128–9, *128*, 134–5, 221,
            229
        Greece *221*, 230
        Italy 120–2, *122*, 126, 128–9, 132,
            134–5, *222*, 230
        Netherlands 127, *223*, 230
        Norway *122*, 123–4, 127, 132–5,
            224, 231
        Portugal *224*, 231
        Spain 123–4, *123*, 138–9, *225*,
            231
        Sweden *226*, 232
        Switzerland 120, 127, *127*, 133–4,
            226, 232
        Wallonia *218*, 228

party competition (*cont.*)
  interaction of mainstream right and
    extreme right, and right-wing
    extremist party vote 129–35,
    141–2, 203, 206, 207
    see also *under individual countries*;
    under individual parties
  position of extreme right and right-
    wing extremist party vote 125–9,
    141–2, 203, 206, 207
    see also *under individual countries*;
    under individual parties
  position of mainstream right and
    right-wing extremist party vote
    114–25, 141–2, 202–3, 206,
    207, 208, 209
    see also *under individual countries*;
    under individual parties
party family see right-wing extremism
party organization and leadership 64–6,
    98, 100n.1, 100n.2, 100n.7
  electoral success 91–9, 92, 94, 95,
    202, 205, 206, 207, 208,
    209–15
  see also *under individual parties*
Perussuomalaiset (PS) 9
Piñar, Blas 79–80
pluralism see democracy,
    parliamentarism and pluralism
political space see party competition
populism see terminology
populist right see terminology
Portugal see institutional environment;
    Partido da Democracia Cristã
    (PDC); party competition

racism 15, 17–18, 28, 35–41, 36, 50,
    50–1, 52–3, 210
  see also *under individual parties*
radical right see terminology
radical right-wing populism see
    terminology
Radikale Venstre (RV) 119, 139
Rassemblement pour la République
    (RPR) 115–17, 120, 132–3
Rauti, Pino 25, 40, 76–7, 82, 126
Republikaner
  electoral laws 188, 191

electoral results 2, 4–5
  ideology
    democracy, parliamentarism and
      pluralism 42, 46
    electoral success 55, 56
    immigration 30, 31
    racism 36, 38
    type of party 51
  organization and leadership 67, 70–2
    electoral success 92, 93
  party competition 128, 128, 134–5,
    221, 229
  see also institutional environment
right-wing extremism
  concept 14–20
  party family 24–8, 49–50, 53–4, 57,
    60–1, 61
  types of party 50–4, 50–1; 60–1; 61
    see also authoritarian xenophobic
      type of party; neo-fascist type of
      party; neo-liberal populist type
      of party; neo-liberal xenophobic
      type of party; neo-Nazi type of
      party
  see also terminology

Schlierer, Rolf 72, 128
Schönhuber, Franz 31, 71–2, 128
Schweizer Demokraten (SD)
  electoral laws 189
  electoral results 4–5
  history 62n.4
  ideology
    democracy, parliamentarism and
      pluralism 42, 47
    electoral success 55, 56
    immigration 30, 33
    racism 36, 39
    type of party 51
  organization and leadership 77, 78–9
    electoral success 92
  party competition 127, 127, 133,
    226, 232
  see also institutional environment
Schweizerische Volkspartei/Union
    Démocratique du Centre
    (SVP/UDC) 9
Socialdemokratiet (SD) 139

Sozialdemokratische Partei Österreichs (SPÖ) 85, 121, 126
Spain see Falangistas; Frente Nacional; Fuerza Nueva; institutional environment; party competition
strong state see democracy, parliamentarism and pluralism
Suomen Maaseudun Puolue (SMP) 9
Sverigedemokraterna (SDk)
  electoral results 4–5
  ideology
    democracy, parliamentarism and pluralism 42, 48–9
    electoral success 55, 56
    immigration 30, 32
    racism 36, 39
    type of party 51
  organization and leadership 67, 74–5
    electoral success 92
  party competition 226, 232
  see also institutional environment
Sweden see Det Nya Partiet (DNP); institutional environment; Ny Demokrati (ND); party competition; Sverigedemokraterna (SDk)
Switzerland see Freiheitspartei der Schweiz (FPS); institutional environment; Lega dei Ticinesi (LdT); party competition; Schweizer Demokraten (SD)

terminology 20–3
  extreme right 21–3
  far right 21, 23
  fascist 21
  fundamentalist 21
  national populist 22–3
  Nazi 21
  neo-fascist 21
  neo-Nazi 21
  neo-populist right 21–3
  new populist 21–3
  new radical right 21–2
  populist 21–3
  radical right 21–2
  radical right-wing populist 21–3
  totalitarian 21

totalitarian see terminology
Trivselpartiet (Cosy Party) 73, 100n.3
Tyndall, John 35, 43, 67–9
types of party see authoritarian xenophobic type of party; neo-fascist type of party; neo-liberal populist type of party; neo-liberal xenophobic type of party; neo-Nazi type of party
typologies
  alternative typology 28–9, 50, 60
  existing typologies and their limitations 24–8, 60

Union Démocratique du Centre see Schweizerische Volkspartei
United Kingdom see Britain

Vanhecke, Frank 88–9
Venstre (V) 118–20, 139
Vlaams Blok (VB)
  electoral laws 188
  electoral results 1, 4–5
  ideology
    democracy, parliamentarism and pluralism 42, 46
    electoral success 55, 56
    immigration 30, 32
    racism 36, 38
    type of party 51
  organization and leadership 80, 88–9
    electoral success 92
  party competition 217, 228
  see also institutional environment

Wachtmeister, Ian 32, 47, 74
Wallonia see Agir; Front National (Belge) (FN(b)); Front Nouveau de Belgique (FNB); institutional environment; Parti des Forces Nouvelles (PFNb); party competition

xenophobia 15, 17–18, 28–34, 30, 50, 50–1, 52–3, 62n.3
  see also under individual parties; immigration